The
Circumnavigators'
Handbook

The
Circumnavigators'

by

INTRODUCTION BY

NEW YORK   LONDON

Handbook

Steve and Linda Dashew

RODERICK STEPHENS, JR.

W·W·NORTON & COMPANY

To our families—
For keeping the lines of communication open during our
wanderings—

Thanks

The text of this book is composed in Times Roman, with display type set in Egmont Medium.
Composition by ComCom. Manufacturing by Haddon Craftsmen, Inc.

Library of Congress Cataloging in Publication Data
Dashew, Steve.
     The circumnavigators' handbook.
     Includes index.
     1. Sailing. 2. Seamanship. I. Dashew, Linda.
II. Title.
VK543.D37   1983   623.88'223   82–19015
ISBN 0–393–03275–2

W. W. Norton & Company, Inc., 500 Fifth Avenue, New York, N.Y. 10110
W. W. Norton & Company Ltd., 37 Great Russell Street, London WC1B 3NU

Photographs not otherwise credited were taken by the authors.

Contents

Foreword   11
  Introduction   19
  Acknowledgments   21

1 Setting Goals   25

2 Preparation   28

      1. *Intermezzo*   29
      2. Ground Tackle   42
      3. Self-Steering   58
      4. Cruising in the Shade   68
      5. Catching Rainwater at Sea   76
      6. Staying Dry Below   77
      7. Refrigeration   82
      8. Communications   87
      9. Dinghies   95
     10. Outboards   101
     11. The Liferaft   102
     12. Harnesses   106
     13. Man-Overboard Gear   107
     14. Securing Interiors for Heavy Weather   109
     15. Storm Shutters   113

16. Chafe   113
17. Lightning   117
18. Heaters   119
19. Fans   119
20. Running Lights   121
21. Sailing Instruments   121
22. Dorades   122
23. Weather Cloths   124
24. Cockpit Cushions   124
25. Bug Screens   125
26. Flashlights   125
27. Wind Generating Systems   126
28. Deck Knives   128
29. Medical Preparation   129
30. Cruising Security   134
31. Sybaritic Sailing Systems   139

3 Seamanship

32. Going to Sea   146
33. Weather   149
34. Working on Deck   156
35. Watchkeeping   157
36. Offshore Visibility   160
37. Performance under Sail   164
38. Spinnakers   167
39. Speed   173
40. Storm Tactics   180
41. Approaching Coral Islands and Reefs from Seaward
        189
42. Piloting in Coral   193
43. Anchoring   201
44. Running Aground in Protected Waters   206
45. Running Aground Offshore   208

4 Emergencies

46. Man Overboard   215

47. Fire   218
48. Collision   219
49. Major Leaks   220
50. Rigging Failure   221
51. Stopping Quickly   222

5 *Navigation*

52. Celestial Navigation   225
53. Passage Planning   227
54. Long-Range Navigation Aids   230

6 *Cruising Life*

55. Foreign Officials   238
56. Getting Along Locally   244
57. Provisioning   253
58. Foreign Marketing   262
59. Galley Equipment   268
60. Precooking Meals for Underway   270
61. Personal Grooming in the Tropics   271
62. Children's Schooling   276
63. The Cost of Cruising   280
64. The Business Side of Cruising   288

7 *The Boat*

65. Crew Size   296
66. Designs   300
67. Multihulls   314
68. Materials   322
69. Positive Buoyancy   326
70. The Rig   327
71. Steering Systems   360
72. Interiors   362
73. Plumbing   393
74. Machinery   396
75. Electrical Systems   416
76. DC-to-AC Inverters   421

8 The "Next" Boat

77. *Masina*   423
78. *Sunflower*   429
79. *Wakaroa*   437
80. *Intermezzo II*   453

Index   489

Foreword

Cruising offshore offers many pleasures: the relief of getting away from the rat race, confidence in your vessel's ability to meet what nature may dish up, the joy of new sights, sounds, and tastes. As self-confidence increases, one begins to realize that it's possible to control one's future. That independence is easier to achieve than previously thought. The longer one journeys, the deeper the rewards become. Eventually new values and priorities assert themselves, even when returning to shore.

To achieve the mental and physical balance necessary to gain the most from one's sailing experiences, it is necessary to remain in harmony with the vessel, her requirements, and your own skills. A partnership based on preparation and confidence must develop.

For every circumnavigator preparing for a transocean voyage, there are thousands of weekend sailors going on their first overnight passage. The gulf in experience and knowledge seems unfathomable, and yet in most respects the basic equipment and seamanship skills required for a safe completion of both voyages are similar.

As cruising becomes more popular, and as once-secluded anchorages are filled, some of those who have gone before talk of the good old days. Derogatory comments on the neophyte's boat-handling antics or his laughable gear echo from under cockpit awnings. But don't forget that even the most hoary blue-water sailor was once a tyro himself.

The authors and their two daughters enjoy a reading session on the foredeck of *Intermezzo II*. (Harrill House)

The thoughts we pass on here have been distilled from hundreds of conversations in anchorages around the world. We have logged some of them under exquisite trade-wind conditions aboard *Intermezzo,* and scrawled a few fighting storm-strength winds and breaking seas. Our intent is to shorten the learning curve for those who come after us.

If your present plans encompass an occasional offshore cruise with day-sailing and office hours in between, some of our comments on lifestyle and equipment won't apply. But once the horizon beckons more strongly, and your vessel becomes a home, the emphasis changes.

Equipment that may seem a superfluous luxury when you are gone for a week or two becomes a "necessity" when the cruising time lengthens. Adding comfort and complexity will increase costs and maintenance, but the extra pleasure derived from many of these luxuries can make life more enjoyable for all aboard. On the other hand luxuries can be expensive. If that means waiting additional years, forget them. . . . Go cruising now!

Throughout our text there runs a theme: you must be prepared at all times for what the sea may throw at you. It's difficult to strike a balance between the pleasurable and positive aspects of cruising and those that simply must be dealt with, come what may. If this book were written to truly reflect our sailing experiences, there would be 20 pages covering seamanship, preparation, and the proper vessel; the rest of the book would be devoted to the enjoyment of life afloat. The problem is that learning to enjoy life afloat is easy, and mistakes are not costly. Mistakes in seamanship, however, can cost you the vessel. Hence our emphasis on the strategically important aspects of offshore sailing.

Our decision to go cruising came rather quickly. I was flying back to California from a meeting in Washington, D.C. It had been a long and difficult week. Once again I was thinking about how dissatisfied I had become with our way of life. I opened the inflight magazine from the seat pocket in front of me. The lead article was about six families who had given up the high-powered, achievement-oriented lifestyle for something different. One of these families had gone sailing. Even reading this, with my lifetime of sailing experience behind me, it didn't take. But at the end of the article, the question was asked "Why didn't you go before?" The answer was "We were afraid to make a change."

I don't know what a religious revelation is like, but I suspect my reaction to that exchange was similar. Lights started flashing and I knew the answer for us was to go cruising. We could view life from a different perspective and reevaluate our priorities. For the rest of the flight I mulled over how to sell the concept to Linda, my wife of seven years. I came up with a carefully conceived, step-by-step plan to bring her around.

On the drive home from the airport I rehearsed my tactics. The sun was shining and it was unusually clear when I pulled into the driveway. Linda was in the kitchen of our five-bedroom house overlooking Santa Monica Bay. She was surrounded by a comfortable home and possessions she treasured. We chatted about the kids, the week I had spent in the East, and I carefully put out the first tenuous feelers of my new plan. With a few discerning questions she cut right to the heart of my proposal and answered—"Let's go." I was dumbfounded.

I grew up on boats. In the late 1940s my dad sold his business in Michigan and bought the beautiful 76-foot Alden schooner *Constellation.* We sailed her down the St. Lawrence Seaway, along the east coast of the U.S., through the West Indies, South America, back to the Panama Canal, and up the west coast of Central America to California. More traditional boats followed, and in my teens I did a stint of ocean racing. Then came dinghy sailing, and finally I became hooked on high-speed multihulls. Up until the instant of my revelation on the airliner, I had spent all my free time designing, building, and racing yachts. On the odd year we squeezed in a week or two cruising with my folks or friends.

Linda's sailing started when we met. I courted her on wet, uncomfortable boats with an occasional sail on something more stately.

At 35 years of age, nothing either of us had done in thousands of miles of sailing had prepared us for a life of long-term cruising. Sure, I knew how to make a boat move, and I knew a little about piloting, but working through the turbulant pass of a South Pacific lagoon, stocking a boat for months at sea, or dealing with foreign officials? These and a thousand questions like them were mysteries to us.

We read every book on cruising we could. And 14 years of sailing magazines were resurrected from the garage and scanned for the cruising articles I had ignored as a racer. We talked with everyone we could find who had spent any real time cruising.

Author Skip Dashew at the helm of his family's 6o′ Alden ketch *Chiriqui*. (S. A. Dashew)

How do you handle children? Do we need a windvane or a an autopilot? What about sail inventory, the dinghy, liferaft, and food stores? Do we take the labels off our cans and varnish them? What supplies can you get in the islands? The list was endless.

But the decision had been made, and we started looking for a yacht. Our stars must have been in the proper alignment for within 6o days we had found, fallen in love with, and bought *Intermezzo,* a 5o-foot Bill Tripp–designed yawl.

Fifteen months of frantic research and work passed before we had the boat prepared and provisioned to go, and still when we left California Yacht Anchorage in Los Angeles harbor I couldn't believe that we were actually getting away.

By the time we had reached Baja California, just a few weeks later, we had started learning about cruising. My carefully repainted boot-

The 76' Alden schooner *Constellation* on which author Skip Dashew (at age seven) and his family embarked on a 20,000-mile cruise. (S. A. Dashew)

top, just a half inch above the water with the boat fully loaded, was continually covered with moss. No calm marinas here, and the continuous lapping of the sea at anchorages along the way was growing a garden for us. Cleaning it weekly became one of the standard chores. I'm sure every one of the dozen experienced people we had talked with knew that you should have three inches, minimum, of bottom paint showing, but they had failed to pass it on. It was too elementary.

Sailing across the Pacific toward the Marquesas, as the weather became warmer and more humid we wilted. *Intermezzo* had no fans aboard, and nothing in the way of a proper sailing awning. Our light clothes were fine for California, but were too heavy for this kind of heat. Furthermore we discovered that the twin jibs we were using took an inordinate amount of time to trim with the shifty northeast trades at our back.

When we arrived in the Marquesa Islands, we found that all our companions at anchor were going through a similar learning experience.

In one major respect we were luckier than most of our new friends. We had had the experience to pick an excellent sea-going boat, one that would hold her value as we cruised and be easy to maintain.

By the time we had reached New Zealand, the main topic of conversation among our cruising friends had switched from amateur radio and refrigeration to the next boat. All were evaluating their experience and discussing what they would do the next time.

But these phases of learning are part of the game. They in no way detract from the overriding conclusion that cruising offers a beautiful way of life, with a sense of freedom not found in any other activity. You learn to be independent and self-sufficient. You find that keeping a diesel engine running isn't difficult, alternators aren't really scary inside, and refrigeration is so simple you wonder how you could ever have paid someone in the service station just to put a can of freon in the air conditioner. The feeling of pride and security derived from a well-stocked, seaworthy vessel ready to sail for a new destination on a moment's notice is unmatched, even if she is sitting at a marina waiting for you to break away from work.

Introduction

It's a pleasure for me to have an opportunity to introduce Steven and Linda Dashew's *The Circumnavigators' Handbook.*

I was able to borrow an early draft of the manuscript, primarily to learn a little bit about the Dashews, for whom we were providing plans for a new offshore cruiser. The primary purpose was accomplished and I did get considerable insight into the preferences and experience of our clients.

Of much more importance, however, was that in almost every chapter I felt that I learned a great deal, all of which would be more than useful not only for someone anticipating a circumnavigation, but really for anybody who enjoys planning an offshore passage.

One does not have to read far to get the message that the secret of a safe and successful offshore trip is careful and thorough preparation for everything that can possibly be anticipated.

I think the authors agree with my own basic preference for simplicity, but at the same time they do not close their eyes to the importance of electronics, perhaps primarily for emergency communication, and secondarily as a backup for more fundamental types of navigation.

An interesting example is a question of anchor chain versus rode lines, and after reading a clear description of some of the areas it was necessary to anchor in, I was forced to accept that there were areas where a chain certainly was necessary, but the fundamental problem of a chain's really snubbing hard in most adverse conditions was very

Elyse and Sarah made many close friends all over the world.

cleverly circumvented by use of relatively light nylon line bridging an area of slack chain and providing that all-important cushion against the sudden takeup which does occur with chain in really bad conditions.

In addition, there was a wonderful explanation with some clear figures of just why any boat equipped with sail should not operate with a standard fixed propeller. While I have argued long and strong against such an unfortunate combination, I was delighted to read some actual figures on the relative performance of the same boat, the same people, the same equipment, comparing the speed under sail with the fixed three-blade propeller versus a folding propeller. I can't wait to get a reprint of this part of the text to carry with me to bolster my own arguments.

Not only does the handbook contain a tremendous wealth of the owners' own wide experience, but they also supplement this with the experience of others whom they have contacted in their long-range wandering.

Perhaps there's one final thing that fueled my enthusiasm, and that was that a great majority of their conclusions quite parallel my own. This is clearly *must* reading, with advice that could and should be followed.

Roderick Stephens, Jr.

Acknowledgments

Every now and then a friend or acquaintance by word or deed will start a process that has profound effects on those close to him. Intentionally or not, John Rousmaniere has had that effect on us. Going back to the days when we had nary a thought of the cruising life, John and I raced together one weekend. Some of his comments and the reactions they triggered started me thinking about a lot of things, including what I was doing with my life. He was there again when, check in hand, I wasn't sure if *Intermezzo* was the right boat or if cruising was the right mode of life. His reinforcement at that point was instrumental in our going ahead with the purchase of what turned out to be a wonderful yacht. When we returned to the States 3½ years later, John encouraged us in the writing of this book, going so far as to introduce us to his own publisher, Eric Swenson at W. W. Norton.

Chuck Tobias, upon his return from his own five-year break with the land, and in the midst of a difficult film project, gave unsparingly of his time and advice when we were desperate for realistic data on long-term cruising. Four years later, in Tortola, we met again after a 37-day nonstop crossing from Cape Town. Chuck was supportive of our writing and gave sound advice on the business aspects of books. Tony Gibbs and Dick Rath at *Yachting,* Keith Taylor, Patience Wales, and Charles Mason at *Sail,* Oliver Moore and Shane

Mitchell at *Motorboating and Sailing,* Phil Thurman and John Wooldridge at *Pacific Skipper,* and Elyse Mintey at *Sea* gave us excellent critical advice and some practical hints on publishing, as well as direct encouragement by publishing our articles.

Chuck and Wendy Adams, Peter and Mary Usmar, Mike and Fred Sidthorpe, Tom and Lisa Miller, and Pony Moore read the manuscript and had excellent comments. Angelo Lavranos took valuable time away from his busy yacht-design practice to point out several weak points in the text. George Sustendal drew on his own substantial experience to critique the text.

Jim and Cheryl Schmidt, Al and Beth Liggett, and Noel and Letara Barrett put up with my questions, requests for photos, and perusal of their yachts.

Tony Mohr took time away from his sound effects business and law practice to proofread the rough-edit the manuscript for us.

Vic Stern and some of our friends at the Ocean Racing Catamaran Association provided the initial impetus that started us thinking about giving up racing and going cruising.

Special thanks are due my dad, Stan Dashew, for his initial support of our cruising plans, and for allowing us to draw on his enormous collection of photographs.

The
Circumnavigators'
Handbook

1
Setting Goals

Once you have made up your mind to try long-distance cruising, the most important item on the agenda is an analysis of goals. This has to be more than what type of boat or gear you'll be working toward. Finances, career evaluation, what you're shooting for in a lifestyle, and a time frame for achieving it—all have to be considered.

Linda and I long ago found that it was best to sit down together and discuss the options. If there were others about who could relate to what we were trying to achieve, they provided a good sounding board. Verbalizing options, and then *writing them down,* helped clarify the direction we should go.

The most important area to be considered is finances. Budgets have to be established for the purchase of a vessel, for equipping it, for monthly expenses while cruising, and for emergencies. This varies tremendously depending on the lifestyle you aspire to, your current career status, and what you have in the way of prior commitments. A lot will have to do with what you're willing to give up in the way of creature comforts.

A person well established in a career, with a good income, a home, and perhaps a boat already down in the marina, will have the most difficult choices. On the plus side, the option is there of reducing a land-based lifestyle and rapidly accumulating a cruising kitty. On the other hand more than a short break from a good career can make it difficult to return to the old niche. Do you go now, or wait a few years?

At the other end of the spectrum are the younger cruisers who are just getting started in life. They have few commitments, are at an age when they can cruise a while and then reenter the mainstream. They can enjoy a more basic lifestyle offshore. Enthusiasm makes up for lack of cash. One thing is sure: no two cruisers are going to have the same set of conditions and options to evaluate.

A really thorny problem is getting back into the same lifestyle you left, should you decide to return to the fold. A lot of people burn their bridges behind them and can't return. Others who didn't (like ourselves) wish at times they had made a clean break before they left.

The matter of housing creates the biggest problems. Most cruisers trade their home equity for a boat. It's a great way to go, and they find their living costs substantially reduced once aboard. But with inflation a fact of life in our day and age, will they be able to move back into a house upon returning?

In setting financial goals, it is crucial to be realistic. If you are to err on living costs, err on the high side. Vessel acquisition is a fixed amount, but the cost of preparation is as variable as the size of your wallet. The gear you add after buying the boat must be carefully budgeted. That budget must be adhered to.

Planning for a certain date of departure is also a must. Your time schedule has to include purchasing and preparing the boat, sharpening personal skills, rounding up home affairs, giving notice at work, and saying good-bye. All of these can take longer than you think if you can't keep to a schedule. There are many philosophies about how flexible to be, but we feel strongly that you should set a date and go. Beyond essential areas of preparation for seamanship and safety, anything else can be done once you're out there. Leaving on time, even if your destination is only 100 miles down the coast, frees you of many of the expenses of land-based operation that invariably hang on until the lines are cut. It improves morale and adds to the time your money will last.

A larger question of timing, mentioned earlier, asks "What's the best time of life to go cruising?" Do you go early, before establishing a career, do you delay until the children are grown, or do you wait for retirement?

Cruisers are going earlier and staying out longer than ever before. It is clearly easiest to cruise without children: a smaller boat is possible and costs are less. Furthermore, the younger you are, the easier it is to overlook some of the niceties of life.

Children complicate the scene. Schooling, space, extra costs while at sea all intrude. Young children are easiest to cruise with because they are flexible. They can keep up with school through correspondence or similar programs, and they thrive on the extra time they spend with their parents; also, the parents have control over their environment. It's more work, but certainly worthwhile. But the decision becomes more difficult when the kids reach teenage status. Older children frequently are reluctant to leave friends, schools, and activities.

Those waiting for retirement age have to weigh the health of youth against the financial security of that monthly check. There are no easy answers.

But through it all, keep the goal firmly in mind—going cruising.

2
Preparation

It goes without saying that the offshore cruising yacht must be properly prepared to deal with whatever the sea throws at you. Proper rigging and safety gear, emergency equipment, backup systems, and ground tackle are all essential. Regardless of the size of the boat or your budget, the yacht must be ready for her sea trials.

On the other hand the average cruiser spends less than 10 percent of his time at sea. The other 90 percent is spent in anchorages where the daily business of living goes on. For a long-term cruise to be successful you must give careful consideration to the various amenities of the cruising life aboard, both at sea and at anchor.

There are certain elements of preparation that are common to all boat sizes and pocketbooks. Nobody can cruise in the tropics without awnings, but you can get by without air conditioning. You must have at least a primus stove to heat food; a microwave oven is nice but not necessary.

In general, cruising lore has had it that a good offshore voyaging yacht should be spartan. Generators, refrigerators, electronic navigation aids could not be repaired in distant ports and should not be relied upon. Our experience is that if they are within your budget, some of the creature comforts of life are worth having, even at sea.

When we bought *Intermezzo,* I had planned to strip her of what I then considered nonessentials in order to simplify maintenance and our lifestyle. The big diesel, refrigeration, radar, even the hot-water heater were all on the scrap list. What I didn't recognize was the difference between living aboard full time and taking occasional extended cruises: after the short cruise we had a warm house, well-stocked freezer, and hot shower waiting for us at home; it's a different story when the boat *is* your home.

I was forestalled in any rash moves not by that realization (at the time), but by a well-honed commercial instinct. What I wanted to do to *Intermezzo* would make it difficult to resell her later. So the amenities stayed. By the time we finally sold her, we not only had learned to appreciate those amenities, but had added many more.

In general, when it comes to making major changes in the rigging, interior, or machinery of a well-found yacht, my advice is to wait. After you have accumulated experience on board, your concept will be different.

1. *Intermezzo*

Every yacht is a compromise, all the more so if you're working on a budget (who isn't?). *Intermezzo* is an excellent example of this. When we first made plans to go cruising I had several criteria for a yacht. First was a budget, including an equipment list of what I considered minimum gear for our purposes. Second, I wanted a stock boat that would have a ready resale market should we change our plans. Third, I wanted the largest yacht we could afford and handle. Beyond these basic parameters and that of a "modern" design, we had no prejudices.

In 1975 there were not nearly as many choices available on the market as today. Economics and practical experience forced us toward ex-racing yachts with good inventories. The IOR racing rule was just really coming into its own and the late designs to the Cruising Club of America rule were selling at a big discount.

I had been scanning the magazines, calling brokers and visiting marinas for some months when I returned home from a New York business trip in May 1975. A new issue of one of the yachting magazines had come in my absence and I eagerly turned to the brokerage pages. My business had finished early on the East Coast and it was midday in Los Angeles as I scanned the ads looking for our new yacht. Something caught my eye and I called a Newport Beach brokerage firm. No, that vessel was not what we wanted, but the broker had another. . . . It had been a long week and I didn't really want to go into the office. Linda and I had a quick bite, jumped in the car, and as an excuse to get away for a drive, went to Newport to see another "deal."

Intermezzo lay in the dock behind her owner's home in a regal manner. Her brightwork gleamed, stainless and chrome were polished, and she looked huge. She was heavier than we had wanted with a displacement of 35,000 lbs., and she had the long overhangs common to most of the light-weather racing designs of the CCA era. Her accommodations were laid out strictly for racing, with nine bunks and two heads all in the center of the boat, the fine ends not being good for anything but appearance. Her equipment list, including 24 bags of sails, was extensive and the price was very right.

We made an offer subject to the owner's permission to inspect the vessel ourselves over a two-week period, prior to survey.

I went down with a sailing friend and took her apart, literally. We checked the entire hull-to-deck bond, all wiring and plumbing, every inch of bulkhead bonding, through-hull fittings, chain plates, rigging, mast tangs, the works. I had never seen such a well-built "production" boat in my life.

From my sailmaking friend Swede Johnson, of Baxter and Cicero, I found that she had been built on a special basis for a well-known racer during the last of the "factory team era" in the late 1960s. That accounted for the structure. But I could hardly believe she had ever been really pushed. Swede, having done some miles on her himself, assured me she had been sailed hard, even though she didn't show it. All the more to her credit.

We had a formal survey done which she passed with flying colors, and it was time to go to the bank.

Linda, the children, and I handed over our check to the brokers and we were off for Catalina.

What a thrill it was to sail down Newport harbor for the first time at the helm of *Intermezzo*. I had covered the same water hundreds or maybe thousands of times in dinghies and racing boats, but there was a difference from the deck of a 50-foot soon-to-be-cruising yacht.

I reviewed her characteristics as we moved along. She was 50 feet on deck (57 feet overall counting the boomkin and bowsprit) with an "extreme" yawl rig to take advantage of the free sail area under the CCA rule in the mizzen staysail. Built originally by Columbia yachts to a Bill Tripp design, she had been a flat-out racing boat. There was no denying she was fast in her conditions-light airs. An impressive string of victories against top Southern California competition attested to that. She was narrow by today's standards at 12 feet, and had a waterline of 36 feet (when loaded for cruising) and a displacement of 36,000 lbs. There was 15,000 lbs. of lead ballast encapsulated in her solid fiberglass keel. The deck was balsa cored forward, with two layers of one-inch plywood sandwiched between three laminates of fiberglass aft to take winch loads.

Underwater she had what was then called a fin keel, with a detached spade rudder, heavily supported. Designed for racing in light airs, she sported a very tall rig and, by the standards of her day, a minimum wetted-surface hull design.

These last two attributes were very beneficial in most of our cruising, since we encountered winds in the 8- to 12-knot range more than anything else.

The trade-off for the speed in the light airs and low wetted-surface hull shape was lack of interior volume. While she had a moderate displacement (heavy by today's standards), the hull volume was deep and in the center of the boat. Her ends were fine, without much room for living or storage. She had the power and comfort at sea of a 50-footer but the accommodation volume of a modern 40-footer. Considering our intended usage and budget, it was an excellent compromise.

Her rig could best be described as a double-headsail sloop with a mizzen stuck onto the back end. The mizzen looked very pretty and it was an excellent place for the radar she carried, but it had running backstays and the seven-foot boom extended past the stern almost four feet. Swede Johnson, who had helped design the rig, counseled getting rid of it. He was absolutely right for cruising as it turned out, but she looked so nice with it back there, and after all, it might come in handy some day—so we left it in.

Once out of Newport Harbor we set course for Long Point on Catalina Island and sat back to see how the Benmar autopilot would behave. With a light sea breeze blowing we were ambitiously carrying our heavy #1 genoa, big staysail, full main and mizzen. As the breeze built with the afternoon heat we pulled down the mizzen, then staysail, and finally took a reef in the main. Soon we were furling sails in the lee of Long Point after averaging almost 8 knots on the wind. I was impressed.

With only three months to go until our projected departure date we listed what we would have to do to prepare the boat for shorthanded sailing. First, I would have to make some choices in sail inventory. It simply wasn't possible to carry her full 24-bag wardrobe with us all the time. There would be no room left for the peanut butter we knew we would have to have aboard.

We eventually settled on taking a light #1 genoa (3.5-oz. high cut) and its matching 2.2-oz. staysail. The heavy #1 was cut down to make a 6.5-oz. working jib of short overlap, good for sailing in and out of tight spots if we had engine trouble and well proportioned for poling out when running. The ¾-oz. drifter with its wire luff stayed aboard and saw many thousands of miles of action both running and reaching. This would frequently be carried to leeward of the main, freed off at the head in blooper fashion. The 8.5-oz. #2 heavy genoa stayed with us as a primary upwind sail. At 540 square feet we could stow it without too much difficulty, and it also served well in a breeze downwind or reaching with the big staysail set underneath. There was a heavy #3 jib, and we had made a survival jib of 50 square feet. For the forestay we had made a 10-oz. storm sail which would balance nicely against a double-reefed main or the mizzen.

There were two racing mains to select from. We chose the "heavy" main, cut for San Francisco Bay racing. I reasoned it would be used mainly upwind and here its flatness would be a help. I didn't expect to use it much off the wind. That was a big mistake, as we soon found that rather than twin jibs we carried a light #1 on the pole and the main, with occasionally the drifter to leeward. Many is the time I rued selling our light-air main.

There were two mizzen staysails and a mizzen spinnaker. We took them all, but used primarily the ¾-oz. mizzen staysail.

Intermezzo had come to us with five spinnakers and I had initially decided to sell them. During a club race, however, Linda, the children, and I had no trouble flying the spinnaker so we decided to take one along. We chose a 1.5-oz. cross-cut for strength and ease of flying, and we were glad to have it.

We found that the mizzen was rarely used, and then usually only in the lightest wind ranges. If the mizzen staysail was set and we forgot to rig one of the running backstays, the mast could come down. After almost making this mistake, we cut the mizzen boom down so a standing backstay could be used, consigning the mizzen to service as a steadying sail at anchor. To ease the chattering when swinging in a breeze, we had the sail fully battened which did an excellent job of quieting it down.

During the balance of our long weekend at Catalina we decided on several major areas of gear to purchase: a windvane to back up our autopilot, an omega set to help us with sightless days in the Pacific, and roller-furling gear for the forward triangle.

We initially chose an RVG vane. This unit with its permanent in-the-water installation, skeg, and trim-tab-operated rudder looked good, but couldn't really handle *Intermezzo* at speed. (We exchanged it for a servo-pendulum-style Aries in French Polynesia; that did an excellent job as long as there was some breeze.) We picked up a Roach omega that was simple to operate and inexpensive. At the time we felt the $1600 price tag a good investment, and in spite of the early problems with omega propagation we would choose it again under the same circumstances. For roller-furling gear we went to the Mariner company and got one of their hank-on furling systems. We put this gear on both the headstay and forestay, and were pleased with the help it gave us in handling our big sails.

Back again in Los Angeles after our first weekend out, we went through *Intermezzo,* clipboard in hand, making a list of what gear should be replaced. The batteries were getting toward the end of their life span, so they were exchanged. Heat exchangers on the 50-h.p. Izusu diesel were changed to Cupra Nicol; a second alternator was added, as was a second set of oil and temperature gauges that could be seen from the navigation area. We installed a Halon manual fire extinguishing system in the engine compartment under the main cabin sole, an extra electric bilge pump, and a 60-gallon-per-minute Jabsco for damage control on the front of the engine. We also bought a second set of blades for our Martec folding prop that had more pitch in them to give us better power when we were motorsailing. We added a wire jackstay that ran on the deck from one side of the cockpit around the forestay and back to the other side of the cockpit to attach ourselves to when working forward, a collision patch, bungs for all the through-hull fittings, and a permanent radar reflector.

It soon became apparent that I wouldn't be able to disentangle myself from business commitments as readily as I had hoped, and with the weather patterns being what they were, we were committed to another year of preparation.

During this period we decided to modify *Intermezzo*'s interior to make her more suitable for cruising shorthanded.

Working within the guidelines of what had already been built, and keeping all the basic structural elements intact, we were able to make substantial-appearing changes for minimum cost. Forward, where there had been two fore-and-aft single bunks that made up into sail stowage bins, we were able to build a large full-size double bunk athwartships. (We found this position an advantage in rolly anchorages as it reduced body movements. While broad-reaching or running there was no problem sleeping across the boat, but when reaching or beating we retired to the main saloon.) There were two heads amidships which we felt to be an extravagant use of space, so in the starboard one we left the basin intact but removed the toilet and added six extremely deep shelves to form our "pantry." It was valuable, easy-access storage, built in such a way that the shelves could be removed and the space converted back to a toilet.

The main saloon was more of a challenge. She had a traditional ocean-racing layout of two pilot berths to a side with a settee below (also used as a bunk) and a double wing table in the middle. The table was supported by two-inch vertical aluminum pipes. Given her 12-foot beam, it was a tight area and anyone subject to claustrophobia would have been in trouble in spite of the light-painted paneling and teak trim.

Our solution was to remove the forward port pilot berth, pull out the support poles, and cut down the table. The port fore-and-aft settee then had an athwartships running seat added to it along the forward bulkhead to form an L-shaped seat, and the table was placed on a single pedestal off-center. This made a tremendous difference in the floor space available, and opened up the saloon visually to what seemed like double the previous space. It had the added advantage

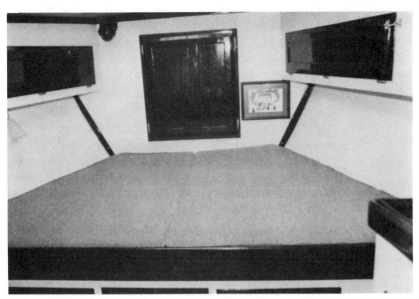

Our athwartships double berth—7′ long at the after end, 5′8″ at the front end, and 52″ across.

Port side of the saloon where we used to have pilot berths.

The starboard side of the saloon with two pilot berths.

of making access to the "engine room," located under the saloon floorboards, a lot easier.

In the galley we built several lockers into the foot area of the after port pilot berth, and a lift-up shelf alongside the companionway.

The navigation station to starboard, opposite the galley, with its quarterberth under the cockpit, was left as it was.

The modifications were accomplished for about 200 man-hours and a modest amount of material. Linda and I did the required paint and varnish work to match up the new materials.

On deck we found the basic racing cockpit layout excellent. There were Barient 32s for primary winches, 28s for secondaries, and 16s for use on the vang and/or the mainmast running backstays. The halyard winches for headsails and mainsail were on the mast and were #22 Barients, except for the main halyard winch which was a reel winch design with which I would never ship again.

The spinnaker poles were large diameter with thin walls that had been chemically milled to reduce weight. I could lift a pole with one hand, and the Barient chain drive on the mast made setting pole height very simple.

We consulted Swede Johnson about a storm trysail and decided that instead we would put a third reef in the main and heavily reinforce the head. The third reef had a permanent pendant rove when at sea, but fortunately we seldom saw conditions that forced us to use the reef.

We acquired a 14-foot "pulling boat" in fiberglass, an 8-foot inflatable (later sold), and enlarged our propane gas capacity to 10 gallons, stored on deck. We added a McCulloch brushless alternator gas-driven by a 4-h.p. Briggs and Stratton single-cylinder engine. This was for backup and we stowed it below, after carefully cleaning out its self-contained fuel tank.

The interior cushions were all recovered using a combination of grained vinyl on one side and an industrial-quality synthetic fabric on the other. At sea we left the vinyl side up and saved the less practical but more luxurious fabric side for port.

A minor addition that was to have a major impact on our comfort and convenience was a Tripp 500-watt, 12- to 110-volt inverter. With this Linda could use a mixer or blender in the galley and run a powerful 110-volt AC vacuum when cleaning up below. It would also handle my power tools, albeit with some difficulty.

Throughout the initial stages of the trip we were pleased with our improvements. But a period of idleness in New Zealand got us to thinking about some additional changes, and we ended up doing a major renovation of the interior.

In the main saloon we removed the port-side after pilot berth altogether, and the old bench seat. Along the hull we built in a 14-foot double bookshelf. Where the forward end of the bunks had been outboard of the port head we put our radio gear, where it would be dry in any conditions imaginable. A new settee was built alongside the hull, which gave us a lot more room at the table while opening up the saloon visually. In the galley we tore down the fridge, reinsulated it, and completely redid the compressor, hold plates, and related hardware, adding a small freezer in the process. The freezer proved to be a valuable asset, and we were sorry that we hadn't made it larger than its two cubic feet (which held 100 lbs. of carefully packed meat).

We really made changes to the after end of *Intermezzo*. I had been seeing all the space in our huge cockpit and lazarette as a liability in the Indian Ocean and rounding the Cape of Good Hope. We had also found that in extreme heavy going it was difficult to keep the large companionway hatch watertight.

At the start of a long project in Green-
hithe, New Zealand.

After three hard months of work our
new cockpit and bridge deck are ready to
go to sea.

So we embarked on an ambitious project to create an aft stateroom from the old cockpit, making a new cockpit farther aft where the mizzen mast and lazarette had been. This seemingly impossible task was accomplished with relative ease by using the existing cockpit combings as cabin sides. Over this was built a multilaminate plywood-and-teak roof. The old cockpit sole, back as far as the cockpit divider, became an athwartships double bunk and the children's stateroom. The companionway hatch stayed the same, but the bottom three feet of it was permanently blocked off to give us a much more secure interior.

The mizzen mast was moved forward from its extreme aft position to the end of the new "bridge deck" over the now aft cabin, which put it just in front of the helm. *Intermezzo* thus was transfigured to a ketch, and the resulting mizzen, now enlarged to 120 square feet (still fully battened), became a much more useful sail.

An all-teak cockpit was built into the old lazarette/helmsman area. The seats were 6½ feet long, giving us more fore-and-aft seating than before, but a much narrower cockpit. We solved the problem of cockpit drains with two large pipes fiberglassed from the back of the well directly through the transom, above the waterline.

Aside from the additional interior space and drier hatch opening, we found two very interesting advantages. First, we had an excellent seat for keeping watch on top of the bridge deck with our feet down the companionway. It was high enough to give us good visibility seated, relatively dry, and physically secure. Second, we found the bridge deck area got a lot more use than the cockpit in nice weather. Last, we were able to rig permanent sailing awnings in the forward shrouds of the mizzen, over the bridge deck, and an awning under the mizzen to cover the cockpit. Both of these fed our water tanks, giving us a rain catcher at sea or in port.

The negatives came in sitting outside in foul weather. We no longer had the protection of the big dodger that had covered the companionway and forward end of the old cockpit. So nobody went on deck if it was wet unless they had to.

The aftcabin project was accomplished in 900 man-hours, and Linda and I once again did the finish work.

The next project was to redo the doghouse windows. These were ⅜" plastic set into light aluminum frames, and I had always been worried about them. We had storm shutters just in case, but if we

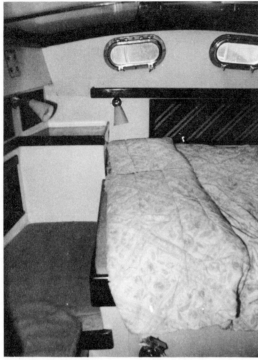

The athwartships double bunk where *Intermezzo*'s cockpit used to be.

lost one the salt water in the navigation area would be an expensive lesson on all our transistors. We ended up ripping out the old windows entirely and going to 1-inch-thick plastic windows, 2½ inches bigger than the openings all around, and set *outside* the doghouse, so they would bear directly on the fiberglass structure and not depend on a frame for integrity. The interior raw fiberglass was covered with attractive teak frames.

With the Indian Ocean ahead and a lot of miles left to go, we replaced the lower standing rigging on the mainmast as well as some of the tangs. Other tangs had shown signs of elongation on the mast and to these we added welded-bearing washers.

The last change we made was in the sail plan. An extra tang was added eight feet above the old inner forestay position. A new forestay was made and longer pendants made up for the running backstays, which were also moved eight feet up the mast. On this higher staysail stay we were able to set our #3 working jib. This enabled us to carry a light #1 on the headstay with the #3 as a staysail rolled up, and change down in headsail size by using our roller-furling gear. We also

The front-opening ports kept the galley and navigation area well ventilated.

A galley that missed only one sea-going meal in 3½ years.

found that the #3 could be flown to leeward when the #1 was on the pole to weather broad-reaching or running. In Mauritius, preparing for the last heavy weather toward Africa, we put the old rig back, which provided better mast support and gave us back our permanently rigged storm staysail. We thus had the capability of picking the ideal rig for either the heavier winds of the high latitudes or the lighter trade-wind conditions.

These changes took us to the end of the trip. They made *Intermezzo* a much more livable yacht, easier to handle, and definitely safer. The cost in cash was moderate for what it accomplished, and we ended up with a heavily built, well-tested vessel that we knew, outfitted in much the same manner as we would have done had we started from scratch with a new yacht.

2. Ground Tackle

Ground tackle and anchoring techniques for a serious cruising yacht differ considerably from the equipment and skills adequate for local sailing. Not only do you have to cope with a wide variety of bottom conditions not found close to home, but you can rarely count on reliable data on weather and current conditions. Obviously the cruiser must be able to cope with the worst conditions and still have a margin of safety. The problem comes in trying to visualize what kind of conditions you may have to face. Sheer weight and size of anchoring gear do not give a full range of protection.

Before going further, we'll describe a situation we experienced at the beginning of our trip. We were anchored inside the lagoon on Takaroa in the Tuamotus, enjoying our first afternoon in a coral atoll. The sky was an exquisite pale blue, and a gentle southeast wind was blowing. It was the first anchorage in six months since we had left Los Angeles that was both clean and quiet, without the roll so prevalent in the Mexican and Marquesan anchorages.

As we entertained newfound friends in our cockpit, we noticed a mast moving toward us from the other side of the lagoon. It was a 23-year-old single-hander from Newport Beach, Dean Kewish, sailing a beautiful Vancouver 27. Dean dropped his hook about 30 yards to the east of us, and when he snugged up he was abeam. After getting acquainted on the last of our Carta Blanca beer, we retired for an early dinner and what we thought was to be a restful night's sleep.

About 2100 the wind veered from southeast to west and began to blow 15 knots, gusting higher. The change in motion woke me, and as I glanced at the telltale compass over our bunk it took a minute for the implications of the shift to filter in. Where before the reef to the east of us had prevented a chop, we were now facing waves building up across 10 miles of lagoon with an average depth of 60 feet. The ensuing nine hours until daylight were the most anxiety-filled I have ever experienced in a lifetime afloat.

From a quiet and peaceful anchorage, with a steady light trade blowing, we were suddenly looking at a building sea and wind with no possibility of slipping out to the safety of the ocean, no reference marks ashore for bearings, and a steep-to reef not more than 100 feet abaft our transom. What was worse, since in the dark we were not sure of our distance to the reef, I didn't dare let out more scope. We were anchored in typical atoll conditions: a coral bottom with a covering of thin sand. The anchor had withstood only half reverse before dragging when we set it, but then we were in a protected anchorage in light airs. Throughout the evening and into the early-morning hours the wind continued to build until it was gusting 45 knots, with a four-foot sea running, accompanied by torrential rains.

I kept the engine running all night, occasionally putting the prop in gear in the heavier gusts. The depthfinder was flashing away but it didn't give much comfort, as it wouldn't show a change until we were sitting on the reef. Our only solace came from Dean's cabin light. If he was not dragging, then we weren't either, as our relative bearing didn't appear to be changing. The radar was going as well, but we were so close in that it was difficult to measure distance accurately.

The worst part of that night was the grating, snapping, and crushing sounds emenating from our anchor chain. The bottom had numerous coral heads scattered about, and as we plunged up and down

Intermezzo's double anchoring system. Both a CQR and a Danforth are carried at the end of the bowsprit. The roller-furling system shown is a Mariner hank-on system.

and occasionally from side to side in the shifts, the chain would foul and then snap the coral heads. The resulting tumultuous assault on our ears was incredible. It sounded as if our chain was alternately going to snap, pull the windlass off the deck, or jerk the anchor out of the bottom.

To ease the strain, we rigged our standard double shock absorber. This consisted of a 30-foot piece of ⅜" three-strand nylon line tied to the chain and secured to the bow so that 6 feet of chain hung slack, and then a second section 8 feet long with 2 feet of chain slack. Normally the first section would be just stretched tight. In the big surges the second would draw tight, and occasionally the gypsy would take some load.

Dawn found us still afloat with somewhat shattered nerves. We were delighted to see one of the locals paddling out to us through the still-rough water. He had his 13-year-old son expertly drop him off on our boat, and then the son returned in the outrigger. He guided us back to the relative calm of the pass where we tied up at the copra wharf. Dean followed us without a guide as he had traversed the pass twice before and was more familiar with it. We considered ourselves lucky to be afloat and determined never to be caught in a similar situation.

This episode illustrates many of the factors facing cruising yachts at one time or another, and while it takes place in an exotic setting, the lessons are universal in application.

The primary problem is that a majority of tropical anchorages are in coral-infested waters with a bottom of thin sand over hard coral or rock. On a smaller boat this doesn't create a big problem as a its anchor will dig into the sand a shallow distance. A plow-type anchor on a 30-foot boat is usually acceptable under these conditions. That night, Dean's 25-pounder held him tight; we, on the other hand, rode to a 60-lb. CQR and dragged about 50 feet. Had the wind or seas increased another 20 percent, our anchor would not have held at all.

The CQR plow is the most popular lightweight anchor among the cruisers, and for good reason. It has an excellent holding-power/ weight ratio and self-stows easily (see illustrations). Since it is a deep-burying anchor it will not trip itself out if the direction of pull is changed. This last factor is significant in tidal anchorages and where you can expect a change of wind direction. The drawback with the CQRs is that they will not hold well in soft mud, which means that they are no good for anchoring off river mouths or in areas with substantial run-off of topsoil. Another problem they have is in the thin sand and coral conditions found in so many tropical anchorages. In many cases there will be less than six inches of sand in which to bury. As Dean Kewish's experience proved, this is no problem for a small boat's CQR. With a larger vessel like 50-foot *Intermezzo,* however, the anchor and anchoring loads increase, requiring a greater bottom penetration for commensurate holding power. With

The raised teak breakwater directs mud from the anchor chain overboard through a forward scupper.

rock or coral under a thin layer of sand, there is no room for penetration and the result is limited holding power.

The Danforth-type lightweight anchors have good points to fill in for the CQR. These anchors have a much greater fluke area and do not require such a deep penetration to gain their holding power. In the thin sand conditions described, a Danforth will give much better holding. But it doesn't bury as deeply as the CQR and has a tendency to trip and require resetting when the direction of pull is changed; in these conditions, a careful anchor watch is necessary. Furthermore, in poor bottom conditions the flukes can become jammed with coral or debris, which prevents them from penetrating. Another problem occurs when they foul coral heads. The difference in construction makes the Danforth-type anchor more vulnerable to damage under these conditions than the CQR.

In soft mud, though, the Danforth is positively amazing. We once tried anchoring with our CQR at Waiheke Island in the Haurakae Gulf of New Zealand. Even with 8 to 1 scope it wouldn't hold. My dad was aboard and observed that we didn't have enough chain out. Having been through this before, I asked if he would care to wager. The terms set, we proceeded to let out all 80 fathoms of our chain in the 2-fathom anchorage. Even the miniscule backing capability of our folding prop was enough to drag anchor and chain all over the bay. After retrieving this system, we set the Danforth with its short chain and ¾" nylon line. With a 5 to 1 scope it dug in abruptly and held against full reverse power.

There are a number of copies of both the CQR and Danforth anchors on the market. I'm sure that some of them are quite good, but with my vessel at stake, I think it best to stay with anchors that have earned their reputation over the long haul.

The Viking company produces an aluminum anchor, similar to the Danforth design, which has some excellent attributes. It combines

These twin CQRs, photographed in Noumea, New Caledonia, held the powerful French ketch *Cologne* on her circumnavigation.

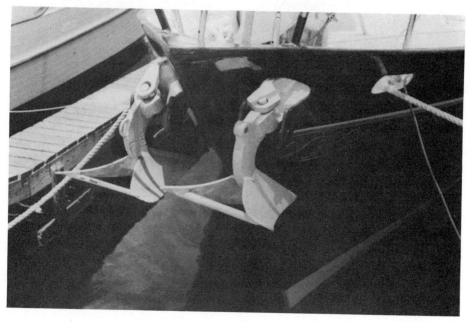

The stainless-steel nosepiece aboard *Swan* in Cape Town, South Africa.

Twin anchoring/mooring bits aboard the cutter *Caticus Rex*.

Intermezzo's aluminum Viking anchor carried on her boomkin.

light weight with extreme fluke area, so that under a majority of conditions it will hold as well as its heavier counterpart. For a kedge or stern anchor, where you are handling it from a dinghy, it's an obvious choice. The Viking has the further advantage of being assembled with bolts, so that spare anchors can be easily carried.

The Northhill stainless sea-plane anchor is a good all-around pick. It has excellent holding power, and on bottoms with more weed than a Danforth or CQR can penetrate it may get the job done. Its disadvantages include bulkiness and a tendency to foul its rode, since it lies with a nonburied fluke.

The Herreshoff Yachtsman anchor (also known in variations as a mariner's or fisherman's anchor) is excellent in rock and weed. Many people feel that one of these of significant proportions should be carried disassembled as the anchor of last resort. For rocky coasts or foul coral bottoms I would agree, but their usefulness in the tropics, compared to a Danforth and CQR, is open to debate. Still, if you need to use it only once in a lifetime, it's cheap insurance.

The Bruce anchor is new to the yachting scene and offers a potential combination of the best points of the Danforth and CQR. Non-

Intermezzo II's Bruce anchor.

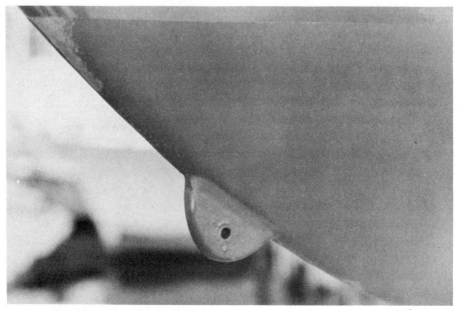

Lug for tying off chain on *Intermezzo II*, located right at the waterline. By lowering the attachment point of the chain we reduce scope requirements or substantially increase holding power.

tripping, with greater fluke area than the CQR, it doesn't have the structural disadvantage of the Danforth when clearing fouls. It is claimed that the Bruce can be utilized at a 30-degree angle and maintain 50 percent of its pulling power. Proven in the North Sea on oil rigs and commercial vessels, it could be the ultimate cruising anchor. On *Intermezzo II* we gave the 110-lb. Bruce a try and found that it lived up to its reputation.

As to size, our experience has taught us that one should carry the largest possible anchor and use it for everyday anchorages. The holding power goes up in proportion to the fluke area, and that goes up dramatically with the weight. Yet going from a 40-pounder to a 70-pounder is only a small percentage increase in the *overall* weight of the total anchoring system. Remember that most of the time you will be anchoring in less than ideal conditions and a few extra square inches of anchor surface are going to make a big difference. For a small overall gain in weight you will achieve a big gain in security.

Aboard *Intermezzo* we started out with a 60-lb. CQR as our primary, everyday anchor. When we left Los Angeles, people laughed at us for carrying such a large weight on the end of the bow. And indeed the data in the various handbooks we read indicated that this should be considered a "storm" anchor for a boat of our size and windage. Yet after a few months of cruising, we jumped at the chance to trade up to a 75-pounder in Fiji. The difference those 15 lbs. made in setting time when anchoring in poor bottoms was really amazing. If we had to do it over again, we would go with a 100-pounder. There is virtually no difference in handling a self-stowing anchor of 100 lbs. compared to one of 60 lbs.; the increase in safety factor, however, is dramatic.

For secondary work we used a 40-lb. Danforth standard, stowed in a chain pipe on the bowsprit. This gave us the option of using either or both anchors quickly. Having the second anchor ready to go at a moment's notice is a big advantage when you want to rush a second hook into the bottom quickly.

A third anchor should be carried for the stern. We use a large Viking aluminum anchor. It has the fluke area of a 60-lb. steel Danforth yet weighs only 22 lbs.

Many boats we have seen use stern anchors half the size of the bow gear. This can be a costly mistake. We have often found that the wind has swung and all the load is on the stern, or worse, broadside, when

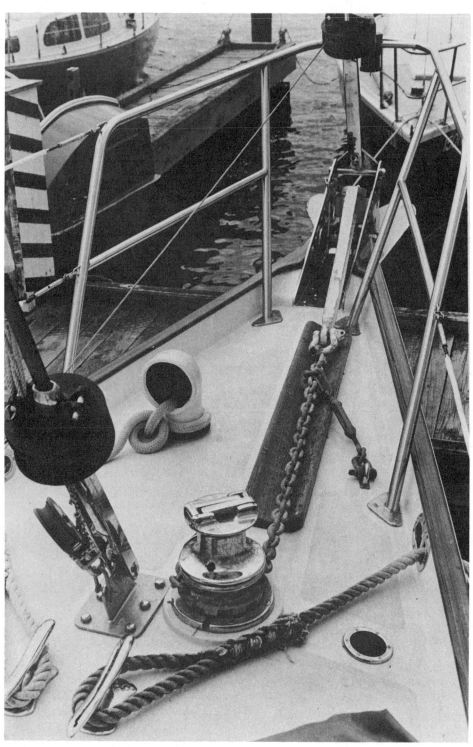

Businesslike ground tackle system aboard the 68′ *Deerfoot* in Auckland, New Zealand. Note the teak chafing strip and spare rode available from the port-side forepeak cowl. The turnbuckle and chain claw ensure that the anchor stays "home" at sea. (S. A. Dashew)

both bow and stern anchors are working harder than under heavy bow conditions.

I prefer to avoid anchoring to more than one hook whenever possible. Being bridled means it will be difficult to exit in a hurry should this be required. Or conditions may be such that it is difficult to recover the second anchor on leaving.

How many anchors you carry will depend on your cruising grounds. If the bottom tends to be foul, or the water murky or especially cold, more anchors will be necessary. In the tropics, assuming scuba gear is aboard, you can count on retrieving a fouled anchor. (We averaged one bad foul every four or five months.) Otherwise, when cruising for an extended period you should have at least two spares over your minimum inventory. This would put you up to five anchors.

Of course, if you're sailing closer to home, with marinas along the way, you can get away with a minimum of three.

Cruisers that risk sailing in cyclone or hurricane belts during the season will want to have aboard not only extra anchors, but the rodes and chain to go with them. Should it be necessary to take to a less than perfect hurricane hole, the extra gear may be necessary.

What's the best anchor rode? I have rarely found an experienced seaman with anything but chain. Nylon is much stronger and has excellent elastic properties which reduce shock loading on the anchor and the vessel, but it cannot stand abrasion and chafe as well as metal. When anchoring in coral-filled waters there simply is no alternative to chain if you want to sleep well without an anchor watch. There are areas of the Caribbean that offer open stretches of sand, but in the Indian and Pacific Oceans this type of anchorage is rare. A slight wind shift and you are working against a coral head.

Chain size is one of the thorniest problems for the cruiser. No body of technical data exists on the proper size of chain for a cruising vessel. Recommendations are generally based on length, and vary between sailboats and powerboats. No consideration is given to windage, hull shape, or external conditions. And the data presented are not backed up by any calculations from which you can interpolate.

In general, though, remember that even in poor weather the loads on an anchor rode are not that high. A 50-footer like *Intermezzo* might generate only 2000 lbs. of load in 60 or 70 knots of wind. We utilized a single piece of ⅜" nylon three-strand as a shock absorber in our anchoring system. This piece of ⅜", without benefit of any chafing gear, stood repeated use, day in and day out, in some pretty good blows for three years!

On the other hand if the anchor chain is snagged on a coral head or some other underwater obstruction, the vertical loads as the bow lifts to a swell are enormous. If there's going to be a problem with chain, it occurs in this type of situation.

In addition to chain size, there are different types of chains to consider. Long link, stud link, proof coil, BBB—these are but some of the terms used to describe the various designs. Then there are grades of chain. As an example, look at what the Campbell Chain Company has to offer for 5⁄16" chain. Their system 3 (comparable to BBB) chain has a working load limit of 1900 lbs. Their system 4 (schedule 40) is rated at 3900 lbs., and their system 7 goes to 4700 lbs. working. (Note: It's normal practice in the United States to rate working load at a quarter of ultimate breaking strength.) Tradition would indicate that *Intermezzo*'s conservative chain size would be 7⁄16" with a working strength of 3700 lbs. In most cases, tradition is talking about 7⁄16" BBB chain, so by going to a schedule 40 higher yield alloy steel, we can drop to 5⁄16" yet still have a higher working and ultimate strength.

We chose to go with the lighter weight, high-yield chain, and carry extra depth: 80 fathoms. Thus we had the strength necessary to protect ourselves and the ability to anchor in deeper anchorages, yet the weight in the bow was the same as it would have been with heavier, shorter link material.

The capability to anchor in deep water means we are able to pick the best anchorages, sometimes well offshore, which allow for ease of exit and clearance of obstacles; as a side benefit, we are visited by fewer onshore flies and mosquitoes. The negative comes in crowded anchorages where it is tight and we take up a lot of swinging room. We generally use a minimum scope of 6 to 1 (the lighter chain requires more scope for a given holding power). This was a problem, for instance, in Pago Pago, American Samoa, where there is one small shallow spot about 100 feet square. All the visiting yachts wanted to anchor there as it is convenient to the dinghy dock and showers; with our large swinging radius we took up more than our share of the anchorage.

The greater swinging requirement can also be an annoyance even when you are by yourself in tight anchorages.

Once you decide on your chain, be sure to get a test certificate. This means that the chain has been tested, usually to 80 percent of its specified strength. Next, be sure it fits the gypsy of your windlass like a glove. There should be a good tight fit. If not, as we found one night in heavy conditions, the chain can jump right out of the gypsy.

Then have the chain galvanized personally. Most chain comes with very thin galvanizing and will not stand up to coral. Two out of three cruisers visiting New Zealand after six months of tropical cruising were regalvanizing their chain. That one night in Takaroa took off enough of our galvanizing to leave us with a rusty mess every time we anchored thereafter. Good-quality, thick galvanizing will last several years of hard use.

If you're using a high-strength, small-size chain, have the chain manufacturer affix an oversize link at each end to accept the anchor shackle; the space between the links is generally not large enough to accept a full-strength shackle.

Finally, don't let anyone sell you two lengths with a joining link. We know firsthand of three cases where yachts or anchors have been lost where joining links came undone.

Give careful attention to chain stowage. Nothing is worse than having to send a crew member below knocking down the chain castles that get built up. We have found through observing many boats that a straight drop into the chain locker is best, with a vertical space for the chain to stack itself about 2½ times its final height. In other words, if after being all smoothed out the chain is in a pile 18 inches tall in the locker, there should be about 45 inches of clearance from the bottom of the locker to where the chain exits through the deck or the end of the hausepipe. The end of our chain is secured to a ⅜″ piece of nylon which is anchored to an eye bolt. It will hold the boat if necessary and is easy to cut in an emergency.

Be sure the chain locker has good ventilation as the chain will frequently come aboard with a few creepy crawlies and a bit of slime. Also, be sure the limber holes are large and numerous. A lot of water comes below through the chain pipe at sea no matter what is done to stop it up. That water, in combination with a bit of grass or related muck, will test any drain system. On the subject of chain muck, in New Zealand we added a teak strip from the bow to the anchor winch and then across the deck to the rail where we cut a scupper. This keeps the mess that is washed or dripped off the chain forward and gets it overboard before it creats a mess all the way down the gunnels. We use a "T" off our engine-driven bilge pump for a deck hose. The hose end is lashed to the bow pulpit to clean the chain as it comes aboard.

Our stern anchor and second bow anchor are each on 60 fathoms of ¾" three-strand nylon behind 40 feet of ⁵⁄₁₆" chain. We also carry one additional 50-fathom length of line as a spare and for occasional use in tying the stern to coconut trees. We would prefer ⅝"-diameter nylon for its elastic property, but feel we need the extra chafe protection of the thicker line.

A shock absorber of some form, as described earlier, is a must on the chain in order to reduce the load on the windlass and anchor, as well as to suppress some of the rumbles coming back up the chain.

If your chain is heavier than ¼", a powered windlass is a must for shorthanded sailing and an extra safety margin. Aside from the obvious advantages under emergency conditions, it allows a much faster getaway. A second major consideration is that it reduces the reluctance to hoist anchor and reset the hook when you don't come to rest where you think is best. I can recall one instance in the Societies where we were trying to anchor in 15 fathoms with 80 fathoms of chain, and it took three tries to get the anchor to bite properly. Can you imagine cranking all that chain up by hand? We might have decided to live with the poor setting, but that would be dangerous.

Another consideration is going aloft. Using the warping drum and spinnaker halyard makes it quick and easy to pull yourself up.

Be sure the winch is well bedded to prevent moisture from getting at the electrical components. Carry spare brushes for the motor and a spare starter solenoid. Hydraulics are really the best bet, but usually more money and hassle. We have an electric and have had no problems.

There is much debate on capacity. Our winch is rated at 500 lbs. continuous and 800 lbs. intermittent. A consideration in choosing windlass power is its ability to pull the boat off a reef. A boat of *Intermezzo*'s size with a hydraulic windlass of 3000-lb. capacity running through a tackle could in many cases get herself off a coral reef at high tide. Whatever the choice in this area, be sure to check the gear oil every few months for water.

There are few joys so great as pushing a button and watching all that chain coming in without effort and stowing nicely below. When picking the hook up or letting it go, nothing is worse than having to stop repeatedly to free chain jams. To make sure the chain strips easily and runs out freely, place the stripper carefully (if the windlass has one). Try to get as long a fall for the chain off the gypsy as possible, and do everything you can to stay away from a chain pipe.

Another problem is stopping up the opening in the deck through which the chain runs. In heavy weather going upwind, it is incredible how many gallons per hour will come through an improperly stopped chain hole.

When securing for sea, never depend on the gypsy itself to hold the anchor. Always safety it with line. A good friend of ours almost lost his boat because of a hole punched in the bow by an errant anchor in heavy weather in the Atlantic.

The bow roller generally doesn't work very hard. With a nice scope its loads are low. But once the anchor fouls a coral head, the load is straight up and down. The roller has to carry the load of the chain sawing through the coral. If there is a sea running, the loads can approach the full strength of the chain. Be sure the roller is good and husky. We have a $5/8''$ bronze pin in our roller and it lasted one year before it wore through to half its original size. The roller should have $1/16''$ inch of clearance from the pin to prevent buildup of salt and dirt. When anchoring bow-and-stern or with a beam wind there is a tremendous side load on the cheeks of the bow roller. Be sure to consider this aspect when looking at the unit's strength.

An important part of our anchoring gear is a riding sail. Under marginal conditions, in a good breeze, keeping the bow head-to-wind instead of skiing from side to side can substantially reduce the loads and prevent the anchor from breaking out. A second advantage occurs in light airs and hot weather. Most boats ventilate best head-to-wind, and the riding sail helps her respond to those little puffs that make life bearable if they find their way below. Single-stickers can use their storm jibs on the backstay effectively.

The last item in the anchoring gear is the dinghy. When a second anchor has to be rowed out, the conditions are going to be pretty bad.

So be sure to have a dinghy that will get you to windward towing that anchor and warp. Don't forget to consider the time necessary to launch a dinghy as well. If the boat goes aground, a minute or two lost or gained in getting a kedge set can be the difference between getting off or not. Make sure the dinghy can unload fast, and always have the sling attached.

3. Self-Steering

Self-steering gear is important, even vital equipment on an offshore cruiser. The development of the high-powered, reliable windvane has done more to promote long-range cruising than any other factor. Being relieved from the drudgery of constantly steering, watch on and watch off, good weather and foul, makes all the difference.

Because it is so key to one's comfort as well as safety, careful consideration must be given to the various kinds of gear and operational philosophies. The characteristics of your vessel will also have a lot to do with the final choice.

Let's consider what we expect a self-steering apparatus to do. First, it must be able to handle the boat into the lower wind ranges. Here we are talking strictly about apparent wind. Upwind, even in the lightest airs, if there isn't too much sea running, most self-steerers will do well. But trouble starts when you turn the boat around and head downwind. Subtracting boat speed from true wind speed does not leave much apparent wind for the vane to work with. Add to this the problem of substantial shifts in apparent wind direction through small increases or decreases in wind velocity and your system isn't going to work so well. The quicker the boat is in light airs, the more substantial the problem. Aside from using an autopilot, the only alternative is to fit an oversize control sail to the windvane under these conditions and accept the poor results.

The other end of the spectrum is heavy weather. You have to be

The Belgian cutter *Kottick* was on her second trip around the world when we met them in Bali, Indonesia. Her transom-hung rudder with attached trim-tab self-steering was efficient, inexpensive, and easy to service.

able to control the boat while she is being buffeted by wind and sea. If she has the capability of handling heavy going downhill with minimum risk of broaching, the vane will have to cope with tremendous steering loads as the boat surfs down following seas.

Reaching under moderate and above conditions is again demanding. With the wind and seas more or less beam-on, the hull will want to swing downwind and back up, sailing a giant S-curve as the vane tries to cope. Substantial rudder corrections by the vane will be required.

Not only should the self-steering gear be able to cope with various wind and course conditions, but we want to be able to carry all the sail the vessel can handle and that is comfortable for the crew. Having to shorten down prematurely or use specialized rigs to accommodate self-steering is a sign of weakness in the steering gear or design of the vessel.

Next, the vessel should be able to keep herself reasonably well on course. Given a moderate speed (10 knots of apparent wind) and

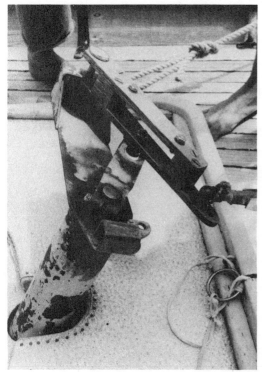

The 56′ ketch *Islander* had her rudder shaft bored out to take a control rod which actuated a trim tab on the keel-hung rudder. The upper end (shown here) was connected to a steering sail on the transom. This gear was installed before the second of her three leisurely, single-handed circumnavigations. We saw her in Port Louis, Mauritius.

normal sea conditions, a variation in course of ±15 degrees should be a maximum. Any more than this will shorten the distance made good drastically.

Last, the vane steering system should be powerful enough so that it isn't necessary to jump up every half hour to adjust sheets or vane settings in order to compensate for moderate changes in wind velocity or boat balance.

Finding the proper vane to match your boat isn't easy. The hardest aspect is getting good data to work from. If you find a similar vessel powered with a given vane, you have to ask yourself if the skipper has the background to evaluate his system's performance properly. Usually the answer will be no. I learned this myself the hard way.

Even though *Intermezzo* came to us with a powerful Benmar autopilot, I felt we needed a mechanical vane, both as backup and because I didn't want to be faced with continuously running the engine for the pilot's electrical needs. Knowing nothing about this type of gear, I canvassed marinas.

I eliminated several types of vanes right off the bat for aesthetic reasons, a move we came to regret. We finally settled on an RVG unit, based on aesthetics and the fact that I had talked to two owners who had fitted the RVG to boats identical in hull shape to *Intermezzo*. In both cases these skippers indicated that the unit worked well. What I failed to perceive was that their units had been tested only under ideal conditions.

Extreme light winds down the coast of Mexico didn't give us much of a chance to try out our vane. Once we were free of the land enroute to the Marquesas and into the trades, we began to put it to work. The first thing we found, was that with the RVG at the conn *Intermezzo* could not carry her full press of sail. With everything up, she would wander all over the ocean, jibing one minute and heading into the wind the next. Since the RVG is a trim-tab/rudder combination, *Intermezzo*'s helm had to be lashed to balance the basic hull/rig configuration. If the wheel was off as little as one half of one spoke, we would be off course again. It required constant and careful tending. Any slight change in apparent wind angle or speed sent the watch on deck to play with the wheel adjustment. Finally, we were forced to sheet some of our sails, not for speed but for balancing purposes.

After 13 days of rolling around with this unit, we hoisted the chute, turned on the autopilot, and took it easy. The problem was essentially this: the RVG unit, while sold as being able to handle a 50-footer, simply didn't have the necessary power. On a smaller yacht it may have performed well, but *Intermezzo* was just too much boat.

In Taeiohai Bay we met Earl Shenk and the beautiful Alden ketch *Eluthera,* a powerful, well-rigged, 48-footer. Earl found that his Aries vane was more than a match for his keel-attached barndoor rudder. Well, if an Aries could handle that situation, it could certainly handle *Intermezzo*'s much lighter hull and spade rudder. We found a 35-footer in love with the RVG concept, sold them ours, put our aesthetics aside, and ordered an Aries from England. We've steered happily ever after.

The moral is simple. Match the vane to the boat.

There are several types of vane systems on the market. The most powerful of these is the servo-pendulum style similar to Nick Franklin's Aries. This unit uses an air rudder that you feather into the wind and lock in. As the apparent wind angle changes, it forces the air

The trimaran *Wind Rose,* photographed in Gizo, Solomon Islands, used an RVG trim-tab-style vane with success. The exceptional directional stability of her fine, deeply laden hulls helped.

A homemade Hassler-style vane aboard the French yacht *Ambrym,* in the New Hebrides.

rudder over one way or the other. This movement is transmitted to a steering oar, pivoted on its vertical axis in the water. Since the oar is moving through the water, this change of angle makes it veer to port or to starboard. Lines are attached to the oar which run to the tiller or wheel and control the vessel via her own rudder. The principle of using the vessel's motion through the water to steer her is simple and provides unlimited free power to turn the main ship's rudder.

The next group of units, such as the RVG or Chrono Marine Chrono Vane, use an auxiliary rudder. In the case of the RVG, the vane rudder is controlled via a small trim tab that gets its input from a feathering vertical-axis air blade. Chrono Marine goes directly from the horizontal-axis air vane to the water rudder. It's simpler, but not quite as good in light airs. Both of these units suffer from the problem of being left permanently in the water. If there is one thing vanes don't like it's a fouled blade or trim tab. They do offer the advantage of providing a means to steer the vessel should the main system develop problems. However, even on well-balanced 35-footers, both of these makes will require close attention to sail setting and trim. Vessels over 40 feet require servo-pendulum vanes.

Smaller craft can make use of the inexpensive direct air control of tillers such as the QME unit. These are very inexpensive and will get you there, but they don't have the power for light airs or really heavy wind that the other models provide.

Another interesting approach is to work out a trim tab directly on the rudder. Tom Blackwell did this with the aid of Blondie Hassler's engineering on *Islander*. To the main rudder he attached a trim tab, driven by a vertical-axis air vane. To accomplish control, Tom had the stock of the rudder bored out and inserted a long rod down its length. This rod was connected to the air rudder via some linkages at its top and to the trim tab with a bell crank at its bottom. By this means he was able to control *Islander*'s main rudder with the force exerted on the tab. With a transom-hung rudder this approach is even easier, as the trim tab can be attached directly to the aft end of the rudder, with its linkage taking place on top.

If you are on a tight budget, don't be afraid to try making a vane on your own. Probably half the people we've met around the world have done it, usually with trim-tab-type designs. They all were out sailing and, allowing for some experimenting, their "home brews" seemed to perform well, costs considered.

Note the direct-drive trim tab on this 32′ ketch in the Loyalty Islands, New Caledonia.

The small New Zealand yacht *Willyet* crossed the Indian Ocean with its Kiwi vane. Home-built from a design developed by New Zealander Pony Moore, it was effective and inexpensive. The photo was taken in Gran Baie, Mauritius, after some heavy-air reaching.

The subject of autopilots is more easily dealt with. There are generally two sizes, small and other. Under 35 feet you are into the small sizes; most of the bigger units will handle up to 70-footers.

There are many styles of the tiller-control unit originally invented by sailmaker Swede Johnson on the market today. They are cheap, effective, and *if kept dry,* reliable. The last precondition needs careful attention. Seals and gaskets must be maintained, and a sheltered location out of direct spray will help. Larry Porter used a tiller master on his Cal-40 *Molly* to control her spade rudder in extreme heavy going in the Pacific without problems. More than once, however, we have met cruisers in out-of-the-way spots who said they wished they had two units aboard. If you don't have a vane for backup, then a spare unit should definitely be considered.

The permanently mounted autopilots are much more reliable. If they're properly installed you don't have to worry about moisture. Units such as the Benmar 14B with which *Intermezzo* was equipped use an electric eye/compass combination for determining which way to turn the wheel. Other units employ what is known as a magnetometer, or electric sensing device, coupled to a compass that directly "reads" a compass's magnets.

Modern units have circuits built into them that compensate for weather helm, following seas, and other conditions that make it difficult to steer. Usually these circuits can be adjusted both manually and automatically. They reduce the amount of steering necessary to keep your boat in the groove, while lowering power consumption at the same time.

When installing your autopilot, try to have it drive the quadrant or rudder directly, avoiding the use of the regular steering cables. If the pilot has its own drive system, the wheel system will have less load, and should a wheel-steering failure occur, the pilot can be used as a backup.

Autopilots have a big advantage over self-steering. They will handle the boat in very light apparent wind ranges, and of course they will do the job when you're under power.

One accessory to consider seriously is a hand-controlled dodger and remote-control course changer. With one of these gadgets you can change course from anywhere on the vessel. I eventually lengthened my control box cord so I could take it aloft to the lower spreaders, where I had good visibility when entering harbors. A word

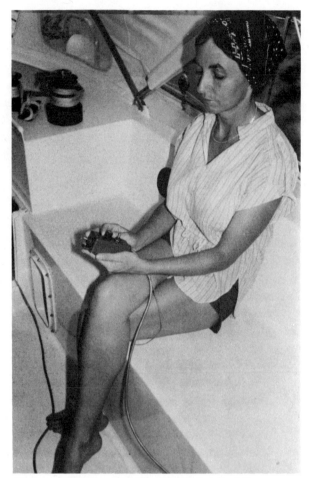

Linda works the portable "magic box" of *Intermezzo II*'s Wagner hydraulic pilot.

of caution, though. Never rely on any electromechanical device, such as an autopilot, if its failure may put you in a dangerous position. For this reason, whenever I was steering from aloft, Linda was stationed at the wheel, ready to take over instantly if anything went wrong.

One way to extend the capabilities of the small automatic pilot units is to tie them into a trim tab on the main rudder or to an air vane on a servo-pendulum vane. Using this approach the pilot only has a minimal amount of work to do, since the forward motion of the vessel provides most of the power required. The Moeslys on *Svea* had a hydraulic pump belted to their Free-wheeling prop shaft which provided the power to operate the rudder when sailing.

The main concern with using an autopilot while sailing is power consumption. The lightweight tiller-steering rigs generally take less than 1 amp per hour, even in moderate going. As you work up in size, however, a pilot can draw as much as 6 or 8 amps at 12 volts, every hour. When you multiply this times 24 hours, it's a lot of current consumption. *Intermezzo*'s current requirement varied between 4 and 8 amps, depending on sea conditions. Several of our friends in 40-footers used between 2 and 4 amps. If the pilot is to be used exclusively for sailing, then some form of underway generating system must be employed, either a towed taffrail generator or shaft-driven alternator.

The ideal situation is to have both a vane and a pilot. The vane handles long sea passages, and the pilot takes care of light airs, running, and powering. Plus, you then have a backup system if one of them fails.

But what if you have to make a choice, due to budget considerations? In this case, I would opt for the pilot. Aboard *Intermezzo*, once we installed a taffrail generator we found that the autopilot was in use about 70 percent of the time we were at sea. We found it less demanding on the crew even than our powerful Aries in moderate weather; and in the 30 to 40 percent of our cruising that was spent in very light airs, it was the only way we could keep *Intermezzo* moving with all her light sails without having to keep a close eye on course and sail trim.

Most autopilots are mechanically simple, and for the electronics have easily replaced printed circuit boards. If it's your only form of steering, take the time to have a service technician show you the various symptoms of ill health and the steps necessary to correct them, and carry a good inventory of spares.

Finally, when the going is good, experiment with sheet-to-tiller or wheel rigs. The possibilities are many, and given a bit of sea room and time, virtually any boat can be made to self-steer on one basis or another. John Letcher's book *Self Steering* has some excellent helpful hints in this regard.

Aboard *Intermezzo*, we found that by using surgical tubing of varying lengths and diameters to one side of the wheel and the small staysail sheet to the other we could get her to hold a reasonable course on all angles of sail except beam- and broad-reaching. Granted, our sails were on occasion trimmed in strange ways, but at least she could be made to steer herself.

4. Cruising in the Shade

On a cruising yacht, awnings come under the category of essential gear. As the latitude decreases, awnings move higher and higher on the scale of importance until they become *imperative*.

Awnings can perform three major roles, and should be designed with an eye to each. First comes shade. How much shade you need depends on where you're cruising, but if you're considering the tropics, you'll want to cover as high a percentage of your vessel as practicable. Awnings can lower the temperature on deck as much as 30 degrees.

Awnings should also be designed to catch rainwater. A well-built system on a 30-foot boat can deliver enough rainwater to keep the tanks topped up, which eliminates the need to go ashore every so often to refill. Rain provides fresh, untreated, healthy water, which can be used for washing dishes, laundry, and most important, daily showering. A 200-square-foot awning will easily catch 8 to 10 gallons of water for each eighth of an inch of rain that falls. It is not at all uncommon to catch 150 to 200 gallons in a single tropical afternoon. Once you're used to drinking really fresh from-the-sky water, piped water will seem unpalatable.

The last major function of an awning is to keep you dry. Since rain and heat frequently go together, you will want to keep hatches open during a downpour and a properly designed awning is the answer.

In developing a design, a primary concern is ease of setting and striking. If it takes more than five minutes for two people to set an awning, go back to the drawing board. You'll find that in short-

The Bermuda 40 yawl *Aventura* made good use of its main-deck awning during the summer of 1979 in Madang, Papua, New Guinea. Note the foredeck hatch wind scoop and the use of the main and mizzen cap shrouds to secure the awning.

Svea, in Bellasana, Papua, New Guinea, with a combination foredeck awning and rain catcher. On her second circumnavigation she was always festooned with a variety of creative awnings.

hopping between harbors it may be necessary to strike the awning, but two hours later the hook is down and you'll want it again. Or assume that you have to strike the awning at 0200, with a 35- or 40-knot wind blowing, with you in your birthday suit. You have to be able to get the awning down in a sequence that keeps it under control without resorting to a knife. Even the most complex design will meet these criteria with thought and practice.

There are as many opinions on the best material for awnings as there are boats in the anchorage. If cost is a primary objective, there are many inexpensive, plastic fiber-reinforced tarps on that market that will serve for a year or two if they have good patches in the corners. Nylon-coated fabric is a bit higher on the price list, will give long service, and is favored by many cruisers. These two materials have some drawbacks, however. First, they tend to mildew. After a period of weeks a black spotty mold begins to grow, which means you have to bleach and use a scrub brush every month. Also, these fabrics take more room to stow than other materials. On the plus side, they don't leak and will keep you drier, and in the case of nylon-coated fabric will let the least amount of sun through.

Materials made specifically for awnings and covers are of woven synthetics such as Acrilan, and are the most expensive. They are favored because they are long lived, fold and stow easily, and don't mildew.

Sailcloth is the last category. We have run into several cruisers, considerably experienced, who prefer filled sailcloth for awnings, citing the benefits of strength and ease of handling. An awning can make an excellent happy hunting ground for a blown-out genoa. The price is right, and it works well.

We have on board, or have at times used, all of the various categories outlined. My favorite on a basis of ease of handling, utility, and cost, is old sailcloth. At the bottom of our list is our cockpit awning of plastic-coated nylon. The mildew causes too much hassle.

A mistake that temperate-climate sailors often make when preparing for the tropics is to use colored fabrics. They look great, but anything other than white absorbs and radiates downward a great deal of heat. *Intermezzo*'s main awning was blue and white striped, and you could readily tell which color you were standing under.

Construction is an area most people are in at least basic agreement on: make it *strong*. Large areas of an awning can be single-layered,

Intermezzo dressed with her rain-catching main and mizzen awnings in the Solomon Islands. Note the weather cloths at the companionway hatch and after cockpit (removed in heavy going).

At sea we would leave up the mizzen awning and rig a small watch awning between the mizzen foreshrouds.

but when it comes to the corners and other points of attachment, heavy reinforcements are the order of the day. The awning should be able to stand gusts of 35 knots or more of wind for short periods of time before you get it down. And it should be able to withstand a constant 15 to 25 knots under normal usage. Major attachment points should have a total of four good-size patches, with regular grommets. Anywhere the awning rubs, such as around the topping lift or end of the boom, there should be chafe patches.

There are as many shapes of awnings as there are yachts flying them. Basic rig configuration is the first consideration. A split rig gives a big advantage here. A number of options are available with a mizzen and perhaps running backstays that are the envy of sloop and cutter owners. I know of one split-rig afficionado who says that even if his buddies in their single-stickers beat him to the next anchorage (upwind), he still has his awning set and is sipping his afternoon drink before they are.

There are four areas for awning placement. Starting at the bow, you'll want to cover as much of the foredeck as possible for coolness and to protect the forward hatches from rain. At the same time you need to be able to get forward to the anchor windlass and spare anchors. Usually these awnings are attached to the lower lifelines, leaving a gap of 18 inches or so between the awning edge and lifelines for air passage. The lower the outside edge is, the easier to step over the tie lines; the awning should be just high enough to allow the hatch to be opened. They usually have lines in the four corners and lifting eye in the center attached to the spinnaker pole topping lift or headsail halyard. Another approach, which does away with the halyard, is to run a center line from some point forward, perhaps the windlass, to the mast. Neither of these approaches works well for catching rain. If you use the forward awning as a rain catcher, you should attach it to the upper lifeline and have it sag in the middle with an attachment for a fill hose.

Next are main awnings. On single-stickers these usually start at the mainmast and attach on either side to the cap shrouds and/or to the lowers. Athwartship battens are necessary, since without them attachment aft is difficult. The awning runs to the end of the boom unless you have an aft cockpit, in which case it should continue to the backstay. This necessitates a zipper to get around the topping lift. Use the heaviest zipper possible. There is some debate on its location.

If the zipper runs fore and aft the awning may be easier to set and strike, but when it rains the zipper leaks right over the middle of the cockpit. Running the zipper athwartships, from the middle out to the edge of the awning, puts the leak in a more tolerable place, but makes the awning a bit more difficult to set. If the zipper does end up athwartship, put it opposite the side from which you board.

Battens are heavy and cumbersome, and are prone to breakage when squalls catch you beam-on. Aluminum, fiberglass, and PVC tubing give the best service. Plain old wood will do, but unless the battens are fairly closely spaced and substantial you will spend a lot of time hunting up spares. *Intermezzo*'s original 24-foot awning had four 13-foot-long athwartship battens on 8-foot centers measuring one by three inches. We lost them in the first good squall to hit us in the Marquesas Islands. On the other hand, friends had a similar-size awning with twice as many battens that survived.

If you do have battens and want to trade a bit of complexity for batten security, a series of bridles from each batten to the main halyard and tie-down lines to the upper lifeline will minimize potential damage. On a ketch or yawl the mizzen shrouds allow you to eliminate battens if you so desire by attaching the aft end of the awning to the mizzen cap shrouds. If you have running backstays they also make good tie-off points.

The edges of these designs should have a tape or double-hem reinforcement. Many people like to have a light bolt rope as well on the edges and down the center.

Main awnings should have vertical side flaps to cut down on the sun in the morning and afternoon. These are usually 18 to 24 inches deep. Some boats have a zip-on extension for the cockpit area to cover really low sun angles.

Rain catching efficiently on main awnings takes a bit of practice and usually a few modifications. It is easiest with a flat awning without battens. The awning is sloped in one direction, and at the low spot, reinforcement patches are sewn and a nylon through-hull fitting is fastened in. You can then pull down on the fitting so that rain from the rest of the awning will funnel its way down. An awning that is supported along its center by the boom takes a bit more work since there is usually a natural cup on each side of the crown. If the awning is sloped slightly aft, a hose can be fitted on each side.

The battened awning gives the most trouble as a rain catcher. The

Sunflower's rain-catching system, on Nissan Island, Papua, New Guinea. The side curtains of their main awning were held open with beer cans. The 1″ hose would be full in a moderate squall.

only effective system we have seen is to tilt the entire awning to one side. An extra flap is sewn on the outside of the side curtain and a few aluminum beer cans are placed to keep the flap open. The rain then runs off the top, onto this side flap to which a hose is attached.

The main awning on a 40-foot boat should have at least a ¾″ ID hose to take advantage of those occasional torrential downpours.

Ketches can rig a cockpit awning under the mizzen boom with a batten at its after end which is tied to the end of the boom or standing backstay. The awning can usually be designed to be left up at sea. If it starts to oscillate in a blow or going upwind, it can be rolled around its own batten and tied up under the mizzen gooseneck.

There is a final category of specialty awnings for use at sea. Cock-

In 1948 in the Caribbean, *Constellation* makes use of Egyptian duck awnings as rain catchers. (S. A. Dashew)

pit awnings or Bimini tops are fine when you're sitting at anchor, but in some parts of the world you will have to spend long periods of time standing up on watch. If you are working through coral, you may be aloft for hours at a time. Special awnings, if the attachment points are available, should be made for these conditions. If you can't work out something suitable, carry a good-size umbrella.

The best small stuff for attaching awnings we have found is parachute cord, which won't slip down on a shroud and which can be tied in a bowknot for easy removal. About half of the awning attachment points will not have to be adjusted, and these can be fastened with spring hooks or old jib hanks, saving time in setting.

Don't be disappointed if your first try requires some modifications;

four or five recuts of the main awning *are not* unusual. In the final analysis, well-designed awnings are as important as well-cut sails.

5. Catching Rainwater at Sea

The capability for catching significant quantities of water at sea is very important from a comfort standpoint. One rarely carries enough water on long passages to shower, wash clothes, and rinse the salt from dishes. Even if a substantial quantity is carried, most people husband their inventory as a precaution against a forced long passage due to gear failure. An efficient water-catching system, however, can go a long way toward improving the comfort of long passages.

When we left Mexico aboard *Intermezzo,* we were woefully unprepared in this regard. The occasional passing squall which should have yielded gallons left us without a drop. Crossing the doldrums with hundreds of gallons falling on us, we were reduced to scavenging water by the bucket from the scuppers and passing it below—cumbersome at best.

Three years later we were better prepared. Our mizzen awning was at the ready, and when the first squalls hit us near the equator off Brazil, after 19 days at sea, our tanks were topped up in less than 30 minutes. Thereafter, they stayed full.

As indicated in Chapter 4, awnings are a good system. Another approach is to take water directly from the decks. After a brief period of rain, perhaps 10 minutes, the salt and dirt will be washed overboard, and if your freshwater tank fills are located at the low point of the deck when sailing (one for port and one for starboard), a good cloudburst will put as much as 20 gallons a minute down the pipe on a 40-footer. John Nichols had an interesting idea on *Heart of Edna.* He raised his freshwater intake half an inch above deck level to ensure that any dirt around would wash by the fill pipe.

Another interesting system was used by the Moeslys on *Rigadoon.*

They built in a solid handrail all the way around the main cabin edge, with a hose bib fitted to the aft corner on each side.

A bucket tied at the gooseneck is good for a few gallons now and then, but if you really want the luxury of fresh water, a little planning will make a big difference.

6. Staying Dry Below

Whether you are at anchor at some idyllic South Pacific port, or are trade-wind sailing enroute, the cruising life is indeed pleasant. But let rain or sea find its way below in any quantity and your pleasure will tarnish in a hurry.

To begin with, assume you are going to get wet below. All gear that can be damaged by an errant wave top finding that one open hatch or leaking deck fitting had better be stowed in plastic bags in the driest part of the boat. Hatches should be located with an eye to minimizing the damage when spray or rain does come through. In the tropics you will often want the hatches open when sailing and during heavy rain. If they are over the cabin sole, water coming below won't hurt anything. But in many yachts the navigation area, with all its fancy dials and knobs, is near the companion way. Going downhill in heavy weather, this area has a high probability of getting wet.

When evaluating gear placement and storage, remember that water runs downhill and that there are two "downhills" aboard, depending on whether you are on port or starboard tack.

Vinyl covers on cushions go a long way toward reducing dampness. They give you a chance to mop up before the foam absorbs moisture. Printed material on glossy paper is very susceptible to ruin if it gets wet. On the other hand the soft paper used in pilots or paperbacks will dry out quite well without sticking.

There are many types of deck hatches. Most of them will leak at

Here's an excellent way to keep an eye on things and stay dry. By the time this 32' yacht had reached Cape Town, South Africa, her observation dome had been put to good use.

some point in their careers at sea. The force of a boarding wave is substantial, and you can be sure it will find any weakness in a hatch seal. Hatches should be rigidly made, with heavy frames and large upstands inside their seals. Medium-soft rubber, not weatherstripping, should fit into a recess or have a sharp edge pressing against it. The hatch should be dogged at all four corners. Gate-type hinges should be used, and the holes enlarged so the pins have a sloppy fit that allows the hatch to seal on its rubber on the hinge side. A good idea is to have double-opening hatches so that in dry conditions they can open forward but in moderate conditions they can open aft to give some ventilation and a degree of spray or rain protection at the same time.

Lightweight molded fiberglass hatches will have to be strengthened. If the hatch is wood composite, be sure it is well bedded. Even a well-made wooden hatch will eventually leak in rain or heavy weather. This can frequently be cured by digging out the joints and filling them with epoxy.

After the hatches have been certified A-1, fit a tight vinyl or acrylic storm cover for heavy going. This cover should overlap the hatch

This storm cover fitted to *Intermezzo*'s saloon hatch protected the hatch gasket from spray and solid water.

Breakwaters are the best way to protect hatch gaskets. All foredeck hatches on *Deerfoot* have them. (S. A. Dashew)

joint to keep out any green water that comes aboard. Additionally, it's a good idea to make a breakwater of light teak on each side and forward to accomplish the same purpose in less than ultimate circumstances.

Opening ports and windows are easier to cope with. Due to their smaller size, they are not as subject to working and are more easily dogged. Ports with heavy metal frames, large hinges, and heavy dogs work best. Carry spare rubber seals.

Companionways present a different problem. Assuming they are well designed and executed, they will keep you dry going uphill or reaching. When the wind swings aft in heavy going, though, things get a little wetter. It is impossible to make hatch slides or swinging companionway doors watertight from heavy boarding seas. The best you can do is design outside storm covers that can be fastened from below to protect the joints from a direct hit. A raised breakwater around the exposed part of the sliding hatch is a must. After all this, in heavy going you can still expect some spray below through the companionway.

Non-opening windows alongside the doghouse or trunk cabin are another perennial source of trouble. The light plastic and aluminum frames favored by most production boat builders don't stand up, and generally won't take really heavy weather. This forces you to make that hard decision to go on deck and fit storm shutters when it's already howling.

When these windows do begin to leak it frequently is next to impossible to remove the aluminum frames without damaging them. Short of removing and replacing the entire assembly, it's a good idea to fit permanent heavy-plastic storm shutters. These take the direct load off the inner window and also prevent spray from reaching the potentially leaky frames.

Every hole drilled through the deck creates a possible drip. Bedding compounds or sealants will not do their job unless the fitting stays put. Winch bases and cleats, for example, must be supported with an adequate backing plate. Most people we meet end up using silicon sealants; it's best to apply to both surfaces a primer made for the type of sealant being used. It will improve the surface-to-surface bond considerably—but it will make it difficult to remove the fitting later.

Of all the fittings on a boat that give leak problems, lifeline stanch-

Only strongly secured lifeline stanchions will avoid deck leaks. Note the attachment to the deck combing on *Deerfoot*. (S. A. Dashew)

ions are number one. Because they usually have inadequate bases and are not well backed up below the deck, they work back and forth, and as a result more often than not they leak. One approach is to glass over the fasteners after they're installed. This works, but it makes it difficult to replace a bent stanchion.

Cockpit lockers, lazarette hatches, and chain pipes contribute mightily to the pumping required in heavy going upwind. They all leak. To mitigate the problem, cockpit lockers and lazarette hatches should have positive seals, heavy latches, and substantial upstands, ideally at least 1½ inches in height. Further, a cockpit seat cover, which prevents solid water from getting at joints, can be fitted. If the chain pipe forward doesn't face aft and have a driven bung or screwed cap, it can easily let as much as 10 gallons an hour get below in heavy going. Be prepared to remove the water with ease.

Take a look at the galley sink drains. If they feed into the cockpit plumbing and if you shut off the cockpit seacocks when going ashore, heavy rain can fill the cockpit and back up through the sink to flood the cabin. To correct this potential problem, the sink must have its own shutoff valve.

When you expect wet going, don't forget to cover the Dorades and/or fit their plates below. They aren't made to take solid water. If you expect really heavy going, remove the cowls and fit the topside cover plates.

Now that the seals have been redone, fittings rebedded, storm covers made, and breakwaters fitted, there are still a few things that can be done to make life more bearable when it gets wet below.

First, stow all unused clothing and bedding, as well as spare parts, in heavy plastic bags. Four mils thickness is about right for cost and longevity. Every month or so, give all the hose clamps and other exposed metal aboard a spray of a moisture-displacing lubricant such as WD 40. Electronic gear should be run at least every week while in humid climates or at sea. It isn't a bad idea to spray the contacts, terminals, and switches aboard every couple of months with a good-quality cleaner. Sooner or later all the switches on deck will go out, so have a duplicate switch panel below; that leaves you with a backup system.

7. Refrigeration

An efficient refrigeration system plays a key role in increasing the enjoyment of your cruise. The farther into the warmer climates you venture and the longer your cruise, the more significant a good fridge/freezer becomes.

If you are going to be cruising in temperate climates, some of the less efficient systems—including an icebox—may do for you. Surprisingly, however, the difference between a really efficient system and a mediocre or poor system lies more in approach and engineering than in cost or complexity. And if you're planning on being gone for a year or more, it's possible to just about pay for your system with food savings.

A "finned evaporator," *Intermezzo*'s secret weapon in the war against engine running time for refrigeration. Note the surface area of the fins and tubes.

When we left Los Angeles, we had what we were told was a top-grade system. With no experience in these things I had gone to several "experts" to have our reefer surveyed. In Southern California it worked fine. It even worked pretty well in northern Mexico. When we got to the Marquesas Islands, latitude 80° south, it was a different story. To use the system just as a reefer, forgetting the freezer, took more than two hours a day running time on the diesel. Among the 14 boats in Taiohai Bay on Nuka Hiva that had refrigeration, two hours a day was considered normal.

Then Phil sailed in. He had installed his own system in his 1906 English yawl. The unmuffled diesel made it easy to tell when he was running to cool down the reefer. Phil's icy drinks in the afternoon confirmed that his half hour a day of running time was for real. We have since run across two other yachts with super refrigeration performance. All of them had several common factors in their systems.

Let's define performance. A yacht with a 10-cubic-foot freezer and a 4-cubic-foot refrigerator, sailing in the tropics with 80 degrees ambient air temperature and 80 degrees water temperature, should not have to run its generator or engine for power more than 75

Intermezzo II's double-gasketed freezer door.

minutes per day. This means that if you are cruising the West Indies (except in the summer) you should be under an hour a day. In the temperate latitudes, the time should be less than 30 minutes a day.

Since your other electrical needs are going to eat up some time, it is best to try to match the refrigeration performance to electrical consumption.

Aboard *Intermezzo,* for example, we found that in the tropics, where we used 12-volt fans in the cabin quite a bit, it was necessary to run the engine about an hour a day. In cooler climates the electrical consumption eases off to a point and then holds steady, while refrigeration requirements drop in proportion to lower ambient temperatures.

This type of performance can be achieved only with a mechanical compressor, belted off an engine, and a holding-plate system.

There is no real mystery about this system. The components are simple. They are easy to install, and most important, easy for the average yachtsman to service.

Let's talk about hardware. First you have to have a compressor. This unit will be run by your main engine or auxiliary generator via V-belts. The majority of all compressors used in this type of system are made by either Techumseh Engineering or York Manufacturing, and find their biggest application in auto air conditioning. The most important thing to know about a compressor is that its capacity is related directly to its R.P.M. A unit built for automotive use will be able to turn at 5000 to 6000 R.P.M. for short periods, and 4000 R.P.M. indefinitely without harm. This means that you want to pick a pulley ratio that allows the compressor to spin as fast as possible at your charging R.P.M. if you are using your main engine, but not exceed its limit at cruising R.P.M. If a prolonged burst of high R.P.M. is necessary in passaging, the system can be shut down. As a rule, 1800 to 2200 R.P.M. at charge and 3600 to 4000 R.P.M. at cruise speed is a good compromise.

So if your engine is comfortable at 1100 R.P.M. for generating electricity and you like to cruise at 2000 R.P.M., then a 2 to 1 or perhaps 2.25 to 1 pulley ratio between the main engine and compressor will be ideal.

The next important piece of hardware is the heat exchanger. This cools down the refrigeration gas by running it through tubes surrounded by sea water. While all systems use a heat exchanger of some type, only rarely have we seen installed units of sufficient size to do an adequate job. From our own experience and observation of others, we feel that what is called a two-ton unit is about right. ("Ton" refers to its capacity.) Note that this is based on a certain waterflow through the heat exchanger. If you are going to put the heat exchanger on the same cooling-water system as the engine that powers it, be sure it is *upstream* of the engine and that the waterflow matches the manufacturer's specs for the heat exchanger's rating. This can easily be checked by holding a two-gallon bucket at the exhaust and timing how long it takes to fill.

The most important part of the system is the holding plates. In most vessels these are a series of copper tubes running in a stainless-steel or plastic tank filled with a solution of antifreeze and water. An average system may have 50 feet of half-inch tubing. It is here that most systems really bog down.

As the tubing cools down, it eventually gets so cold that the holding liquid around it forms a frost. This frost then inhibits the heat transfer system, just as excess frost causes your home freezer to run longer. The ultimate capacity of the short length of tubing is way below that of your compressor.

There is a cheap and efficient way around this problem, called a finned evaporator. Don't let this fancy-sounding term scare you. A finned evaporator is one of those radiator-looking things you see in your air conditioner. The one we used in our main box had 240 feet of copper tubing with aluminum fins every eighth of an inch to further enhance heat transfer. The total surface area is hundreds of times that of the average tubing-only system. As a result, the compressor can be used to full capacity, and you get a quick pull-down.

The cost difference between holding plates with finned evaporators and those with plain copper tubing is about 30 percent. On plates built for us in New Zealand in 1978 it worked out to a difference of $150.

The next major element to consider is the box itself. For tropical cruising the freezer should have six inches of polyeurethane foam on the bottom and four inches in the sides and top; if you have the space, use six inches of foam all the way around the freezer. A fridge should have a minimum of four inches on the bottom and three inches on the sides and top. Equally important on the freezer is the seal on the door. It has to be positive, and there should be inner and outer seals. This is vital to keeping the holding plates frost free.

Finally, consider the relationship between the fridge and the freezer. Your type of cruising will dictate the percentage you will devote to each in different areas. The best engineering approach is to put all the holding plates in the freezer and use a small opening between fridge and freezer for a bleed-off of cold air to the fridge. When your freezer is loaded with food, each item becomes a miniature holding plate which lengthens the time you can go without pulling the temperature down mechanically. If you are doing some powering between anchorages and then sitting for a few days, chances are you won't have to touch the system until you next power since the well-frozen freezer will keep the fridge cool enough.

On the other hand, if your refrigerator has its own holding plates, there is a limit to how long it can be run since overrunning will make it too cold and will ruin your fruits and vegetables. Thus although the freezer may be fine, you are forced to run the engine within a day or so due to lack of holdover power in the fridge.

A lot of people are scared of refrigeration systems. Stories abound about freezers going bad in remote anchorages, hours of engine time, and constant headaches. In some cases they are true. We have seen systems on yachts in far-off places that were an unbelievable mess. And more than one of our cruising friends has been badly ripped off by "experts" in out-of-the-way places.

But the truth is that marine refrigeration is very simple to understand, to maintain, and to repair at sea. Take the time to find out how to charge the system with freon gas, how to change an expansion valve or drier, and how to evacuate the system. There are thousands of refrigeration and air-conditioning schools all over the world. A serviceman can show anybody in less than an hour all that is required to keep a refrigeration system running. It's worth the effort.

8. Communications

The subject of communication gear on the long-range cruiser is one of never-ending debate. There is the school of thought that one should be cut off from outside news and from any sources of help. Self-sufficiency, after all, doesn't include getting on the radio and yelling for assistance.

However, good communication gear can make life more interesting, provide valuable data to assist in making plans for the future, and allow you to stay in touch with loved ones. And in a real emergency, long-distance radio gear can make a tremendous difference.

Our own leanings, gradually acquired, are toward this last argument. The longer we cruised aboard *Intermezzo,* the more complete our inventory of radio gear became.

VHF is what people usually look at first. A *V*ery *H*igh *F*requency radio is good only for short distances, line of sight plus a hair. At best, if your antenna is at the masthead and the receiving antenna on shore is on a hill, you might get 60 miles of range. More normal is 30 miles. Two yachts talking to each other are restricted to perhaps 15 miles.

In U.S. coastal waters, parts of the Caribbean, and some areas of Europe, VHF can be handy for talking with marinas, lighthouses, or a local harbormaster. But it is not essential. In the less developed areas of the world—anchorages such as Papeete, Rabaul, or Benoa, for instance—it is rare to find more than one or two yachts with their VHF on.

Intermezzo didn't carry VHF gear when we started our cruise. I couldn't see the necessity for it where we were going. By the time we had reached New Zealand, I was ready for a set, but not for the usual reasons.

Crossing the Tasman Sea we twice had scares when large ships came by to take a look at us. The trouble was that we didn't know if they saw us and were taking a look or if they didn't see us and were going to run us down. From the New Zealand Marine Control, I learned that New Zealand and Australian shipping is required to investigate any small yachts they see and report their position to the proper authorities. It made us feel good knowing somebody cared, but that didn't change the fact that on two occasions we had been scared out of our wits by what we thought was imminent collision. To rectify the situation, we bought a used VHF. Equipped with channels 6, 12, 16, 28, and 68, it subsequently served its purpose. On virtually every passage thereafter, we contacted all ships, usually when they first became visible, to advise them of our position, get an update on the weather, and have a nice chat. Off the east coast of Africa, twice caught in heavy weather, we were continually advising ships of our bearings relative to them and asking them to stand clear as we were having difficulty maneuvering in the heavy weather (and I didn't want to get wet on deck).

A fancy, synthesized set is not necessary unless you intend to do a lot of communications with shore stations in crowded waters. We found that almost everyone monitered channel 16 and would switch to one of the few crystals we had aboard when contact was established.

Marine single sideband has come onto the scene since 1975. The

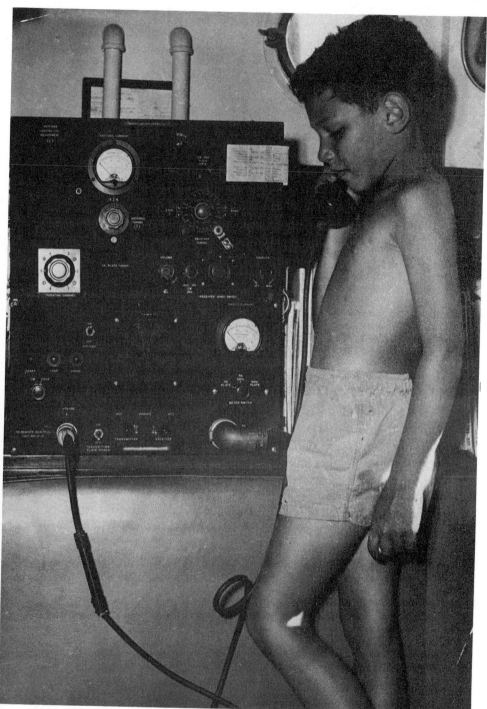

How things have changed! Not too many years ago this 20-watt set was considered very compact. (S. A. Dashew)

switch from the old-style AM-model radios to the newer SSB has produced an increase in the quality of communication and an increase in range—but it has also boosted the expense.

Communication via marine SSB isn't much use outside the well-established industrialized countries. There is no end of stories about people sitting right outside Papeete Harbor trying vainly to raise the French on 2182, theoretically the worldwide distress frequency; or failing to get the USCG on 4125 from a thousand miles offshore. For business communications, working through high-seas operators like KMI, WOM, or WOO can be more successful, if their directional antennas are pointing your way. If not, and if they are using multidirectional low-gain antennas, you may have a difficult time raising them. The 4-, 6-, and 8-megahertz (MHz) ship-to-ship channels are perhaps the most useful, but we have never raised a passing ship on SSB.

When we left the States, certain business commitments required me to communicate frequently with shore. By the time we had reached Papeete this was no longer the case, so in New Zealand we removed our marine SSB and made room for what many consider to be the greatest advance in cruising gear since the steering vane: ham radio.

Amateur radio has been around since man started using the ether to communicate. Only recently, however, have advances in microelectronics made it feasible for the average cruiser to have aboard, and successfully operate, an amateur set.

Today, fully transistorized and pretuned amateur transceivers are available at higher power ratings than regular marine communications gear for less than half the price.

Ham gear has a tremendous advantage over marine SSB: there are literally hundreds of thousands of hams around the world anxious to talk with their sea-going counterparts.

From a safety standpoint, ham gear is by far the best. Maritime "nets" or groups of amateurs exist all over the world. Land- and sea-based, the members of these nets trade information and keep track of the positions of voyagers as they travel. Land-based hams can get detailed weather synopses from the local meterological bureau covering the region in which you are traveling. If a medical problem occurs aboard, a specialist in the area can be brought to the phone in a matter of minutes.

At the time of our first crossing of the Tasman Sea in 1977, our friends the Marriotts, aboard their 44-foot steel ketch *Makaretu,* found how valuable the ham network is. Belinda, their one-year-old daughter, developed mouth ulcers and was unable to eat. Via the Pacific Maritime Mobile Net, they were "patched" into a specialist in children's mouth diseases in Honolulu, Hawaii. He discussed the problem with them, reviewed their onboard medical supplies, and advised temporary treatment. Four days later, when they made port in Opua, New Zealand, a doctor was on hand to treat Belinda—all courtesy of ham radio. Is it any wonder that 80 percent of cruising boats in the outer areas carry ham gear today?

Take the time we were leaving Suveroff Atoll in the northern Cook Islands. We were undecided whether to go to Tonga directly or via American Samoa. We had been out nine months and need to reprovision. If we went direct to Tonga, some 1100 miles to the west, the reprovisioning would have to be done in Suva, Fiji. On the ham radio we talked with yachts in Pango Pango and Suva. Comparing prices and availability of the stores we needed, we found that American Samoa at that time was the cheapest place in the Pacific to reprovision. The money we saved by having that knowledge would have paid for the radio we were using.

At sea, there are annual migrations of yachts from one cruising ground to another. The weather herds them into flocks, and we have found in our many crossings that one of the high points of each day was our daily roll call. It's a chance to catch up on gossip, trade sea stories, check on the vagaries of weather and sea state. On long passages this becomes a real morale booster. It's always good to know someone else is suffering with you or that the weather is better a few hundred miles ahead.

Equally important is the intelligence gained on where to go and what to see. Circumnavigator Carl Moesly told us that the biggest change between his first time around the world and now is the ham radio. Through it he was able to find protected, shallow, anchorages that he had not known about the first time around.

Our experience in the Reef Islands, at the southern end of the Solomons in Melanesia, is another case in point. At the suggestion of some people we met in Graciosa Bay, Santa Cruz Island, we made a wet, miserable beat across the channel separating Santa Cruz and the Reef Islands. There we met the Gibbs—Bernie, Carol, Dean, and

Darren. They were bush traders in the old-style sense, and led an incredibly interesting, if somewhat isolated life. We spent two marvelous weeks with them, one of the highlights of our circumnavigation. They were anxious to extend their hospitality to other yachts, and at their request we put out the word to some friends behind us. Where they used to average one visiting yacht every other year, the Gibbses now receive three or four visitors a season. And Bernie has become a ham.

The final benefit of amateur radio is the contact it provides with home. I'm sure this was a major reason we were able to enjoy ourselves for so long away from our families in the States. We were able to talk with them on a weekly basis via ham friends ashore.

The licensing procedure for getting an amateur licence in most countries is not difficult. You have to learn Morse Code (useful anyway for copying weather broadcasts) and a modest amount of theory. Anyone can do it, given a few months of study time. There are literally thousands of ham clubs all over the world that run classes to assist the neophyte. Once you get a U.S. license or a license from a country that has what is known as a third-party agreement with other countries, it is possible to have a shoreside amateur plug you directly into the telephone lines. In effect, you can talk via his phone, and at his phone rates. If it's a local call for the ham, that's the only cost. If you want to talk with friends or family on a weekly basis, as we did, the cost is minimal.

As to the system itself, the most important element is the antenna, the means of radiating the power of the transmitter to the outside world and of receiving what is coming back through the ether.

For a boat, the simplest antenna is an insulated backstay, i.e., a long wire antenna. This is an "unbalanced" system, and as such requires what is called a counterpoise or ground plane. This is usually formed by the ship's hull if metal, her machinery and through-hull fittings, or by a special ground plane fastened to the hull underwater. The ground-plane/long-wire combination work together, and you can't have a good long wire without a good ground plane, which means you have to have everything you can think of tied into the ground plane: metal exhaust line, engine, through-hull fittings, genoa cleats, winch bases, etc.

Next, with a long wire you need an antenna coupler or tuner. This device fools the transmitter into thinking that the wire is a different length than it really is, so that the radio waves will radiate properly. On marine SSBs, the coupler is usually automated and can easily cost as much as the basic radio by the time it is installed and tuned. With a ham radio, the coupler has one or two control knobs that you adjust while watching a signal meter on the set and that peak up for best readings.

Once the radio waves leave the tuner, they are "hot," that is they are radiating, so it is important to have the coupler as close to the base of the antenna as possible. If there is a substantial distance between the two, part of the signal will be trapped inside the boat and lost.

Next in the way of antennas come the balanced "whips." These are short antennas usually set up for specific frequency ranges. Coils are built into their bases again to fool the radio into thinking they are something they are not. For marine SSB work it is usually necessary to have several of these to cover a wide range of frequencies. In amateur radio, whips are available that cover all the available frequencies with or without adjustment. A second family of whips is available with removable tips. In this case, each tip is a different length and has a special resonator coil in its base. If you want to work a given frequency, select the proper tip and screw it on.

Whip antennas, especially at low frequency, should have a good ground. Some manufacturers say that coupling the ground to the lifeline stanchions and wires is sufficient. We have found the best bet is a 15-foot piece of braided battery cable from the base of the whip trailing in the water when the radio is in use.

Depending on the rigging of a boat and the conditions of use, the long-wire antenna will usually be a little better performer than the whip, if the coupler can be mounted closeby. If that's impossible, the whip is the way to go. In any case, most yachts carry a whip for use in the event of dismasting if their other antennas are lost.

Other forms of antenna are available that are infinitely more efficient than whips or long wires. The most basic of these balanced antennas is called a half-wave dipole. It will deliver eight times the output radiation of the whip or long wire. I know this seems hard to believe, but it's a fact. It also hears eight times as well. This means a 200-watt radio with a dipole will have the same punch as one with 1600 watts used with a long wire. ·

What is this marvelous piece of gear? Nothing more than a two-piece antenna fed in the center with coaxial cable. They are easy to make and easier yet to install. Being a balanced antenna, no ground plane is required.

Most cruisers eventually end up with a dipole, if not permanently rigged at least for use in port. The problem with dipole antennas, however, is their length. If you are using ham gear, 14,300 KCs is the most popular frequency area, and this requires a 32-foot antenna. On *Intermezzo* we just had room to permanently rig such an antenna between the main and mizzen mastheads. Others without such facility usually hoist the center of the dipole to the lower spreader and stretch out the ends fore and aft.

A dipole can be made in an hour for less than $10. The instructions are found in any radio manual or can be obtained at your local ham radio store.

There is a slightly more advanced form of dipole called a "trap dipole." These have electrical "traps" worked in so that antennas will resonate on a series of frequencies. If you're not really into the ham game, it's best to buy one of these.

A step up in sophistication and price are the Cat's Whiskers antennas manufactured by the M2 Company in Palos Verdes, California. Seen on most of the West Coast fishing boats, these will radiate on four marine SSB or amateur bands, with the efficiency of a dipole, but with less directional characteristics. They weigh in about 14 lbs. and are mounted on the masthead. Again, being balanced, they don't require a coupler or ground plane.

Choosing a radio receiver today is a lot more fun than it used to be. Advances in electronics now put digital readout sets with very accurate tuning and minimal drift within everyone's budget. A good shortwave receiver with digital readout is a must for picking up weather broadcasts. Since these are broadcast on marine frequencies, it may not be possible to tune in on a signal before the weather report begins. If signals are weak, the first half of the report can be lost before it is zeroed in on the dial. Digital readout alleviates this problem.

A good receiver is also a source of excellent entertainment when offshore. You can pick up the broadcasts of the next country to get a feel for what is happening. The BBC and Voice of America provide interesting listening, and the Armed Forces Radio and TV network broadcasts major sporting events and has 24-hour news coverage from the major U.S. networks.

As with broadcasting on the ham or SSB, reception is only as good as the antenna. Early on our trip we acquired a special switch so that we could divert the transmitter antenna to the receiver. This device is called a co-ax switch, and is available in any radio shop. It simply switches the coaxial cable used in antennas from one operation to the other.

Your long wire, or better yet dipole, will enhance the performance of the receiver. The whips don't work as well.

I remember sitting in Rabaul, Papua, New Guinea, listening to the Super Bowl game on my cheap Radio Shack shortwave receiver working through our masthead dipole. Our neighbors, with much more expensive receivers but inadequate antennas, were unable to pick up the signals.

Here's one last thing to consider on the subject of radio communication. It is possible today to buy rather inexpensive weather facsimile chart printers. These printers operate on radio waves broadcast worldwide and can give up-to-date weather charts for any ocean on earth. Inexpensive models are available for under $3000, and with a good receiver and antenna system, they do an excellent job of letting you know what's coming. If you're planning on doing a lot of high-latitude sailing or spending time cruising during the hurricane season, a weather facsimile printer machine is worth considering.

9. Dinghies

The dinghy has to perform a number of vital functions. From a safety standpoint it must be able to go to windward under adverse conditions towing a spare anchor warp. It may become a liferaft or important adjunct to the raft. And of course it forms basic transportation when anchored.

Oar-powered workboats all over the world have one thing in common—they're long and narrow. (S. A. Dashew)

Let's explore these requirements in more detail. To begin with, sooner or later (probably sooner) you will find yourself aground. Under certain conditions you may urgently need to launch the dinghy and pull out a kedge anchor. If there is a sea running or you're fast on a reef, a few minutes can spell the difference between another learning experience and disaster. You may find yourself in a situation of having to row against a strong wind, and perhaps seas. So the dinghy has to have some sea-keeping ability. And it must be stored and secured in such a manner that it is ready to go over the side quickly.

This last point was brought home to us in a very embarrassing manner at the beginning of our trip. We had just made a radar and depth-sounder entrance to fog-shrouded San Diego Harbor. I was tickled at our successful use of these new toys even though I had been in and out of the Point Loma breakwater many times in other boats with nothing guiding me but my ears and nose.

The fog lifted as we worked closer to the Shelter Island Basin. I had Elyse, then seven, read the depth sounder (for practice) as we headed for the marker dividing the channel entrance. When Elyse started reading 3 instead of 30, I thought she was confused until there was a thud and *Intermezzo*'s bow lifted a foot out of the water.

I had forgotten "red right returning," and we were hard aground on a mudbank. What a way to start a cruise! It was apparent that the tide was at the top of the flood and ready to start ebbing any moment. We couldn't back off, so I began to get the dinghy overboard. Out came the sail covers, awnings, fenders, three sets of oars, sailing gear, dinghy anchor, and dock lines. By the time this was all on deck it was difficult to get near the dinghy, let alone try and tie up the lifting sling. It was at least ten minutes before I had the boat over the side and had set a kedge. As it turned out we were able to get off on that tide, but another few minutes of messing with the dinghy and we would have been stuck for the night. Under different conditions, what was then rather comical could have been serious.

Thereafter we always stowed the dinghy only with essential items, and left the sling attached.

With these thoughts fresh in mind, consider also the use of a good dinghy as either a liferaft or in conjunction with a raft. The Robertson family in *Survive the Savage Sea* tell how they used their solid dink first as an annex, and later as their primary life-support vessel when the raft deteriorated.

Where the dinghy will be most used is as normal means of transport in harbor. On a basic level, the dinghy will take you ashore and to visit neighbors. That is a necessity, but you will find yourself getting much enjoyment from exploration trips, jungle river rides, poking through mangrove swamps, or lazy cruises over the Bahamian flats. These are some of the finest moments in cruising; but since some of these exploration trips will be in secluded areas, you must have a dinghy that will get you back, regardless of what happens.

The ability to take repeated beachings on sharp rocks or coral must be considered, along with the capacity to be pulled on and off the shore by lighter members of the crew. Linda is just able to handle

Not too many years ago some of the finest surfboat men were found right in the West Indies, on the island of Saba. (S. A. Dashew)

our 115-lb. dinghy if the beach surface is rough sand or coral. If it's smooth sand or mud, she needs help. Inflatables are more difficult to pull up and back than solid boats of comparable weight.

Next, the dinghy must be easily rightable when swamped. Any centerboard sailor knows the importance of this aspect, but it means more buoyancy than is generally built into the standard dinghy. We have seen dinghies with handrails fastened to their bottoms to act as runners on coral beaches and handholds to help flip the dinghy back up in the water. The less freeboard the boat has when she is turned back up but still swamped, the more difficult it will be to bail her dry, even with large bailers.

Another consideration is getting ashore or back out to sea when a sea is breaking on the beach. The techniques for this are covered in our seamanship section, but in general, speed and directional control are the essential elements.

The inflatable dinghy has opened up a new dimension in yachting. Regardless of size, a yacht can have a good-size tender with an easily stowed inflatable. It's not unusual to see a combination of inflatable and solid dink on 35-footers.

Inflatables are lightweight, will make excellent lifeboats if properly prepared, and when powered adequately do very well in the surf. Rowing an inflatable is another question. Of primary importance here are the size of oar blades and the length of the oars. The standard oars that come with inflatables are much too short. At least seven-foot oars are necessary for the average eight-foot Zodiac or Avon.

Solid floorboards make a tremendous difference in the performance of inflatables, both under power and rowing. These can be simple pieces of ⅜" plywood or more elaborate premade floorboards available from the manufacturer.

The boats I like the best are those with the inflatable floors and solid floorboards. These units plane and have a much greater range of utility. The 10-foot Avon or Zodiac, with a 6-h.p. engine, will move two people at 13 knots—fast enough to really expand your exploring horizons. With that sort of speed at your disposal, the dinghy becomes more like an automobile for going to town, getting supplies, or visiting. There are many spots on the cruising circuit where the best anchorages are some distance from the center of town and local shore transportation may be infrequent or nonexistent. Without a good high-speed dinghy, the in-town anchorage becomes mandatory. Tahiti is a good example of this. The anchorage in downtown Papeete is crowded and noisy; after a few days tied up stern-to, it wears a bit thin on charm. You can take a 15-minute ride by inflatable in either direction from Papeete and find quiet, beautiful anchorages.

If you go one step up in size, to an 11-foot boat, you can then add a 20-h.p. motor for waterskiing. Before laughing this off, let me say that waterskiing in the tropics is an exhilarating sport. The warm water, incredible colors, and flashing shapes beneath as you zoom across coral heads really adds to the enjoyment. The one size up in inflatable also makes for a much drier ride.

A planing inflatable is probably the best boat for handling surf. It has excellent maneuverability and acceleration, and its extra speed means you don't have to time your moves quite so precisely as with conventional boats.

The negative side of the inflatables is expense. They are initially expensive and don't last forever. You must be careful with them around coral and jagged rocks. And although they will take a tremendous amount of punishment, punctures do occur. Simple punctures are fairly easy to repair, however, and facilities for repairing inflatables exist all over the world in major ports.

In the small eight-foot units, Avon is the most popular. Once you get into the size of boat that has the inflatable keel and hard floorboards, the verdict is unanimous: Zodiac. Because of its size and weight, the larger unit takes more abuse from the beach and sun. But if you are careful about sharp edges, and keep a cover over the inflatable when it is not in service, ten years of use can be expected. If you never cover it and really beat the tar out of the unit, three to four years is about par.

When towing your dinghy, make provisions to run the towing line through the forward towing eye(s) and back to eye bolts in the dinghy's transom, being sure to put PVC plastic chafing gear over the lines where they are in contact with the hull. Damaged towing eyes are among the most common problems, and this system will minimize abuse.

As the long-distance cruiser gets more experience he begins to work away from the inflatable. Most of our friends who have been there before, like the Liggetts or Moeslys, carry solid dinghies. They last almost forever, are easier to pull up on the beach and easier to get aboard, and are much cheaper. The size varies with deck space, but a 9-footer is about the minimum, with 10 feet a lot more desirable. One of the problems with solid dinks is their length/width ratio. Most commercially made units are designed to carry as many people as possible, with a minimum of tippiness. This is fine in a calm anchorage, but the squat shapes are difficult to row, especially into a chop, and difficult to handle, even in small surf.

Aboard *Intermezzo* we devoted space to a 14-foot "Wherry" or pulling boat. A joy to row, good in the surf, with reasonable performance under power, it gave us close to the best of both worlds. By attaching the towing eye directly to the mainmast, and providing a chock on the doghouse, our Wherry was carried right-side-up at sea, and was ready to go over the side quickly. *Intermezzo*'s fenders were lashed to the gunnels to provide extra buoyancy in case they were needed to augment our raft. The crew of the 47-foot *Dawn Treader* of Lune created an interesting dinghy when we were together in the Bay of Islands, New Zealand. They made up two punts, or square-ended dinghies, that nested inside each other. When they wanted to go exploring, they bolted the boats together, transom to transom, and added a 6-h.p. outboard. Their lightweight, flat-bottomed 14-footer literally flew over the water with that small engine. At other times it split into two dinks.

A lot of boats with children aboard carry a second dink. Allowing the kids, even when they are young, to go off on their own is great for them and for you. In this case, the choice is usually one inflatable and one solid. We made use of inexpensive lightweight inflatables for our children, and at about $60 we certainly got our money's worth.

Many carry sailing rigs for their dinghies, and in theory it's a great idea. But our experience seems to parallel others; we found that it was rare that the dinghy was set up to sail. When it wasn't sailing, we had sails, mast, boom, rudder, and centerboard to stow.

More and more boats are carrying windsurfers aboard. These are compact, and in warm waters are great fun; they can be lashed, on edge, to the lifelines or else stowed flat on the cabin top.

10. Outboards

If you have a good rowing dink, an outboard is a luxury. But if space limits the dinghy waterline, or your choice is an inflatable, the outboard becomes a necessity.

There are so many makes and models on the market today that it's hard to single out any specific unit as best. In general, though, most cruisers agree that even in the small outboards a two-cylinder model is worth the extra weight. It isn't at all unusual to see a two-banger operating on one or one and a half cylinders. With a one-lunger you don't have that security.

Plastic fuel tanks are a must. In spite of your best efforts, it's impossible to keep steel outboard tanks from creating a rusty mess.

In the smaller outboards, up through 6 h.p., Johnson and Evinrude are the most popular. Their 6-h.p. units are probably the best they ever built; if they are kept dry, they'll give years of relatively trouble-free service. And for waterskiing behind a Zodiac, the 20-h.p. Mercury can't be beat. It is relatively light, and has enough power to jerk up even a 200-pounder on double skis. Surprisingly, once on top of the water, even our heavyweight can drop a ski and slalom. The ride isn't fast, but the quick acceleration of the inflatable makes for exciting cutting back and forth.

The Japanese have made big inroads with outboards in all of the island areas of the Pacific and Indian Oceans. Mariner, Daihatsu, Suzuki—all appear to be well built, lightweight, and reliable. Service is also good. But for worldwide service, you can't beat the Johnson and Evinrude.

There are some (not many) among the cruising fleet who believe we should still be fighting the Battle of Dunkirk and use the Seagull outboards. There must be a magic formula to these ancient creations that I cannot master. Nor have I met many long-term cruisers who will keep a Seagull running, much less aboard, for more than a year. Thereafter it becomes an anchor, or is traded for a carving such as the elegant creation the Hast family picked up in the Solomon Islands for their Seagull.

Of course, some of us are more stubborn than others. When we last saw Emory Moore, in Bali, Indonesia, he had three Seagulls on his stern pulpit: a big one, a small one, and one for parts. None of them worked, but he and DeeDee kept in good shape rowing their Avon through the water.

11. The Liferaft

I have many doubts about the suitability of a standard yacht liferaft for an offshore cruiser.

To begin with, the odds are infinitesimally small that you will ever have to take to a raft. In this regard, we can't stress too strongly the foolishness of abandoning ship before it is absolutely certain that she's going down. There are far more stories of sailors whose vessels have survived after being abandoned than there are of sailors who have survived long sojourns on liferafts.

The problem is that the standard yacht liferaft is effective really only in areas where help can be summoned quickly. Most of the long-distance cruising tracks, of course, are out of the shipping and aircraft lanes, and the odds are that if you take to the raft you're going to be there for a good while. That means you need to look at your abandon-ship materials in the light of an extended stay.

Prior to purchasing *Intermezzo*'s raft I read the Baileys' *Staying Alive* and Dougal Robertson's *Survive the Savage Sea.* Both are excellent, graphic accounts of long periods on ill-prepared lifesaving gear. And while I'm sure they would not like to repeat their experiences, it does show that you can survive for quite a while under terrible conditions.

After digesting these two books, I met George Siegler of Survival and Safety Designs. George and his partner had a different philosophy from the standard raft people. They felt you had to be self-sufficient for long periods, and needed to be able to make progress toward a destination.

George and his partner had enough courage in their convictions to take a 12-foot Zodiac equipped with a sail and their survival gear on a 2400-mile passage from San Francisco to Hawaii, a 58-day trip.

We ordered a C. J. Hendry six-man raft, and while there were only going to be two adults and two small children as potential occupants, I felt the additional space was warranted for "comfort." At George's suggestion we had packed in a heavy-duty Sears air mattress, to act as a floorboard and lift our bodies out of any residual water that might find its way into the bottom of our raft. We purchased the usual Transpac safety gear and George's Sig II survival kit. In addition we had packed in several extra solar stills for greater distillation capacity of that most precious item, drinking water. We added a variety of glucose and protein supplements to the inventory, wool clothes, and wool blankets. An emergency locating transmitter was packed, as were a dozen 25-mm parachute flares.

All of this extra material required going from the standard six-man fiberglass cannister to the next size up. In the raft tie-down system we used a hydrostatic release, required by the Coast Guard for commercial vessels, that would automatically let the raft go if it was submerged to 15 feet.

When the raft was ready to be packed in San Francisco, I flew up for the afternoon to observe how the gear went in, learn the raft-testing procedure, and to be sure I was familiar with the operation of the bellows, patching gear, and solar stills.

We serviced the raft on two occasions during the 3½ years of our cruise. The first time was by a professional. The raft was in good condition, but some of the accessory items were not. I was glad to be on hand to tell the chap working on the raft what I wanted rejected.

The second time we had the raft apart I did the work myself. What I learned this time was really of interest. First, batteries left in the flashlight had burst and corroded, although they were only one year old and had been kept dry. The flashlights were ruined. Next, moisture either from condensation or leakage had puddled in the bottom of the cannister. We replaced the food supplements, purchased nickel-cadmium batteries and new flashlights, and sealed the various small items inside the pack in separate plastic containers.

We decided to fit a PVC-coated nylon fabric cover to our raft, to prevent rain or sea water from forcing its way into the cannister. Made of light material, and held loosely by a shock-cord drawstring so as not to restrict the cannister opening, it was well worth the investment.

I got a real surprise trying to maneuver our well-packed raft. With molded handholds of minimal value, I had a hard time getting the raft back where it was supposed to go. How I would handle the reverse chore, perhaps on my own, under adverse conditions was open to speculation. We felt that protruding handles attached to a reinforced spot on the cover would be a real help. So would separating the extra material packed into the raft to reduce the bulk and weight to a more manageable size.

Three and a half years later, and looking toward equipping a new boat, I would take a different approach. I feel George Siegler's original ideas to be the only valid system for an *offshore* cruising vessel. Equipping a good inflatable dinghy with awnings, a small rudder, and a sail would give you the capability to make 30 to 50 miles a day in the direction of salvation. Considering the constant abuse these inflatables take day in and day out, they would certainly stand up to a long-term voyage better than any standard liferaft.

The key is proper preparation. You must have a means of staying dry, and more important, keeping out of the sun. This can be accomplished with an awning or tent attached to the edges of the inflatable and supported by aluminum struts. The sailing rig and rudder can be easily made. On the Italian Whitbread round-the-world racer *R and B,* they worked out a pair of leeboards so they could sail upwind in their Zodiac liferaft.

One big problem is inflation time. The safest procedure is to leave the inflatable partially filled with air, with floorboards in place, lashed down to the deck. A scuba tank, with an air nozzle, will take care of the rest of the work in a matter of minutes. Spare supplies must be carried in a sealed container, either in the raft or at some convenient spot nearby. We have met people who use their everyday inflatable dink in this manner. If the dinghy is kept in good shape, and covered, there is no reason why it won't do double duty. But toward the end of its life span, one must consider replacing such a raft a bit earlier than would be necessary if the only consideration was for shoreboating.

From a cost standpoint there are advantages as well. As a general rule an inflatable dinghy is going to cost 20 to 25 percent less than a comparable liferaft.

A negative aspect is stability in heavy weather. It can be argued that without ballast pockets an inflatable of this nature is more subject to being rolled over than a stabilized raft. Without an inflated center support tube to the canopy, the Zodiac or Avon type of dink will be more difficult to right once upside down. True enough, but the excellent turned-up bow shape and natural buoyancy of these designs, coupled with a good sea anchor, should do much to offset the risk.

Also, one must evaluate this risk against the potential for the type of weather that would create a dangerous situation. On a long-term cruising vessel the chances are you will be using the trade-wind routes, staying out of the bad-weather regions of the world. And of course if your sailing is to take place principally along shore, or in areas with good commercial ship and air traffic, then you should take a longer look at conventional rafts.

Ralph Naranjo had a very clever piece of gear in his survival kit. He built up a five-watt Heathkit Morse Code transmitter that ran off dry cells and would work on the ham radio bands. Five watts of code may not sound like much, but you can be sure that somewhere, someone with a powerful directional antenna will pick up the signal. It is inexpensive to build and the necessary code is easy to learn. The ability to broadcast not only your trouble but your position is a tremendous asset, especially considering the short range of the standard EPIRB.

It is of vital importance, whichever approach you choose, that forethought, planning, and some practice go into abandon-ship drills.

12. Harnesses

No single piece of safety gear is as important as the safety harness. Without it, on a shorthanded cruiser if one of the crew members goes overboard, the odds of getting him back, especially in heavy going, are minimal.

The harness itself should be heavily made. Two-inch nylon webbing with four rows of stitching at structural attachment points is the minimum for an adult. The harness must be comfortable to wear and easy to put on and take off.

The simplest design is one that incorporates a strap around the chest and under the arms, with two shoulder straps worked in on a fixed basis. D-rings can be used for width adjustment. A ⅜″ to ⁷⁄₁₆″ three-stand nylon line is necessary for attachment. I prefer to have two lines on my harness. The first is a long working line, which will clear my feet when snapped back on the D-ring. The second is a short three-foot tether for use at the wheel or working in severe weather. The hook itself must be strong, equal to the breaking strain of the nylon, and capable of being operated with one hand. Be sure to keep the action working well with an occasional freshwater bath and a few drops of oil.

A child's harness can be made of lighter gear all around. The harnesses we built for Elyse and Sarah were of 1″ webbing with ⁵⁄₁₆″ line.

Next, work out convenient attachment points. This is most easily done by installing a heavy pad eye (again equal to the breaking strain of the rope) alongside the companionway. It must be placed so you can attach either in the cockpit or from down below before coming on deck. An extension line should be made up that will allow you to work anywhere in the cockpit, or to go forward just a bit, and then return to your below-deck watchkeeping station, all the while remaining hooked up.

For going forward, a jackstay is best. Aboard *Intermezzo* we rigged a piece of nylon-covered $\frac{3}{16}''$ 1 $\times$ 19 wire. This ran from one of the genoa cars on the toe rail, forward and around the intermediate forestay, and back to a car on the opposite side of the cockpit. Once hooked on, we could work anywhere on deck and walk right around the bow without having to change hook-up points. The advantage of wire over rope is that the connecting hook will slide more easily when dragging behind.

Before cutting the jackstay to a specific length, be sure that the long tether, when attached to the jackstay, will allow you to work around the headstay as necessary to hank on or remove a headsail. Since the length of your own tether is limited by what can hang on the harness without tripping you, any additional distance will have to be made up by slack in the jackstay.

Before leaving California we took our float coats to a sailmaker to sew in two-inch webbing around the chest and under the arms. With double D-rings attached to the end, it was easy to add a safety line when we wanted to go on deck. For sailing in colder climates, where a jacket or rain gear is necessary, this system saves a lot of time.

13. Man-Overboard Gear

One should look at what experience has taught the ocean-racing fraternity is necessary for man-overboard gear. As a minimum, one set of pole, horseshoe ring, and strobe light should be carried.

The pole should be 15 feet in length, and the flag at the end must have a batten to keep it extended in light airs. The strobe light must be checked every three months for operation, and the battery renewed at a maximum of six-month intervals. Since the odds are that there will be quite a bit of wind blowing when this gear is employed, a good-size sea anchor is a must. The 6-inch units normally sold are a joke. If it's blowing a gale and your lifesaving gear is being swept rapidly to leeward, a proper 12-inch or better sea anchor is called for. It's a good idea to use a long floating line between the sea anchor, horseshoe, and pole. They will spread out in a line, giving the person in the water the greatest target for which to aim.

The lines should be checked every six months or so for sun rot. Most floating lines don't take to ultraviolet radiation and about a year is all you can expect from them. Keep an eye on the straps on the horseshoe ring as well. They will go rotten after a year or two.

If the system is not ready to go over the side at a moment's notice, it is of little value. The usual practice of tying the various elements here and there just won't do on an offshore boat. The best approach we have seen is the forespar launcher. By pulling one wire, the entire system—pole, strobe, and horseshoe ring—is let out. Another system for those of you building a boat is to utilize a tube through the hull for the pole and a standard holder for the ring and light. When the ring is tossed, its drag and that of the sea anchor will pull the stowed pole from its hull tube.

If you have a mizzen, the mizzen cap shroud is an excellent place for the launcher and its load of gear. Otherwise, the pole can be placed horizontally along the rail.

Some offshore races require their entrants to carry two sets of gear. This won't be practical on small boats, but larger yachts; budgets permitting, would do well to emulate the practice.

In some of the stronger blows we've encountered, I always wondered if a wave top would take some of our man-overboard gear. More than once I watched solid water break across the after end of *Intermezzo*, expecting to see our strobe light flashing off behind us. However, with the exception of one time when we were *anchored* in Cape Town, with a 70-knot southeaster howling about our ears, the gear stayed put.

14. Securing Interiors for Heavy Weather

Every sea-going vessel should be able to take a full knockdown without damage. It's no doubt a little hard on the crew's nerves to put the spreaders in the water, but it should not put the boat out of commission.

The problem usually comes in cleaning up the mess below. Drawers have all emptied from the windward side, the reefer may have emptied itself partially, and even floorboards may be adrift. The resulting chaos can take days to clean up, and if it happens during a long voyage, with bilgewater thrown into the equation, it will be

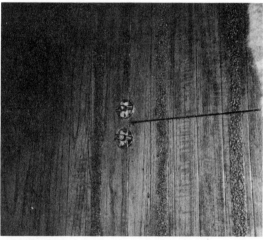

Floor buttons kept *Intermezzo*'s cabin sole hatches in place in the event of a rollover. Note the nonskid pattern of walnut shells on the varnished floor.

sitive outside latches kept everything ts place if *Intermezzo* was knocked on ear.

Aboard *Intermezzo II* hooks can be used for keeping lockers either open or closed.

demoralizing. The answer is to take simple precautions, easy and inexpensive to execute.

Have a look through the interior and assume that the vessel was actually rolling through a 360-degree somersault. What would go flying? Heavy gear must be carefully analyzed. Batteries must be secured in a positive manner from coming adrift; the electric cables by themselves won't guarantee this. Even the engine and generator motor mounts should be looked at with this in mind. The average marine engine at 700 or 800 lbs. would cause an incalculable amount of damage if it came adrift. Properly installed engine mounts should handle the job—but they must be checked. So should the mounts on the galley stove.

Simpler to deal with are doors and drawers. These should have positive latches, not just spring clips or detent ball-and-socket assemblies. There are many ways to accomplish this. We found that a simple hook and eye, adequate for the load intended, was the easiest approach. When securing lockers, be sure to consider the hinges of the doors as well. If heavy gear is stowed behind, will the door stand the load of that gear if it is flung at it? Heavier objects, such as portable gasoline generators, should have their own lashings.

Floorboards and reefer top-opening doors must have latches to prevent their coming adrift.

To keep goods stored under our settees in place we used ¼ " yacht braid over all interior cushions. This held the cushions in place, and the cushions held the access doors closed.

The companionway hatch should have a positive inside latch; slamming into large head seas can cause it to open. And of course the wash boards must be held in place by some form of lock or barrel bolt.

Books create a more difficult problem. If they are really well secured, it will be very difficult to get them out when you want them. For this reason we rig fixed lines to hold them in place. When we're at anchor, these lines are removed.

Lee boards or lee cloths on bunks must be stout enough to keep a crew member in place during a violent knockdown. In most cases when a vessel is badly rolled or knocked down, the crew occupying pilot berths with good protection come out unscathed. It's the crew members in open berths or sitting about who are subject to injury.

Arion III had sailed halfway around the world when this photo was taken in Bali, Indonesia. Permanent storm shutters had been installed over the large doghouse windows.

Intermezzo's permanent storm windows after installation in New Zealand. They were 1″-thick Lexan, and literally bulletproof.

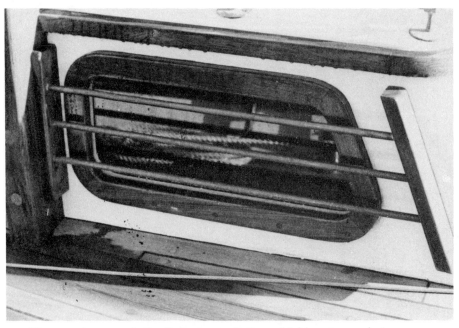

These ports are ready for their storm windows. Making storm windows easy to use helps ensure that they will be used when necessary.

No cruising boat should go to sea without a sump of reasonable depth. This usually takes the form of a pocket in the keel behind the ballast. There is always some water in the sump, usually of doubtful origin. To prevent this from gaining access to lockers during a severe knockdown, add a perimeter edge to the sump. The edge will retain water until the vessel is well past horizontal.

15. Storm Shutters

Unless your windows or portlights are of immensely strong construction, you'll have to have storm shutters aboard. *Intermezzo*'s production doghouse windows left something to be desired in this regard. When we left California we carried ¾" high-density plywood shutters. These were affixed by means of lanyards to eye straps. After our first really good blow, when I never got around to attaching the shutters, I decided we needed a better system. As a result, we redid our windows, exchanging the light-duty plastic for 1" Lexan, in effect putting permanent storm shutters in place. We dispensed with all but one sheet of our plywood inventory.

There are many approaches to this problem, but a vessel meant to cruise offshore for any distance must have some form of permanent shutters quickly at hand.

16. Chafe

Sail chafe with modern materials is not a major problem. With a combination of Dacron sailcloth, heavy synthetic threads, and stainless-steel wire, the situation is well in hand. A few commonsense guidelines in preparation and sail handling will minimize any problems that you may expect to encounter.

The mainsail presents the biggest chafe problems. When you are broad-reaching and running, the sail will lie against the spreaders and after lower shrouds despite the best efforts of your boom vang. Smooth off the trailing edges of the spreaders to a 600 sandpaper finish; it can be quickly done and will pay real dividends. It's also not a bad idea to rub down the aftershrouds with a rag every once in a while when you're aloft to reduce dirt stains on the sail. Extra patches of sailcloth should be sewn to the sail, extending from the luff of the sail to six inches beyond the spreader tip on both sides of the main. These chafe patches will take whatever wear there is, leaving the primary sail untouched. It's a good idea to have similar chafe patches for the first reef as well. We considered adding vertical chafing strips to lie against the after lowers; I kept looking for wear but it never proved to be a problem.

The topping lift must be watched for chafe against the mainsail leech. The wire should be plastic covered and have a good shock-cord slack-control system to prevent its whipping around in a seaway.

If you use your mizzen most of the time, it will require the same preventive treatment as the main. If it's primarily a riding sail, and is furled when the breeze picks up, it can be left as is; but pay attention to those spreaders.

Headsails present their own problems. The basic concern here is chafe against the spreader tips. Leather is the traditional material for chafing guards, and it looks very nautical; plastic spreader boots, however, are much easier on the sail fabric and stitching.

The pulpit will bear watching if the headsails are tacked right down to the stemhead fitting. Be sure there are no sharp edges, and then have chafing strips sewn over each headsail where it rubs. Be sure to check while broad-reaching and running as well as close-reaching.

Spinnakers will inevitably work themselves back and forth against the headstay; a layer of ¾-oz. fabric loosely stitched along the foot so as not to interfere with stretch will be well worthwhile.

Mizzen staysails have a tendency to hang up on main boom out-haul fittings and any cleat or winch on the boom. Since these sails are of very light construction, a tear is probable. Large-size reinforc-

Mainsail chafe patches for running. The upper patch is
in use when the main is reefed.

ing patches are necessary in the potential problem areas, since the
mizzen staysail will be wandering around when you are well off the
wind. Chafe isn't as much of a problem here as catching and tearing.

When reefing either the mizzen or the main, be sure that there are
no sharp protrusions along the boom that could chafe or tear the sail
as it is lying reefed. In a good breeze, the reefed portion of the sail
will be flopping steadily even if secured by its cringles.

Headsail hanks also require watching. On a long passage they are
going to see a lot of wear. The hanks on our light #1 jib were just

about worn through at the end of our Atlantic passage. At that point they had about 6000 miles on them, with perhaps another thousand to go. Hanks *can* be rebrazed, and if you're in a country where labor is cheap, this may be the way to go. But in the higher priced sailing areas, new hanks will probably cost less. Carry spares.

Chafe with running rigging isn't much more of a problem than with sails. The main thing to watch is that the leads on sheets and halyards are fair, and it doesn't hurt to change the nip on them by an inch or two every once in a while.

A sheet working against the side of a block won't last long even under light loads, and it could chafe through in hours if the line is working hard. Conversely, it could work all day long against the side of a smooth stainless-steel lifeline stanchion and not show any damage.

The biggest chafe hazard comes between lines. When broad-reaching, we found that our headsail sheets always wanted to interfere with the boom vang. This necessitated constant changing of the relative positions of the vang and sheet blocks. We never did find a satisfactory solution except keeping an eye on things. We have not had much success with chafing gear on running rigging. If you get it in place for a certain wind angle, things will surely change or the chafing gear will slip. We found it better to adjust leads so they were fair to begin with.

Eventually, something will get by you and a large ragged spot will appear on a line. If this is close to the end of the sheet near the clew of the headsail, simply reverse the line and you're in business again. If the chafe spot is put into a nonstructural part of the line, the core will carry the load easily. If it's three-strand line, seize the chafed area to keep it from unraveling, and reverse it. Occasionally we have taken the core out of braided lines and inserted another core where the line is not under load.

Spinnaker halyards will give excellent life if run over large-diameter sheaves. We found that about once every five days it was necessary to drop the chute and cut off the chafed end of the halyard.

Nylon anchor rodes are very resistant to chafe, but they should always be protected at the bow roller, just in case. For chafing gear we used flexible, reinforced PVC tubing secured with marlin through the ends.

17. Lightning

There are many theories on how to deal with lightning on a small boat. My first exposure to the problem occurred on a lake in the Ozark Hills of Missouri, when I was in college. We were out sailing in a small catamaran when a front came through bringing with it the usual rain, hail, and lightning. We could see lightning striking the ground on either side of the lake as the front came toward us. My initial reaction was "My God! Our mast is aluminum and higher than the surrounding scrub." Deciding that discretion was the better part of valor, I capsized my cat and swam for it. That was *not* a smart move. I didn't think about the conductivity of fresh water if it took a direct hit and we were in it.

At sea, properly protected, a small nonmetallic vessel presents little physical danger to those aboard from lightning strikes. There is considerable financial risk, however: a good hit can wipe out all electronic gear aboard, including clocks, alternators, radios, radars, and long-range navigation gear.

The American Boat and Yacht Council, in its safety standards for small craft, recommends bonding chain plates, masts, and through-hull fittings together. This gives lightning a path to exit, probably without blowing a hole in the boat. But a really substantial bolt could still take a through-hull fitting with it.

If you opt for this technique, remember that lightning does not like sharp angles or bends. Its preference is a straight line, or at best a gentle curve. If the mast-to-keel angle is too sharp and there is a nearby through-hull fitting with a circuitous bonding wire running to it, the lightning may take the direct path rather than the ground strap and perhaps blow a hole in the side as it goes.

I was concerned from the beginning by lightning, and although we rarely encountered conditions that gave rise to risk of taking a direct hit, the thought of our electronic gear going up in smoke gave me nightmares.

In Darwin, Australia, I discussed the situation with Charlie Hast aboard his 54-foot schooner *Sunday Morning*. Charlie had formerly been in aerospace work, doing research with microwave antennas.

Part of his job was deciding what to do about lightning. From our conversation I learned a number of interesting things. First, the better the ground system, the more likely it is that you'll take a hit. For every bolt from the clouds to the ground, there is one that goes the other way. If you are too well grounded you may invite trouble. Second, lightning hits vary in intensity. Electronic gear can be protected from a moderate strike. A real whopper, however, will overcome almost any precautions.

Charlie felt it was best to keep the lightning out of the vessel altogether if possible. This meant unbonding the spar(s) and carrying the bolt down one of the cap shrouds. To protect masthead gear you should install an insulator on both cap shrouds, at the masthead, and affix a lightning-arresting rod to the cap shrouds that points above the masthead. Getting from the chain plate to the water is a little more complex. An ideal solution would be to have the cap shroud chain plates run down the outside of the hull right to the water. Since not many owners would tolerate this solution aesthetically, the next best approach is to use a wire from the shroud to the water.

This is the method we adopted. A #6 size wire provides plenty of strength for flexing back and forth when at sea. We attached it with a hose clamp on the lower swage terminal. It's a good idea to seize the wire above and below the insulation to keep it from flexing too much.

There are some areas in the world where lightning displays and occasional hits are common. The east coast of Florida, the Gulf of Panama, and the north side of New Guinea have all claimed their victims.

I asked Charlie about protecting electronic gear. His first comment was that by twisting positive and negative wires together, the incidence of transmitting static energy could be reduced. Using a common ground or a "ring" wire system is inviting trouble. Last, provide for easily disconnected electrical gear. This includes antennas. The disconnected leads should have a plug nearby in which to be placed, so they are tied back to the ship's ground system. This reduces the chance that static electricity will gap between the antenna plugs and electronic gear.

Metal vessels appear to have a better chance of surviving lightning strikes unscathed. Their greater surface area more effectively dissipates the power in the lightning bolt, thus reducing risk to electronic gear.

18. Heaters

Carrying a heater on most small boats is a nuisance. They take up quite a bit of room, and unless you are sailing in really cold climates they are unnecessary.

If you make only occasional dips into the higher latitudes for a summer's cruising, you will never encounter temperatures below the 50s Fahrenheit. Coming from the pleasant 80s closer to the equator this may be a shock, but between warm sailing gear and the galley stove you can survive. (A couple of old-fashioned flower pots inverted over the stove burners provide solid warmth.) Additionally, the Aladdin-type mantled kerosene lamps give off a tremendous amout of heat.

The one thing these forms of heat will not do is dry out the interior. For that you need vented combustion, i.e., a permanent installation of a kerosene-or diesel-fired heater. There are some excellent inexpensive makes on the market that really put out the BTUs. The Dickenson heaters, made in Vancouver, B.C., are one of the most popular units.

When positioning a permanent installation, remember that you might want to use it at sea; it must be placed where no one is liable to reach out to it for a handhold if caught by a sudden lurch. In addition, be aware that for any unit that works with natural drafts, the size, length, and on-deck position of its stack is critical.

19. Fans

A simple automotive-type 12-volt fan can do wonders for your environment in the tropics at anchor or at sea. A six-inch oscillating fan with a permanent-magnet motor will use just 1 amp at 12 volts DC. The most popular units available around the world are made by

Sanyo. They have a plastic blade and motor casing. (The blade cage and stand, however, are of cadmium-plated steel and are subject to rusting.)

We installed our first fan in Papeete, Tahiti, and by the time we had left Australia for the Indian Ocean crossing we had added three more: one in the galley, one in the saloon, and the other two in the staterooms.

An inexpensive 12-volt fan delivers more cool per unit of cost than any other system. These are indispensable in the tropics.

Close to the equator, where the trades die away at night, a fan moving the air over your body makes a tremendous difference in comfort, as it does at sea with the vessel closed up in heavy going or rainy weather.

20. Running Lights

Various international regulations require yachts over 13 meters (about 42½ feet) in length to carry an assortment of running lights that are virtually useless from the standpoint of visibility when offshore.

Yachts under 40 feet can legally use the tricolor masthead lights now available. These units are excellent and give amazing range. A small amount of amperage provides all-around visibility for an amazingly long range; the electrical requirements are within anyone's battery capacity. Many of our friends with larger boats now carry the masthead tricolor lights despite the unrealistic restrictions of the rule.

Strobe lights are to be used only for emergencies. Still, there are parts of the ocean where it is commonplace to see them flashing, usually while commercial fishermen are asleep. To a ship, they mean trouble: either a collision is imminent or there is a problem to be investigated. Their application on a vessel going offshore is marginal.

A good anchor light is handy for finding your way back to the boat at night in the dinghy; if hooked to a signaling key, it is useful for contacting other vessels if radio gear is not aboard and you know your Morse Code.

21. Sailing Instruments

The only place sailing instruments are really necessary (if at all) is down below. If you're standing watch below with an occasional look topside, dials showing apparent wind angle and speed give you a good idea of what's going on up on deck, especially if you're carrying a spinnaker.

Those of you just getting to know the sea are better off without these gauges: you'll develop sea sense much faster. Well-placed telltales are almost as effective, and much more reliable. (Use recording tape from old cassettes; it lasts, flies in very light breezes, and does well in soggy weather.)

A speedometer is strictly a luxury, but a log is important. Whether to use a taffrail log or an inside electronic or cable-driven log is a difficult decision. We carry a Walker log, which is quite accurate, except when we're surfing downwind, when it underreads a bit. We also have an electric log and find that we rarely bother with the Walker. If you do stream a taffrail log, be sure to check the line where it comes out of the rotor and where the sinker is attached. We found that every 500 miles the line had to be shortened because of chafe. We lost two rotors to chafe before we realized that it wasn't a shark back there with a taste for bronze.

22. Dorades

There will be times at sea, and in port, when inclement weather will make it impossible to crack the hatches. In this case, the more Dorade ventilators you have the better.

Each compartment of the vessel should have its own ventilators. There is no such thing as too many vents for fresh air. The diameter of the incoming pipes should be as large as possible. Remember when figuring sizes that a four-inch vent pipe has 80 percent more cross-sectional area than a three-inch pipe. The air scoop itself will vary from the low-profile (and inefficient) units to the extended-hood variety. As with pipe diameter, cross-sectional area is all-important.

There are on the market today combination ventilators and water

The proper cowl-area/vent-pipe relationship is shown on this Dorade box.

traps that work well enough in rain or light spray. But any solid water will quickly find its way below. The best ventilators, like the original Dorades, separate the incoming and exhaust pipes with an effective baffle leading to on-deck scuppers in the box. This will keep the water of even a solid hit out of the cabin. Even so, you must be able to cap the vent from the inside for heavy going. And if you're going to be sailing in cold climates, you'll want a way to adjust the airflow from below decks.

23. Weather Cloths

Weather cloths are a mixed blessing. Under certain conditions at sea —especially in aft-cockpit boats reaching in moderate seas—they'll effectively protect you from those occasional dollops of green water that pop over the quarter. They also provide additional privacy in port.

On the other hand, if they're too strongly made and catch a heavy one at sea they can bend the lifeline stanchions they're attached to; and furthermore, there are many times in port when it's nice to see the view from the rear porch.

So if you want weather cloths, we think the best approach is to make them from the lightest cover material possible, and then do what Jim Moore did on *Swan:* he used Velcro to attach the bottom of the weather cloths. This provides a strain-relieving breakaway panel when the cloths are down in heavy going, and makes them easy to roll up when you want to look around.

It also makes sense to have pockets sewn on the cloths for holding a deck chart, pilot, and perhaps even binoculars.

24. Cockpit Cushions

Cockpit cushions are great for short cruises. They are comfortable, dressy looking, and can be stored out of the weather when not in use. But once you begin to travel for longer periods they become a real nuisance. You're not likely to have space available below for storage when it's wet on deck, and the result is soggy, mildewed, and malodorous cushions.

We have seen nonabsorbent, flexible foam used for cockpit cushions. Those we have tested in the time-honored manner have been of such high density that after a short period we might as well have been sitting directly on the wooden seat. If a low-density, nonabsorbent, flexible foam could be found, that would be the answer. In lieu of this, most people end up with a few of the sealed, square deck cushions and a pillow or two used only on deck but stored below during inclement conditions.

25. Bug Screens

Surprisingly, bugs are rarely a problem in the tropics if you anchor far enough offshore. Even the infamous "no-nos" of the Marquesas (and now the Tuamotus) usually reserve their ardor for those who venture ashore at sundown. But in some of the higher latitude cruising areas in the summer, bugs can be a real nuisance. The east coast of the United States, for instance, is one of the worst places on earth for pestiferous gnats, mosquitoes, and flies.

Bug screens substantially restrict airflow and may make it difficult to adjust your hatch openings. They are also a maintenance problem, particularly the fitted screens with wood or aluminum frames, which are also expensive and hard to stow. Still, if you're going to cruise in areas with lots of bugs, you're going to need screens. The most practical system is to use Velcro around the hatch opening and sew the mating Velcro to the edges of heavy-plastic screening cut to the right size. The permanently fixed Velcro is not pretty to look at, but the screens will keep the bugs out when you need to use them and roll up compactly when you don't.

26. Flashlights

Nothing is more frustrating than a boat full of flashlights that won't work when you need them.

There are two answers. One is to invest in top-quality underwater lights. The other is to buy the cheapest lights you can find and dispense with them on a regular basis.

We started out with the first approach, but after losing our four super lights to Poseidon in various exotic anchorages, we opted for the latter.

Our first Christmas in Mexico, Sarah received a miniature light that was powered by two AA-size batteries. Six months later it was still being borrowed by the captain. Thinking there must be a message somewhere in this fact, we bought eight of the miniatures and scattered them around the boat. With simple parts inside, they were easy to keep running, and 2½ years later were still part of our inventory.

Along with your normal lights you'll want one really powerful portable beam to be used in the dinghy or on deck under special conditions. It's also a good idea to have a red hood to put over it when night vision must be maintained.

AA-, C-, and D-size batteries are available worldwide.

27. Wind Generating Systems

Imagine lying peacefully on your hook, with the palms ashore swaying in the trade wind and the surf booming on the outer reef. In one hand is a cold drink and in the other a good book. During the evening you turn on all the lights you want, and cook your dinner in a microwave oven. Throughout all this the engine is never run. No maintenance, no expense, and it's *quiet.*

A dream? Not anymore. Ex-cruiser Wardy Ward has developed the aptly named Soma windmill. Using highly efficient permanent magnets and a beautifully simple variable-pitch prop, built heavily and sealed in epoxy to resist sea water, these windmills can generate up to 500 watts of power in a 20-knot breeze. The blade diameters run from 6 to 10 feet. The larger the diameter, the lower the wind-speed range in which the generator works. When you reach port, the unit is quickly assembled and hoisted up the headstay until the blade

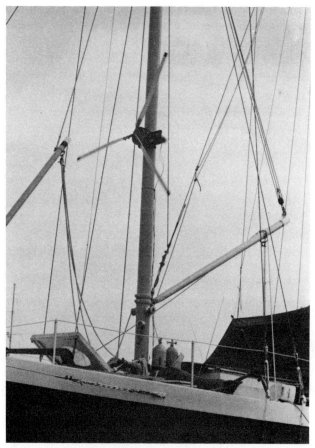

A home-built step-up wind generator in the Virgin Islands. More and more yachts are going to wind generators to avoid running the engines when anchored.

tips are well above head level. The windmill is allowed to head itself into the wind, and off you go.

We first met Wardy and one of his prototypes on Mike Moorheartd's 79-foot ketch *Armanel,* as we were clearing out of Opua, in the Bay of Islands, New Zealand. I would have bought a unit on the spot, but since we had only a mechanical refrigeration system run off the engine, we still would have had to use the engine every day. If we'd had time I would have installed a heavy DC motor, powered by the windmill, to take over the reefer from the engine when the windmill was working.

As it was, for the next two years I dreamed about windpower. Keeping careful track of the wind conditions we found at various anchorages, it appeared that in the trades the windmill would be capable of taking care of 70 percent of our cooking and all of our refrigeration, as well as the normal DC needs of the vessel. Out of the trades, we figure cooking would be strictly with propane, while the wind would provide about half the refrigeration and all the DC.

28. Deck Knives

Deck knives are important both for safety and for convenience. Aboard *Intermezzo* we ended up with a knife at the mainmast and

Intermezzo's deck knife (one of two) was carried on a backstay.

one aft in the cockpit. In both cases they were handy to halyards and sheets should one or the other have to be cut in an emergency.

The cockpit knife doubled occasionally on fish duty (very occasionally), and both blades saw frequent use for whipping and maintenance chores.

It didn't take long to learn that the plastic diver's sheath was better than leather for a holder. We also found that by applying a bit of Vaseline now and then we could keep the blades free from rust and relatively clean.

In port, we normally removed the knives and stowed them below to remove temptation.

29. Medical Preparation

If you are going to make long ocean passages and cruise in out-of-the-way places you must be well prepared for medical emergencies. Fortunately, there are a number of good books on the subject that provide valuable guides to supplies, diagnosis, and treatment.

Foremost among these is the *International Medical Guide for Ships,* written and published by the World Health Organization in Geneva, Switzerland. It was compiled as an international guide for ships' captains and gives excellent material on symptoms and treatment. Less extensive but equally valuable is Peter Eastman's *First Aid Afloat.* His is perhaps the most popular of all the yachting medical guides. Peter's book has an excellent section on medical inventories, both equipment and medicines. It would also be a good idea to take along a home medical guide as another backup.

Serious medical problems are rare at sea. We know firsthand of only one major problem among all our cruising friends. (There must be something about salt air and a relaxed lifestyle that drives the evil spirits from our bodies.) But you have to worry about medical emergencies when preparing for offshore cruising, to say nothing of your shorebound friends who will constantly ask, "What do you do if . . . ?"

We were pleasantly surprised by the number of doctors out cruising. I think it is safe to say that in any moderate-size anchorage with more than half a dozen boats together, the odds are substantially in favor of finding a trained physician aboard at least one of them. (We have also frequently found doctors ashore in remote places.) People tend to make major crossings at one particular time of the year because of weather, so usually there are a number of boats going at the same time. On every one of our major ocean crossings, there has always been a doctor somewhere in the fleet within a week's steaming.

If you have a ham radio, you'll always be able to find a local cruiser who is a doctor, or get advice from one on the phone via a shorebound ham. In this case, of course, you must be prepared to supply your own medicine. Go over your list with a local doctor before you leave and ask him to write out all prescriptions to be filled. If you have a federally documented vessel, some pharmacies near major commercial harbors will fill your needs at a discount, without a prescription.

There are several areas of training that are worth looking into before leaving. A basic first aid course seems a must; if time permits, an advanced first aid course can be of real help. Next, you are going to have to know how to put in stitches and give shots. If this gives you pause, try what Ralph and Lenore Naranjo did before leaving. A doctor friend arranged for them to view emergency room procedures before doing a little practice work. (No, they didn't practice in the emergency room, just watched.) The sight of a little blood and gore in advance can prepare you for the worst should it occur, and help you remain cool and in control if messy work has to be done.

Don't neglect your dentalwork. Have a complete checkup by a dentist and bring all requirements up to date before leaving. If you plan to be gone more than six months or a year, find a local dentist to clean and check your teeth enroute.

Women can get gynecological checkups in most foreign ports.

Along with the normal medical kit, you will want to have aboard a large inventory of salt tablets, especially for the tropics. We were to find out how valuable these were in Rabaul, New Guinea. One evening we were having drinks at the Rabaul Yacht Club with Dr.

Emory Moore and his lovely wife DeeDee. Emory had been in the tropics during World War II and had quite a bit of experience with heat-related medical problems. When I complained of lack of energy and a head-achy feeling, he asked if we were using salt tablets. My quick recovery of vitality was amazing, just a few hours and four salt tablets later.

Vitamins are another consideration. On occasion you may be eating less than balanced meals and high-potency vitamins will fill in any gaps. While pharmacy items such as vitamins and salt tablets exist everywhere in the world, discount brands sold in the United States are generally much cheaper.

Just the opposite is the case with antibiotics and related medicines. We have found these available in just about every stop we have made, but at generally less than half the U.S. prices.

The subject of inoculation against the various diseases of the world is very difficult to get hard data on. Regulations and requirements will vary depending on whom you talk to and how old their data are. The best sources of information in the United States are the county health departments in major cities. They're used to handling inoculations for people traveling overseas, and most of their inoculations are free.

Out of the country, when you arrive at a port the medical people there will tell you "It's not necessary here, but up the line. . . ." Before we left New Caledonia for the New Hebrides Islands, for instance, we were told that due to the regulations of the next country, and for our own protection, we needed to update our cholera and typhoid shots. I decided to wait, since local scuttlebutt was divided about this "official view." In Vila, New Hebrides, nothing was required on our yellow health card, but we were advised that we needed the whole range of inoculations for the Solomon Islands and Papua, New Guinea. The doctor looked as though he could use the business, so we allowed ourselves to be punctured with a raft of inoculations, having our wallets lightened at the same time of Australian currency. In the Solomons we were told that the shots we had just received weren't necessary, but that they would be for New Guinea. In New Guinea they weren't necessary, but they would be for Australia, and so on.

Smallpox vaccinations are required in a number of the under-developed parts of the world by the *local* health authorities. It appears that the World Health Organization's declared victory over smallpox hasn't reached places such as New Zealand and Australia, so be sure you're up to date. Yellow fever shots are suggested for some areas of Africa and Central and South America, but not required in any of the Pacific or Indian Ocean areas we visited. Cholera, typhoid, and diphtheria shots were not required in any of the areas we cruised, although we were told in Melanesia, as a general rule, to stay with our own water supply and avoid eating directly in the native villages, just in case.

When eating locally procured fruits and vegetables, avoid picking up bacteria by first washing all fresh produce in a potassium permanganate or mild chlorine bleach solution.

Malaria in its various forms is something else. It is necessary to start taking antimalarial tablets at least two weeks before entering an area known to have malaria. Since you can have a malaria parasite in your body and have the tablets keep it at bay unbeknownst to you, it is advisable to continue taking the prophylaxis for a month after you have left the tropics.

Be careful of the type of tablets you take and the dosage as you travel from place to place. Some resistant strains of malaria have developed in parts of Papua, New Guinea, Indonesia, and South America. Check with a local pharmacist or chemist, because there are many types of malaria and as many types of antimalarial tablets. Even within a single country, such as New Guinea, you have to change the tablets as you move around. We learned this the hard way. Not realizing the tablets we were taking in Madang weren't strong enough for the east coast Papua region, I caught a case of rare cerebral malaria. As it turned out I became ill just after losing out in the next-to-last round of a rock-and-roll dance contest at the Port Moresby Yacht Club. Fortunately, a malaria specialist in the capital city of New Guinea gave us excellent assistance, and told us what we should have been taking.

Health care outside the U.S. is much less elaborate than what Americans are accustomed to, but for most normal illnesses you can count on good treatment at much-reduced rates. (I was in the Port Moresby Hospital for ten days, undergoing numerous tests before the form of malaria I had was isolated. The final cure was quinine—not very exotic, but it worked. The bill? A total of $220, including tests and specialist!) Also bear in mind that it is possible within a day or two at most to fly from virtually anywhere to a major country for special treatment should the need arise.

Among medical problems encountered while cruising, none is more common in the tropics than open sores that develop into staph infections, and these are difficult to heal. Here are a few ground rules: First, you must treat every nick and scratch as a *potential* major medical problem. This was vividly brought home to us by the experience of our friend Craig Porst in Taeiohai Bay, Nuka Hiva Island, in the Marquesas. Craig had scratched his foot aboard the Cal-46 on which he was crewing. He thought nothing of it and went diving. Three days later he was in the hospital with a huge infected crater on the top of his foot. For five days Craig had to stay in the hospital, receiving massive doses of antibiotics and having his wound cleaned and drained daily by the doctor.

After Craig's experience, we became more careful. Topical antibiotic creams and powders such as Neosporin did well for us. For any scratch, nick, or cut, no matter how small, we would clean the spot, apply the ointment, and stay out of the water until it had healed over. If going into the water was essential or if we coudln't avoid getting wet in the dinghy, we would rinse the sore place with fresh water, then clean and reanoint it with Neosporin. Once an open sore begins to look angry, soak it in a hot water and chlorine bleach solution. And in Polynesia a local custom for treating coral cuts and scratches is to apply lime juice directly to the wound. It is most important to keep salt water off any open sore as staph infection thrives in the sea. Take especially good care of your lower legs and feet, as it's virtually impossible to keep them dry.

Another problem frequently found among those first cruising is constipation. The abrupt change in diet and lack of fresh vegetables in some areas contribute to this problem. Mineral oil was recommended to us by the French doctors in Atuona in the Marquesas. They had seen the same problem aboard other yachts and among newly arrived French colonists. Increasing your freshwater intake also helps.

Linda had to see a doctor in Papeete, Tahiti, for a small growth on her eyeball. It turned out to be a common ailment among the cruising people, caused by not always wearing polarized sunglasses.

The hot, humid tropical weather breeds tropical skin fungus infections. A young Australian doctor in the New Hebrides told us that the skin fungus problem was the biggest ailment he saw among visiting Europeans. Carry along an antifungal cream. And for women and girls, a "thrush" infection will very likely develop in the vaginal area. A periodic douche with vinegar and water will keep it at bay; if it does develop, a doctor or chemist will prescribe suppositories.

Remember, also, that your body's liquid requirements are higher in hot climates, so drink lots of water daily.

The final medical problem which may occur in cruising is fish poisoning. Always check with the locals before eating your catch. Fish may be fine to eat in one area and be poisonous in the next bay. Large pelagic fish caught offshore are generally not poisonous, but once in a while one will have a high level of toxin. Most fish poisoning is cumulative. If after one or two meals of a given fish you notice a slight upset stomach, numb lips, and tingling limbs, don't eat any more of it.

30. Cruising Security

From the standpoint of personal security, cruising must be one of the least hazardous ways of spending one's time. Yet given the state of crime statistics flashed across our TV screens, people contemplating cruising often are concerned with potential hazards of this nature.

From time to time we are asked, "Don't you feel a little insecure lying on your anchor in some deserted cove?" Occasionally stories of missing yachts, or sea-going shoot-outs are magnified out of proportion to actual occurrences.

The bottom line to crime when cruising is that it's virtually nonexistent. With the exception of certain areas of the world such, as the east coast of Colombia, the southern Philippines, and some of the islands off the Arabian Peninsula, risks are few and far between.

As with other aspects of cruising preparedness, however, you should consider the security of your vessel and crew before setting off.

To begin with, you need to take stock of the risks, and establish an overall philosophy of dealing with them. Theft can be a problem in the States, but is rarely encountered elsewhere in the world. Among the 15 or so yachts that circumnavigated at the same time we did I'd be surprised if over $1000 worth of gear was lost from all the yachts combined. And most of that would have been in the "big" cities.

When cruising, you spend most of your time aboard; the yacht is left unattended for a relatively small percentage of the time. Usually during these periods there will be other yachts around to keep an eye on things. Many of our cruising friends lock their yachts only occasionally when away for short periods. Protecting a boat from forceable entry can be fairly difficult, and in some cases leads to more damage, if someone tries to break in, than if the vessel had been left with a relatively easy access. Usually a thief is looking for something that can easily be disposed of locally: tape cassettes, cameras, portable radios, and so on. Some cruisers advocate leaving a few easily noticed items right on the saloon table as incentive for a thief to make a quick trip on and off their boat.

Personal safety is a different matter.

Many of our Stateside friends living in cities are reluctant to take an evening stroll these days. Out in the islands, on the other hand, with the exception of certain U.S. "vacation islands," I can't think of a place we have ever been where we felt at all nervous in the evenings ashore. Violent crime of the type endemic to the U.S. just doesn't exist in the parts of the world frequented by the cruisers.

Still, there are some undeniably villainous types abroad in some cruising areas, particularly in parts of the Caribbean and the Bahamas, where the drug-smuggling trade flourishes, and every cruiser must ask himself the inevitable "what if" question. Suppose you are sailing peacefully along and another vessel accosts you. Or you're boarded in a secluded anchorage. Do you acquiesce or fight? One's response to this question goes right to the heart of the philosophy of self-reliance and cruising preparedness.

Nobody likes to be caught unawares, so the first aspect to consider is some form of alarm system. The most efficient alarm of all comes with four legs, sharp teeth, and a loud bark. A dog is the best all-around guardian there is, and many cruisers have one aboard. There are some negatives, of course, and if you're allergic to animal hair, as we are, your options are limited. Some governments try to discourage visiting dogs. Hawaii, New Zealand, and Australia are chief among them. But the bureaucratic problems can be and are dealt with by the canine cruising fraternity.

A simpler alarm system can be made with a piece of thread stretched across the decks and attached to a bell.

One single-handing buddy of ours used a variation of Joshua Slocum's tacks. He strung treble fishhooks on monofilament line around the perimeter of his vessel above the lifelines, trusting he would hear the results soon enough if someone climbed aboard uninvited.

More sophisticated electronic systems have difficulty coping with open hatches (necessary for ventilation in the tropics), blowing awnings, or the boat's motion at anchor.

Assuming you awake to find an intruder below, what do you do? One cruising couple we know had this happen in Jakarta, Indonesia. When they awoke, the thief had already passed a suitcase full of their gear down to a waiting canoe. A battle ensued involving nonlethal weapons, and the thief escaped, shouting "I come back and kill you!" Several nights later they were awakened by this same persistent thief. Another battle ensued and this time they were able to rescue the valuables he had gathered. When I asked these friends why they had not resorted to the more substantial forms of force which were at hand, their reply was sobering. If they had shot the intruder, his friends waiting in the canoe alongside would most likely have gone to the police. Endless hassles could have developed and they might still be in some Indonesian jail.

On the other hand, what if the intruder himself had been armed, perhaps with a knife or something more deadly?

Guns on cruising vessels are the subject of heated argument. At the heart of the debate is the question of if or when armed response is appropriate. If you decide you should cruise with an armory, then you must be aware of some basic rules.

1.   You must be proficient with your weapons in a variety of circumstances. They must be practiced with regularly, and kept clean and in good operating order.

If you are going to carry firearms and are prepared to use them, practice is a must. (S. A. Dashew)

2. Never show a weapon unless you intend to use it. Your opponent won't know you are only trying to scare him off. If his life is threatened, he will probably take action against yours if he can.

3. Have an understanding among the members of your crew as to what general course of action you will take in any situation that could result in the use of gunplay.

What type of gun should you carry? The most popular weapon in the cruising fleet is a shotgun. Usually a short-barreled "riot" gun is carried, loaded with heavy shot. If you have never practiced with this kind of weapon you are likely to be surprised how little "scatter" there is to the shot, even on a short barrel. It takes a reasonable amount of skill to hit a target even at 100 feet with this weapon. If you're really serious, a semiautomatic model should be employed that will automatically pump a round into the chamber each time you pull the trigger.

Next on the list comes the civilian version of the M-16. Sold as the AR-15 or Mini-14, these carbines are lightweight, short-barreled rifles. They shoot a smallish projectile at an extremely high velocity. As a result, it has a lot of stopping power for its mass. The high velocity makes correction for distance and cross wind less of a factor. These are sold as semiautomatic weapons with magazines holding up to 30 cartridges at a time, and at a moderate distance, in the hands of a skilled marksman, they can do substantial damage.

But there is the question of range. If you perceive an approaching vessel to be threatening, at what point do you want them to realize it will hurt to take you on? A military-style carbine has a relatively limited range. To fill this gap in the on-board arsenal, the experts recommend a larger bore, longer barreled rifle with a low-power scope. This sort of weapon, in the hands of someone with a moderate amount of experience, and in relatively calm conditions, is good at several hundred yards.

What you use on board is another question. A riot gun or rifle won't be much good in the confines of a cabin. A pistol is the answer, and those of our cruising friends who have only two weapons aboard usually make the pistol their second choice.

If there are children aboard, and you're concerned with their playing cops and robbers, then a semiautomatic weapon with a heavy action will be the safest form of pistol. The 9-mm Browning is a popular example. You need a sure, strong grip to crank a round into the chamber on such a weapon, something beyond the ability of most preteenagers.

Some experts feel that if you're not overly familiar with weapons, and if the children question doesn't apply, a good-quality long-barreled revolver is best. They generally have more "kick" than a semiautomatic, but don't have jamming problems. In either case you must be familiar with the feel and use of your weapon.

Gun maintenance in a salty environment is difficult. If you can afford it, consider a stainless-steel version of your weapon. It will cost about double, but be worth it in the long run. Your guns must be kept dry and well oiled to prevent rusting. They should be checked monthly to be sure that they and their environment agree with each other. This also applies to the magazines of the semiautomatics, and to a lesser extent your ammunition supplies. For best results, the latter should be kept in sealed containers.

What about the red tape of carrying firearms into foreign ports? This is perhaps the thorniest question of all. Attitudes vary substantially in different countries, but one aspect is consistent. Handguns are what foreign Customs officials are most concerned with. New Zealand is a good example: you can keep your rifles and shotguns aboard, but handguns must be stored at the local police station, to be retrieved upon your departure.

Some ports will require that all your weapons be stored at the local Customs or harbormaster's office. If you have a sealable or bonded stores locker, Customs will generally allow you to seal your weapons aboard, which saves the hassle of retrieving them when you clear.

One tempting thought is to not declare weapons. We think that this is a serious mistake, as it puts your vessel at risk. Most countries give their Customs officials the right to impound any vessel found bringing contraband into the country, and undeclared weapons certainly fit that category.

In the final analysis, your approach to sea-going security will probably parallel your attitudes ashore. When considering the various aspects of the subject, though, it's nice to know that the odds of ever being caught in a situation that requires violent action are extremely remote.

31. Sybaritic Sailing Systems

For my money nothing is as important at sea as taking a nice shower before turning in for the evening. In the tropics particularly, getting that sweat and salt off your body makes the sleeping much better. If it's cool out, a hot shower is one of the joys of life. And how about a bountifully stocked freezer with good cuts of meat for dinner, an inventory of cheap island lobster, fresh frozen fruit for dessert, and a reefer keeping salad fixings fresh and crispy? Would the cook like to use a microwave oven to defrost with, have hot salt water for doing the dishes, use a favorite electric frying pan for the evening meals? How about cooling the boat off in the evening when it's at that in-between state with the day's heat locked inside and the night air stuck on deck. Want to run your 12-volt fans all night and have decent lighting?

All this and more is available to you for a modest capital investment but little or no increase in operating cost. The secret is to utilize the capacity of your auxiliary diesel when it is charging batteries. If you are using one of the smaller, popular diesels in the 107-cubic-inch range, you have 12 to 15 h.p. going to waste while the engine is idling turning the alternator in your daily charging cycle. With the proper set-up, that little diesel and its two quarts of diesel fuel an hour have the ability to do everything I've mentioned, and much more.

Let's review the jobs we want to do and what they will cost in horsepower. First, that 50-amp alternator that comes standard is way too small for a really efficient operation. A good cruising boat needs something in the range of 150 amps, from either a couple of alternators or one large one. At 150 amps you will be pulling about 2½ h.p. Next comes the reefer/freezer compressor. A belt-driven automotive-type unit will be knocking down 2 h.p. at the beginning of the cooling cycle, if you are set up well. Automotive-type units are the most popular with long-range cruisers, and the most efficient. Allow another ½ h.p. for a saltwater pump on the reefer system. There are a number of lightweight AC generating units on the market that produce 3 to 5 kilowatts of power. Assuming 5000 watts (5 kw), and the fact that you are using all of it at once, you are using another 7 h.p. We probably have another 2 or 3 h.p. to play with, and in these days of conservation it's better not to waste them, so let's throw an air conditioner into the pot. Assuming the AC electrical system is busy, I would belt another mechanical compressor into the system for the air conditioner. Since we are using the same compressor and heat exchangers as in the freezer system, they can act as a spare parts inventory ready to go in case there is a problem with the freezer unit in a remote spot. That will take another couple of horsepower. The hot-water heater doesn't take anything but waste heat from the engine.

Efficiently set up, the above system will generate in one hour of engine time a day enough energy to provide the sybaritic lifestyle to which we all secretly aspire. It won't be necessary to run the engine any more than your neighbor does, nor does it mean making an electromechanical nightmare of your vessel.

Take a look at what that two quarts of diesel fuel is gong to give you each day. First, you have a usable inventory of 12-volt DC from the batteries in the range of 100 amp-hours. That means lots of 12-volt DC fans, the occasional use of a 12- to 110-volt inverter for a vacuum cleaner, blender, or small microwave, and lots of reading lights. Next is a good 15 cubic feet of freezer and fridge. The air conditioner can pull an easy 25,000 BTUs of heat out of the interior in the evening, and the hot-water shower will be ready to go. In the galley, you have up to 5000 watts of cooking power for an hour in the evening, or if you prefer, split up between morning and evening. (Note: We don't advocate relying on electric cooking. We prefer a propane stove with electric accessories: frying pans, microwave oven, etc.) If you're into diving, you have also been filling up your airtanks for the next day with a belted air compressor.

These systems, individually, are in use in thousands of yachts in one form or another. The big difference here is that instead of having a large, heavy, and expensive diesel generating plant, powering a bunch of cumbersome electric motors, we use the low-end capability of the main propulsion engine. Most of the accessories that usually are electrically driven are now belt driven from the engine. This means that a much smaller AC generator is required to handle cooking and/or maintenance chores.

There are two approaches to setting up this gear. The first is by mounting it directly on the engine. Assuming there is already an emergency bilge pump hooked up, there may be room for one compressor, a large alternator, and the big AC generator. But what happens if you lose the main engine? After becoming used to the good life, reversion to the bad old days would be intolerable.

There is a way to have your cake and eat it too. That is with the use of a lay shaft. This is simply a metal shaft, supported by bearings, alongside the engine. Power is transmitted to the lay shaft via V-belts, and the various accessories then get their power from the lay shaft.

This has the further advantage of allowing a small backup diesel plant to be placed in such a way as to take over the job of the main engine should it develop problems. My vote is for an inexpensive lightweight diesel in the 3- to 5-h.p. range. This is plenty with which to handle the essentials such as refrigeration and DC charging, with some AC capacity thrown in when the other accessories aren't at peak load.

When you're sitting in a marina and want to take advantage of shore power, belt a 5-h.p. electric motor to the lay shaft. It then drives the accessories as required.

If you want to stay simple, the changeover from one mode of operation to another is accomplished manually, by removing and replacing V-belts. But electric or manual clutches are readily available to do the job at the touch of a switch.

Once the decision is made to go ahead with this system in full or in part, consideration has to be given to a number of factors. The most important of these is what R.P.M. the engine will be running at when charging and when at cruising speed.

The average high-performance alternator generally reaches about 90 percent or more of its capacity at 4500 alternator R.P.M. They can be run, however, for indefinite periods at 10,000 to 12,000 R.P.M. This means that if you are charging at anchor and want to get maximum power out of the alternator when your engine is turning over at 1200 R.P.M., you are limited to about 2500 R.P.M. cruising. If the cruise R.P.M. is higher, you then have to work the pulley ratios so that they turn the alternator more slowly at anchor. Conversely, the engine must be run faster at anchor to have the same DC power output unless you settle for a longer charging cycle. With mechanical refrigeration compressors, on the other hand, the performance past a certain R.P.M. is more or less proportional to the speed at which they are turning. If you have a 2 to 1 pulley ratio set up for cruising R.P.M., you are going to have only half the compressor capacity in use at anchor because of the much lower engine R.P.M. when the engine is just charging. Or if you spend most of the time at anchor and are not concerned with powering performance, arrange the belts so the compressor works best at anchor and turn the compressors off when you're powering.

The AC generator is simpler. It has a fixed R.P.M. at which it must be run to generate the proper voltage and cycles. So you must decide whether you want it set for powering or sitting at anchor (unless you use a variable-speed unit).

What will become readily apparent is that low-R.P.M. engines are a lot easier to work with in this regard than the higher R.P.M. units. However, the higher R.P.M. engines offer lighter weight, and in some cases quieter running. This is a moot point if you're working with an existing installation. But if you're building now, or repowering, you are on the horns of a real dilemma. If the weight of the slower turning engine is not a concern, I would go for the slower engine.

Another aspect to consider is how much horsepower is available when the boat is under power. It is normal, at cruising speed, to have about a 30 percent reserve of horsepower. If the prop is large enough to absorb the extra horsepower, there won't be much difference in speed as the wind and sea start to kick up. When it's calm, that 30 percent unused horsepower is going to waste. If that's the case, you can put that excess horsepower to work. It will help cool the boat and the freezer, and help run your female crew members' hair driers. If the sea kicks up and you want to maintain speed, something has to be shut off.

For hot-water heating, you have an abundant supply of calories being dumped overboard via the engine's heat exchangers. There are numerous hot-water units on the market that tap into the freshwater side of the cooling system; in less than an hour they can generate 12 gallons of very hot water. We have found that adding a layer of extra insulation to the outside of the hot-water cylinder helps keep an evening's hot water steamy for the next day.

While we're on the subject, we saw a very clever set-up on a yacht in Mauritius: a return line from the hot-water pressure system to the water tank. Instead of wasting a quart or two of water waiting for the cool water in the lines to be displaced with hot, they simply opened a valve and dumped the water back into the main tank until it began to run hot.

We learned another trick for the saltwater side. Depending on the size of the water tanks and the availability of fresh water, more often than not you may be washing with salt water in the galley and even occasionally in the shower. If you tie your water pickup into the saltwater line on the engine, just before it dumps into the exhaust system, you will have available, as long as the engine is running, water that has been heated for free. With this system we have found galley water in the tropics to be so hot that it has to be left standing before it is comfortable to use. If the saltwater flow through the engine is too great, it won't be heated enough for this purpose. The simplest way to correct this is to restrict the incoming water, *up-stream* of the raw water pump. The restricted flow will have more heat to carry away and consequently will be proportionately hotter. *(Remember to open that gate valve again before running the engine up to cruising R.P.M.)*

Obviously, some thought and attention has to go into the detail of what to use in your system and how to install it. Our main point is that you should not be misled by the tradition of spartan cruising. If you can afford it, there is no reason not to have a comfortable lifestyle with some of the shorebound luxuries.

3
Seamanship

There simply is no substitute for experience when it comes to seamanship and handling a yacht under the variety of conditions you can expect to meet in cruising. Reading the accounts of others will help, and dockside chats with the more experienced can't hurt. But none of this is a replacement for actual hours spent sailing, anchoring, reefing, or working into an unfamiliar harbor.

On the other hand, more than two-thirds of the people we have met in far-off anchorages had little or no experience before they set out.

With the hours required for preparing the yacht, putting personal business in order, and holding down a job, most people find little time for actually sailing, aside from a short shakedown. Yet there is a crash course in sailing skills available to most sailors almost every weekend: racing.

Racing is the fastest, most concentrated way to learn what a boat will take and how to make her move in varying conditions. A summer's racing can teach you more about moving a boat quickly through the water than a circumnavigation.

But for the one most important thing you need for successful cruising, however—*respect* for the sea and its mate the weather, and how their changeable moods can affect you in various situations— there is no substitute for learning the hard way.

What follows are mainly suggestions as to what you need to learn.
Where we have learned practices and procedures that can generally
be applied across the board, we pass them on. If we dwell on safety
and preventive measures it's because we have been taught that the
best way to stay out of trouble is to stay alert to the negative possibilities in any given situation.

And when you're lying on the hook in the Virgin Islands after a
beautiful sail down from the States, or maybe rafted in Durban,
South Africa, having survived the Aghulas Current, or are tied up
at home after a boisterous day's sail, there is a sense of accomplish-
ment that makes all the hard hours of learning worthwhile.

32. Going to Sea

Depending on the type of passage you plan, there are various levels
of surveillance you should perform before putting to sea. Going for
a three-hour hop through the reefs of Fiji will require different
standards of readiness than preparing for a departure across the
Atlantic.

If the engine isn't a necessary ingredient to safe arrival, and your
trip is a short one, a cursory glance at gear will do. When your sailing
follows this pattern on a repetitive basis, a total review of all machinery and systems should be made once a month.

Voyages that require the engine to operate flawlessly, such as a trip
under power through a pass or across a breaking bar, need more
detailed preparation.

The first thing to check is the engine V-belts. Look for worn spots
on the inside as well as outside edges. Black fuzz around the pulleys
of the engine or its accessories is a telltale sign that wear is taking
place on one of the belts. Identify the culprit and be sure to correct
the situation. Have a quick look at the motor mounts and the engine
oil (don't forget the injector pump), and check the coolant level. Are
the throttle and shift linkages working freely? Is the saltwater flow

out the exhaust up to standard? If the water flow appears a bit thin, take a quick look at the rubber impeller on the pump to be sure all the blades are still attached.

Next, review the steering gear. Check the steering cables for meathooks, paying special attention to the end of the swages where the cable attaches to the quadrant. If eye bolts are used for adjustment of cable tension, check the threads from time to time for cracks. Are the cables tight enough so that if the rudder is hard over and further force is applied to the wheel, the loose wire won't jump the sheaves?

Check out any gear that may be necessary later in the trip. If you have hydraulic steering, look at the cylinders and helm pump for signs of leaking fluid. Depth sounders, autopilot, radar, and long-range navigation aids should all be given a run in.

The next level of readiness comes with an offshore passage in moderate climates. Check all turnbuckles for safety wires, being sure to glance at threads for cracks. Look over swage terminals for cracks, being especially careful to observe the wire where it exits the swage for broken or cracked strands. Have a look at halyards right at their nicropress sleeves, and 18 inches after for meathooks. A quick trip aloft is in order to check spreader bases, seizing of spreaders to shrouds, tangs, and swage terminals. Are the halyard sheaves free running?

Before starting out on any ocean-sailing passage we dog all hatches and fit storm covers, just in case. Once things have settled down, we open up a bit, but only after we have had a chance to gauge the sea.

When preparing for an offshore passage that includes the probability of severe weather, and this takes into account just about the entire nontropical world, we go a step further. Double lashings are prepared for the dinghy and liferaft, although they're not employed until actually necessary. (Extra lashing means more time should we need to launch either one in an emergency.) We then have a look at any gear in the ends of the boat or above the center of gravity to see what can be concentrated.

Most cruising boats accumulate piles of gear—outboards, spare anchors, dive tanks, etc.—usually stored in areas which hurt your sailing capability. Under normal conditions the extra work of moving this gear to gain speed and comfort for a short passage is not worth it. But if you're looking at the potential of bad weather or a longer passage, it can make a real difference.

Preparing *Intermezzo* for her first trip across the Tasman Sea, we took stock of what we could get off the deck and stow below: four 72-cubic-inch dive tanks, 60 lbs. of lead weights, a 70-lb. gas generator, a 45-lb. outboard motor, 70 lbs. of miscellaneous dock lines, hoses, and junk. That's about 400 lbs. physically lowered an average of 6 feet, or 2400 foot-pounds, which represented a significant chunk of our righting moments. In addition we sold off 60 lbs. of gasoline stored on deck and dumped overboard 70 lbs. of fresh water that we had carried next to the liferaft in trade-wind conditions. These materials had accumulated gradually, and as a result we hadn't noticed the change in performance. But when we close-reached out of our last Fijian pass toward New Zealand, *Intermezzo* felt like a new boat. Had we encountered really severe weather (which we didn't) the extra stiffness could have made a substantial difference in her performance.

If you expect heavy weather on a long passage, check the watertight integrity on deck. Disconnect your anchor rodes, and firmly lock and caulk the access caps. Remove the chain from the main anchor and drive a plug into the chain hole. Ventilator cowls that are not absolutely necessary should be removed and capped. Make sure the inside caps are handy at the remaining Dorade points. If storm windows are aboard, are they easy to get at? Take a look at the cockpit locker gaskets.

Before going to sea we always give the lifelines a good going over. We check all the tension on the lines and the end fittings, swages, turnbuckles, and stanchion attachment points. They are all prone to failure at embarrassing moments. And of course the stanchions themselves must be solid.

If any major masses of metal have been moved toward or away from the compass, be sure to take a couple of bearings as you depart to check for deviation changes.

Once we are free of land, the vigil is continued. On watch, in spite of bilge alarms and an automatic bilge pump (on separate circuits), the bilge is checked every four hours. At least once a watch a glance is given to sails and running gear. Each morning we take a turn around the deck inspecting turnbuckles, swage fittings, goosenecks, and running rigging.

Only once in our entire trip was my vigilance actively rewarded. Between gales off the coast of Africa I found a shroud starting to strand. At the time I didn't realize we were in for the worst weather of our circumnavigation, but I replaced the offending shroud anyway. Twelve hours later we were battling 60-knot winds and the replacement shroud was working hard. You can bet that one payoff made worthwhile all my checking of the previous three years.

33. Weather

The "science" of weather forecasting is one of man's oldest prognostic endeavors. From the days of "red sky at night, sailor's delight" things have improved somewhat. The advent of yacht-size weather facsimile recorders and weather satellites has given a sizable edge to the cruising yachtsman in his confrontation with the elements.

The basics of weather forecasting, using the sky, barometer, common sense, and a little technical background, can be mastered by any sailor. Racing skippers learn the value of on-board forecasting or find themselves at the tail end of the fleet. No less important aboard a cruiser, but for different reasons, on-board forecasting is the subject of numerous well-illustrated books.

But one learns in this field by doing, and a good place to start is with the daily weather chart in the newspaper. For years I practiced daily forecasting in Southern California based on data gathered at home, and then compared the results with what Mother Nature contrived. It was essential to success on the race course, as you soon learn if you are on the wrong side of wind shifts out there. The cruising sailor is more concerned with large-scale weather patterns than which side of the course a lift is coming from, but this information, too, can be gleaned by anyone willing to track it down.

There are numerous sources of weather data available all over the world today. Broadcast-band and VHF weather are available for local conditions. Most high-seas marine radio services offer area-wide forecasting services, as do national authorities on special fre-

Drying out aboard *Intermezzo* in Noumea, New Caledonia, after a hard Tasman Sea crossing.

quencies, such as the U.S. Coast Guard. The important thing here is to be aware of the frequency and time.

A tape recorder is essential for SSB reception, for frequently you will want to play the data over again to make out hard-to-hear passages. As we mentioned before, digital-readout radios save a lot of time hunting for a very narrow and perhaps weak signal. Be sure your set has a BFO (beat frequency oscillator) for tuning in SSB broadcasts. Both the U.S. government and British Admiralty publish lists of worldwide weather broadcasts, which are sometimes accurate. However, before heading to a new region it is better to find out firsthand what the up-to-the-minute frequency and time schedules are.

As mundane as it may seem, television weather forecasts can sometimes be the best source of data, if not the forecast itself, that brief glimpse of a synoptic chart they show. In some areas of the world the harbor officials will have on display daily weather charts. This is especially true of commercial harbors.

We have found that the best system for getting local advice is to talk with airport meteorologists. If you explain your course, desired patterns, and boat speed, they will frequently assist you with the best time for departure.

Many of the larger yachts we have met cruising carry weather facsimile recorders aboard. These are now small and relatively inexpensive, considering the service they can give. In addition to straight synoptic charts they can also provide satellite cloud patterns and wave height and direction data.

Of the various weather situations that face cruisers, the trickiest is the equinoctial journey from temperate high-latitude cruising grounds to the tropics. This usually involves leaving a sheltered area and heading across a stretch of ocean at the mercy of frontal passages until the more stable winds of the trade-wind region are reached. Our second passage across the Tasman Sea is an example.

Opua, the northernmost clearing port in New Zealand, was bustling with activities as the cruising fleet made ready to go their separate directions. We happily greeted many old friends first met in Tahiti or Fiji. Some were heading northwest with us for New Caledonia; others were going back to Fiji or heading directly for Australia and a quick passage west via the Indian Ocean.

The main topic of conversation was weather. The locals told tales of fierce winter gales, and after a prolonged, beautiful summer, we were expecting the worst of the infamous Tasman Sea. For the preceding three weeks a succession of lows had been moving from the Bass Straits south of Australia and across the Tasman, bringing winds of up to 70 knots and large confused seas. It definitely was not our idea of cruising weather. On our sail down from Fiji the previous season we had been fortunate to have light airs, missing severe gales a week either side of our passage, and we assumed the Tasman would get even with us this time.

We had completed our preparations for going to sea and said our good-byes, so it was time to make our break with shore and see what the Tasman had in store for us. As we pulled up to the wharf at Opua to clear Customs and tied alongside Jim and Cheryl Schmidt's 70-footer, *Wind'Son,* a few wisps of altocumulus and cirrus clouds presaged a change in the weather. Our dock lines secured, Jim showed me his latest weather fax chart. A large high was slowly approaching from eastern Australia. As word spread among the half dozen yachts lined up for clearance, a perceptible change in countenance was apparent.

We pulled away from the wharf heading out of the bay on a close reach in a gentle southeaster. *Wind'Son* was just behind us. We had decided to pick a quiet anchorage on the outer edge of the bay for a last good night's sleep; we chose Whangaroa, 60 miles up the coast. It was on the way, reputedly a beautiful anchorage, and had excellent steamer clams along the beaches. More important, tomorrow would be Friday, and as everybody knows, it isn't prudent to start a passage on a Friday.

An exhilarating reach up the coast with an offshore wind soon had us at the gorge-like entrance to Whangaroa Harbour. As we motor-sailed through we had our pick of three lovely fjord-style bays. Following *Wind'Son* into the placid waters of the northwest bay was easy.

The rattle of the anchor chain died away and the diesel was secured. A quiet serenity settled over our private haven. Fair weather and warm days, not to mention buckets of clams, delayed our departure three days. While Jim and I anxiously reviewed the daily synoptic charts, Elyse and Sarah listened to their voices echo off the adjacent cliffs and explored a nearby stream. Our friendly high was almost stationary. Relief at having pleasant prospects instead of a certain hammering dulled our sense of weather tactics, for highs can deal out wind as well, and they don't stay put long in the Tasman.

On May 7, four days after clearing, we headed north. The weather looked fine as a gentle southeaster greeted us. The basic strategy in leaving New Zealand is to get at least 400 miles north of North Cape as quickly as possible; this puts most of the severe depressions behind you. So we motor sailed along at 7 knots, hoping for an increase in breeze.

A few hours later the southeaster started to fill in. We set our bicentennial red, white, and blue spinnaker, spinnaker staysail, and mizzen staysail, and doused the iron genoa. *Intermezzo* flew along at just under 8 knots in the baby whitecaps. Her 2800 feet of light-weather sail soon overtook *Wind'Son* as she, feeling the breeze herself, had started sailing. Our thoughts were on a record crossing to Noumea, hot french bread, and palm trees. We should have known better. Later that evening, as the breeze began to lighten, Jim and Cheryl powered by us and soon were out of sight over the horizon. Whoever said we were racing anyway.

The next morning greeted us with a wind shift to the east and an increase in the breeze. It was soon blowing in the high teens and we were sagging off to leeward a bit from the rhumb line, but still looking for as much northing as possible. As we surfed down the waves, Martin, our new Aries windvane, did a remarkable job of keeping *Intermezzo*'s 18 tons on course. Hanging onto the spinnaker till the last moment, we had already doused the two large staysails when the wind started to increase in velocity. Down came the spinnaker and none too soon, as the wind continued to back and freshen. Soon we were beating into a stiff northeaster blowing a steady 30 to 35 knots and gusting higher. Our stay in Whangaroa was going to cost us. As we dallied, the high had started its movement east and we were now feeling the counterclockwise circulation off its backside.

We were snugged down to our large staysail and reefed main, and with the wind in the 40s and 50s, we spent the next three days below in the quiet, dry confines of our cozy cabin, checking the horizon every 15 to 20 minutes for shipping. Linda and I read, played word games, caught up on sleep, of which our four-hour watches allowed plenty. Sarah and Elyse pursued their new stock of coloring books and gleefully slid down *Intermezzo*'s varnished cabin sole on their pillows. School was temporarily in recess due to inclement weather. In spite of the building seas, Martin performed flawlessly.

On our fifth day out the breeze started to moderate back to the high 20s. It seemed like drifting. Another 24 hours found us in the lee of the New Caledonias' barrier reef. Hove-to for the night awaiting daylight to fix our position, we contemplated the passage up. *Intermezzo* had averaged 165 miles per day and taken a pounding. She had solid water on deck at least once a watch, and while we had found a couple of small leaks, she was ready for more. Her crew, however, was definitely not ready for more, and putting our purist theories behind us, we fired up the diesel and motored the remaining few miles in the light morning airs to Noumea's main pass.

We were greeted first by the sight of the beautiful old ketch *Armanel* at anchor. Mike Moorhardt and crew had cleared the same day we had and sailed directly up. They had the front-side circulation of the high and had broad-reached the whole trip! Jim and Cheryl, by powering out ahead of us for 20 hours of light airs, had gotten away from the worst of the winds and had a freer sail. Our tactics in this case definitely left something to be desired. We had broken a cardinal rule of prudent cruising: never waste a spell of good weather, whatever the temptations, if you have a difficult passage ahead of you. (On the other hand, we'll never forget those three blissful days in Whangaroa.)

As with other aspects of cruising, one must learn to become self-reliant in weather forecasting, trusting your own data and instincts ahead of the "professionals." And you must be able to judge the quality of the forecast data you receive.

The South African weather bureau provides data to a huge area of shipping and their clients are mainly commercial vessels. When they say strong winds, you can assume they mean that the lulls are strong and that they are thinking about supertankers not yachts. Coming back to the States on our last passage, we picked up the Florida weather forecasts warning of small-craft signals and winds gusting to 25 knots. What a difference. By South African standards that meant day-sailing weather.

In some areas of the world it is hard to develop weather data as there are few ships or land-based stations to pass on information. In South Africa, the easterly moving depressions may come unannounced from the southern ocean. Tasmania has the same problem. On the other hand New Zealand has the benefit of all that data coming to it from upwind Australia.

Where there are substantial changes in water temperature you must carefully watch local conditions. The weatherman with a good handle on continental winds may be unable to anticipate what happens to a weak front when it hits a body of warm water such as the Gulf Stream. That is one of the reasons Cape Hatteras has such a bad reputation for unannounced gales.

Boat speed is all-important in judging your weather chances. The faster you go and the better your range at speed under power, the less likely you are to get caught. Another factor is your direction relative to the course for weather systems. If you are going the same way, they will be overtaking slowly. If you are heading into them, as on the trip from Mauritius to Durban in the Indian Ocean, you are certain of encountering several frontal passages during a trip.

Once you've made the autumn passage to the tropics, avoiding, you hope, the full wrath of winter storms and the chance of a late hurricane, the rules of the game change considerably.

Trade-wind sailing is usually dominated by the circulation around large, relatively stationary high-pressure systems. These tend to keep out any frontal weather and your local wind will usually vary with the development and position of the high.

Trade-wind tactics are dictated by the comfort of your boat and her ability to stretch her legs. Larger boats will want more wind than is usually found in the trades and will look to the outer edges of a high if possible, with tighter isobar spacing for breeze. If you have a smaller boat, sailing closer to the high's center will reduce wind velocity, but expose you to the danger of getting stuck toward the windless center.

One of the surprising things we found in our sailing is how light most trade winds are. I would guess we averaged not more than 10 knots of wind.

The longer the passage, the more difficult it is to predict the best time to leave. Most cruisers approaching long hauls try for the right season, based on the pilot charts (which must be used with a grain of salt), and play the cards as they are dealt.

With the exception of the South Atlantic, all major oceans offer annual revolving storm seasons. Usually the late summer months are the worst, and even if you don't plan on cruising where these storms are frequent, you should know how they behave, about the navigable semicircle and the dangerous quadrants of the storms.

Because of today's forecasting methods, especially satellite photography, many of our cruising friends feel safe sailing during the summer in hurricane belts. They keep an eye on the weather and stay close to a good hurricane hole. We prefer to go to the higher latitudes where the chances of storms are remote.

Whatever your choice, remember that any unusual movement in the barometer is cause for concern, especially pumping (quick changes up and down in pressure) or a drop of more than 2 or 3 millibars below the diurnal norm for the area.

The U.S. government has several excellent publications dealing with revolving storms available at most chandleries.

One cannot consider cruising weather without a discussion of trade-wind squalls. They are generally more prevalent at night but without severe increases in wind velocity, usually under 30 knots. If you are cruising with radar, they will show up clearly at distances of up to 20 or more miles. Radar returns showing up as small targets, perhaps a few miles across, will rarely have more than 20 knots of wind in them. Those that present a frontal-like appearance, sometimes shaped like an open horseshoe, will have a lot more punch, up to a maximum of 50 to 60 knots. If you are without radar, it is frequently possible to gauge the size of a squall by starlight, or if you are lucky, by moonlight.

Our experience has been that squalls in the doldrums can be more severe than their higher latitude counterparts. With a well-found 50-foot yacht, only once crossing the doldrum belt in the Atlantic did we shorten down before the wind forced us to. This was based on a radio discussion with friends ahead of us who had been nailed by 50 plus knots of wind and a very disturbed sky at sunset. We sat there all night under storm staysail and double-reefed main and nothing happened.

The doldrums can frequently be crossed in a day or two, even by small yachts using their engines. If that sort of range isn't available, you must work hard to make every favorable breath of air move you along the way. The pilot charts can give some indication of the best longitude to cross the various doldrum belts (they usually run east-west), but since conditions vary so much from year to year the pilots are as often wrong as right. Still, none of our friends has ever taken more than a week to cross the worst stretches of doldrums, and even they didn't have to eat their horses.

34. Working on Deck

Required reading for anyone going offshore should be Hank Searle's novel *Overboard.* * The portrayal of the heroine's falling overboard under pleasant conditions when on watch alone at night is worth the price of the book. The author's choice of pleasant conditions for his accident, rather than during some tempest, shows his familiarity with the sea and its ways. Most accidents of this nature happen not in severe weather, but when the boat gives an unexpected lurch on an otherwise calm sail.

*New York: W. W. Norton & Co., 1977.

The answer is to be conservative, and always wear a harness when working out of the cockpit, night and day. If the harness is easy to use, and if a jack line is rigged, you will be so used to working with a harness on after a few days that you won't even notice it.

We *never* go on deck at night, even to read the log, without first hooking up. Elyse and Sarah are not allowed even into the cockpit without their harnesses. Since the tether lines attached to the pad eye at the companionway should be long enough to allow one to run from the saloon to the end of the cockpit, this isn't an inconvenience.

Our general rule is that whoever is on watch wears a harness so that if a quick trip on deck is required, he'll be ready to go.

Even with a harness on, it's better to stay aboard. To accomplish this, there are several basic rules to follow. Always keep one hand for yourself. Don't rely on lifelines. Never step on anything that will move under you. When walking on deck, keep your center of gravity low. It won't take long to learn how a vessel moves, and it will become second nature to anticipate her plunges and gyrations in heavy going. If it's necessary to extend full height, keep one hand on a shroud or other fixed piece of gear. Never rely on a boom for support when leaning outboard. If something were to give and the boom went free, guess where you'd end up. If it's necessary to work extended over the rail using both hands, hooking your knees under the linelines will help maintain balance. And above all, *don't get careless.*

35. Watchkeeping

The question of keeping watch in a seamanlike manner is often avoided by many cruisers. Shorthanded on long passages with self-steering, many feel that the odds of collision at sea are just too long to justify having someone on deck 24 hours a day. The sleep-through-the-night proponents feel that, well rested, they are better able to deal with any adverse situations that might arise.

On the other side are those who feel that leaving the deck of a small boat unattended is like flying blind in the Grand Canyon, that it is irresponsible to other vessels and to those aboard your own.

I suspect that the best course lies somewhere in between. Considering a voyage offshore outside of shipping lanes, the odds of even sighting a ship are pretty long. And the odds of meeting on the same patch of ocean at the same time are even longer. There may well be other cruising vessels out there too, but the chances are they'll be going in the same direction as you. Pride and paint are most likely what's at stake should you collide with a fellow cruiser. So as a general rule I think a constant deck watch at all times in all parts of all oceans is an unnecessary extreme of caution. On the other hand, near shipping lanes or land, a rigorous watch system is a must.

When we first started cruising offshore, Linda and I stood our watches four hours on and four hours off. Perhaps it was my years of sailing in crewed vessels, but I couldn't get used to the concept of leaving *Intermezzo* to her own devices, even in mid-Pacific. Sleep would have been impossible for me anyway: I worry too much.

Four hours on and four off, all night long, sounds like a grind. But in fact it became a pleasant routine. During the evening watch in mid-ocean we would check the horizon every 15 to 20 minutes; the rest of the time we sat at our comfortable navigation station and read. We had rigged lights that would give us concentrated illumination when we were braced on either tack. We had the boat, the stars, and our thoughts completely to ourselves. That sort of quiet pleasure I had forgotten existed.

It usually took me three days to adjust my sleep patterns to the demands of this on-again, off-again routine. Some of my sleeping was done during daylight hours, and I found that using an eyeshade helped. Linda was able to sack out anytime, and from the beginning of each sea passage her sleep routine adjusted nicely.

If we became tired during a watch, we would catnap, using a kitchen timer to wake us at the desired intervals.

I found that the evening watches were a good time to catch up on navigation. Even far offshore, if we had a clear sky or perhaps a moon I would work several sets of sights during the evening.

We kept the log on an hourly basis. In it we indicated our course for the hour, wind direction and apparent velocity, distance covered, the barometer reading, and any electronic LOPs.

Once each watch we would update our DR or fixed position on our working chart, and indicate the latitude and longitude of this position in the ship's log.

If we were carrying extra sail, if the winds were shifty, or if we were watching for navigational waypoints, I would leave written instructions in the log for Linda.

By the time we had reached Cocos Keeling in the Indian Ocean, after almost three years of cruising, we had relaxed a bit. From Cocos to Mauritius, and from Cape Town toward the West Indies, except when near land or in the shipping lanes, we did away with a formal watch system. Instead, Linda and I both bunked down. In practice we found that every 45 minutes one of us would be up to take a look around and see how *Intermezzo* was doing and if there were any lights on the horizon. We were so refreshed when we arrived at Rodriguez Island near Mauritius after our 11-day run across the Indian Ocean that it was then I began revising my ideas about the best routine for safe ocean crossings. (We also subsequently found, when we were keeping regular watches, that three hours on and three off worked better than four and four.)

Voyaging close to land is another subject entirely. A clear delineation must be made between casual or nonwatch when standing offshore, and the routine necessary anytime you're near land or underwater obstructions.

The definition of "near" is equally important. We always allowed for a 50-mile margin of error, in our worst possible position, when approaching dangerous territory. This may sound overly cautious, but consider some of the possibilities: perhaps the last sight or sights were off; current may have been assisting you in an unknown manner; maybe a couple of days earlier a mistake was made when transposing a position from one chart to another. Any one of these could put you onto a dangerous coast well in advance of your ETA. As a result of this, we always stand formal watches when within 75 miles of land.

It goes without saying that if you're not on deck, you can't see what's coming at you. And while we're not overly strict about making a cup of coffee now and then, or getting a snack, we have learned from several near-disastrous experiences that when anywhere near reefs, low islands, or hard-to-see coasts, *someone must be on deck and alert, at all times.*

To protect night vision in these circumstances, we make it a habit to replace all bulbs aboard with ones painted with high-temperature red paint.

It is necessary that all aboard fully understand how to read running and range lights of sea-going vessels. Having been confused a time or two myself I know how easy it is to get mixed up, and I always insist on being called when lights are within a few miles. Tugs with tow, commercial fishing vessels, and drilling rigs all may have special lights; you have to know how to read the various positions and colors and what they mean. The worst problem is with ocean liners. They are so lit up it's often difficult to tell the range lights from the rest. Add to this their high speed and propensity to give their passengers a look at anything unusual at sea, and they can be scary.

36. Offshore Visibility

We were four hours out of Nissan Island in Papua, New Guinea, heading for the bottom of New Ireland. The trades had disappeared, and the sea was like glass as we slipped along at six knots with our little diesel purring below. Since our radar hadn't seen much action in the previous month of day-sailing, we had it running to keep things loosened up. The moon had set, but a beautiful net of stars hung overhead. It wasn't too long before we were crossing the favored track of ships heading to and from Kieta on Bougainville Island. On this evening I was surprised by the amount of shipping: six moderate-size vessels and one super-size bulk cargo carrier. What was even more surprising was that only one out of the six showed up with radar interference on our set. The other five were not running their radars. Had there been a moderate sea running, and had we used the running lights legally required on a vessel over 13 meters, we would have been virtually invisible to this shipping.

The problem of small-vessel visibility becomes even more acute at

Look at the bow of the baby supertanker (just 100,000 tons) in the background of the Royal Cape Town Yacht Club docks. Offshore, you certainly want to see him first.

sea, out of the shipping lanes. As the sea increases and mist starts to hang, things worsen. Out of the shipping lanes there is still a surprising amount of large-vessel traffic. The watch on the bridge, if they are looking at all, are intent on other big ships. A small speck of a hull or sail may well not catch the eye of the deck officer or watch.

Needless to say, under these conditions it behooves the offshore cruiser to keep a sharp lookout. Nobody will be doing it for you. Yet most offshore vessels today are crewed by two-person teams, and even the most zealous take a break now and then, fall asleep during watch, or decide to snooze through the evening. On the other hand, conditions can deteriorate on deck to the point where you can't keep a good watch even if you're fully alert.

How then do we improve our chances of being seen? It's easier at night. A new generation of high-powered masthead tricolor lights has recently come onto the market. I first saw a unit made by Marine Spec. on the mast of a Vancouver 27 in Fiji. Its brilliance was amazing. Ignorant of the IMCO regulations which ban tricolor running lights for vessels over 13 meters (about 42½ feet), I decided to get one at the first opportunity. Several months later in Auckland, New Zealand, we picked one up at a marine chandlery and installed it at *Intermezzo*'s masthead.

On our way north toward New Caledonia, we conducted an experiment with some friends sailing in company. With Jim checking his radar for range and then viewing the green sector of our light, we were clearly visible at 5½ miles! We were more pleasantly surprised by our masthead light when rounding Cape Aghulus at the tip of Africa. We were in the grip of a severe southeasterly gale, with spume flying everywhere. We had spotted a supertanker on radar about 10 miles downwind of us. At 8 miles we called him up on VHF and gave him our coordinates. At 7 miles' range, a few minutes later, he called us back to say that he had our masthead light in view.

What if eyeball contact won't work due to weather or sea conditions? How visible is a small yacht on radar? I've talked to officers aboard large ships in ports all over the world and the answer is disconcerting. If a good sea is running and there is some water in the air, a small yacht, even with a radar reflector, is going to show up as an occasional dot among the other dots of what is referred to as "sea return" on the ship's radar.

A fixed radar reflector of large size at the masthead will help substantially, but the return it gives is so small in relation to what is seen on a radar screen that you cannot be positive you will be identified.

Numerous times in foul weather off the coast of Africa we called ships to advise them of our position; the answer would usually be "Ah, yes, we see your target, now!" (translation: "Now that we're looking for you in the spot you told us to look, we can pick out your return from the other radar echoes").

The moral of this story is: Don't count on being seen on radar.

The biggest problem, it seems to us, is during the daytime. Everyone at sea relaxes then, aboard yachts as well as big ships. But this is the time, in many cases, when small vessels are the least visible.

Radar reflector and *fluorescent* masthead light in Durban, South Africa. With the amount of shipping traffic on Africa's east coast, most yachts did their best to be seen.

If a good breeze is blowing and there are white caps, a ship will have to be quite close to you before the lookout can distinguish your sails and spars from the waves. And that's too close for comfort.

What can you do? Well, several yachts we know have tan sails. These are not only easier on the eyes at sea, but are definitely more visible. Another approach, not quite so traditional but nonetheless functional, is to have a colored stripe across the top of the main and working headsail, or even to make the whole top section colored. It may look strange, but it's effective.

Finally, though, there is no substitute for eternal vigilance. This basic rule of the sea was underlined for us at the end of our last voyage, when we were sailing through the northeast channel of the Bahamas toward Florida. It was our last leg after 3½ years of foreign waters. I was on watch and keeping a careful eye out for both the confines of the channel and the tremendous amount of shipping around.

It was Linda's turn to be in the sack, but she was restless and as keyed-up about our Florida landfall as I was. Checking the horizon carefully, I slipped below for a cup of coffee and a hug. The coffee had not had time to cool down to a drinkable state when I felt, or perhaps heard, a strange sensation: a steady vibrating throb. It took just a second for it to register that I was hearing the screw or engines of a very large ship vibrating through the water. A rush topside shocked me with the sight of a 20,000-ton cargo ship sliding by our port side, not more than 50 feet away. Had he seen us? Not if he passed that close. How had I missed his lights? I don't know. But from then on, in shipping channels, we resolved never to leave the deck unattended.

37. Performance under Sail

Speed to a cruising yacht is an essential ingredient of safety and seamanship. Too often new cruisers are misled into associating performance with unseamanlike practices and the racing fraternity. Talking to cruisers with thousands of miles under their keels, in anchorages all over the world, we have realized time and again that the performance reported doesn't come up to the potential of the yacht they are sailing.

More yachts are lost due to being set off course by current than any other factor. The length of time current has to act on your boat, obviously, is related directly to the time you spend in it. A fast boat is going to be less affected, and that may be the difference between clearing that reef and being set on it. Generally a quick passage means reduced wear and tear on the boat, less exposure to bad weather, and a happy first mate. In many cruising areas, speed is extremely important when considered in relation to weather systems. Leaving New Zealand, for example, the trick is to wait for a big high-pressure system over the Australian end of the Tasman Sea,

The 70' ketch *Wakaroa* reaching at 11 knots with her cruising spinnaker.

then go like blazes the 400 miles north necessary to get past the track of the worst depressions before the next one comes along. You can normally count on three days of good weather. The fourth day you may be slugging into 60 knots of cold wind. The same holds true for rounding the South African coast from Durban to Cape Town: wait for good weather and then run like the devil. Speed is essential.

When you are cruising in areas with difficult landfalls you're going to want to make the anchorage before dark. In coral, you need to be there even before dark so that the sun is still at a proper angle for bottom viewing. An extra knot many times makes the difference between a quiet, safe night and one spent hove-to off an unlit, dangerous coast.

Most boats are more comfortable with an adequate press of sail. This is especially true off the wind.

Last, when you make your next harbor and somebody asks where you've come from and how long the passage took, there is pleasure in being able to report a fast time.

The myth of the 100-mile day dies hard. For many years the "happy hundred" was a magic number for cruising vessels, regardless of size. With modern gear, sails, and hulls, any well-designed, properly sailed 35-foot cruising yacht with the right gear should be able to do 30 percent better than that.

As a rule of thumb, a speed of 1.05 to 1.1 times the square root of your waterline length should be easy to hit. For most of the boats we met cruising, this adds up to 130 to 140 miles per day. Yet only about 5 percent of them were getting this kind of performance. How do they do it?

First, you have to learn what the boat will take, how fast she should be going, and how hard she can be driven. In effect, you have to raise your anxiety threshold, the point at which your concern for the vessel outweighs other factors. Once again, the best possible way to do this is to go racing. When somebody in a similar vessel is pounding along beside you and your genoa is improperly trimmed, you'll know it soon enough. If you don't have the gear, or don't want to take your home through all that work, go racing with someone else. There's simply no better way to learn how to make a boat go.

A majority of people cruising offshore today have beautifully equipped boats. They are, on the average, much stronger and more seaworthy than those that have gone before. Aluminum spars, Dacron sails, roller furling, and self-steering have made cruising easier, safer—and they should also make it faster.

The key to fast passaging is keeping the boat moving. That may seem self-evident advice, but few offshore cruisers follow it. In the name of conservatism and seamanship, smaller and heavier sails are carried, the sail area is reduced at night, and anything remotely resembling a squall is cause for anxiety.

Our first *Intermezzo* liked light airs as long as she had enough sail up. In the temperate climates we carried a light genoa on the head-stay, with roller furling, and a #3 jib on the forestay. This allowed us to carry maximum sail until we were forced to reduce. Then we rolled up the big jib and went with the smaller and heavier #3. Off the wind in a good breeze, the #1 was carried to weather on the spinnaker pole with the #3 sheeted to leeward. It helped keep flow attached on the main and was easy to douse if necessary.

In lighter airs, downwind, we frequently carried our drifter to leeward. Since it had its own wire luff, it didn't interfere with the genoa on the headstay. The extra sail area, which is projected higher and farther away from the mainsail, added substantially to boat speed.

38. Spinnakers

It wasn't until our 13th day out from Mexico toward the Marquesas Islands that we rediscovered our spinnaker. The doldrums were very much in evidence, and the steady southeast trades that Mr. Maury's pilot charts forecast showed little promise of making an appearance. We were hot and uncomfortable as *Intermezzo* rolled her way slowly downhill.

Bored with reading, I decided to drag out our spinnaker, just for the afternoon. A short time later, having rigged the necessary paraphernalia, I was amazed to find us clipping along at 6 to 7 knots,

Intermezzo reaching in the southern Atlantic trades with a jockey pole helping to hold the spinnaker pole off the headstay.

steadied down, with a refreshing bit of air finding its way into the cockpit and down below—the fact that it was apparent wind made it no less cooling. Five days later, in the lee of Nuka Hiva, we pulled down the chute.

During our subsequent journeys across the Pacific, Indian, and Atlantic Oceans—a total of 118 days at sea on long passages—we had the spinnaker flying on 33 days.

Intermezzo was designed and rigged for the light-air Southern Californian racing scene. She carried a tall rig on a minimum-wetted-surface hull, with longish overhangs. Most "experts" would agree she's not a good candidate for cruising with a spinnaker. Yet Linda and I have found the spinnaker an essential part of our cruising sail wardrobe.

It is no secret among our cruising buddies that I don't enjoy going slowly, but the major reason we carry the chute in light airs is comfort. The additional speed it lends to the boat steadies her motion down tremendously. The apparent wind angle usually moves forward and increases the airflow over the boat. Anyone who has slowly run downhill in the moisture-laden air of the tropics will understand the value of this bonus.

Most surprising, though, is that we have found the spinnaker to be less work than twin jibs. Our sailing at the beginning of our Pacific crossing with twin jibs was reasonably fast, but rolly, and the sails required a lot of tending. In 30,000 recent miles at sea we have yet to find those steady trades that allow you to go for weeks without touching a sheet. We were always taking the leeward jib off the pole as the wind went forward and then putting it back on as the wind went aft. The windward jib sometimes had to be doused altogether as the wind went forward. With the spinnaker there is only one pole to deal with, and the sail can be carried much closer to the wind than the weather jib of a twin rig.

And what of those black squalls bearing down out of the night to tear the heart out of our stout vessel? I have always assumed the worst that can happen under normal circumstances in the trades is a moderate knockdown. A well-found boat won't find this taxing at all, and if your lockers are properly latched it won't even create a mess. Has it happened to us? Once. The last night out before making our landfall on the Marquesas, one squall, stronger than the rest, caught us unawares. At the time we were carrying our big mizzen staysail as well as the chute. With 30 knots of wind on the beam it wasn't long before the spinnaker was in the water. Once the mizzen staysail sheet was let go, however, and the autopilot turned off, we were able to head back downwind; 15 minutes later, as the squall passed, we were back on our way, shaken a bit but no worse for the experience.

There are some areas of the world and conditions where prudent seamanship dictates against carrying a spinnaker. Crossing the southwestern end of the Indian Ocean, for example, if you have anything above deck lighter than bulletproof, one of the severe south-westerly gales that quickly come out of clear air will be sure to take it from you, and possibly everything the sail is attached to as well. But in the trades, spinnakers are the thing.

Handling a cruising spinnaker is an entirely different story from when you're racing. Aside from the lack of hands and perhaps confusion associated therewith, you have lots of time. It's not a matter of jibe sets and takedowns at mark roundings. Your spinnaker can be designed to be stable and easy to fly. *Intermezzo*'s spinnaker was nothing special by the standards of her racing days. It was a plain 1½-oz. nylon crosscut, of maximum size for her rating. But being a crosscut and having a much narrower head angle than today's spinnakers, it was stable and easy to fly. The full shape meant it wouldn't carry well on a reach, but it was a dream in light stuff downhill, and that's where we wanted it to behave. Except for entering or leaving ports, *Intermezzo* was never hand-steered. Our Bendix autopilot or Airies vane did the work. And the spinnaker, too, tended to itself, sometimes for days at a time.

We don't bother with stopping the spinnaker but usually launch it from a turtle. Downwind, the turtle is attached to the pulpit forward of the headstay. Reaching, we attach it to the rail under the jib. We preset the pole in its desired position before hoisting and trim the sheet about halfway. We also carry a spinnaker net anytime we're running, or if the winds are light or shifty. I hoist and Linda then trims the sheet. On perhaps half a dozen occasions my hasty packing of the turtle has resulted in an hourglass in the spinnaker, but except for one time in the South Atlantic, these have always freed themselves without our having to drop the sail. As a safety precaution we never knot the ends of the halyard sheets or guys. The guy is run through the pole so that the clew of the spinnaker is free to run in

Intermezzo with her #3 jib to leeward and light #1 jib to windward as she runs toward the coast of Brazil from the South Atlantic. The main (not shown) is also up.

the event of a knockdown. If someone goes overboard, it's easy to get the sail off the boat.

We don't try to trim the sail right to the edge of its pulling power. Rather, we normally carry the pole about 25 percent farther forward than conditions warrant; if we're broad-reaching or running, we trim the sheet a little too much and lead the sheet farther forward than normal. This allows us to swing through a range of apparent wind angles and strengths without having to make adjustments; and since the boat is self-steering, she needs this latitude. We don't often carry the spinnaker when reaching unless the winds are very light and somebody is keeping an eye on things. In these cases, the sheet lead is farther aft than normal and the sheet is eased more.

The surprising thing about carrying this sail is the lack of maintenance required on the gear. After half a dozen snap-shackle openings at the masthead we have taken to using bowlines on the halyards. I normally retie these every three days, but they don't seem to have much chafe. Oversize halyard blocks and a halyard a size or two larger than normal will help in this regard. The spinnaker afterguy, where it passes through the pole, has to be watched as well. Most pole fittings are alright if kept free of scratches or burrs, but we find more chafe here than at the masthead. *Intermezzo*'s spinnaker was carried for over 5000 miles without sign of wear or any maintenance except for replacing the bronze shackle between the swivel and halyard.

Now you might say I have left the hard part for the end. That is, getting this beautiful powerhouse back into its bag. Surprisingly, two-thirds of the time we have dropped the spinnaker has been for lack of wind where the breeze just wouldn't fill it, or where rain showers had made it too heavy to fly in the light airs that prevailed. In these cases, if Linda was busy or asleep, I handled the chore myself. The procedure is the same as in a breeze, but with fewer hands. The first thing we do is run off dead downwind. The main is eased against the shrouds. The spinnaker sheet is trimmed till the clew is right at the block. Then the guy is eased until the other clew is six or eight feet to leeward of the headstay. Unless the sea is very calm, I usually move the pole foreguy aft to prevent the pole from banging into the headstay. The sail will then collapse in the vacuum behind the mainsail.

I release the halyard with one hand and pull the sail down with the other. A halyard stopper, foot activated, would have been an ideal addition to *Intermezzo*'s sail-handling gear. When it's blowing over 10 or 12 knots, Linda eases the halyard and I use both hands to gather the sail.

Only once have we really been caught in too much wind. We were running down the coast of New Zealand toward Auckland in a beautiful northwester. The wind was offshore, the sea was calm, and *Intermezzo* was flying. I was enjoying the sail so much that I failed to notice the gradually building wind as soon as I should have. When the sea began to kick up off the Whangarei River we started oscillating. A particularly sharp roll pitched Elyse from her reading perch, and Linda inquired politely if I might consider reducing sail. By now it was blowing a steady 30 and gusting to 40—but even so our takedown system worked quite well.

The final decision on how long to carry a spinnaker will depend on the size of the sail relative to the boat's stability, and the boat's ability to self-steer. Most modern cruising boats, with moderate rigs and spade or skeg-hung rudders and short ends, will find the spinnaker even more useful than an older design like *Intermezzo*.

39. Speed

There is nothing more annoying than an undercanvased sailboat in a seaway. When running, you will want to carry more sail to steady down. Even when broad-reaching, higher speeds can usually be attained without an undue amount of motion. On the other hand, under certain sea conditions you may be more comfortable going slow. One of the interesting things about ocean sailing is that the sea is always showing you new combinations of wind and wave. Constant adaptation is necessary to maintain fast, comfortable passages. For a given set of sea-conditions, most boats will have a threshold above which even a slight increase in boat speed will be accompanied by a substantial decrease in comfort.

Intermezzo II reaching at hull speed in light airs. (Les Abberly)

Aboard *Intermezzo* this threshold was at 185 miles per day. Regardless of what was happening it seemed, reaching to running she could go to this level (about 7.75 knots average) and still be comfortable. But if her speed was stretched to 190 or 195 per day, it became difficult to move about and sleep.

As the sea conditions become rougher, or when beam- or close-reaching, a further reduction in speed is necessary to maintain comfort at a reasonable level. With a constant sea condition, however, when the breeze starts to die away you will have to add sail and boat speed to maintain a reasonably steady ride.

Dinghy and catamaran sailors learn early in their racing careers an old adage: up in the lulls and down in the puffs. As the wind dies down, to maintain boat speed you head up, bringing the apparent wind forward in the process. When the breeze picks up again, you head off to gain stability and ground to leeward so you'll be able to head up in the next lull.

These same tactics apply to many offshore passages. Take our trip across the middle Indian Ocean from Cocos Keeling atoll to Rodriguez Island 2100 miles to the west. Two days out of Cocos, the mid-Indian Ocean trades hit us with a vengeance, as predicted by the pilot charts. The 35- to 40-knot southeasterly, occasionally shifting to south or east, combined in the early part of the passage with a southern ocean swell to make it wet and uncomfortable aboard. Early on we adopted the tactic of keeping the wind as far aft as possible when it was blowing hard to make ourselves more comfortable. By running off an extra 15 degrees we brought the apparent wind from 115 to 130 degrees, allowing the southern swells to hit us on the quarter rather than the beam. There was a marked improvement in our comfort. Through daily radio schedules we learned from boats a week or more ahead of us that the southerly swell had died out farther west and that the trades had dropped into the low teens. By heading off initially we would be able to head up later on and keep the apparent wind forward where we wanted it in the light stuff.

As the passage progressed, we found that with the breeze constantly shifting in direction and velocity we were sailing a zigzag course either side of the rhumb line, but eventually tending just a bit north. Some 300 miles from Rodriguez, when the wind went into the east and lightened, we came up 20 degrees to the south and were able to keep moving while some of our friends who were on the rhumb line (or great circle) were running dead before the wind.

Our erratic course had cost us less than six miles per day in extra distance sailed, which we more than made up in those last few light-air days.

Tacking downwind is another racing tactic well adapted to cruising vessels. On long ocean passages, unless the wind is blowing hard enough to move you at a speed/length ratio of 1.20 to 1.25, you will probably benefit on a pure boat-speed basis from tacking downwind. As you approach hull speed, you lose the benefit of more speed from this maneuver, but the comfort benefits may still be substantial. Coming up even 20 degrees from a run, which will cost you less than 8 percent in distance, will allow the leeward headsail and the mainsail to draw well. That's an increase in usable sail area of at least 35 percent. In addition, with the wind more to one side, the tendency to oscillate will be dampened.

The trades are constantly shifting, and not infrequently these shifts will take place on a regular basis between daylight and evening hours. On our passage from Cape Town to the West Indies in the southern Atlantic, we noticed this diurnal shift once we got into the tropics. Since our course followed the edge of the South Atlantic high, we had the winds almost continually right up our stern. We found that by jibing to starboard in the evenings and back to port each morning we were able to stay out of phase with the shifts. This allowed us to carry the true wind at 150 degrees (apparent at 135) while only deviating from our actual course by 15 degrees. It made for a little extra work, but our schedule in mid-Atlantic wasn't that busy.

Closer along shore, tacking downwind will pose more work and navigational problems that mitigate against its effectiveness. On smaller boats whose ability to windward deteriorates in heavy going, coastal cruising has to be looked at from an entirely different standpoint. Sea room and the margin of safety become the major concerns, lest the nearby coast become a dangerous lee shore. This is especially true voyaging east of the Bahama Islands or rounding Cape Hatteras. If a severe northeaster should strike, plenty of sea room may be necessary.

Offshore, going to windward poses different problems. Speed becomes secondary to comfort. Just as with downwind sailing, each boat will find a groove where she has the best combination of boat speed and motion. There are some vessels that in certain wave shapes must be driven hard to maintain boat speed. Backing off results in going up and down and sideways—uncomfortable without attendant progress. Others can be made to sail upwind comfortably at reduced speeds. *Intermezzo*'s hull design and weight distribution made her really good in heavy going. With a longer sea running, even if the waves were breaking, she had a very moderate motion. But in the short chop generated by a 20-knot wind, she had to be pushed hard or she would sit in one spot and hobby horse. So in the normal upwind conditions we gritted our teeth and got the passage over as quickly as possible.

Sail shape has a tremendous impact on comfort as well as speed. If sails are too baggy, the boat heels over instead of going forward. If they are too flat they have no drive in the lighter air, and in a chop you bob around and go nowhere. With modern fabrics, outhauls, luff tension adjustment, and varying sheet leads and angles, a great deal can be done with a working suit of sails. Experiment with the craft controls in different conditions, watching the steam gauge as well as noting motion. You'll be surprised what a difference sail shape changes that are hardly discernable to the eye will make in the boat's performance.

Don't get lazy about your headsail sheet leads. Move them around as conditions change. When the wind goes aft and the headsail sheet is eased, the lead block on the toe rail will have to be moved forward to keep the sail properly trimmed. This should be done so the sail luffs evenly, top to bottom, when it needs trimming. If the upper part of the sail is flapping around and the bottom is pulling, the lead has to go farther forward. As the wind increases, you may want to move the lead aft to allow the top of the sail a small luff, opening up the slot between the mainsail and jib in the process. This eases drive aloft and heeling moment, and can extend the range of a headsail when you would otherwise be overpowered and ready for a change down.

The importance of a good boom vang cannot be overemphasized. Reaching and running, except in light airs, the leech of the main

Here the mainsail is vanged to the rail while running free. Note the midships weather cloths used to protect the main saloon hatch from occasional spray.

should be held as straight as possible. Drive is improved this way and heeling thrust is limited. At the same time chafe is reduced on the leeward side of the sail.

When running under sea conditions that cause the vessel to oscillate, motion can sometimes be effectively dampened by overtrimming the mainsail. If you are using twin jibs and start to oscillate, try setting the main reefed down to the upper spreaders and trimmed to a close-reaching position. This will act as an air brake on the side-to-side motion.

We have talked about squalls, and made the point that they are the prime reason people substantially reduce sail at night. But remember that in most of the world's cruising grounds a good squall means no more than a 50 percent increase in wind force. If your sails and rigging are in good condition, the vessel will cope. *Intermezzo*'s ¾-oz. drifter, light as it is, is still strong enough to hold the boat flat in the water, so we have never been unduly worried about blowing out sails in the occasional squall that does have wind.

With roller furling on the headsails (see Chapter 70), you have the luxury of waiting to see how things develop. The old adage of reducing sail in time, valid in the days of lesser boats and gear, doesn't necessarily apply in our age. So we recommend that you don't slow yourself down by reducing sail for long stretches unless it really is necessary.

Below the waterline lurks another source of reduced performance. In light airs, the difference in speed between a clean bottom and an even slightly dirty one is fantastic. We find that if our bottom paint is nearing the end of its life, and if cold water, sharks, or crocodiles have kept us from properly cleaning the bottom, the resulting film of scum can cost us 15 miles a day in Force 3 conditions. Another factor is comfort. A hull with a clean bottom moves more smoothly at speed through the water, will steer better, and will be much easier on her crew and gear.

Intermezzo sailed with a Martec folding prop, which we figured was good for an extra 6 to 8 miles a day over the fixed three-bladed prop in moderate conditions, and 15 miles in the light stuff. When we left the Marquesas Islands, we switched props, thinking we would need the backup and stopping power of the three-bladed monster in the Tuamotu atolls. It felt as though we were dragging an anchor in the light southeast trades, and in Papeete we put the Martec back on and left it there.

Intermezzo's main reefed down and tied off awaiting a heavy southwest gale off the east coast of Africa.

40. Storm Tactics

The definition of heavy weather at sea varies greatly. As your confidence and experience increase, the gales become fewer. As the size of your vessel grows, the furies seem to abate. Many is the time we have swapped sea stories after a long passage and heard of severe weather within miles of us of which we were unaware. Perception and sea kindliness are key ingredients.

With so many combinations of wind, wave, and vessel, not to mention crews, it is impossible to create a universal heavy-weather syllabus. What we can do is make you aware of our thoughts, based on our reading and our own experience.

Unless you decide to circumnavigate in the roaring 40s, the odds are that perhaps once in a lifetime of sailing you might experience a truly severe storm. But afterward, how do you know how bad it really was?

Linda and I always find that after the fact things weren't as bad as they seemed at the moment. I have seen perhaps a dozen blows in the 60-knot range, twice of long enough duration to generate good-size seas. In these conditions at sea, we have been fortunate in having singular wave systems to deal with; and while we have been in confused swells and waves in moderate gales, we have never had to deal with them on a monumental basis.

A modern, well-found cruising yacht, properly secured for heavy weather, at worst can expect a rollover, and perhaps dismasting. Providing you are well secured below, that's certainly no more dangerous than a moderate fender-bender on your local highway. Yet storms at sea are what get the press. In every port we have ever visited, the question is invariably asked "Have you been in any bad storms?" A vision of monster waves far from land seems to haunt the subconscious of our shorebound friends.

Far offshore, out of the coastal currents, with long fetches for mature seas to develop, the risks are few. Closer in, especially in confined areas, you will have to be more careful in your seamanship and decisions.

Wind per se should give you little cause for concern. Rarely is a stoutly rigged vessel going to be damaged by a squall or strong winds in protected waters. Most high-latitude storm systems are fast moving, and exposure, at worst, will generally be less than 18 hours.

It is the wave systems that are our concern, and in bad circumstances even a 40-knot wind can generate seas large enough to create problems. To begin with, wave height depends on the duration of the wind that is driving them, and the fetch they have to travel. The farther a wave goes, the taller and longer it will be. Even so, a mature sea in open water gives us little to fear. As waves are opposed by an ocean current or a tidal flow, their period shortens and their faces steepen to create the square waves or overfalls that occur in the Gulf

Stream, many areas along the European coast, or off South Africa. The rising sea bottom will also affect sea conditions. Shallow water, while limiting wave height, causes waves to steepen and break.

Changing bottom conditions, underwater canyons, mountaintops, and plateaus, even though hundreds of fathoms deep, can also affect surface waves. The most infamous of these areas is off the southern tip of Madagascar, in the Indian Ocean. More than 100 miles offshore there are undersea mountains and plateaus, relatively small in extent, and separated by large distances from the Mascarene Shelf itself, that create tumultuous seas on the surface. Yet some of these obstructions are 200 fathoms below the surface. The fact that they come up abruptly from much greater depths disturbs current flow enough to upset the balance topside. The cautious offshore sailor studies bathrhythmic charts and plots a course to avoid such undersea irregularities.

When sailing closer to shore in substantial currents like the Gulf Stream or Aghulas, you must keep a close eye on the weather, with alternative ports of refuge charted along the route, just in case. Even a moderate gale that encounters a swiftly flowing ocean current is nothing to trifle with. Beyond these precautions for offshore passaging, it behooves the cautious skipper to make quick progress through the potentially bad areas. If this entails the use of the engine, so be it.

As we mentioned before (in another context), there is an axiom about crossing the Tasman Sea, from New Zealand north, that has its corollary in many other parts of the world. Go like hell to get out of the depression tracks. Most cruisers follow this advice, using whatever means necessary to get them above the latitude of Lord Howe Island as quickly as possible.

Modern boats are infinitely more seaworthy than their earlier counterparts. Higher ballast ratios, more reserve buoyancy and freeboard, and better hull shapes all contribute. The Whitbread Round the World race is a great example of how far modern gear and designs have progressed. Racing for thousands of miles in the roaring 40s and 50s these boats drive at speed continuously, seeking to stay with the easterly flowing depressions that move them swiftly on their way. Even with their hard sailing, severe knockdowns are rare.

Given sea room, a moderate-displacement boat with good control will do well to maintain speed in heavy going off the wind. Our experience going from Bora Bora in the Society group to Suveroff Atoll in the northern Cook Islands is a case in point.

We left Bora Bora on a rainy morning. Unusual thunderstorms dotted the sky as we worked our way out of the pass and into the open ocean. With the sun gaining altitude, the minor frontal condition appeared to pass. We were left with light airs and a calm sea. With the spinnaker and mizzen staysail set and a moderately rising barometer, we were in excellent spirits.

During the day the breeze gradually increased until the spinnaker became a bit dicey. We dropped it in favor of the light #1 jib top, sheeted to leeward. Early in the evening, with the apparent wind in the low 20s and *Intermezzo* logging a steady 8 knots, I turned in. Two hours later Linda roused me to help furl the big jib. The breeze had increased and we were dipping the cockpit combings now and then in the slop to leeward. With an overcast sky and a still high barometer, I wasn't particularly worried; after all, we were still in the trades. But rather than get wet at night changing headsails (something I abhor) we opted for rolling up the jib and going with the storm staysail which always lived hanked onto the forestay. This necessitated taking a single reef in the main to balance our helm; and since we were doing so well, I decided to toss in the second reef so we would be comfortable for the evening. Cutting our sail area by 60 percent accounted for a drop in speed of from 8½ to 7¼ knots— not much of a penalty.

During the rest of the night and into the next day the wind continued to strengthen, still from the southeast, until we had a steady 50 knots apparent at the masthead. The gusts were into the 60s. On our Zenith transoceanic radio I was able to pick up a weather broadcast from Honolulu, indicating that a trough of high pressure was feeding us the breeze.

Shortened down as she was, *Intermezzo* continued to steer herself with the Benmar autopilot. In this early storm stage, with the waves not yet above 15 feet but rather steep, we were continuously surfing. For the next two days the wind continued to blow southeast in the 50s, occasionally reaching higher for an hour or two at a time. Throughout it all, under double-reefed main and storm staysail, *Intermezzo* continued to look after herself. Every now and then we would hear a whoosh as a wave larger than usual sent us on our way down its face, and the person on watch would see the inside speedometer needle sit against the 12-knot mark. With the wind at 140 to 150 degrees apparent and the seas almost the same, we were comfortably riding across the wave faces in the classically prescribed manner.

As *Intermezzo* headed down the seas, there was never the slightest indication she might broach out of control or dig her bow into the sea in front. The large spade rudder controlled her beautifully, and the ample freeboard forward provided the lift necessary to keep her head up in the troughs.

Only during momentary lulls, when the breeze dropped into the low 40s, did we become worried and consider hand-steering. In these periods, with boat speed under 7 knots, *Intermezzo* would oscillate on the waves, and if slapped by a cross sea, give evidence of wanting to broach. Since the lulls were short lived I didn't want to put up more sail, and we carried on without a problem. We eventually made Suveroff Atoll, having averaged over 200 miles a day during the heavy-weather period.

What I learned from this experience has been demonstrated on other modern, well-designed boats: keep them at speed, so plenty of way is available for good steering control.

We were fortunate in that blow in that the wind stayed from the same direction, there were no opposing currents or undersea mountaintops to deal with, and the swell was for the most part consistent with the wind waves.

It would be unusual to find a blow of this duration in higher latitudes, in those areas where frontal lows predominate. Depending on the weather system, and your position relative to it, very abrupt changes in wind direction can occur. When this happens, sea conditions can become chaotic. The best description I have found of dealing with this situation is in Bernard Moitessier's *The Long Way.* *
In it he describes the tactics he developed to keep *Joshua* at speed, taking the most dangerous of the seas from behind as the waves fought each other after frontal passages. Under such severe high-latitude storms as Moitessier describes, and in more moderate blows, the key factor is always to match boat speed to sea conditions, being careful to keep up enough speed for good control.

If you are not knocked down and rolled over, how do you know if you have been in a "survival" storm? We may have encountered our ultimate blow off the coast of South Africa. This storm was made

*Garden City, N.Y.: Doubleday, 1975.

all the more interesting by the fact that we shared the experience with three other vessels, of widely differing designs and sizes, each of which adopted a different tactics to deal with the conditions.

The blow came on like most southwesterly gales in that part of the world. We had been charging along at midday under the #2 jib, staysail, and mizzen (our main had blown a seam in the previous gale), when the breeze started to swing from north to northwest and then west. I considered going down from the #2 to the #3 jib, but since our previous three southwest gales in this part of the ocean had been short lived, I left things as they were. About 1735 hours the breeze began to lighten, with the barometer stabilizing in the low 29.7-inch range. I knew it wouldn't be long before we were into the southwesterly portion of the front. Within 20 minutes a lightning display off our port bow heralded the frontal assault, and shortly thereafter we were getting 50 knots from the predicted direction.

Immediately we shortened down to staysail and mizzen, and although the motion was a bit strange, with a north to northwest sea and a southwest breeze, we were riding well at 40 degrees apparent.

The next morning I talked with Chip Vincent on his 40-foot ferrocement Ingrid ketch *Eos,* on our daily radio schedule. He was 50 miles north of us and had experienced the same frontal passage several hours later than we. Our conditions seemed to be similar: wind steady at about 35 knots, gusting higher, with seas rather steep, being stacked up by the opposing Aghulas Current. Chip was sailing to weather, under reefed mizzen and storm jib, and indicated he didn't think he could continue much longer. He didn't want to run off, as that would take him away from Durban, but if the seas got any larger he felt it would be the only safe thing to do.

On the air at the same time were our friends the Schmidts, aboard the 70-foot Sparkman and Stephens ketch *Wind'Son.* With a 60-foot waterline and 16-foot beam, even though she was short rigged, *Wind'Son* was an able sailor, especially in a blow. Jim's comment: "What gale?" He was just behind Chip, about 20 miles to the east. Our next radio schedule was set for 1700 local time. In the ensuing period the wind freshened and steadied at 50 knots. With the barometer back in the 30.2-inch range and holding, we figured we might be in for a spell of bad weather. It appeared that rather than moving by quickly, as the weather systems normally do, the high that was feeding this southwesterly to us had become stationary. By 1700 the

Linda making bread as *Intermezzo* beats to weather.

seas were extremely steep, averaging perhaps 15 to 20 feet, with the top 3 feet breaking.

Intermezzo continued under mizzen and storm staysail, with the apparent wind at 35 to 40 degrees. The Aires windvane was working hard trying to keep us at the designated wind angle, as *Intermezzo* was buffeted by the breaking seas. About once an hour a breaking crest, bigger than the others, would rumble aboard, sweeping right over the doghouse and into the cockpit. I considered running off, but we seemed to be holding up well into the seas, and although our 2 or 3 knots wasn't much to brag about, at least it was in the right direction. *Intermezzo*'s buoyant hull, semiflush deck arrangement, and efficient rig made this tactic feasible.

We talked with Chip first at 1700. He was running off, under storm jib alone, having a difficult time steering. He had been knocked down twice by large cresting seas that had caught him inattentive to *Eos* 's needs. In both cases the masthead was laid flat in the water, and the second knockdown took his VHF antenna as a prize. But each time, with only a single wave to deal with, *Eos,* with her high center of gravity and mediocre ballast/displacement ratio, was able to recover.

Wind'Son had split her main, and taking advantage of her dependable GM 6-71 diesel, was powering at 6 knots for Durban. Jim reported having watched from their doghouse as an extra-large wave boarded the back of a primary sea and broke across his bow at a height above the furled genoa clew. That made it at least a 30-foot breaking sea.

Unknown to us, at the same time and 50 miles to the west, 747 captain and man-about-town Frikki LaRue was lying a-hull in the 40-foot *Senta,* a modern design, with a good ballast/displacement ratio. Frikki had been through this before. *Senta,* with her fin keel, sloop rig, and spade rudder, was lying with the seas hitting her on the quarter. They had been drifting in this manner since the advent of the storm, not wishing to lose ground to leeward but unable to continue into the steep seas. About the time of our radio schedule, Frikki and his crew were discussing whether the seas had increased to the point where they should run off, hoisting sail to help control. There was a roar and a crash as a large wave knocked them on their beam ends. Seconds later, before *Senta* could right herself, they were rolled over by a second wave. Frikki reported, "It was like being in a cement mixer." In the process the top hatch slide, unlocked at the time, dropped out, allowing copious amounts of water below. Later, the crew agreed that it felt as if *Senta* had tripped on her deck edge. The mast, which had been stepped on deck, was now trailing alongside. It eventually broke free, so they ran *Senta* off to present her stern to the seas. No further problem was encountered and they made Durban under jury rig and engine.

By the following morning a few altocumulus clouds were creeping into the sky and the breeze was back down in the 40s. While the seas were still quite something, *Intermezzo* proceeded on her way. During the previous 24 hours all hands had been restricted to their bunks with leeboards in place, as a precaution against a severe knockdown. The galley had been closed for the only time in our voyage. But with conditions improving into the afternoon, a hot lunch was served as the wind dropped into the 30s, cat's paws by South African standards. We set our #2 jib and got moving in earnest.

About this time Linda spoke via VHF to one of the many supertankers enroute to the Persian Gulf.

"Are you out for a pleasure sail this afternoon?" he pleasantly asked.

"No," was the reply, "we're ten days out of Mauritius and expect to make Durban tonight. Originally we left from Los Angeles 3 years ago."

Silence, and then "Oh my God!" followed with "Do you ever have any bad weather?"

Chip let things die down before pointing his nose once again to windward, while *Wind'Son* continued moving her 130,000 lbs. under power in the direction of a welcome harbor.

Discussing our experiences later on that week, after enjoying some of the hospitality for which Durban and the Point Yacht Club are so famous, we reached several conclusions. First, everyone agreed that lying a-hull in anything like the conditions encountered was dangerous. Second, it was vital to keep enough sail on so that good steering control could be maintained. For my part, I wondered whether I had adopted the proper tactics. True, we had survived unscathed, and had even made good an average of 3 knots upwind during the storm. But was our approach the most cautious one given the circumstances and *Intermezzo*'s weatherliness, or had we missed that wave with our name on it?

And what of other storm tactics? Caught in a severe depression in the Eastern Atlantic, Chuck Tobias was forced to slow down his extreme heavy-displacement ketch *Mar* by towing warps. Chuck had installed a large reel on the after end of his cabin top, attached to which was 600 feet of two-inch rope. In the 60- to 80-knot winds and accompanying seas, *Mar* was uncontrollable. They were forced to stream warps to help keep her stern to the seas. The combination of heavy displacement and attached barndoor-style rudder wasn't up to the conditions. Even when towing warps in older boats it's important to vary speed to the conditions encountered.

Lying to a storm anchor is not much in vogue these days, unless there is a lack of sea room. No modern yacht we have met cruising actually carried this gear. Given the incredible force of breaking seas, it is difficult to see how any rig would be able to hold up the head of a high-freeboard yacht. Failure in this regard would leave the vessel at the mercy of beam seas.

One last thought: Too often under the stress of heavy weather and its accompanying exhaustion we let events take control of the judgmental process. Rather than acting in advance of need, perhaps changing our approach to the storm before a severe knockdown or rollover forces us to consider alternatives, we lay below listening to the elements topside.

If you find yourself in this situation, observe the wave pattern and your vessel's behavior. If on occasion it appears that you have just missed being caught by a big one and that more or less speed is required, force yourself to take action—before it's too late.

41. Approaching Coral Islands and Reefs from Seaward

More cruising yachts are lost approaching reefs and coral islands from seaward than from any other cause, even in broad daylight. No risk faced in cruising offers as much potential danger to a vessel than these outcroppings from the ocean's floor. And yet simple prudence, being alert to sea conditions, and being on deck with your eyes open can virtually eliminate the danger.

One of the worst passages that a cruiser in the Pacific will face is from Tonga to Fiji. Because of Fijian Customs regulations, entry must be made at Lautoka, Suva, or Ovalau. Coming from Tonga, the best landfall is Suva, about a three-day sail for *Intermezzo*. A close examination of the charts will indicate that you must thread a series of narrow channels fronted on either side by islands, with barrier and detached reefs.

After waiting for a full moon and clear weather, we worked our way out from Vavau, Tonga, in company with our friends aboard the Australian ketch *Makaretu*. We chose to leave in the late afternoon, believing this would put us at the first bad stretch during early-morning daylight, about 36 hours later. We would be shooting for the center of a 20-mile channel, with a fairly steep island to the south and a series of detached reefs and low islands and barrier reefs to the north.

The full moon would let us work star sights or moon LOPs during most of the evening, and would provide good visibility up through early-morning hours.

With both radar and omega aboard, we felt we would have some backup in position finding. The trades were doing their thing, and once free of land *Intermezzo* began to stretch her legs, readily leaving the somewhat smaller *Makaretu* behind. The southeast trades were steady at 25 to 30 knots, and with the #1 jib on the pole we were averaging a little better than 8 knots. The next day we worked a round of stars in the morning and sun lines during the day, checking the omega for accuracy. It was apparent that something was disturbing the omega LOPs and they couldn't be relied on. Still, with a full moon and clear sky we weren't worried.

Our progress over the bottom, with helping current, was close to 200 miles per day, and it appeared that we would pass by our first danger spot in the dark. If the wind held, this meant we would be able to clear the next reef to windward of Vitulevu and Suva in daylight. That would eliminate the necessity of heaving-to offshore during the evening if we were late, a possibility I didn't relish with the reefs and uncertain currents fronting Suva Harbor. So we pressed on.

That afternoon, 24 hours out of Vavau, a thick overcast started to build. We snapped a last sun line and crossed it with a couple of dubious omega LOPs. Still, we were certain of our position within four to six miles.

We set the watches so that I would be on deck from 2000 onward, and while I didn't expect to pass through the danger area until 0300 the next morning, I wanted to have my more finely tuned nose and ears awake during the critical hours. Later in the evening Linda woke me. I was chagrined to see we still had our thick overcast. A slight amount of light was dimly perceivable now and then from the moon, as the overcast thinned.

Thinking I might get a moon shot, I brought the sextant on deck. With Linda still awake, I worked out a "worst possible" position— not where I really thought we were, but where we might have been set by errant current. This showed that at about 0200 we would pass within four miles of the reefs farthest offshore to the north, a reasonable margin for a "worst possible" position. I chatted briefly with Brian behind us on *Makaretu* during our evening radio schedule. He felt that we couldn't be as far north as my "worst possible" position indicated.

Linda bunked down and I assumed my watch on deck, enjoying *Intermezzo*'s glorious ride through the dark night, but just a bit apprehensive about our position.

About 0145 the moon popped through. I was so surprised that I almost missed it, and wasn't really sure that my sextant altitude was accurate. I considered waking Linda while I worked the sight, but decided to let her sleep. I wouldn't be below for more than a few minutes. Nervously I calculated the moon LOP and plotted it. When it showed us 16 miles north of our expected position and 6 miles north of our "worst possible," I shot up on deck. From my perch in the cockpit I called Brian and informed him of what I had worked out, adding in the process that I didn't believe the results but would keep a close watch just the same.

With the #1 jib on the pole to starboard, the main vanged and prevented to port, *Intermezzo* was putting her long flat run aft to work and surfing beautifully off the trade-wind seas.

At 0203 we rose to a large wave and ahead of me I thought I saw a white line. I blinked, and as we rose again, I thought I saw it again. Instinctively I grabbed the autopilot control and turned *Intermezzo* hard to port. As she started to jibe, I grabbed the cockpit knife and cut the main preventer and vang lines which restrained the main boom. It jibed over, fetching up on the starboard running backstay, and forced *Intermezzo* up into the wind. Within 15 seconds of my "vision" we were motionless in the water.

The commotion woke Linda. She bounded on deck, breathless from adrenalin flow. We cleared our large jib from the pole as quickly as possible. I still wasn't sure I had really seen anything, but we weren't taking chances. Instead of running off in 30-knot trades, we now were faced with working our way back to windward. With the jib furled on the headstay, we set a staysail and reefed the main. As soon as possible I called *Makaretu* and advised them of what I might have seen, and that I was leaving our masthead strobe on just in case they were close. Brian replied he would slow down until daylight.

For the next three hours we tacked back and forth, working our way slowly to windward, keeping a very wary eye open. It was possible that we had been set into a horseshoe shape of reefs, and since we couldn't be certain of our position, all we could do was try to hold our own until daylight. Brian called up on the radio at first light.

"Have you seen what's behind you yet?"

"No," Linda replied. We had been too busy looking forward. Glancing aft we saw clearly in the first rays of sunlight that we were right in the middle of the horseshoe reefs.

That we had escaped was due as much to luck as to any seamanship involved. I had made what could have been a decisive mistake when I went below to work the moon sight, leaving the deck unattended for five minutes. Thereafter, whenever we were within 30 miles of reef-strewn areas, somebody was always on deck.

The fact that I had been able to see the breaking surf at a reasonable distance, even with a full overcast, brought home even more the value of keeping a good watch.

Another important factor when working inside lagoons and passing by reef-strewn coasts or low islands is to know the state of the tide at all times. There are places in the world where at high tide without a sea running, a barrier reef will not disturb the wave action. Low and intermediate tides will almost certainly show some disturbance. Under more normal conditions, with higher reefs or a bigger sea running, it's possible to see and *feel* underwater obstructions a long way off.

The sea breaking on shore will send back a reflected wave that can be felt at a quarter mile or more away if you are at all attuned to the pattern of the open-sea waves. Any change in wave pattern in these waters is cause for alarm. Coming up on exposed reefs when going to windward presents a different problem. It isn't unusual to have quite a bit of current running with the sea, close along shore. Where this is found, the sea will quickly smooth itself down and stretch out —again a danger signal not to be ignored.

Another immediately noticeable sign is a lee that occurs when approaching from dead to leeward. And of course, land can be smelled for a long way especially if it's a fragrant tropical isle.

Given a clear night, without moonlight, a coral atoll with palm trees can be spotted by starlight at a distance of four to eight miles. We verified this one night coming back from Tiki Island in the Tuamotus with a boatload of Takaroan seamen. We had been to their favorite fishing and lobstering grounds over night, and I felt safe working back in the dark with these experienced Polynesian navigators to guide us. Sure enough, when the outline of the leeward side of Takaroa first became visible, the radar indicated a range of eight miles.

One of the dangers with atolls, however, is that they are not always covered with palm trees. Approaching from seaward, it will appear that there are areas of clear sailing between islands when in reality those are barren motus or barrier reef. If visibility is good this won't prove a problem, but if you aren't on deck to look, you can't tell what's coming at you. Even if it's *necessary* to go below, be sure to call the off watch on deck.

David Lewis's *We the Navigators* has an excellent section in it on sensing reefs and land by the feel of the elements. It should be carefully studied by anyone journeying to coral-filled waters.

42. Piloting in Coral

Nothing strikes fear into the heart of a newcomer to cruising like piloting in coral. Stories of the horrors of Tuamotu passes abound, and the droll comments of the Admiralty or U.S. pilot don't do much to instill confidence. And yet, given proper preparation, evaluation of the factors involved, and a little help from the weather, the risks can be minimized.

Our first experience was typical. Having read everything I could lay my hands on (which wasn't much) I was terrified at our first encounter with a coral atoll and its entrance pass. A pleasant sail in light southeasterly trades had brought us up to the windward coast of Takaroa in the Tuamotus in the early-morning hours. On our chart of the island the pass looked barely wider than our 12½-foot beam. Studying the Admiralty pilot aboard didn't help matters as it talked about 8-knot currents and 6-foot overfalls. We slowly sailed along the barrier reef with the surf booming in our ears and I considered our options, such as going on to Papeete (another pass), and

Intermezzo working her way through the Langa Langa Lagoon in the Solomon Islands. Note that the main anchor is run out and is ready to go in an instant. (Brian Marriott)

wasn't very happy. If we were going to cruise these waters, we would have to learn sometime.

In reality the problems we faced were minimal, but I didn't yet have the perspective to understand that. By interpolating from our Pacific Basin tide tables, we established that slack high water would be just after noon. Arriving at the pass at 1100, we stood off, jibing back and forth. Through the binoculars I could see triangular markers outlining what I supposed was the edge of the coral entrance. Also apparent was a bit of turbulence as the water rushing out the narrow pass met the slight trade-wind swell that was still evident.

It appeared easy as I studied the layout, but all those stories I had heard. . . . As slack water came I still hesitated. Maybe we should go on to Papeete and request a pilot. But our timing was off for the narrow gap between Tikehau and Rangiroa, and even with a full moon I didn't want to attempt that at night. Still undecided, I saw a small boat pulling toward us. As it drew alongside, Henry, a giant Tuamotuan, introduced himself as the "official" yacht pilot. He had been through this with other sailors before and was aware of our concern. With Henry in the bow, we worked our way into the pass, veered slightly to port, and came to rest alongside the concrete copra wharf of the village. The entire operation, *given good visibility,* was less difficult than working into a slip of a crowded marina on Sunday afternoon.

While most piloting through passes and in coral lagoons is just as easy, there are certain prerequisites to a safe journey. As with all things associated with the sea, one must maintain a constant vigil lest an innocent-looking passage turn into disaster.

To begin with, you must study whatever data are available about the area to be traversed. Pilots and charts are a help, but that data will at best be marginally accurate. They can be relied on for a general lay of the area, but nothing further. Picture postcards are a much better source of information, if obtained ahead of time.

Next, your vessel's capabilities must be considered. How handy is she under power? What's her turning ability, how fast will she stop, and should the engine fail, can you sail her out of a tight spot? How about construction? Steel, aluminum, heavy solid fiberglass all have a much higher tolerance for error than wood or cement.

Next is weather. Is it settled? Can you expect to have good sunlight and visibility? What about the time required? A short passage isn't a problem, but longer passages through coral may mean that a stop is inevitable due to loss of sun angle.

Eyeball navigation, de rigeur under these circumstances, requires proper equipment and preparation as well. To begin with, good polarized sunglasses are a must. The polarizing action filters out much of the reflected light from sea water, making it easier to see underwater obstructions. On board should be lightly shaded glasses for partially overcast days, and heavily tinted ones for bright, cloudless days.

You will be spending a lot of time aloft, in some cases hours, and a comfortable perch is required, one that can be maintained in a

A comfortable, secure perch aloft helps when you stand long periods of time keeping a lookout.

seaway. The higher you are, the better you will be able to see out in front. It's best to have a perch on the upper spreaders (small boat) or lower spreaders (big boat) that can be used in calm water. For bouncy conditions, steps or ratlines lashed to fore and aft lower shrouds are best.

You want to wear a good shade hat, or better yet, sun visors. They tend to stay put in a breeze where a full or floppy hat will require a helping hand.

There will be times when you want a chart aloft too, and for this purpose nothing works better than an old-fashioned clipboard. The chart can be folded until the section needed is exposed, and if a snap and line are attached to the clipboard, it can be hooked to a lashed

The spreader platform on the 29′ sloop *Sea Love,* in Rabaul, Papua, New Guinea. In the coral-filled waters of Melanesia it saw lots of use.

ring so your hands are free when not consulting the chart. Working with binoculars aloft when wearing polarized sunglasses isn't easy, but on occasion is essential, so have good straps on both.

With your own house in order, and the vessel's capabilities considered, let's review those factors which are not under our control that affect visibility.

Foremost is water clarity. There are some lagoons in the world where you can see a shackle on the anchor in 60 feet of water, and others where you can't see the bottom in 10 feet. Generally, though, visibility will not be a problem. But if you're working in coral associated with a high island and there has been heavy rainfall, beware. The runoff from the rain will muddy the water, and on occasion it can take several days or more for visibility to improve. Another factor that will affect clarity is man-made activity. Blasting, dredging, or dumping all can have substantial and lasting effects. We learned about this in Maieva Bay just south of Papeete. We had come down inside the lagoon from Papeete, looking for a quiet anchorage, and the indentation in front of the Maieva Beach Hotel looked like the spot. They had been building a small marina and the water was disturbed. Linda, keeping a lookout from the bow pulpit, didn't realize that the water was shoaling, since its color stayed dark. There was a thud, our stern rose abruptly out of the water, and as you can imagine, there were a few inquiries from the cockpit as to what was going on forward. Subsequently we stayed completely out of anything but clear water if coral was about.

After water clarity comes the sun. The best visibility is with the sun over your shoulder. Not only the sun's angle overhead must be considered, but its declination as well. If the sun is on your latitude in the morning, you'll be able to see well to the west, with the sunlight beaming from the east, and the reverse in the afternoon. Visibility to the west will be best about 2½ hours after sunrise until an hour before the sun is directly overhead. Very low sun angles can be used, but they are good only for narrow directions of viewing.

The question of visibility is a little more complicated when the sun is north or south of your position. If the sun is north of you 15 degrees or so, you will have good visibility to the south; the opposite is true if the sun is to your south. If you're making a short journey, you can pick the optimum time; but on a longer trek you'll have to figure out ahead of time where the sun will be at any time you're going to have to make any course changes that will require good visibility.

Other factors to consider when making longer journeys are the reliability of your speed under sail or power, and the possibility of intermediate stopping points should a delay occur and visibility be lost.

Then, of course, there's the weather. If it's absolutely calm and the water surface is glassy, it will be difficult to see below the surface, even at good sun angles. Fortunately, this is a rare situation, and a slight rippling of the surface will give you the necessary clarity.

Even worse than glassy calm is an overcast sky which will make it virtually impossible to see what's lurking below. We are fortunate in that most coral cruising areas are blessed with clear skies, but some regions, such as the Fijis and New Caledonias, can be overcast for long periods. In this case you have no choice but to stay put, although in a metal boat there is more margin for error than with others. And, of course, if you have been over the route before it may be okay.

Don't rely on coral or channel marks to show you the way. They are frequently misplaced, missing, or confusing.

The most difficult passage we experienced in coral took place on the back side of Vitu Levu in Fijian waters, when we wanted to go from Lautoka to the islands of the Blue Lagoon. The Fijian government had recently completed a series of aerial survey charts, detailed but without soundings, that were supposed to be accurate. The distance was too far to make it in one sun even at 7½ knots. Thinking it would be simple to find a spot to anchor overnight and then finish the journey the next day, we were up at first light readying *Intermezzo* for her trip. As the sun climbed, we worked our way out of the well-marked ship channel in a northerly direction, looking for the break in the reefs shown on the chart.

Moving north, away from Lautoka, the water cleared until we found the channel markers indicating our left-hand turn to the west. For the next three hours we wound our way through deep channels, well defined with steep-to coral. Toward noon we started to search for a good place to anchor for the night. With the sun 30 degrees to our north, we figured good visibility until 1400. Time droned on and still no anchorage appeared. There had to be one somewhere I reasoned, but no luck. At 1415 it appeared as if someone had pulled a switch: we could no longer see. We turned *Intermezzo* around and backtracked toward Lautoka at full speed, racing the sunset for visibility. The next day, being familiar with the early segments of the route, we left at daybreak, spending three hours inside the reefs before the sun had climbed to give us good visibility. This headstart made it possible to make the Blue Lagoon Islands in one shot.

Between the two extremes of pure sunlight and overcast are the occasional clouds. They can be disconcerting as they cast shadows over the bottom. In many cases these shadows look just like coral heads. Experience, as always, is the best teacher, and after a while you'll be able to tell which is which.

One of the factors to be considered is the type of coral and bottom conditions you'll be working with. In most areas you'll have a hard bottom with a thin layer of sand at a pretty constant depth. Up from this will rise coral heads, the sides of which will be virtually perpendicular. These configurations are the easiest to navigate in. The contour of the coral is usually even, jutting fingers with small isolated heads being uncommon. Water will be deep, right up to the edge of the coral. The top of the coral will be covered with a small amount of water at low tide or perhaps slightly awash. If contact is made, it's usually not serious.

Much more dangerous for navigation are uneven bottoms with "bombies." Here you may have a bottom that rises and falls, and large circular or hemispherical coral growths. They can occur all over, and on occasion be well below the surface, lurking just at a height to snag you. When piloting in these conditions, favorable light is obviously required.

You will learn to discern water depth by the play of colors. Dark blue means security: deep water. As the water color lightens up but stays in the light-blue range, you still have plenty of depth to work with. When the white starts coming up, it's time to keep a close watch and slow down, depending on your draft. Yellows, browns, and purples are definite bottom crunchers.

As we mentioned before, you should always know the state of the tide during a passage. If visibility turns poor and you have low tide coupled with a bit of sea, you will generally be able to tell the location of the coral heads by surface disturbances and wave patterns. A swift current in a pass will also show their location by eddies and swirls.

Passes through barrier reefs are a different story. To begin with, the data shown in the pilots and charts are liable to be more accurate. Most passes are steep-to along their edges, since the action of the current causes the coral to grow in wall-like structures. The entrance to the pass may also be well marked.

You may encounter various degrees of current at the mouth, depending on the sea state. A large lagoon that has miles of reef and one or two outlets can generate tremendous flooding currents if a sea is running. The waves breaking on the outer reef pour huge quantities of water into the lagoon. Much of this must find its way out of the passes.

Only once, however, did we find it difficult to enter a pass, and that was at Suveroff after 3½ days of gale-strength winds. When we approached the entrance to the pass, which fortunately was in a lee, the current was really boiling. At full throttle, with our storm staysail and double-reefed main drawing as well, it took us over an hour to beat through a quarter-mile pass.

If a substantial current is ebbing and there is a sea opposing it, there will probably be a good break across the entrance. As the current changes to flood (if enough sea has been running it may continue to ebb until things calm down), the break will become manageable. If the vessel is handy at surfing and if you have been through the pass before, it may be worth a try. But if it's your first time through, or you're not adept at running on a breaking sea, don't attempt it.

Once the threshold of the entrance has been crossed, a pass should not be hard to navigate. If you are fighting current, the eddies close to the coral will have substantially less flow or even a countercurrent. If the current is flooding and you are flying over the bottom, remember that you must maintain enough speed beyond that of the current to have good maneuverability.

If the wind is blowing across the pass, and it often does, work along the windward side, other factors allowing, just in case it should be necessary to sail your way out.

A last point: Should you find yourself in a situation that requires piloting in coral at night, it's good to know that a barrier reef will show up very well under a powerful spotlight. Be sure the spotlight cable will reach to your perch aloft, and take a look once or twice at night when you're at anchor to get a feel. An emergency might crop up where this bit of practice will come in handy.

Lest all the foregoing sound daunting to you, remember that it wasn't that many years ago that these passes and lagoons were navigated on a regular basis by unwieldy, heavily laden, sail-powered copra schooners. If they could do it, so can you.

43. Anchoring

No matter where you stop on your cruise, the most important rule of seamanship is to anchor defensively. Always assume the worst will occur, and consider your position in that light.

First is how to get out fast, if conditions deteriorate and the anchorage becomes untenable. Can it be done at night or when the sky is overcast? If not, you'd better be sure you're well protected: many tropical anchorages require good sunlight to exit, with the sun at the right angle behind you so that the reefs or heads can be seen clearly. Even if the steady trade winds are blowing, consider what will occur if a sudden trough of low pressure develops and the wind veers and picks up to gale force. It can happen in the trade-wind season. Remember that even though you may be inside a lovely lagoon there can be a long fetch for chop to build up if things get nasty. What happens if the current turns against the prevailing breeze? Know the times of ebb and flow so that you aren't fooled by slack water when anchoring, and then find the tide changing against the chop after dark.

Obviously, you want reference points for bearings to check your position against dragging. The trouble is that many out-of-the-way anchorages have no good landmarks in the dark. If they exist, take bearings and note them in the log. If not, and if you have reason to be concerned, drop the dinghy anchor alongside with a float attached. You can check the position of the float to see if you've moved.

The new breed of digital depth sounders with alarms are an excellent anchor watch tool. If there is shelving between you and the beach, the alarm can be set to give warning should you drag that way. In order for a depth sounder to be effective, though, the alarm must be loud enough to be heard from where you are sleeping. And it must have a variable-depth capability. On some sounders the alarm can be set at only two or three specific depths. These won't do the job.

I like to have a telltale compass over the bunk. The compass, mounted above my head, allows me to crack an eye, glance at our heading, and fall back asleep without getting up or disturbing Linda. Before we added the telltale, I was up and down like a jackrabbit all night when we were anchored in unprotected waters.

The technique of anchoring itself, under most circumstances, is quite simple. When considering where to drop the hook, you have to allow for a distance of dragging before it will set, especially with a CQR. Then, looking at where you think you will come to rest, make sure there will be room to swing 360 degrees. If other boats are nearby, you must assess their ground tackle and swinging radii.

Those that came before you have first call. If it turns out that you're interfering with their swinging room later on, it will be your duty to reanchor. Vessels of similar shape, lying to chain of the same proportionate size to boat windage, will tend to swing in the same manner. Those on light chain will tend to wander more, and any vessels lying to rope must be given a wide berth. Swinging room will vary with scope, of course, and again you must assume that those on light chain or rope will have a much greater swinging radius than others.

Nothing is more annoying than to be sitting in a pleasant anchorage with good swinging room and have a newcomer anchor right on top of you. Don't be guilty of that yourself. Make sure when you fetch up that there is plenty of room between yourself and the others in the anchorage.

Be sure the hook is ready to run out, with the rode flaked cleanly on deck or below. Wait until the vessel has a bit of sternway before letting the anchor run, and be sure not to allow the chain to drop on top of the anchor. If anchoring on a fouled bottom, drop the hook, back up a few feet, and drop your pile of chain in one spot. Then with a riding sail set, allow the vessel to drift back in a straight line from the anchor. If the wind doesn't shift, you'll be able to recover the chain without fouls.

Once the rode is run out, let the vessel come up into the wind, then back down. Slowly at first, give it a good bite in reverse, using at least 75 percent power with a folding or small two-blade prop, and 40 percent power with a feathering or three-blade wheel. This will set the anchor securely. If the anchor won't stand a good backing down, it should be reset until it does. If you can't get a really good bite, and if no other anchorage is possible, you will want to keep a close eye on it through the night.

When the anchor is being set by the engine, feel the rode with your hand and it will telegraph the bottom conditions and what the anchor is doing. A rough, jogging sensation indicates that the anchor is skipping over a hard bottom, possibly rock or hard sand and coral, and having a difficult time digging in. If it catches now and then, and then jumps as the anchor slides free, be especially wary of the final set. It may be that you have just caught a rock or coral head, and a good gust or wind shift will break the anchor free.

The telegraphy is more pronounced with chain, which has the further advantage of continuing to send an unmistakable message during the evening. If it is moving or dragging over a fouled or poor bottom, you'll hear it below.

An anchor that has set will stop its low-frequency rumble and set up a high-pitched flutter as the rode is pulled tight and into a straight line by the power of the engine reversing. You can hear it in the foc's'le even over the engine noise.

If you're using a rope rode and the bottom is foul, it's a good idea to attach a float to the end of the anchor lead chain to lift it off the bottom. Lightweight nylon that floats, or polypropylene of sufficient diameter should be utilized in these conditions. The combination of the chain float and floating line will reduce the risk of bottom fouling and chafe. In crowded anchorages, however, with powered dinghies about, floating line can be a hazard.

If there is any question about the bite of the anchor or the bottom conditions, put on mask and flippers and have a look for yourself.

A Danforth-type anchor, even one that is really set, will break free with a modest amount of vertical strain. This makes it ideal for stern anchors which on occasion must be picked up from a dinghy. A burying anchor, such as the CQR, may require up to 50 percent of its holding power to break free. If the anchor is really buried, bring the boat over the anchor and tighten up on the rode. If there is a gentle swell running, the lift on the bow will break it free. If the swell is more than gentle, control the rode tension with the windlass clutch rather than the chain stopper. This will allow some slippage before damage occurs, if you keep an eye on things. In the absense of a swell, the engine, running forward, will eventually dig the anchor out.

Fouls on coral can usually be freed in the same manner. In this case, by tighting up on the chain and then waiting with the bow slightly depressed, the chain will eventually saw through the coral. If that doesn't work and you don't want to go in the water, try running at the obstruction from different angles. This will frequently break the chain free. As a last resort, get out the diving gear.

If the bottom is known to be foul and diving gear isn't available, you will want to rig a trip line to the head of the anchor. If the anchor fouls, it can be tripped out backward.

When lying to double anchors in heavy weather, keep the load on the rope rode. This will ensure that it stays off the bottom and free of chafe. The second anchor on chain is there as a backup. If conditions get really bad, you will want to have the rodes set so the rope

An unusual "anchorage." *Intermezzo* and her Australian "mate" *Makaretu* are tied between the masts of an unfortunate World War II Japanese freighter in the Solomon Islands.

takes the initial load and then the chain comes into play. If the chain were to come first, the rope would only get to work if the chain failed or dragged.

You must know how to sail an anchor in and how to sail it out. The specific techniques will vary from vessel to vessel, but the basics are the same. If you are concerned about weather conditions and want to get the hook in really well (and if you have plenty of room to maneuver), set the hook with a bit of way on. Our technique is to run straight over the anchor and let the rode out rapidly. Then, just before applying the windlass brake, we head up quickly. This moves the hull away from the chain and prevents damage to our bottom paint. On a modern design with shorter overhangs, it might be better to sail in on a rope rode to prevent damage to the bottom.

The other approach is to sail head-to-wind, position the bow where you want it, and let go, relying on the wind pressure to set the hook. The problem here is that you are never sure the anchor is really set until it starts to blow. Obviously, in these conditions you must have room to drag, and be sure you have good holding ground.

Sailing the anchor out, assuming you're working with a powerful windlass, is quite easy. Bring the boat almost over the anchor, then hoist the main and let it luff. If you have a mizzen, it will help keep you head-to-wind. If you're using only a main, be careful that you don't start sailing off before you're ready. As the hook breaks free, hoist the headsail and back it to the tack opposite the one on which you want to depart. It will blow the bow across, and can be sheeted in to leeward as the anchor is brought home. This technique presupposes enough room to fall off, gather way, and accelerate to the point where you can maneuver before running into trouble. If that isn't the case, and you have enough windlass or manpower to get the anchor aboard quickly, a running start may be better. In this case you will actually sail up to the anchor, and will have a bit of way on before breaking the anchor free.

Anchor handling under sail should be practiced whenever possible. We always sail on and off the hook if conditions permit. It's a nice way to end a passage, and it keeps our skill level high, in case it should be needed in an emergency situation. There is no substitute for practice.

44. Running Aground in Protected Waters

Running aground is a common experience to anyone who sails. Whether you are in San Francisco Harbor, the Chesapeake Bay, or some beautiful English river, you will find bottom if you go out often enough. In most cases, given a few simple precautions, and assuming protected waters, little or no damage will result (except to the skipper's pride is his faux pas is observed).

When you're sailing where the risks of running aground are high, it's a good idea to write into the log the state of tide during the next 24 hours. If caught on a slack tide or the beginning of ebb, you must work with all speed to avoid being stuck for the next 12 hours or so. If the tide is rising, then you can usually set an anchor and let the moon do the work for you. If your day's run will take you across a shallow spot, be sure to get there before high water. If you don't make it, there is still a bit more coming in to float you free.

Also, remember to consider the monthly tidal cycle. If you get caught at high-water springs, you sit a month or more waiting for the next extremely high tide. I remember how upset the local yachtsmen at the Matavia Bay Yacht Club in northern New Zealand were one year when a visiting yacht went aground on the grid (telephone poles driven into the mud to support the hull when the tide runs out) at high-water springs, and couldn't get off for an entire month!

Current, wind, the possibility of a change in the weather—all have to be factored in your consideration. The design of the vessel will have much to do with attempts to float or pull her off. Older designs with low freeboard and heavier displacement have to be carefully sealed to avoid flooding on an incoming tide if they are lying over on their sides. More modern boats, with lower displacement/length ratios, have enough buoyancy in their topsides to float them quickly with a rising tide.

If you're stuck for the duration of the tidal cycle, and expect the water to go out far enough to lay the vessel down, take a sounding pole or oar and check around the vessel for underwater rocks or obstructions. You may want to induce the boat to lay over in the right direction as the tide falls. If there are rocks about, cockpit cushions and fenders can be used to protect the hull.

Boats with wide keels will tend to stand erect, but the risk is that something will cause them to topple. Even a large boat supported only by its keel will not tolerate much of an eccentric load before she'll go over. As a result, it's best to induce your boat to lie down in one direction or the other with the dropping water level. Many of our European friends cruise with "legs" they can fit to their hulls to support the yachts when they're dried out.

Once the tide has gone out, you might as well make the most of the situation by checking the prop, zincs, and through-hull fittings; give the bottom a cleaning, and touch up the paint if necessary. To anyone waiting to have a laugh at your expense, you can blithely explain that you had been planning this for some time!

There are several standard steps to take in all simple grounding situations. The first is to set an anchor uptide (that is, the direction the water will be returning from) and/or upwind, as the situation dictates. Then, if a powerboat is about, you might ask the skipper to make a few high-speed circles around you; the attendant wake may be enough to bump you free. If you have a good-size prop with powerful reverse thrust, you may be able to excavate the sand or mud from beneath the keel with prop wash. Swinging the rudder back and forth can help when using the engine in this manner. Keep an eye on engine temperature, and give a periodic look to the saltwater strainer—odds are it will be picking up a bit of mud and debris in the intake. If you are concerned about the shaft seal and rubber impeller on the saltwater pump, it may be better to wait for the tide to float you off.

Kedging will often provide that extra oomph required to break you free. Hauling your vessel down by the masthead will lessen her draft and can be effective with smaller boats.

45. Running Aground Offshore

Hitting an exposed reef with breaking surf is like a bad motorcar accident: it always happens to the other guy. The sad truth, of course, is that given a lapse in seamanship, bad luck, or a no-win situation, it could indeed happen to you. But being driven ashore on an exposed reef or coastline does not need to mean the end of a voyage. A careful study of serious situations and how you should handle yourself and your vessel during one, coupled with a modest investment in special materials, can lengthen the odds of getting back to deep water.

Two basic things can happen. The first is where you strike and are driven out of reach of the sea by surf. In such a case, there is time to evaluate the situation and decide what to do. The second is where the vessel is held at the surf line, perhaps by rocks or coral pockets. Here, time is all-important. Regardless of your state of exhaustion, the weather, or the visibility, within the limits of safety for yourself and crew, you must make every effort to free the vessel in the shortest period possible.

A few hours can make the difference between breaking free with the hull intact and having a hole ground or broken through the hull which will make refloating impossible. If your vessel is metal or heavily built fiberglass, you have more time than if she is wood— even a stoutly built wood hull won't last as long under the same conditions. In most cases a ferrocement boat can be written off as soon as she hits.

Aside from time, the most important ingredient is faith in the future. Never give up hope until the hull is destroyed. If the hull is intact, somehow, at some time, in some manner you will be able to float her free.

In the tropics, where navigation aids are few and currents unreliable, coral reefs are the biggest hazard. This is a mixed blessing. Coral by its nature is abrasive, and will chew through anything less than metal, sometimes in an incredibly short time. On the other hand most coral is easily crushed, and as such is not as liable to puncture a hull as rock. Also, the coefficient of friction between a hull and coral will be substantially less than between the hull and mud or sand.

A majority of accidents happen with barrier reefs, where there is a buildup of coral fronting a lagoon or estuary. The reef width can vary between 30 yards and a mile or more. It isn't unusual to find two or three feet of water over the reef at high tide. This type of grounding is the easiest from which to recover, given time and hard work.

Take the case of Dixie Lee and his 44-foot steel ketch *Pagan Lee*. Dixie is a caricature of the beer-drinking, fun-loving Australian hell-raiser. In love with life and the fairer sex, at 54 he is still as strong as a mule, and perhaps as stubborn. His twinkling blue eyes and great shock of white hair belie an exotic past as coast watcher in the Solomons during World War II, and weekly trips into the New Guinea highlands as a surveyor today.

Dixie, another male crew member, and several lady friends were sailing *Pagan Lee* from Cairns, Australia, to Kieta, on Bougainville island in New Guinea. At 0230 on a dark, overcast night, they struck Long Reef, in the Louisidade Archipelago, southern New Guinea. With a 15-knot southeaster blowing and four- to five-foot breaking seas, it wasn't long before *Pagan Lee* was quite a way up on the reef.

After getting out an SOS, Dixie and crew took stock. With a steel hull on the stoutly built *Pagan Lee,* and moderate sea conditions, they decided to wait until daylight to take action. The SOS, broadcast on the 2182 distress frequency at night, was heard by several ports in the Pacific islands. Information was sent to search and rescue in Port Moresby, which launched two twin Otter aircraft at first light. Since Dixie wasn't sure of his position, not having had a fix since leaving the northeast coast of Australia, it was several hours after noon before he was spotted.

Aerial photos taken at that time show that *Pagan Lee* had been driven 100 yards in from the edge of the reef. With that much distance between the boat and the face of the reef with its breaking seas, and over a mile to go toward the inside lagoon, most skippers would have started removing valuables and salvaging what gear they could. But that wasn't Dixie's style, and the ensuing struggle should be considered carefully by all those who go cruising coral-strewn waters.

Dixie decided to work the boat toward the lagoon. He wasn't sure if there was a pass out of the lagoon, but he reasoned that he could always blast one with dynamite once he had *Pagan Lee* floating. They adopted a system of putting the bow anchor, a 45-lb. CQR on chain, out at a 45-degree angle toward the lagoon, coupled with a 50-lb. fisherman anchor angled on a nylon rode from the stern. With *Pagan Lee* thus bridled, and with the sails hoisted to heel her over, they winched like the devil for two hours on either side of high tide. At high tide there was 2½ to 3 feet of water over the coral reef. On good days they moved her more than a quarter mile. During the low periods, aside from resting the crew set out with two metal staves scavenged from hull repair stores and broke up large coral heads blocking their way.

Five days later, exhausted, with *Pagan Lee* in need of a bit of paint, they kedged her into deep water.

In retelling his story, Dixie made three important points. First, under no circumstances allow the vessel to dig a hole in the coral when she first hits, thus trapping herself at the reef's edge. If it happens, without outside aid the game is over. Second, carry tools aboard suitable for breaking up the coral, such as a pick axe. And third, if you are serious about wanting to have the maximum chance of freeing the boat, learn to use and carry dynamite.

Pagan Lee was a moderately heavy, hard-chine steel design. Built of ³⁄₁₆″ plate framed on 16-inch centers, with longitudinals spaced at 12-inch intervals, she was as close to bulletproof as you can get. Yet Dixie thought that any modern, well-built fiberglass boat would also have survived. A lighter boat, with more freeboard, would have the advantage of floating more of her weight on the incoming tide.

The other route out of this kind of trouble, obviously, is to get the boat back to the edge of the reef and through the surf. I had figured this would be impossible without outside help, until I heard the story of DeeDee and Emory Moore's experience on the reef at Taka Lambaena in the central Indonesian archipelago.

The Moores have been sailing for a lot of years. DeeDee was one of the terrors of Newport Bay in her Southern California racing days, while Emory cultivated his bedside manner as a top cancer surgeon. When the Moores decided to go cruising, they had a Bill Lapworth–designed Cal 2-46 built to their specifications. With roller-furling headsails, a modest rig, and a GM 4-53 diesel turning a three-blade 26-inch propeller, she was a conservative boat, easily sailed by a couple in their 60s.

They were heading for Singapore, with DeeDee handling the navigating; not having had a sight for a while, both she and Emory were on deck keeping watch. They were aiming for the center of a 10-mile-wide pass. Taking visual bearings on Kompo Isle in the early-morning mist, they thought they were clear. Emory wasn't feeling well, and at the end of his watch went below. Not much later the sun peeked through for a moment and DeeDee raced to get her sextant. The sight recorded, she considered asking Emory to come back on deck while she worked it, but he was resting peacefully and she decided not to disturb him. (This was the same mistake I made on our passage to Suva, when I went below to work a noon sight; see Chapter 36.)

Arion III was sailing along under full main with the #1 genoa rolled down to 110 percent in a 20-knot southeast trade wind. The autopilot was out and they were using their Sayes self-steering rig with marginal results.

Toward the end of her worksheet, when she was just about

through with the sight reduction tables, DeeDee felt *Arion III* round up slightly. With horror she realized that the water through the starboard windows had changed color, and in a matter of seconds had run the gamut of blue, green, brown, then slam! They were hard on a fringing reef with a trade-wind sea breaking over the boat.

Rushing on deck, they threw the sheets off, then tried to free the stern anchor from its chock, but the release pin was frozen. The engine was thrown into reverse, but to no avail.

Within minutes they were 50 feet in from the edge of the reef with seas breaking over their stern. While Emory shipped the self-steering rig and dropped the sails, DeeDee got off an SOS on the 15-meter-band ham radio, which was received in Guam. A group of amateur radio operators stood by to monitor the situation.

At this point in the story, Emory said, "I was starting to plan our new boat." I suspect that would have been my own reaction as well. But DeeDee wasn't about to let that "goddamned Indonesian reef" beat her. Putting their eight-foot Avon dink over the side, they decided to try to set the anchor and winch themselves off. Bringing the Avon around *Arion III*'s stern, they found the seas too rough to transfer their 35-lb. CQR anchor. The Avon was moved amidships and tied fore and aft. They laid the anchor in the bow and the chain in the stern. *Using her seven-foot stoppered oars,* DeeDee rowed this blunt-nosed little inflatable, towing a one-inch nylon rode through the breaking surf. Gaining the edge of the reef, she paused to drop the anchor and chain, only to be blown back into the break before she could get the anchor over the side. Once again, now rowing at an oblique angle to the waves, she worked her way seaward and this time succeeded in dropping the hook over the vertical edge of the fringing reef.

When DeeDee got back aboard *Arion III*, exhausted, she and Emory started to grind in on their #28 Barient two-speed cockpit winch.

With the tide rising, they felt a first tentative thump, as *Arion III* eased toward deep water against the spring-like tension of the stretched nylon anchor warp. For hours they cranked and rested, then cranked again. Gradually, they began to edge into deeper water. An occasional wave, bigger than the others, would give them extra lift and a few additional feet of seaward progress. By early afternoon they fired up the engine, and with 100 h.p. working in tandom with the Barient, they began to make real progress through the surf. Resting for a moment, they decided that on the final lunge the anchor rode would have to be cut free so that it wouldn't foul the propeller. Their strength somewhat recovered, they gave a last effort, revved the engine up to full reverse, and cut their rode. With another wave they were free of the coral and backing out to sea.

The damage sustained by their fiberglass hull was superficial, and their spade rudder, although it was abraded and had shifted the quadrant, was in good condition.

By saving their vessel without outside aid in such a difficult situation, DeeDee and Emory Moore set a brilliant example of what determination and seamanship can do.

The most interesting technical aspect of this story is the dropping of the anchor over the face of a reef. I had never considered this approach to working out of a fringing reef grounding, but as we've seen, it's a valid method.

It may be that help is available to pull you off, and in this situation a bridle will have to be rigged that can take enormous loads without doing major damage to the boat. Bob Parks, an experienced salvage diver, explained how he helped Dr. Peter Eastman rig such a bridle on his Cal 2-46 after it had been driven ashore on the barrier reef of Huahine in the Society group, French Polynesia. Using anchor chain as the basic bridle, completely encircling the yacht and heavily padded around the hull, and supported every three feet in a vertical direction by tie lines to the toe rail and stanchions, they were hooked up to the hawser of a French naval vessel. In this manner the yacht was pulled off the reef with only moderate damage below the waterline.

There are several pieces of gear that you may want to consider carrying aboard, besides those already mentioned. First are several large rope sheaves, in the range of 8 to 10 times the diameter of the anchor rode. These can be attached to the end of the chain lead, coming from the anchor, and used to increase the mechanical advantage of the deck winches or windlass. Next is heavy-duty flexible foam, such as used in wrestling or gymnastics mats. This material is extremely tough, doesn't absorb moisture, and will make an excellent fender between the hull and coral or rocks.

Consider an auxiliary-powered centrifugal pump. Usually a combination of a three-inch pump and a 4-h.p. gas engine, they are available all over the world at modest prices. Centrifugal pumps of this nature can extract 200 gallons per minute, and can be run from on deck, picking up the water via a long, flexible hose. In the event that the hull integrity is broken, or damage occurs while pulling off, a pump of this nature may be the only way to keep the water in check.

If you have outside ballast on your keel, take a good look at what is necessary to remove it under adverse conditions. It may be possible to gain enough clearance by ballast removal to float free. Obviously, pumping fuel and water tanks and removing interior supplies, and even joiner work (as a last resort), will add to the chance of success.

Draft can be reduced if you heel the boat by pulling your masthead down. If you fill your dinghy with water, attach the spinnaker halyard to it with a strong bridle, and guy the halyard out abeam with the main boom, you can heel a 40- to 50-footer 25 to 30 degrees by cranking down on the halyard.

A last cautionary word: Of the nine firsthand cases I know of where vessels have been stranded on reefs, only twice were lookouts on deck. Keeping your eyes open topside when close to underwater obstructions, or land, will go a long way toward making this subject simply a mental exercise.

4
Emergencies

Most of the cruising people we know have never had to use the emergency procedures discussed in this section. Reading about them is important, though, because as you figure out your reactions to situations that pose danger to your vessel or crew, you will develop confidence in your overall ability to cope at sea. And should you ever get into an emergency, it will be crucial that you have thought ahead of time about how to handle it.

46. Man Overboard

I can think of no worse situation on a cruising yacht than for one of the crew members to go overboard, unattached. As a result, we have always been cautious about wearing a safety harness and hooking up.

Still, the worst can happen, and a few lessons can be learned from single-handers. Chip Vincent, aboard *Eos*, trailed a trip line that would disengage his Monitor windvane should he reach it as *Eos* went sailing by. From Dean Kewish I picked up the idea of a trailing long floating polypropylene line, knotted every two feet, as a means of catching hold and getting back aboard (if the vessel isn't moving too fast). We adapted this to our two-crewed vessel by keeping a knotted and coiled line in the cockpit, ready to go in case one of us went overboard.

The problem of getting the vessel back to the spot of the accident is the most difficult. As indicated in our "Preparations" section (Chapter 13), man-overboard gear should include at least one (preferably two) 15-foot man-overboard poles, strobe lights, and horseshoe rings. If these are tripped immediately, they'll give a good indication of the general locality of the swimmer. But what if you're below at the time? We carried ACR personal strobes that could be attached to a jacket or harness, along with whistles, to help mark our position in the water. Available from Manhattan Marine in New York City is a compact inflatable balloon which when filled with gas ascends to the end of a tether to mark your location.

The time-honored advice for man-overboard procedure is to have one person at all times keep his eye on the swimmer, while the rest of the crew works the ship around. That's fine if you've got extra hands and they're on deck at the time. But with only two of you the situation is different. In any event, before doing anything note the course, calculate the reciprocal, and then turn the vessel around.

Once you get back to the swimmer comes another difficult part. Assuming that he or she is in reasonable physical condition, that your freeboard is moderate, and that there is some breeze blowing, we feel it best to drift down from windward, in a hove-to position, so that the swimmer can come aboard from the leeward side. For this reason, I keep the lower lifeline clear of the boarding gate area so it will be easier to scramble aboard. Another approach is a fixed boarding ladder on the stern, but it must have very sturdy hinge points to take the eccentric loadings that can be expected when the vessel is heeled and weight is applied. If you're building, consider adding a swim step to the transom. The step not only makes it easy for the swimmer to board, but it can also make an excellent platform from which to work in other situations.

Getting aboard a person who is unable to help himself can be almost impossible when you're shorthanded. The best approach is a

Dena Jenson coming back after a visit to a neighbor in Rabaul, Papua, New Guinea. *Sea Love*'s built-in boarding ladder was used for swimming and boarding from the dink.

Intermezzo's man-overboard pole, strobe light, horseshoe ring, and drogue could be released by a pull of one wire. She carried twin sets that could be dropped a short distance apart to line up on when returning.

line slipped around the shoulders to a halyard or block led from the top of a doghouse.

Better yet, use your harness and stay attached.

47. Fire

On a properly wired vessel, protected by circuit breakers or fuses, the odds of having a serious fire on board are extremely slim. Of those that do occur, the worst ones usually have to do with the engine or generator exhaust systems. The first precaution, of course, is to keep

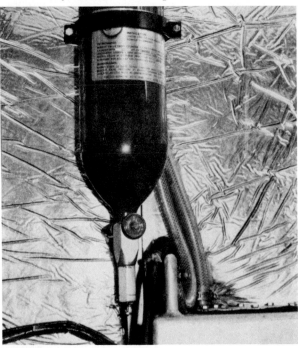

Automatic Halon-type fire extinguisher in the engine room of *Intermezzo II.*

all your machinery areas clean, free of oil and greasy rags. An automatic extinguisher system fitted to your machinery compartment will reduce the chances that a fire there may get out of control. If you have a Halon system, though, remember that the engine must be shut down or else it will exhaust the Halon fumes.

Galley fires are rather more common, and can be dealt with by using properly placed fire extinguishers, flour, baking soda, fire blankets, wet clothes, etc.

The paramount factor is time. You must act quickly on *any* fire to stop its spread. This may mean some personal danger or even injury from the flames, but speed is of the essence. If you're not sure of the source of fire, immediately shut down your machinery and turn off all power. It may be necessary to remove beautiful joiner work in a rough manner to find and stop the problem. The joiner work can be replaced, but the boat can't; for this reason, many people carry a fire axe aboard.

48. Collision

Collisions at sea are rare, and when they do occur, assuming you're keeping a watch, they will be between you and a floating log, cargo hatch, or the like. Depending on your vessel's construction, you may want to make more or less elaborate precautions. Wood vessels planked on ribs, being made up of a series of small structures bonded together, are more subject to leaking from minor impact than metal or fiberglass boats are. A metal boat, with collision bulkheads and perhaps a double bottom, will have little worry in this regard. Fiberglass vessels molded in two halves are potentially more fragile than one-piece hulls. Aboard *Intermezzo* we carried a five-foot-diameter pentagonal collision mat, filled with ½″ closed-cell flexible foam and fitted with lines tied to reinforced grommets around the outside on five corners.

After collision, it is essential to find quickly the location of any leakage so you can assess the chances for stemming the flow. The odds are that the impact and damage will take place in the forward sections of the vessel. You will still have the advantage of working in a narrow part of the vessel's structure. This means that mattresses stiffened by locker doors or galley countertops can be forced against the leak and wedged in with timbers pressed against the other side of the hull. If the damage is at or near the waterline, going about and heeling her to the other side may bring the water flow under control until you can make repairs.

49. Major Leaks

Areas of potential leaks in every vessel should be catalogued and reviewed for control. The worst problem areas are keel bolts, through-hull fittings, and stuffing boxes (both rudder and propeller shafts). Soft-wood plugs should be available for through-hull fittings, along with a large quantity of underwater epoxy, which has many uses aboard. One possibility to consider when chasing a leak is a source above the waterline. It's amazing how much water will find its way below through unstopped chain pipes and cockpit lockers when you are reaching or beating in heavy going.

On our second crossing of the Tasman Sea, from New Zealand to New Caledonia, a high-pressure system passed over us the second day out, turning our lovely reach into a shy beat. The wind picked up into the 40s, and since we wanted to get forth before the weather got worse, we kept pushing. I thought we must have a hull leak, as we had to pump the bilges for five minutes every hour. I made sure all through-hull fittings were tight, the shaft and rudder glands were okay, and the cockpit lockers weren't leaking. Two days later, still pumping hourly, I opened the sail locker forward to get a smaller jib ready—and saw a steady stream of water working its way down our chain. I had left the chain secured to our main anchor and had simply stopped the pipe with rags. The sea had taken them quickly, and our hours of pumping were the result.

Just in case, I always keep a mask, snorkel, and a set of fins in the cockpit locker where they are available should an underwater inspection be necessary.

50. Rigging Failure

With modern materials, fair leads on standing rigging, and careful maintenance, rigging failures are rare. When a failure does occur, furthermore, quick reflexes and fast action can often keep the rig standing.

A piece of primary rigging seldom fails without your being aware immediately. Normally there is a loud crack that can only mean one thing. The first concern is to get the spar unloaded as quickly as possible. You will accomplish this by tacking or jibing, depending on the situation, and with luck you'll keep the spar in the boat during the process, which allows the previously slack lee rigging to take up the load while you effect repairs.

The headstay is the least critical piece of major rigging. Many boats have been known to lose the headstay in heavy going uphill and still keep their sticks. The wire luff in the headsail, coupled to the headsail halyard, acts as a backup; even if this is gone, the intermediate forestay and forward lowers will help out.

The backstay, on the other hand, is probably the most critical. If you're sailing downhill in anything but light going, only a quick luff may save the day. Even if you have running backstays, immediate action should be taken as they may not carry the load for long.

Cap shrouds are next; boats have lost cap shrouds and retained their spar, especially on double-spreader rigs. If you tack fast enough you may keep the spar aboard.

Failure in the forward or aft lowers usually gives you some time to act. The after lower is the more highly stressed of the two in most rigs, and its loss will allow the mast to pump. But modern spars will go a long way out of column before buckling, especially when they have conservative wall thickness.

It is essential on any offshore passage to have the rigging tools and materials aboard to effect repairs at sea. This means spare shrouds, Norsemen or StaLok terminals, and a long piece of wire that will serve for the cap shroud, head, or backstay. The spare shroud and long wire should have one end fitting in place, and have measurement points delineated for the other end, depending on what wire it is to replace.

Bulldog clamps will also come in handy, and smaller vessels should have a nicropress tool capable of handling the largest wire aboard, together with sleeves and thimbles. It's amazing how much load can be carried by $3/16''$ to $1/4''$ double-braid line, when it's rove dozens of times between large shackles. In some cases this can substitute for a turnbuckle or make a short piece of rigging do a longer job.

51. Stopping Quickly

There are several reasons why you may want to stop your boat quickly while under sail. Reefs or other obstructions ahead or a man overboard will both require fast action. Taking your vessel's rig and characteristics into consideration, decide how she can be stopped in the shortest time. *Then practice.*

Beating clearly presents the least problem: a quick luff head-to-wind and you're dead in the water. If you're carrying a moderate headsail for the conditions, chances are you'll be able to heave to with complete loss of way, so know your expected direction and rate of drift from previous experience. If you are required to fall off quickly and the wind is up, it may be necessary to ease the main sheet to allow the head to pay off fast enough. Remember that if the headsail is still cleated when you jibe, it will be backed on the new tack.

Stopping the boat when she's running is the most difficult, but even then you can stop in very quick fashion if the boat is properly set up. It is important to have spinnaker pole foreguys and the main boom preventer gear lead aft to the cockpit. This not only eases trimming at sea, but means you can quickly release the preventer if you have to stop. Then you can jibe all standing, and the mainsail will fetch up against the running backstay and force you into the wind against the windage of the now-backed jib on its pole. If you don't have runners and your vang is on the new weather rail, it will do a similar job, providing it is strong enough. If the vang is fastened to the mast base, you will want to trim the main sheet as the boom comes across, before there is a load.

Carrying a spinnaker under the same conditions requires more activity. To begin with, the spinnaker guys, sheets, and halyards should never have their bitter ends made fast or knotted. With all attachment points free to run, cast off the sheet and guy first; then letting go the halyard will free you of the sail (note the order of casting off: never let the halyard go first or you'll end up running it down). However, because of the extra time involved, perhaps a minute, we make it a practice never to carry a spinnaker if we're navigating under conditions that could possibly warrant a quick stop. (We also make it a point always to wear safety harnesses when the chute is up.)

The importance of sharp, well-placed deck knives is not to be underestimated. A sheet or halyard, under load, will part almost instantly if a *sharp* blade is applied.

Once you are stopped, resist the temptation to start the engine until you have checked and double-checked that all lines are aboard. If you don't, the odds are that you'll end up in worse trouble with a mess around the propeller.

5
Navigation

"Caution! The whole of the area on this chart is as yet very imperfectly examined and charted and mariners are cautioned accordingly."

This comment could apply to most of the tropical Pacific Basin and Indian Oceans, the shores of the Red Sea, and many other areas of the world. It might also be amended to include most of the sailing directions cruisers use, as well as lists of lights and radio aids to navigation.

In short, once you leave the "civilized" world for good cruising country, you are left more and more to your own devices for accurate piloting and navigation.

If you learned your navigational skills, as I did, surrounded by RDF beacons, Loran, excellent long-range lights that were kept operating, good charts and piloting data, then sailing into areas without these aids will be a challenge.

With a little luck, a lot of careful watch standing, and help from those who have cruised before you, these challenges to the navigator's skills can safely be overcome.

52. Celestial Navigation

Probably nothing is of more concern to the neophyte offshore cruiser than navigation in general and celestial navigation in particular. The mysteries of celestial navigation are often taught in a manner that would do credit to an advanced calculus professor. Yet in essence, all that is required is a moderately steady arm for using a sextant and the ability to add and subtract. That is the sum total of celestial navigation.

At the beginning of our trip I had the usual qualms about putting

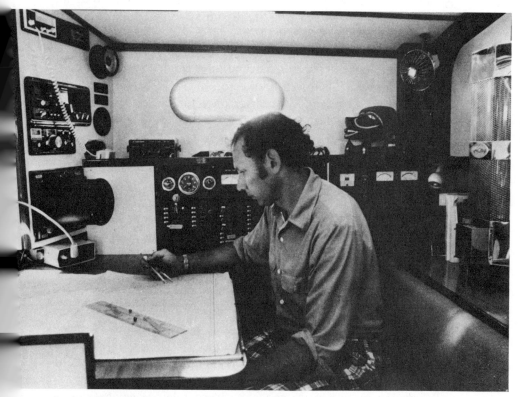

Author Skip Dashew at work in the navigation station of *Intermezzo II.* (Willie Haynal)

my newly learned celestial navigation to work. Our first long passage, 2800 miles of ocean, without landmarks, seemed a daunting proposition. The morning of our 18th day at sea I had gotten a good star fix and was relatively certain of our position. Yet I had a knot in my stomach and a lump in my throat. With the clear conditions we had, Ua Huka in the Marquesas should be visable from 20 miles. We should see it anytime time from 0900 on . . . if we were where I thought we were. I knew perfectly well that it could be a couple of hours before we saw the island, and yet by 0920 I was beginning to sweat. The thrill I felt three minutes later when Ua Huka popped up, right where I had predicted, was one of the greatest of my life.

Three years and three oceans later in the West Indies, I had a little more confidence in my abilities as a navigator. We had been at sea 35 days from Cape Town bound for Tortola. Working from an early-afternoon sun shot, I told Sarah, our seven-year-old, to take a look for land off the port bow. When 10 minutes later she spotted Désirade island, the thrill was still there, big as ever.

The most important factor in navigation of small craft is thoroughness in your work. It is too easy for errors of transposition, addition, or subtraction to creep in. More than once Linda has come over to find out why I was tearing at the few remaining strands of my precious hair, to find me searching for some elusive error in my calculations. Usually she would look at the worksheet and say something like "wasn't it 0400 instead of 0500 when you took the sight?"

Usually in a navigation course you have to solve problems in a much more difficult context than will be the case at sea. Sometimes in the same lesson you will be working in east and west longitude, north and south of the equator, on different days. This means flipping back and forth through the various workbooks and constantly using different formulas. Yet in actual practice, you sail consistently in the same area, perhaps changing the page in the sight reduction tables every other day and the nautical almanac every third day. The sight times will normally be similar day to day, and you will know pretty much how the calculations should turn out. It's easy to tell when an error has been made. In short, it's a lot simpler to navigate a yacht at sea than a desk in a classroom.

When you go to a night school to learn celestial navigation, as Linda and I did, take a correspondance course, or teach yourself, you must practice constantly once you get to sea. Under normal conditions the skill level required with a sextant is minimal. You can expect to have good visibility with which to take sights and make a landfall. Every now and then, however, you do run across poor visibility, and under these situations you must be ready to snap a celestial body that is among the whirling clouds. It may only be visible for a second, and you may not be sure you got it. But perhaps it is your only chance after several days, and you're nearing land. You must have the ability to get a good sight, and the confidence to rely on it. This takes *practice.*

The cruising sailor is faced with another problem in this regard. Months go by in which he uses the sextant constantly. Then he begins to day-sail, or perhaps an ideal anchorage has a grip on his anchor. It may be six months before he uses the sextant again after he hits New Zealand. And yet the landfalls in the Fijis or New Caledonia, after leaving New Zealand, are among the worst in the world. The answer is simply to shoot and shoot and shoot some more. When we start a passage under these conditions, I make it a habit to take at least two rounds of stars, three suns, and a couple of moons every day. If my skill level is reasonably good, I still go for one set of stars and three suns or moons every day.

From all of this practice comes not only manual dexterity, but also confidence in your abilities. Then when a bouncing horizon or poor visibility gives you only a glimpse at a celestial body, you'll be less unhappy having to rely on your quick sight.

53. Passage Planning

Preplanning on the navigational aspects of a voyage is essential for many of the world's best cruising areas.

First, carefully analyze the quality of the charts, pilots, and navigation aids that you have to rely on. Then examine the navigational hazards in each area with attention to those that will require good

Intermezzo with everything set leaving Bali at the start of our Indian Ocean passage. (Mik Madsen)

visibility to negotiate. These factors have to be weighed against the prevailing weather conditions in each area, along with the vessel's ability to get you to there when you expect to.

Intermezzo gave us a fair amount of speed, even in lighter airs. Early in our cruise I got into the habit of doing a time-versus-speed chart for each leg of the projected voyage. By varying our projected speed between 5½ and 7½ knots I could figure out what our options were for arriving at the next destination within the proper time limit.

As an example, take our trip from Sand Fly Passage in the Florida group of the Solomon Islands to Ndina in the Russell group, a distance of 51 miles. The route through Sand Fly Passage had numerous outcroppings of reef to be avoided, and numerous currents and whirlpools. A reasonably high sun angle was required for safe eyeball navigation. On the other end, there were a series of islands to be threaded. Since the sun was north of us and the approach to Ndina would be from the southwest, a late-afternoon arrival would be okay, since the sun would be over our shoulders at the pass. With the spotty trade winds encountered at that point, we didn't feel we could count on more than 5½ knots of boat speed. As a result we would have to allow a little over nine hours, at the worst, for the trip. Allowing for a 1700 arrival at Ndina, we could leave Sand Fly Passage as late as 1000 in the morning; since we could see well by 0900, we were alright.

In the South Pacific there is a strange rumor concerning a cult of moon worshippers in the cruising fraternity. Entire anchorages in the Marquesas and Tuamotus become restless on the approach of a full moon. Tension rises perceptibly in these yacht-filled anchorages, and then, as the full moon appears, the yachts vanish. They are taking advantage of moonlight for making star fixes during the evening, and for better overall visibility to get a start on their next passage.

A little preplanning in the celestial area is also a help. Figure out the relative declinations of the heavenly bodies you intend to use. If you are more or less under the sun, for example, you'll get great longitude LOPs all day long, but you'll be hurting for latitude. If your landfall can be made on a north-south axis, it's a perfect situation. But if you're making an east-west approach, then some additional navigation may be necessary.

It goes without saying that when there is a danger of grounding, or when approaching a partially submerged reef, the ups and downs of local tides must be noted in advance.

In some places it is crucial to know the moon cycle and its relationship to tide and current. Darwin, in northern Australia, is one such area. With 24-foot tides and commensurate currents, weaving your way into that port for the first time during spring tides is to be avoided.

There are other long-term aspects to look at in passaging as well. In journeying from the tropics to temperate climates, you must look to the period between the end of the equinoctial gale season and the start of the cyclonic storm period. Generally there is a month or six weeks in which the odds are most favorable. Late October and early November each year sees an exodus of yachts from the southern hemisphere tropics toward the equator and northern latitudes or south to New Zealand, Australia, or South Africa. Come April or

May, at the end of the cyclone season but before the winter gales, everybody moves back with the sun. (In the northern hemisphere it's just the opposite; November is the time to head for the islands.)

Another way you can avoid trouble by preplanning is to look at the deep-sea charts for underwater ridges or mountains, especially in areas of substantial current. As we mentioned before, for instance, south of Madagascar in the southwestern Indian Ocean the water goes from thousands to a couple of hundred fathoms in a few miles. This geologic upheaval, coupled with strong currents, occasionally produces incredible seas, even in modest weather.

I also like to have a good look at the topographic features of landfalls we expect to make on a passage. If there are mountains with extensive valleys between them, the landfall will first appear as a couple of small islands. If there are some real islands in the area, you may have trouble sorting things out before you get close enough to discern the low ground in between the mountain peaks.

The last thing I do when planning a difficult landfall is to make a list of all the negative things that could happen and then figure out what the proper reactions to them would be to minimize risk and discomfort. Poor visibility, of course, tops the list; then comes current, either favorable or adverse, but in any event unknown; and finally boat speed beyond the normal upper and lower reaches. If the wind gets really light, do we fire up the engine or slow down and wait for the following day? If we're moving too fast, at what point do we slow down or heave to?

Close attention to all these factors before leaving on a passage will make your landfalls a lot more comfortable.

54. Long-Range Navigation Aids

After our own wanderings in some of the worst navigational areas to be found, I have learned (the hard way) several rules to keep in mind.

The first and most important is to *stay alert.* Unless you are well away from any land or known dangers, and to us that means a minimum distance of 100 miles, always have someone on deck keeping a lookout (see Chapters 35, 41, and 42).

As mentioned, the printed aids we have to work with leave much to be desired. Our experience with light lists has shown that they are not to be relied on. The best solution we have found is to radio ahead to fellow cruisers to ask what they have found. Frequently it is possible to get a light list or almanac from the country you are about to visit, via mail. These are sometimes accurate. But even with these data, beware. I remember going to the Marine Office in Honiara, the capital of the Solomon Islands, to get the latest navigation data. We were shown an impressive bulletin board on which were listed the current locations and characteristics of all lights and beacons. We later found that about 30 percent of the time what we saw didn't agree with the bulletin board.

RDF beacons present the same problem. New ones are added, frequencies are changed, and locations are moved without your knowing. We ended up sailing an additional 50 miles through reef-strewn waters when approaching Suva, Fiji, because of reliance on year-old RDF data. The station we were using had the right call sign and frequency alright—but it had been moved.

Pilot books often give you too much of the wrong type of data. They are mostly written for big ships. Frequently the warning material in them doesn't apply to cruisers. Having used both the U.S. pilots and British Admiralty pilots, we have found the latter to be a bit more accurate and relative to our needs. But the data presented must always be taken with a grain of salt, and updated with local knowledge.

Charts must always be used with caution as well. Whenever piloting in difficult areas, we refer to our detailed charts, but we don't rely on them. We have found uncharted reefs and even islands where open water was shown. The answer is to avoid those passages where the data could be in doubt, generally in the poorly charted tropical areas, until you have good eyeball conditions and need the chart only as a general reference.

When cruising offshore in low-traffic areas, be particularly careful. It's not unusual at all to see notations on charts about islands that have been reported to be five or six miles from where they are charted, or reefs that have extended a couple of miles farther off-shore.

By taking all printed material with a grain of salt, keeping good watches, and picking your passage times for weather and moon, you will find successful navigation in the challenging waters of the cruising world a rewarding experience.

Long-range navigation aids can substantially reduce passage times, vessel risk, and crew fatigue. Used properly, with caution, and backed up by other data, they can materially add to the pleasure of offshore passaging.

You must always keep in mind, however, that these devices do not qualify the data they give out. That job is still left to the navigator, and is an essential part of the successful utilization of these new tools.

There is no better way to familiarize yourself with the idiosynchrasies of your navigation aids than to use them in a situation where the data are not critical and can be backed up by other position-fixing means. For example, when we left on our last trip, we were using omega for the first time. Since the initial leg of our cruise was along the coast of Baja California, we were able to check the omega against hourly radar fixes.

Many people we have met cruising in out-of-the-way places will run their omega, Loran, or satellite navigation on a continuous basis for a day or two before departing on their next passage, to verify the accuracy in that particular area of the world.

I am by nature a "nervous navigator." While I have used various electronic navigation aids, my first preference has always been direct observation and/or the sextant. It is our rule on long passages to do at least three celestial sights daily and compare them with the electronic fixes. In this manner we make a continuous quality analysis of the electronic position, so that we are aware of what we have to work with if it becomes necessary to depend on the electronic gear.

We never rely solely on any one navigation aid. If we get consistent readings from two or more pieces of gear, then I relax a little. A careful DR plot is always kept, and any major deviation from that by our electronic gear is cause for a careful review of that data.

Keeping a "worst possible" position vis-à-vis any local dangers, along with where we actually think we are, is another safety feature.

When making landfalls under poor visibility conditions, a set of go/no-go criteria are established taking into account the present reliability of our navigation aids, the relative risks of making a mistake, and the problems of standing offshore until visibility improves.

Perhaps the simplest, and certainly the most popular navigation aid is the depth sounder. The digital-readout units are excellent when working on shore in shallow water, but for navigation I find the recording units better.

Only once in our voyage did the recording fathometer really pay its way: in the Torres Straits between New Guinea and Australia we were able to ascertain our longitude, based on the bottom curves shown on the depth recorder, in an area of dangerous reefs. And yet, I'd carry it again.

Radio direction finders (RDFs) are of some benefit close onshore in many places we visited. However, we've learned to treat RDF fixes with great caution. A bearing error of ± 6 degrees is always allowed for. An RDF can be valuable for homing in on a beacon, but relying on RDF fixes should be avoided if a mistake is going to be costly. One method of improving the accuracy of RDF bearings is with a fixed-loop antenna at the masthead. Friends using this system report that they are able to get quite sharp nulls by pointing their vessel at the beacon.

As a caution, let me relate the story of a friend of ours in a 56-foot schooner. Sitting in Port Moresby in Papua, New Guinea, Charlie was demonstrating the accuracy of his super RDF and explaining how he would use the various stations toward and in the Torres Straits to find Bramble Cay. The set had been reliable in the past and was certainly giving sharp bearings at that moment.

They left a day ahead of us on the passage. When we met up later at Sue Island in the straits, we heard a horror story of having sailed into the entrance of the Fly River, complete with 15-foot breaking seas, after continuous fixes. They were 40 miles north of their intended position.

The next most common aid we have seen is radar. Without a doubt, radar gets my vote as the most useful aid aboard. While not a long-range aid, DR, celestial, or luck can usually get you within the range of today's sets. I would consider 24 miles a minimum range for unfamiliar waters. Power consumption on a sailing vessel really isn't that important as we have usually found that it's not necessary to run the radar continuously for position fixing.

Our approach when making a landfall in the dark or under inclem-

Deerfoot shows off her tilting radar mount near Auckland, New Zealand. Note the satellite navigation antennas on top of the radome and the two SSB antennas on either side. Being able to bring the radar antenna horizontal when sailing substantially extends its range. (S. A. Dashew)

ent conditions via radar is to go within 15 miles of the spot we are seeking via DR or other electronic means, and if no target shows on the radar, we heave to. In practice we have always had target acquisition within the prescribed time, and proceeded on course.

The advantage of radar for making landfalls, especially if you're shorthanded, is not to be underestimated. After a particularly boisterous passage from Ureparapara in the banks toward the Solomon Islands, we raised Santa Cruz just before dusk. Seas were running in

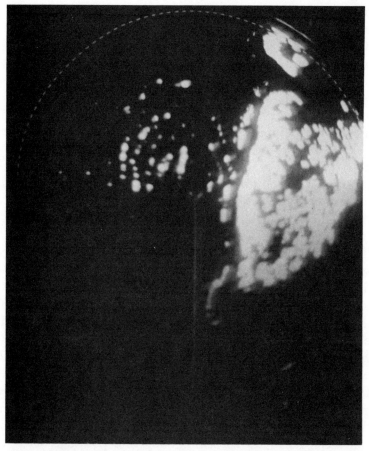

A radar trace of the east side of Vitu Livu in the Fijis. The scattered blips in the lower port section are returns from seas. On the starboard side halfway up the scope an offshore reef can be seen breaking.

the 12- to 15-foot range. By using radar, we were able to work our way around the island, staying three miles off to avoid any dangers, ending up in the lee, hove-to for the evening. Leaving the radar on allowed us to take short catnaps before sun up.

The alternative would have meant heaving to in a rough sea with the possibility of losing contact with the island, waiting for a morning star fix, and then a long sail back.

Another advantage of radar was brought home to us off the coast of Africa. Caught in a severe southwesterly gale in the Aghulas

Current, we found it impossible to keep watch on deck. We were in the middle of the Cape of Good Hope / Persian Gulf shipping lanes, with supertankers going by hourly. During the 36 hours we were pounding forward under storm staysail and mizzen, we contacted ten large ships via VHF that had appeared on our screen, and advised them of our position.

Of the long-range position-finding gear, satellite navigation is for me the most exciting. Several of our cruising friends have acquired this exotic form of guidance and all report that they wouldn't be without it. When a group of us crossed the Indian Ocean together, you could always tell the ones with satellite navigation—they gave their positions down to seconds in our daily radio schedule. Today, with full-function satellite navigators available for under $3000, they are an excellent investment.

The one problem with satellite navigation is the time between passes. In some areas of the world, at certain times you can go as long as nine hours between fixes. On the other hand a fix every nine hours with prudent seamanship and/or a radar will keep you out of trouble. Those using satellite navigation have not experienced the interpretive type of problems found with Loran and omega.

Omega initially came on the scene with a great amount of fanfare as a worldwide navigation system. In the areas where it works well, off the east coast of the United States, for example, we have found consistent fixes within a mile or so. However, there are many other parts of the world where it requires careful analysis and interpretation of the signals received before fixing your position. Where the reception is weak or not totally reliable, automatic lane counters should not be relied on. A strip-chart recorder should be used to count lanes crossed. In this manner, even if you lose tracking for a period of time, with the knowledge of your DR track and a strip-chart record you can interpolate your position.

We have found that the published diurnal correction tables in some areas are off as much as four or five miles. For this reason, when making short passages we have always developed our own diurnal corrections by sitting at a known location for a few days and running the strip-chart recorder.

Since our first *Intermezzo,* fully automatic computer-controlled omegas have come onto the market. They have the ability to select the best stations and automatically make diurnal corrections. Ship captains and large yacht owners who have these machines aboard report that they are generally, but not always, reliable.

Twice after passages of 500 or more miles without a sight, we have been right on our landfall via omega. On the other hand, when approaching dangerous coasts or obstructions, we always assume an error of eight miles to be on the safe side.

Loran C is fantastic if you're in an area where it is operative and if you remember, of course, to watch the corrections and local anomalies. Unfortunately, it's a short-range system, and isn't found in most of the better cruising areas. But at less than $1000 it's hard to beat on a value-for-cost basis.

What about maintenance of these electronic marvels? First, modern gear is generally very reliable. The move toward plug-in circuit boards has eased the potential service problems tremendously. Even in the Solomon Islands or New Guinea you can get air-freight shipments within a week. Most areas have technicians qualified to service radar and radios. Frequently we have found among our cruising friends people qualified to do this type of work. On the other hand, if there is a problem with a satellite navigator or omega receiver, my feeling is that it's better to air-freight it back to the manufacturer. If he's on his toes, you'll have it back within two or three weeks.

A word of caution in ending: A friend of ours put his boat on a reef in the Society Islands while he was below waiting for his radar to warm up. Keep your eyes open!

6
Cruising Life

55. Foreign Officials

Are you apprehensive about dealing with foreign officials? Do you lie awake at night wondering if some beady-eyed and sweaty island republic gendarme will be asking for his mordida? Fear not. Most of the foreign officials we have dealt with around the world have been courteous, efficient, and pleasant. Compared to dealing with many U.S. bureaucrats, in fact, our experiences abroad have been positively uplifting.

Clearing procedures may be time-consuming, and often entail sore feet, but they usually give you a good idea of the local lay of the land by the time you've finished.

Let's start at the beginning. You must have proof of ownership of the vessel. If it is documented in the United States or carries another national flag, there will be formal-looking papers attesting to the ownership. With state registrations, which are a little less daunting in appearance, it may occasionally be more difficult to clear in. Always keep on hand copies of the ownership papers, stowed separately, in case of theft or loss of the originals. It is not unusual for the local Customs official to ask to keep the ship's document until you sail. Sometimes the copies will suffice.

Friendly Customs officers are the rule throughout the cruising world. These two men in Port Sandwich, New Hebrides, were no exception.

A word of caution, if you own a U.S.-documented vessel. If you lose the papers, the U.S. Coast Guard requires a form to be filled out and notarized by a *U.S. notary* before it will issue a new document. If you are in a foreign port and there isn't a U.S. consul around, you're in trouble. Having been through this trying experience with U.S. bureaucracy, I suggest you carry a copy of the form filled out and notarized in advance, just in case.

Every crew member must have a *valid* passport. Check to see that there is plenty of time before the expiration date. We've seen lots of people hopping from foot to foot, trying to enter or leave a country with passports that had expired en route. If you're in an area that doesn't have a consul from your country, you must mail away for the new passport. And in many of the popular cruising spots, mail can take a couple of months.

Know in advance which countries on your itinerary require visas before you can enter, and be sure of where there are embassies or consuls along the route at which you can obtain the visas. For French Polynesia, for example, it is much simpler to get a long-term visa in Los Angeles, San Francisco, or Panama, than when you arrive in Papeete. In New Zealand you can get a six-month visa at any New Zealand consulate in the South Pacific islands. If you should arrive in New Zealand without a visa, it will have to be renewed every 30 days. Most visas must be used within a certain time frame, so be sure you can make it to the country in question before its visa expires.

In addition to visas, some countries require the yellow United Nations health card. This is a record of your inoculations and vaccinations. Requirements vary from place to place, and rarely is the data obtained about your next port of call accurate. Our policy on shots has been, when in doubt, don't.

A few foreign countries require that some form of financial resource be presented upon entering. These regulations seem to be arbitrarily enforced. In Papeete, Tahiti, it wasn't uncommon to see the cruising people pooling their cash each time a new boat arrived, so the local officials would be happy. In 1978 they were requiring $300 per person per month of visa, and not many yachts carry that kind of cash. Frequently, a statement of net worth from an accountant or a letter of introduction from your local bank will go a long way toward alleviating this problem on the few occasions it arises.

The clearing-in procedure varies from port to port. Many countries require you to clear in and out of every port you enter, a tiresome procedure. Others, such as New Zealand and Australia, get you coming in and departing, and leave you be in the interim.

The clearance procedure generally starts with the port doctor, a local physician, who will issue a "practique," or clean bill of health. On occasion it is necessary to certify that no one has died of the plague enroute and other such important medical data. After the medical clearance, the yellow Q flag is removed and if you are on a quarantine buoy, as in Durban, South Africa, you can then move to the docks or normal anchorage. Next aboard will be Customs. They will inspect the vessel if they see fit, but more usually just chat, fill in a few forms, and depart. Customs will want to know if you have liquor, firearms, or narcotics aboard. They will usually give you a form to fill out listing all of these items. Officials in New Zealand and Australia are real paper-pushers. They want you to list every bit of gear aboard, including serial numbers. Since this will happen more than once, it's best to make up in advance an inventory list of cameras, radios, outboards, etc., with serial numbers, makes, and ages, and have copies to attach to the forms in question. The medicine angle is a little bit trickier. Most vessels carry various forms of controlled drugs for emergency purposes. The question is always asked, "Do you have narcotics aboard?" We answer this by supplying a list of all our medical supplies to Customs. They can then make their own decision about what is in the dangerous category in their country. Only in Bali, Indonesia, were any supplies removed from the boat, but they were returned when we cleared out.

If small arms are carried aboard, the easiest way to handle them is to have a lockable cabinet that Customs can seal. Even so, in some areas the officials will take your guns to the local police station until you depart. For this reason it's best to leave really high-quality weapons at home. A gun fancier seeing something special is going to want to try it out. Before New Zealand we had no sealable locker, and we had to trudge to Customs or the police with an armload of artillary on the way in and again on the way out. The sealable locker reduced this nuisance by 75 percent.

Some people feel it better not to declare the guns. I used to feel that way myself until an incident that changed my mind. We were clearing into Papeete, Tahiti. We had lost our ship's document with some other papers in Mexico, and the new one hadn't reached us. As a precaution, the chief of Customs in Papeete asked his men to have a look at *Intermezzo*. I wasn't at all concerned. In fact, I was pleased that they were taking an interest that people really owned their boats. The men were courteous and apologetic as we drove down the quay toward where *Intermezzo* was anchored bow-out with stern to the wall, Mediterranean style. One of the two men took a perfunctory look around at our neat interior and sat down. The second man went forward and a minute later came back with a pained expression on his face. In his hand he held a .38 pistol I had just cleaned and which had been lying in its case on top of the locker in our stateroom. They referred to my Customs forms, filled out originally in Nuka Hiva in the Marquesas Islands, and there were no weapons listed. They shook their heads. "This is bad, very bad," the senior official said. At that point, legally, he had me between a rock and a hard place. Like many cruisers, I hadn't declared the weapons on board. If they wanted to seize *Intermezzo,* I couldn't do a thing about it. If they wanted to fine me an astronomical sum, I had to pay. What could have been a very serious and/or expensive incident ended up costing me a $200 fine. To say I was relieved four weeks later, when I paid the fine and we were allowed to go, is an understatement. After that, you can be sure I declared *everything.*

Remember that you are a guest in the officials' country. You must obey their regulations. If their procedures appear cumbersome and onerous, you have to relax, grin, and bear it. When I got upset about the time it was taking to clear-in somewhere, I used to think about going into the California State Franchise Tax Office to get a question answered—it made the foreign bureaucracies seem efficient by comparison.

The last people you normally see are Immigration. They will stamp the passports and ask you to fill out more forms. On occasion Immigration will ask to hold your passport. It isn't supposed to be done, but it happens. If you're going to be collecting mail or funds from a bank, or cashing travelers checks, you will need the passport as ID. Immigration will usually allow the skipper to keep his passport in these cases.

We have always carried photostats of our passports aboard, again in a separate and safe place from where the passports are generally kept. Having on hand a copy of your birth certificate is also a help in case of losing the passport. We feel it's better for each of the children to have a separate passport.

One last comment on dealing with foreign officials: it helps immeasurably to present yourself and your vessel in a clean, neat manner. We always work very hard as we are coming into a new port to get cleaned up below. If we are going ashore to clear, we try to respect the dress codes in our host country. Generally a skirt or dress is expected for women, and long pants for men.

The last aspect of these procedures is language. Officials dealing with tourists will speak enough English to get their message across. But nothing breaks the ice like a foreign yachtsman *trying* to speak his host's language.

When cruising, you undoubtedly are going to hear stories about official problems in various spots along the way. In late 1976, Mexico was having public relations problems with its yachting visitors. One or two minor stories in *Sea* magazine and an unflattering TV report had cut yacht visits in half. I remember cruisers at the San Diego Yacht Club who, because of these rumors, were going to Hawaii instead of Mexico before turning south for the Marquesas Islands. And yet we found Mexico fantastic, and the officials all helpful and as courteous as any we have met.

We also heard bad reports of officials in Fiji, New Zealand, and Indonesia. Yet in Fiji they were as kind and courteous as you can imagine. We thought we might have a problem when Sarah, then four years old, was attracted to the stamp used to seal our liquor locker. She was unable to resist tearing it off and adding it to her stamp collection. The next day, as we stood at the bus stop in the rain waiting for the bus to town to report the incident, Sarah, concerned at how Customs would react, asked if they put children in jail. She waited outside the office door while Linda explained the situation to the Customs officer, who had trouble keeping a straight face— especially when he called Sarah in and she entered hiding her eyes. In New Zealand we were treated to strawberries and ice cream by the local Customs man, and in Bali, Indonesia, the port captain visited the yachts in Benoa Harbor every week or so to see if there was anything he or his office could do to assist people.

In retrospect, generally, the worse the stories we heard about an area, the better it has turned out to be.

One last point: If you have animals aboard, things can become more complicated. Some countries, like Australia, simply will not allow them ashore. In New Zealand, you can expect to have a vet visit you every day to be sure the animals are still aboard. After a period of time it is possible to get permission to take them ashore, depending on where they have been before. If you're cruising with animals, be prepared for a host of contradictory data from consular offices outside the home country. They always seem to have a different story on current regulations.

56. Getting Along Locally

It is amazing what hunger will do. It will even drive a person with an absolutely deaf ear for language (Skip, for instance) to learn to communicate in a new tongue. And when you get down to it, learning the few words and phrases necessary to make your way in a foreign country isn't that difficult.

First, there are only a few things you really need to be able to say: "hello," "good-bye," "thanks" (and "thanks very much"), "my name is . . ," "what's your name . . ?" "how much is it . . ?" "do you have a better price . . ?" "where is ——?" and so on.

We carried several compact dictionaries, but found that aside from studying them prior to arrival and taking them with us shopping in urban areas, we rarely used them. The day-to-day contact one is forced into with local people when cruising soon gets you on a modest communications basis.

French is the main cruising language, aside from English. It takes care of a great deal of the Pacific and Indian Ocean, where many people who speak another native tongue will speak French if not English.

Pidgin English is a joy to listen to, but takes some getting used to.

An adjustable V-belt sold in many Third World countries. It's useful for low-power applications, and very handy to have aboard.

The best way to get to know "locals" is to ride their public transportation. It's an informative, inexpensive means of getting around, especially on market day. (S. A. Dashew)

It's an essential language in parts of Melanesia. In the Solomons alone, more than 40 languages and dialects are spoken, and Papua, New Guinea, has 700 languages and dialects. So pidgin is the lingua franca. Some of the translations are fantastic. A wood saw, for instance, is "you push him, he go in, you pull him, he come out, he kai-kai [eat] the wood all." A helicopter is "mixmaster belongum Jesus Christ." And my favorite, for a government building in Papua, New Guinea, is "house bullshit."

Where pidgin is spoken there will invariably be someone with a smattering of straight English to translate.

We have found a few rules that help in difficult situations. First, speak very *slowly,* in a normal tone. Remember that the unintelligible rush of a foreign language whizzing past your ears at a mile a minute is exactly what the other fellow hears when you rattle off English to him. And saying something louder does *not* make it easier to understand.

Try to ask a question from several angles, and make sure the answers agree. Avoid asking questions that can be answered yes or no: nobody likes to look as though he doesn't understand when being spoken to, and if a simple yes or no will suffice, many people will use it, even if they're not sure of the question in the first place.

When it comes to buying technical items, where a limited vocabulary won't work, a picture makes all the difference. Al Liggett learned on his first circumnavigation to carry a Sears catalog, and passed this word of wisdom on to us. Armed with this piece of vital gear, you can walk into the local hardware store and point to the item in which you are interested.

We have always been able to find an Anglo or native wherever we've been to help translate if it was really necessary. And there are always schoolchildren anxious to try out their English. But nothing helps get you into the swing of things like making an attempt to communicate in the local tongue. When you are in primitive areas, where languages may vary from island to island, at least pick up "hello," "good-bye," and "thank you." In French Polynesia, learn a few words in Polynesian as well as French. (The best English/ Polynesian dictionary is available from the Mormon church in Salt Lake City, Utah, through their missionary department.) Rarely do outsiders make this small effort, and when you do, it brings immense rewards in the form of acceptance and friendship.

The first thing any cruiser should do after clearing into a foreign port is head for the marketplace to sample the epicurean delights of the new landfall and drink in the incredible blend of smell, color, tastes, and motion of a native market.

It's the norm in most parts of the world to haggle over prices. To some it comes naturally; for others it takes a bit of learning. On occasion the locals look so poor you feel it isn't right to haggle over a few pennies' worth of coconut or papaya, but it's their way of life, and if you don't drive a reasonable bargain you lose respect. Also, it makes it more expensive for the yacht following in your wake.

The difficult part comes in knowing what is a proper price to pay. Short of actual experience, it's tough to decide where to draw the line. Don't make any purchases until you have compared prices. A cruising friend of ours bought a stalk of tangerines for $1 on her way to the market in Tonga, to find them selling for 10¢ at the market itself. We found that the best approach was to quiz locals about the proper price range of various items in the markets before we went. Linda kept a notebook of all purchased items and noted from time to time what we were paying. Armed with this initial bit of intelligence, it wasn't difficult to get down to the base price quickly. In many parts of the world, such as Dempesar, Bali, locals can be engaged to do the bartering for you.

When we buy in the merchant stores, we always ask for a discount. Most of the shopkeepers in the Indian and Pacific Oceans are either Chinese or Indian, and they have a very fine sense of pricing. It pays to shop around, and nothing was ever lost by walking out the door while waiting for a lower price. Numerous times I have been called back when half a block away to be offered something at a price that was rejected while I was standing in a store. After a while, this form of bargaining becomes fun. It's like liar's poker.

As you sail into the more civilized areas for a change of tempo, the pricing game also changes. You're back to the fixed price tags and corporate outlook on merchandising. But there are many levels of pricing in every marketplace, and I always ask for a "trade" or quantity discount. Surprisingly, it's usually granted. "Trade" discounts can run from 15 to 50 percent, depending on the item and area.

Another good deal is to buy things duty or tax free, especially on major items. Most countries have large import duties and sales taxes on retail goods, but a foreign yacht, known to Customs officials as a "yacht in transit," is frequently eligible to buy "bonded stores" or nondutied goods. The most obvious item in this category is spirits. Usually the booze is ordered ahead of the departure date and delivered to Customs. When you leave, Customs puts it aboard, at something on the average of a quarter the normal price. In New Caledonia, you can buy Johnson outboards and Zodiac dinghies at about a 40 percent discount by purchasing out of bond. Also, by presenting your passport, any taxes on over-the-counter purchases are waived by local merchants.

Many of the cruising areas have felt the impact of the general tourist in the past few years. If cruise ships are calling, the locals will have developed a good sense of hype on their native wares. It takes some patience on the part of the cruiser to convince the local people that he isn't in the same class as these wealthy (in local terms) tourists. In the Langa Langa Lagoon on Malaita Island in the Solo-

Port Louis, Mauritius, has one of the most interesting outdoor markets in the world.

mons, so many tourists visit that the artifacts are displayed with *price tags*. After a bit of a discussion you can usually bring the inflated prices on native goods back down to earth.

Tonga is a great example of this. Nowhere else we have been is the commercial instinct so strong as among these gentle Polynesians. Half a dozen cruise ships a year pulling into Nukalofa and Vavau Harbors have generated a demand for large quantities of shell jewelry, carvings, and baskets. As a result the quality of the work has deteriorated, prices have risen, and it's difficult to get the really good items. Yet if you are patient, look over the wares carefully, and bargain a bit, the Tongans will eventually bring around the good work, at a fair price.

Bartering is another game altogether, and the farther into the primitive areas you go, the more successful and fun this form of commerce becomes. (Some of our cruising friends think bartering is good training for their return to civilization, if government mints around the world are going to keep turning their printing presses.)

The value of barter goods is relative, and it is usually cheaper to buy them in quantity at home than at the local level. Find out what the local price is on the items you have to trade, so everyone gets a fair deal. After that, the rules of supply and demand take over.

We have found it best to keep moderate inventories of a limited variety of trade goods aboard. Most prized are sheets and towels. Even very inexpensive sheets and towels are treasured items in the islands. Fathoms of calico (i.e.,) five-foot pieces of colored print cloth) are the best all-around low-value item. Next comes stick tobacco (or cigarettes, depending on the sophistication of the region). Flashlight batteries are always in demand, as are fishing hooks, stainless leader wire, waterproof matches, and light line (³⁄16″ and ¼″). Clothes are one of the best all-around trade items. Many native youngsters have proudly displayed Elyse's or Sarah's shirts resurrected from the "trade" bag. Used clothes are good, but new clothes are the best in many cases. Inexpensive T-shirts and men's shorts go well, but the leader is blue jeans.

We found that the clothes the kids outgrew and we wore out generated enough trading materials, augmented by calico picked up along the way, and tobacco. There is a limit to what can be carried aboard, after all. And don't forget to have small "hostess" gifts for when you are invited ashore—chocolate bars, sweets of any kind, tinned corned beef.

There is a definite technique to overcoming shyness with the locals and getting trade started. The best bet is to attract the children. They are always curious, and in the more remote areas are usually more aggressive in making contact than their elders. A good inventory of bubble gum, cookies, hard candy, and balloons works wonders. Small sets of crayons and paper to go with them are treasured above the stars. Once the ice is broken, the kids are always good for lobster, oysters, crabs, or clams, and will bring coconuts and local fruits if they aren't the personal property of their neighbors. Once the activities have started, the elders will come along.

Trading for foodstuffs is a necessity, but dealing for carvings and artifacts is one of the most interesting aspects of cruising in primitive areas. Once you're off the beaten path, it's possible to find artifacts of excellent quality in many of the villages. Getting the locals to bring the good materials out, however, requires time and patience. You have to acquire a lot of "junk" in the process of lighting the fires of consumerism.

A good example was our stay in the Reef Islands in the southeastern portion of the Solomons. At the time we visited in 1978, the locals saw a yacht perhaps every other year. They are very quiet and shy people, and it took work to get them aboard and talking. After a while people brought things out in their canoes to see if we were interested in buying or trading. Some coconut bowls, then a necklace, a model canoe an old man had been working on were brought. As we acquired these things, more and more people started to go home and look through the rafters. By the time we were ready to leave, a continuous stream of artifacts was working its way aboard. At some point you have to be selective, but it's necessary to start the tide rolling.

Sometimes you will see a beautiful basket or necklace in use and inquire if a trade would be possible. Asking the question empty-handed and asking it with a beautiful new piece of calico on your lap will generate quite different results.

Making friends with the locals, learning how they live, sharing some of their experiences are some of the major reasons to go cruising. It takes work to become accepted. But after that initial shyness is overcome, the people are always curious to see how we live. They're amazed that a miniature house exists within the confines of a small boat. The finish, fabrics, conveniences are a source of wonder and delight. Picture books and maps of your home area are of great interest. *National Geographics* magazines that show your culture are good conversation pieces. Friends of ours had some Fijians aboard who asked them if they believed the stories about men walking on the moon. If they had had the magazines covering the story, they could have shown them photos.

Musical instruments are wonderful icebreakers in many parts of the world. *Intermezzo* carried a veritable band aboard: two guitars, maracas, tamborine, drum, and more. In Polynesia we had some memorable jam sessions. Every native village, even into the heart of New Guinea, has its resident musicians, and the chance to get their hands on a guitar that hasn't been ravaged by the tropics is rare. Our guitar was once borrowed in the Banks Islands to serenade some newlyweds. It has seen many a harrowing canoe trip. If you have a good-quality guitar, take a second as a loaner.

Your own children open another dimension. Elyse and Sarah have found good friends in many of the villages we visited. The local kids are fascinated by our picture books, and it's wonderful to watch them playing with Legos or dolls.

There are usually expeditions to be organized to some point of interest. One of the things to watch out for when going on such an expedition is the local concept of distance. I have never heard a local answer the question "Is it far?" with anything but a negative. If you ask a Marquesan how far it is to those burial caves, and he says two hours, what he means is two hours for him and probably two days for you. We normally use a factor of three or four times the local time estimate to allow for the difference in our leg conditions.

If you are at all handy with tools, which you will be if you've been out some time, repairing outboards, chain saws, or radios is the number one way of making friends. Usually the problems are like those found on board . . . something very simple needs to be put right.

Meeting European colonials is another interesting facet of cruising. After all, you are living the dream of many people who live in the cities you visit for a night on the town and a restocking of the larder; they are continually coming by, staring, and asking questions. It's easy to start up a conversation. An invitation to come aboard and have a look around, and perhaps a drink, is almost always met with enthusiastic acceptance, and later a return invitation to visit on shore. Perhaps a drive around the countryside will be offered, or the use of a washing machine awaits.

With a less hurried lifestyle than found in the cosmopolitan areas, it's much easier to break down the artificial barriers we seem to build up at home. We have friends on the islands around the world who after only a few weeks of contact remain as dear to us as lifelong friends back home.

You can expect hospitality on a very large scale to be laid on for you. Continuous visits ashore, perhaps the use of a car, even a stay for a week or two in your new friend's home ashore are not unusual. It is impossible to reciprocate in kind from a small vessel, but sharing your adventure makes up for a lot. A dinner aboard, routine to you, can be the event of a year for a shorebound dreamer, and a short afternoon sail. . . .

One of the things we wished we had taken with us is a slide projector. A presentation of the home country to our native friends and the places on our journey to our European acquantances, via slides, would be a wonderful way to entertain. A Polaroid camera is also a good investment. In many parts of the world it's considered a miracle of some magnitude to be able to produce an instant photographic reproduction. In the "if we were doing it again" category comes black-and-white photography. We would definitely carry on board simple gear to develop our own black-and-white photographs. To be able to give an 8 × 10 photo to guests as a souvenir of their visit aboard would be priceless.

Going ashore in primitive areas involves some special guidelines. In many parts of the world, especially traditional Polynesian islands, it is considered bad taste to become friends with anyone before the chief has been visited. It's customary in many Fijian villages to send a gift to the chief (usually kava root or tobacco) and ask permission to visit the village before coming ashore.

On Tikopea Island, at the extreme southeastern end of the Solomon group, it is bad form to turn your back to the island chief.

It's not difficult to get a handle on local customs as you clear into a new ethnic region. Most big ports will have a library or museum where inquiries can be made.

For women there are taboo areas in many Melanesian villages. It wasn't so long ago that the penalty for trespass was instant death.

You must be careful of expressing admiration for a host's possessions: in many places you will instantly be presented with the admired item. In the Tuamotus this created some embarrassing situations for us until we learned the system.

It is not unusual to run into "official greeters" in many of the out-of-the-way places where yachts have visited before. These self-appointed guardians of the cruiser's interests can provide an introduction to island life and customs, usually with passable English. On the other hand they are sometimes possessive, and can be a bit of a problem. If you check among the yachts that have visited your next stop, you'll usually be able to pick up the names of these chaps, and find out if they are a benefit or a hindrance.

The matter of privacy presents a problem in some primitive cruising grounds. In some parts of the world, the concept of individual privacy is quite different .from our own. Where some locals might have to be coaxed aboard, others will come clambering aboard all day long. It's not unusual for one or two local "fr· ends" to attach themselves to you and your boat more or less permanently. When you want to have some time to yourself, it may be difficult to invite your guests to leave. We have found that the easiest approach is to be direct. Simply state that it is time for you to work, and that your guest must leave for the day.

In Takaroa, in the Tuamotus, *Intermezzo*'s musical instruments were the centerpiece of nightly jam sessions with our Polynesian friends. But if Linda or I so much as yawned, the group would quit playing at once, return the instruments, and pad off quietly to their homes. On other occasions there is no remedy except to find a quiet, uninhabited anchorage.

The best "crowd control" device we have seen is a dog. If you have one aboard, your local friends will circle at a distance in their canoes. The dog will usually have to be put below before they'll come aboard. And if it's time for him to come on deck for exercise, well, that's a good signal to desert ship.

57. Provisioning

The focal point on most boats is the galley. All eyes turn toward the galley three times a day. With planning and preparation, the cook's job of turning out appetizing, nutritious meals, even under adverse

Things haven't changed much in some of the cruising spots we have visited
from when this photo was taken 30 years ago. (S. A. Dashew)

conditions, can be relatively easy. In 3½ years and 30,000 miles of
cruising, we missed only one hot meal on *Intermezzo*. We celebrated
holidays at sea with fancy meals, always had our traditional turkey
at Thanksgiving and Christmas (including all the trimmings), tried
new foods discovered along the way, and enjoyed our favorite recipes
from home. Here are our recommendations for approaching the task
of provisioning.

Before that first cruise, figure out how long you'll be gone and
what types of food will be available along the way. Know the
capabilities of your refrigeration system or icebox, test your oven for
baking, and work out the precise amount of storage area available.
Keep track of your menus at home for a while to determine: How
many times do you serve meat a week, and what kinds? Vegetables?

Fruits? How much bread will you need, and how much of it can you bake along the way? What other baking will you do? How much flour will it take? (Self-rising flour obviates baking powder and salt in many recipes.) If you're going for a short time, plan to use the prepackaged baking mixes. How many eggs do you serve per week, including those used in baking? (Powdered eggs work well in baking recipes.)

What staples do you use? How fast do you go through a jar of mayonnaise? (Be sure to take all you need of this product, for it's hard to find outside the U.S.) How much cooking oil do you use, and how much shortening for baking? How much sugar do you use, including what you'll use for powdered drinks? Do you use it in coffee, on cereal? How much brown sugar and powdered sugar do you require for baking? Do you use honey as a sweetener? Figure your requirements for baking soda, powder, yeast; and go through your recipes to make up a thorough list of spices and herbs. Be complete with the spice list, as many of them will be hard to find in out-of-the-way places. Buy extra bay leaves to put in bulk flour (bay leaves help keep out weevils). Start with fresh spices and herbs, as they have a finite shelf life.

Now for drinks. How much coffee do you consume? How will you brew it—stovetop perk or drip, or instant, or do you have power aboard for an electric perk? Do you drink tea? What about powdered drinks, including tea mixes and fruit punch? What about milk? Australia has a good-tasting Long Life Milk product available in areas of the Pacific and Indian Oceans (it's also available in South Africa). It comes packaged in paper milk cartons and doesn't need refrigeration. Canned evaporated milk is good for recipes and for making yogurt, but the most popular among yachts is powdered milk. Powdered whole milk tastes better than nonfat, but in the U.S. it's hard to find. If you must use the nonfat powdered milk, add a teaspoon or two of nondairy creamer. Powdered milk tastes best if mixed up ahead of time and chilled. A blender is best to use for mixing. Children like it with chocolate powder added, and warmed up it's good on night watches. Put marshmallows on the list, to serve on top of the hot milk and for roasting over campfires ashore or over a charcoal broiler.

Choose your type of fruit juices, and determine how many servings you'll need per day. Canned fruit juices take a lot of space, but are

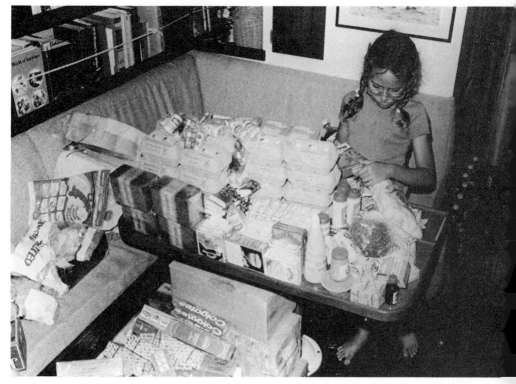

Elyse helps provision for our 6000-mile Cape Town-to-Tortola trip aboard *Intermezzo.*

good. Frozen juices are delicious if you have a freezer and space, but you'll probably find the powdered variety, like Tang, the most practical.

How much soda pop will you require? Cans are bulky for storage, and aluminum ones are short lived in a salty environment. We ordered a case of two-liter plastic bottles of Coke for our Atlantic crossing, and it tasted awfully good every night around 1700, with lots of ice. Soda and mixes are generally available throughout the world. Or take your own carbonation and syrups to mix your own. How much beer, if any, will you want on board? (If you're a dedicated beer drinker, one of the joys of cruising is sampling the incredible variety of beers to be found in the ports of the world; but it's not good being hooked on your favorite brand—chances are you won't find it a few hundred miles from home.) Will you carry wine? If it's not practical to carry a large supply, you may want to follow the tradition of breaking out a bottle at each new port. Think about including a bottle or two of champagne to celebrate special occasions, like New Year's Eve and wedding anniversaries. Will you be stocking a bar? Hard liquor can often be bought duty free when you're clearing out of a major port. (This goes for tobacco as well.)

For breakfast, hot cereals store well. Cold cereals must be packaged properly: Familia in its foil pack will keep for months, but light, airy cereals tend to get soggy, take up a lot of space, and go buggy fast. Eggs and pancakes with syrup taste good, along with canned fruit, fried potatoes, and bacon. French toast is a good way to use stale leftover bread. Look for a stovetop waffle iron (Nordic Ware makes a good stovetop Belgian waffler).

How many pounds of butter or margerine do you use weekly? Margerine stores better without refrigeration than butter, but many out-of-the-way places sell tinned butter.

Go through your cupboards and make a note of all the condiments. Your list will probably include plain vinegar and wine vinegar, peanut butter, jam, jelly, ketchup, mustard, pickles, soy sauce, Worchestershire sauce, and Tabasco. Include items like parmesan cheese, tomato sauce or paste, maple syrup, and bottled lemon juice (for those fish you catch when you don't have fresh lemons on hand). Include pimentoes, olives, and maybe marinated artichokes to dress up a plain salad. Don't forget birthday candles if you'll be out any length of time. (We devoted an entire shelf to peanut butter because of the captain's and third mate's affinity for it.)

Think about snacks. Dried fruit and raisins taste great at sea, and are nutritious. See about buying raw nuts direct from health-food stores, and ask about having them sealed in cans for longevity. Will you want canned walnuts for baking recipes? Popcorn goes a long way, and it's fun to serve in the islands. We've had island children aboard whose eyes grew big as they watched the transformation as the corn popped. And in Takaroa, in the Tuamotus, we popped corn for the entire village for a party we held one night, working in relays with Dean Kewish. Look for well-packaged crackers that will stay crisp. Metal tins with tight-fitting lids are best. When you get to a spot where they sell ship's crackers, buy some. They're hard to chew, but taste good and are filling. The tins they come in, once emptied, are handy for storing other things.

You may want to include packaged or canned puddings, and Jell-o if you have refrigeration. Will you need mixes of nondairy whipped toppings for desserts? Do you use packaged salad dressing mixes, or packaged chili or taco spices. Do you bake with chocolate? Canned cocoa stores better than chocolate squares. Hard candies are good for appeasing a sweet tooth while underway. You may want a supply of candy bars to break out for special treats. (Note: Chocolate chips are scarce outside "civilization.")

Will you take canned or freeze-dried vegetables? We'd recommend using a combination. The beauty of freeze-dried goods is that they taste fresher, are light, and are available in a great variety, including things like chopped green pepper that you can't find canned. On the other hand, freeze-dried foods require fresh water for cooking, and are harder to digest. When researching freeze-dried products, ask about sprouters. It's easy to raise alfalfa and mung seeds underway, and their crunchiness is appreciated when the lettuce runs low.

Use canned fruits and meat if you don't have a freezer. With refrigeration or an icebox you can start out with fresh meat. If you have difficulty finding canned meat, ask your supermarket manager. He may get it for you, or give you an address to write direct. You can get roast beef, corned beef, ham, pork, chicken, turkey, and spare ribs. Danika hams are available worldwide. (When buying canned ham, be sure it states on the label that no refrigeration is needed.) You'll probably want canned tuna and maybe some stew or chili. Canned bacon can be a real treat, although it's hard to find and expensive.

Many cruisers can their own meat. This way they know the quality of the meat, and canned unseasoned hamburger, beef, or pork chunks can be added directly to recipes. Long-term cruisers should consider putting canning equipment aboard to take advantage of good buys along the way.

If you have a freezer, ask the butcher to flash-freeze your meat so that it's rock hard when you put it aboard. Chops, steaks, sausages, and hamburger cook quickly, but plan to include a few roasts too, for special dinners. Chickens are always good, although they take up a lot of freezer space. We eased the space problem when we bought

24 chickens in Darwin, Australia, by cutting them in quarters before stowing.

Beef may be pricing itself off menus in the U.S., but it's still reasonable in other countries, including New Zealand, Australia, South Africa, and many islands with local beef production. We were able to fill our freezer with 110 lbs of choice cuts of beef for $60 at a plantation butchery in the Solomons in 1978.

If you can find an economical silverside cut you may want to try making beef jerky. Nancy Wolfe on *Rhodora* taught us how in Honiara. Slice a nonfatty, boneless roast into very thin strips, about two inches wide. Marinate them for a few hours in soy sauce seasoned with pepper, garlic, and a little fresh ginger. Spread the beef in the hot sun, bringing it in at night and protecting it from moisture. In two days you will have a delicious snack that will keep indefinitely in an airtight container.

Consider the soy bean protein meat substitute. And for added protein, plan to use dried beans and lentils. The problem with cooking dried beans on a propane stove is that they require hours of slow simmering, so those with a primary propane cooking system should consider carrying a small portable kerosene unit as a backup.

When purchasing canned fruit, make a list of each type you'll use and test a few brands before buying by the case lot. Not only are they great for desserts and breakfast but they're good to add to fresh fruit salads. Don't forget to include a few cans of berries, apple slices, and cherries for special pies and cobblers. Be aware, though, that canned berries don't last as long as other canned foods; about 9 to 12 months is the maximum.

On the vegetable list, include mushrooms, kidney beans, garbanzas, and olives, which can be used in casseroles and for jazzing up salads. Specialty foods like canned pumpkin pie filling, yams, and cranberries make good treats. Do you like Mexican food? Then add green chilis, salsa, and refried beans.

The pasta list will include rice, spaghetti, noodles, and macaroni. And you might think about using dried potato flakes. We were always able to find fresh potatoes, so we never carried the dry variety, but it may be convenient for mashed potatoes. South Africa was the only country we visited where cornmeal was available.

Processed cheese does not need refrigeration. Wax-covered cheese keeps well if it's kept cool, and fresh cheese can be stored by wrapping it in vinegar-soaked cheesecloth. We always kept a lot of cheese aboard, finding it great in cooking, and for snacks and entertaining. You can find both processed and refrigerated brands of cheese everywhere you go in the world.

When stocking up on bread, ask to have it double baked. It lasts for weeks. We discovered a heavy wheat-germ and cereal loaf under the Aida brand in South Africa that has long life and stays good until its plastic wrapper is opened. With refrigeration and freezer space, you can take bread enough for an entire passage. A great treat in new countries is finding the bakeries and sampling their bread. One of our best recollections of Mexico is waiting at the bakery for the bread and pastries to come out of the oven.

If you decide to bake your own bread aboard, use aluminum or glass bread pans, as they won't rust; bread can be baked in a pressure cooker too. Biscuits and muffins are good, quick bread substitutes.

Soups always taste good at sea or at anchor. The dried soups are easier to store than the canned variety. Carry some Cup a Soup for fast pick-me-ups on late-night watches.

There are several nonfood items you should buy in bulk: toilet paper, paper towels (these are hard and expensive to replace), napkins, detergent (Joy works best in salt water and is fine for overboard shampoos), face soap, bug spray (like Cutter's) toothpaste, deodorant, shampoo and conditioner, cockroach spray (don't scream, sooner or later you're going to see one). We take paper plates along with woven bamboo plate holders for beach picnics.

Just before departure, buy the fresh produce. Potatoes and onions head the list as long-term staples. If bought fresh and unrefrigerated, stored in baskets or on shelves with good ventilation where air can circulate around them, they last three to four months. Pumpkins and squashes come second. Then come cabbage, beet root, and carrots. (If a cabbage starts to go bad on you, cut away the slimy part, being careful not to infect the remaining good part.) All of these have quite long shelf lives without refrigeration.

Some fruits keep well if bought fresh and kept cool. We had one batch of pamplemousse (the Polynesian grapefruit) stored under the floorboards of the galley for two months. On the other hand, before leaving Cape Town we used the method of tightly wrapping oranges and lemons in foil, which is supposed to guarantee at least two or three weeks' freshness, and lost 75 percent of our citrus one week out to sea. The large bag of apples purchased direct from the orchard in Bay of Islands, New Zealand, lasted five weeks. Green bananas and plantains (the cooking variety) may take up to a week to ripen, but once ripe, must be used quickly.

With refrigeration, carrots, beans, eggplant, green avocadoes, green tomatoes, and citrus fruit keep about three weeks. Lettuce will keep up to six weeks if you buy it *unwashed,* wrap it in newspaper, then place in a plastic bag, refrigerate it, and change the newspaper weekly. You might lose a few outside leaves, but that's all.

Celery and red tomatoes, even refrigerated, are short-term items.

Salamis can be hung, but will often drip grease or develop a mold that must be cut off. It's better to refrigerate them as well.

Eggs keep very well without refrigeration if you buy them fresh and unrefrigerated. The shell must be sealed, either from the outside by rubbing it with Vaseline, or from the inside by dipping it in boiling water for five seconds. Then keep the inside of the shell moist by turning it once a week. We've never needed to use these methods, because we start moving the eggs into the reefer as soon as we "eat down" our cold inventory to make more room.

Once your list is complete, start comparing prices. Talk to the market managers about quantity discounts. Some stores will deliver to the boat as well. See about buying wholesale. Many countries have wholesale warehouses that will sell direct to foreign yachts.

When it comes time to stow the provisions, make a sketch of the boat interior and label the storage areas. Allow for easy-access storage in the immediate galley. Make a notebook listing the type of food, where it is stored, and the quantity. Check off the items as they're used. Then when it comes time to reprovision, you can tell at a glance what you need.

If you have space around the water heater, it makes a great place for storing flour and pastas, crackers, and cereals. The dry heat keeps them fresh.

Never bring a cardboard carton aboard. Always remove the contents on deck and quickly discard the cardboard carton. Cockroaches like to lay their eggs there. If you must bring cardboard cartons aboard, spray them first with insecticide. If canned goods are stored where they might get wet, remove the labels, then varnish and mark the cans. Aboard *Intermezzo* we never bothered with these procedures because the cans stayed dry and rust was not a problem.

58. Foreign Marketing

Once you leave home, what will you find in the way of fresh produce? In industrialized countries you'll do most of your marketing in supermarkets. In some countries, such as New Zealand, you can actually pick your own fruit in selected orchards.

You'll also find supermarkets in many nonindustrialized, or Third World countries. But the trick is to find one that is air-conditioned, since the shelf stock keeps better. Still, you must examine the products carefully. Peek under boxtops; if you see little cobwebs, don't buy. Cobwebs are a sure sign of movable forms of protein. Check for weevils or bugs in the flour and rice. In some of the islands in the Pacific, flour is packaged in airtight tins, guaranteeing freshness.

But in these countries the most economical and most fun way to shop is in the native markets, where you'll find the biggest selection of fresh goods. Once you clear into port, ask where the open-air market is located. What day and time are best to attend? In Noumea, New Caledonia, for instance, the best shopping is at 5 A.M. on Sunday. In Rabaul, Papua, New Guinea, things are more civilized: Saturday morning at 9 A.M. is the time.

The people you deal with are usually friendly, helpful, and courteous. If you see a food that is new to you—and chances are you will —they'll gladly tell you what it is and how to prepare it. They're interested in what you're doing too,

Native markets are established in all major population centers and in many smaller villages as well. If local transportation is available, the odds are the bus line will end at the market. If there is no public transportation, you may want to arrange to share a cab with a fellow yachtsman.

These markets are not equipped to package your purchases, so

This native market could be in almost any good cruising spot. (S. A. Dashew)

take your own containers. A two-wheeled cart is excellent for getting produce back to the boat. Heavy canvas ice bags work well, as do the stretchable woven shoulder bags called billums in New Guinea. Take extra plastic bags along for herbs and crushables such as tomatoes and ripe avocadoes. Eggs will not be sold packaged, so take containers for them as well.

You will need plenty of small change in local currency. It saves confusion if you pay with correct change.

Your senses will be overwhelmed with the colors, sights, and sounds. The food all comes direct from people's gardens and is much fresher and tastier than what you might be used to. Sanitary conditions have always been acceptable, in our experience.

How will you know how much to pay for items if they're not marked? Ask locals ahead of time what they're used to paying, and make a note of prices. A notebook comes in handy for jotting down prices in a foreign language also. If you have the venders write the price for you, it's often easier than the spoken word if the language is new to you. In some places things are easy: in Vavau, Tonga, for instance, almost everything sold for 10¢.

What kinds of food are you likely to find in a tropical open-air market? Usually you find all or some of the following: tomatoes, cabbage, Chinese cabbage, green beans, egg plant; and very often beet root, carrots, onions, potatoes, a tropical potato called kumera (similar to a sweet potato), and taro, a starch root popular on many islands. The fruit will most likely include bananas in various eating and cooking varieties, coconut in drinking and eating varieties, papaya, mango, pineapple, varieties of watermelon, and citrus fruits, including a brown-skinned orange (very sweet and juicy) and bush limes rather than lemons. There's nothing quite as good as a Polynesian pamplemousse, and frequently you'll find avocado. I'll never forget our first taste of papaya from the market in Puerta Vallarta, Mexico. You're in for a real treat when you sample these tropical fruits. Lichee nuts, star fruit, and the great Indonesian variety of fruits are fabulous.

We were introduced to breadfruit in the Marquesas. In season, they are available on all the islands. Sliced and french-fried, they're similar to potatoes. This staple of the islands has a delicate flavor and can be roasted, boiled, and made into a soup. Here is Cheryl Schmidt's recipe for her exceptional Breadfruit Soup:

Breadfruit Soup

2 oz. butter	1½ pints chicken stock
4 oz. onion (chopped)	1 teaspoon salt
1 teaspoon garlic (chopped)	¼ teaspoon pepper
6 oz. peeled, cored, finely chopped breadfruit	⅜ pint cream or milk (optional 2½ teaspoons chopped chives)

Melt the butter, add the chopped onion and garlic, and cook for 5 minutes. Add the breadfruit and chicken stock, cover the pot, and simmer for 20 minutes. Then pour into a blender or puree by pushing through a collander. Add the cream or milk, put back in the pot, and heat—but do not boil.

Coconut is delicious eaten raw, and the water is good to drink. If you shred the meat and squeeze it through a piece of cheesecloth, you'll get a cream that is wonderful in various fish and vegetable dishes, such as Poisson Cru. We were first served this dish at a picnic on the beach in the Marquesas Islands. It was prepared right at the beach with ingredients that were either right at hand or had been brought. The fish was caught fresh, the coconuts were picked from a tree, the limes and sweet green peppers, scallions, and tomatoes were brought in a small woven basket. There are many variations of this recipe.

Poisson Cru

Fish Marinated in Lime Juice with Onions

To serve 6

2 lbs. skinned, boneless, fresh, whitefish steaks, cut 1½ inches thick

1 cup strained fresh lime juice

½ cup coarsely chopped onions

2 teaspoons salt

½ cup coarsely chopped scallions, including 2 inches of the green tops

¼ cup coarsely chopped sweet green bell peppers

1 cup rich coconut milk

With a cleaver or large, sharp knife, cut the steaks lengthwise into ¼"-thick slices, then cut each slice into pieces 1½" square.

In a deep bowl, mix the lime juice, onions, and salt together. Drop in the fish and turn it about with a spoon until the strips are evenly coated. Cover and marinate at room temperature for at least two hours, or in the refrigerator for three to four hours, stirring the fish occasionally.

When done, the fish will be opaque and fairly firm, indicating that it is fully "cooked." Taste to make sure; if it seems underdone, marinate it for an hour or so longer.

To serve, drain the fish and squeeze it slightly to remove all the excess moisture. Place the fish in a serving bowl, add the scallions, green peppers, and coconut milk, and toss them all together gently and thoroughly. You may also add celery or other "crunchy"-type vegetables according to taste and availability.

To prepare the Coconut milk, pare the brown skin and chop or break the meat of a mature coconut into small chunks. To make the coconut milk by hand, begin by grating the peeled coconut, piece by piece, into a bowl, then adding a small amount of warm water (only a few drops of water are used in the Pacific for a rich, thick "cream").

Scrape the entire contents of the bowl into a fine sieve lined with a double thickness of dampened cheesecloth and set over a deep bowl. With a wooden spoon, press down hard on the coconut to extract as much liquid as possible. Bring the ends of the cheesecloth together to enclose the pulp and wring the ends vigorously to squeeze out the remaining liquid. Discard the pulp. One cup of coarsely chopped coconut meat combined with one cup of hot water should produce one cup of coconut milk. The creamier Pacific version, using less water, requires slightly more grated coconut for one cup. An average coconut weighs about 1½ lbs. and will yield from three to four cups of chopped or grated meat.

To open the coconut, puncture two of the three eyes of the coconut by hammering the sharp tip of an icepick or screwdriver through them. Drain the coconut water (and save it if you wish to use it as a beverage). Hold the coconut with one hand, and with the other, give the shell a sharp blow with a hammer or the back of a cleaver a little more than a third of the way down from the top. Turn the coconut an inch or two and tap again. Keep on turning and tapping until you hear the sound of the shell cracking. A thin, visible crack should run all around the shell now, and the top of the nut can easily be pried up.

Cumera, or green peppers, are often available, as well as a variety of cucumbers, including the small pickling size. If you're hungry for crisp, sour pickles, try Beth Liggett's recipe. The beauty of this recipe is that there's no cooking involved.

Dill Pickles

2 quart jars
small, firm cucumbers
2 teaspoons dill seed *or* 4
  heads of fresh dill
(optional: 2 to 4 cloves
garlic, peeled)

1½ cups vinegar
2 cups water
¼ cup (scant) salt

Use enough small, firm cucumbers to fill two quart jars. Wash and cut cucumbers into 1½″ chunks, or slice lengthwise into quarters (do not peel). Pack the cucumbers into the quart jars and, for each jar, add 1 teaspoon dill seed (or 2 heads fresh dill) and (optional) 1 or 2 cloves of the garlic.

Bring the vinegar, water, and salt to a boil and pour the fluid over the cucumbers and spices in the jars. Seal the jars and let set for two days in the refrigerator.

In those areas with an Indian population, the smell of curry spices will drive you wild, particularly in Fiji and Mauritius. After purchasing all the curry spices, we got a curry recipe book, and the tastes were delicious. Use your mangoes to make a chutney to accompany these dishes.

We often found raw peanuts, and in the Solomons and New Guinea we discovered nolly nuts, a cross between almonds and macadamias in taste; they're excellent raw or roasted.

Fresh herbs are usually available in the French islands—such as the Marquesas, Tuamotus, Society Islands, New Caledonia, and the New Hebrides. And where there are French people, can baguettes be far away? These crisp, delectable loaves of bread are irresistible. We always bought twice the amount we wanted on board, knowing full well that they would be half eaten by the time we got back to the boat.

Many of these markets also offer a large selection of baskets and handiwork.

To find the temperate-climate fruits and vegetables of home, you will have to go to the supermarkets. But things like broccoli, cauliflower, or strawberries will have been flown in and will cost a fortune.

We paid more than $3 for a small cup of strawberries in Papeete in 1977. It was Skip's birthday and we splurged for a strawberry short-cake. That's why it's so exciting to come from a tropical country to a nontropical country like New Zealand, the States, or South Africa. You go crazy for the temperate-climate fruits and vegetables.

Meat, poultry, and cheeses, plus dry goods, are always available in one form or another. Often the meat will have been frozen and flown in from another country.

The fact that you can't depend on finding what you want all the time makes each new discovery a thrill, and makes each provisioning trip to another market a fresh adventure.

Whenever we buy fresh produce in a nonindustrialized country, we take the precaution of washing everything in a potassium permanganate solution before eating. (It's also a good idea to give things a quick rinse off to rid them of possible spiders or cockroaches *before* taking them aboard. These pests particularly like to hide in pineapples and bananas.) Potassium permanganate crystals, available from a pharmacist, turns water purple and stains the hands. A little bit goes a long way: just a few crystals, dissolved in a pot of water, will destroy any bacteria on the food you're rinsing. The stains wash off your hands after a few hours, but because of the mess some people prefer to use a mild chlorine bleach and water solution instead of the potassium permanganate. We prefer the latter because it doesn't affect the taste of the food. After the "treatment," rinse your vegetables in fresh water to remove the chemicals.

One of the pluses of traveling by yacht is that it introduces you to new countries on a more personal level than by other means of travel. And shopping locally, native style, is one of the best ways to capture the essence of a new culture.

59. Galley Equipment

You've organized the provisions and know where you're going to stow them. But what about the galley equipment? Do you have all the tools you'll need? Make another list. It should include a handmixer or wire whip, wooden spoons, cheese grater, garlic press, a heavy, geared can opener (it's really important to get a good one), potato masher, measuring spoons, measuring cup, a good set of sharp knives (try to limit them to galley use), a sharpening stone for the knives, kitchen shears, poultry shears, spatulas, corkscrew, bottle opener, nutcracker, cheese slicer, food steamer (to sit inside a saucepan), lime squeezer, potato peeler.

For baking you'll want to include all or most of the following: stainless mixing bowls, cake pans (including angel tube pan and bundt pan if you use them at home), pie tins, casseroles, bread pans, cookie sheets, muffin tin, stovetop waffle iron. For the stove you'll need deep stainless saucepans with lids in a variety of sizes, a double boiler, pressure cooker, large and small fry pan (we used Linda's favorite cast-iron pan with no rust problem), a small saucepan for melting butter, making sauces, and a roasting pan. If you don't have a broiler oven, look for a stovetop skillet broiler. It's smooth on one side for grilling and has ridges on the other side for broiling,

For serving dishes you'll want a cheese and cutting board, a good-size tray for transferring drinks or snacks topside, nut bowls, salad bowl with servers, vegetable serving dishes, gravy bowl and ladle, salt and pepper shakers. The latter should be a type like Tupperware, which has a lid to seal out moisture. Salt flows more freely if you mix a little rice with the salt in the shaker (the rice absorbs the moisture). You'll want a pitcher, fruit basket, and bread basket.

If your galley has electricity, stow an electric handmixer (uses about 200 watts) and a blender (uses around 350 watts). They can be run off an inexpensive inverter and use little battery power.

Another handy item is a vacuum flask for storing cold water in hot weather and hot water in cold weather. The vacuum flask allows you to pour one drink at a time at the push of a finger, eliminating the need to open and close the reefer or light the stove.

You'll need good storage containers in a variety of sizes. Tupperware holds up the best. We found a bag sealer came in handy, and used it for sealing food for the freezer, as well as spare parts, important papers, etc.

What about dishes? You'll want a sturdy set, but if you're planning on living aboard for a long time, you may get tired of plastic, as we did. The Heller brand is popular, and the lip on the plates eliminates spills when the boat is heeled over. But the plates scratch with repeated use. Other choices would be a heavy ironstone, pewter, or a Corningwear dish that is break resistant. You may want to consider something nicer. After a year's cruising, we asked Skip's parents to bring a six-place setting of our china and silver when they came to visit in New Zealand. We stowed them very carefully while underway, wrapped in towels and wedged onto a shelf. In port it was nice to be able to bring out the china for special occasions.

Mugs are handier on board than cups and saucers. Plastic ones tend to crack, so look for heavy pottery. They can always be used as flower vases while in port. We used cheap wine glasses, replacing them as they inevitably broke, and for glassware you can choose among plastic or shatterproof glass.

Other niceties that even a weekender could tuck in are a colorful tablecloth, pretty placemats, and small glass candle holders.

Keep a small flashlight handy to the galley for searching through lockers and reefers.

60. Precooking Meals for Underway

Before leaving port for a passage, it's a good idea to cook ahead of time a roast, spaghetti sauce, a couple of chickens, a casserole, or a stew. Then food will be available for the first day or two while everyone, including the cook, gets his sea legs. Carol Marriott on *Makaretu* made stacks of sandwiches for lunches and stored them in the reefer. Each crew member could choose his own with no bother for the cook. Sue Moesly on *Svea* never leaves port without a fresh and abundant supply of homemade cookies. A large potato or macaroni salad is easy to prepare ahead of time. Some cooks prepare and freeze several casseroles. I prebaked and froze a birthday cake for Sarah's seventh birthday, which took place at sea between Mauritius and South Africa.

If you have two or three meals precooked and still feel like cooking the first day or two, go ahead and cook, saving the prepared dishes for emergencies.

Preparing meals for a short cruise allows the cook more time to enjoy the sailing. And be sure to include extras so if the mood moves you to invite someone from the anchorage over for dinner, there will be plenty.

61. Personal Grooming in the Tropics

Cool and neat are the key words for dress in the tropics. And "cool clothing" in a temperate zone may not feel so cool when worn in the tropical heat. Men's shorts should be slightly shorter than the standard Bermuda length, and of the lightest weight fabric. The shorter length is more comfortable. Make sure your T-shirts are as light as possible, too. Polo knit shirts are versatile and can be worn with either shorts during the day or trousers at night. But most comfortable are the short-sleeve tailored shirts with button fronts. You can wear them partially buttoned, and the air is free to circulate.

Long pants are frequently required by protocol for night wear, except in some British-influenced countries, where shorts are acceptable *if* worn with knee socks. Skip took a sports coat and wore it an average of once a year. (Even then, he felt that he could have gotten away with slacks and shirt in those instances.) We were told by friends in California, who had traveled through the South Pacific, to take formal clothes for such spots as the Royal Suva Yacht Club in Suva, Fiji. "Being without formal clothing may force you to miss out on some social situations," they said. A year later, with our good things duly stored away in plastic bags, we sailed into Suva Harbor on a Sunday afternoon, and went ashore to the yacht club for a family barbecue. To our surprise, shorts and bare feet was the dress code. Times obviously have changed.

On board, bathing suits are our normal tropical dress. The light-weight nylon type are the most practical because they dry quickly and don't restrict your movement. If you are going to be in the sun steadily, cut a white T-shirt just about at the armpits; then your shoulders will be protected but you won't get too hot.

The pareu, or lava lava, is the traditional garb for Polynesians from Tahiti to Fiji, and it's a good, all-purpose cruising outfit. It is simply a length of fabric wrapped around you—at the waist for men, higher up for women—and worn knee length. The simplicity of buying a strip of a beautiful print fabric and tying it, strapless style, is appealing to women. It's comfortable and cool, and all it takes is a simple hem to keep edges from raveling. A variation is to make a seam down the back, shaping it slightly and adding straps, which can be crossed and tied around the neck.

Shorts and cool tops are common on-board apparel, but in many tropical countries you should be careful about wearing shorts ashore. Outside the U.S. and some of the more touristy cruising areas, people expect women to wear simple dresses or skirts when conducting business in town. So respect this protocol when going marketing, sightseeing, or dealing with officials, and always keep your legs covered. Wrap-around skirts are cool, and it's simple to make a dress by sewing a tube, with a few rows of elastic on the top to hold it up.

If you wear long pants, the cotton variety with a drawstring waist are the coolest. Leave tight-fitting polyesters at home, or store them with your temperate-climate wardrobe. You'll want one or two nice dresses for going out to dinner and special occasions.

Most cruisers go barefoot aboard the boat. We knew we were close to New Zealand on our passage from Fiji when night watches started getting cold enough to make us put shoes on. In the tropics, though, you'll need a pair of "reef" shoes for walking on coral and rocks. Rubber-soled tennies or sneakers work well, or the plastic reef sandal, which buckles securely over the instep of the foot and around the ankle. Rubber thongs don't work, as the foot tends to twist and slip out of them. Thongs can be worn on the beach and ashore during the day, but have a nice pair of leather sandals for night wear on the town.

Although nights are usually balmy, you'll occasionally want a light wrap or sweater. Foul-weather gear can double as a raincoat, and umbrellas are good to have for two reasons: use them when it rains, and also for shade in the sun. Umbrellas with telescoping handles are easiest to store.

The long-term cruiser will eventually spend time in the temperate climates as well as in the tropics, and so must have a double wardrobe aboard. Some of the items overlap, but heavier clothing will probably be in storage until needed.

We stored our "good" clothes in hanging plastic zip bags with a mildew-cide bag tucked inside. Be sure to secure the hangers from moving while underway; otherwise they will chafe holes in the garments. Sweaters, socks, and pants can be stored in heavy plastic bags, again with mildew-cide, and tied shut if placed in a locker that might get damp in bad weather. That's an important "might" to consider in many boats.

Store leather shoes and purses in heavy plastic with mildew-cide, putting a little Vaseline on metal buckles to prevent corrosion. You probably won't wear much jewelry, but if you're going for a long time, take one or two favorite pieces. Inexpensive shell jewelry is offered locally, and looks pretty with tropical clothes.

Choose clothing that will be easy to maintain. Wash-and-wear is the best, as we only saw two dry cleaners in the tropics. Laundromats are usually nonexistent, except in marinas in the West Indies. There is one in Tahiti, but at several dollars per load it's too expensive to use. Cotton fabric is the coolest, as it breathes, but it needs ironing. Coleman offers a kerosene iron, or the old-style cast-iron stovetop models are sometimes available. Most ship's electrical systems can't handle an electric iron, but an auxiliary generator can.

If you're using the boat as more than a weekend retreat, consider putting a compact washing machine aboard. This is especially important if you're cruising with children. We found room for a miniature Hoover model (16″ × 16″ × 30″) with a hand wringer by removing the hand sink in the head. We had friends who stored their machine under the main saloon table; they transferred it to the cockpit on laundry day. Ours held 8 gallons of water. By allowing a week or 10 days' laundry to accumulate, and using the same water to wash first whites and light colors and then dark colors and heavily soiled items, we kept water use to a minimum. Our average consumption, including rinse water, was 12 to 14 gallons. Getting water usually isn't a problem in the tropics since there are frequent rain showers; with a good water-catching system on the awnings, the tanks stay full. A

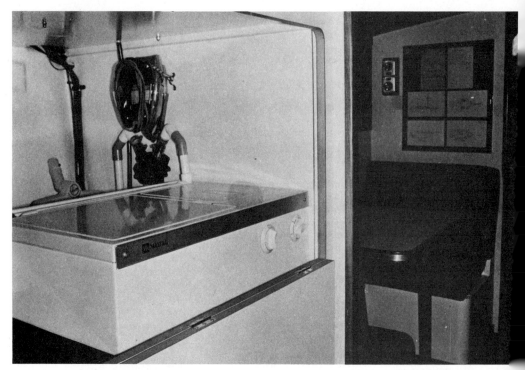

This compact Maytag twin tub measures only 24″ long, 24″ high, and 15″ deep. (S. A. Dashew)

washing machine keeps clothes in better shape than scrubbing in a bucket, and only by machine can you get towels and sheets really clean.

If you do have to wash clothes in salt water, you should rinse them thoroughly in fresh water. Any salt remaining acts as a sponge to soak moisture out of the air, so unrinsed clothes remain damp and scratchy.

Start out with an abundant inventory of clothespins. The wooden variety hold up better than plastic. Laundry can be hung from the lifelines, but by stringing a line higher off the deck, they dry faster. The higher the line, the more breeze, and the faster they dry. Some cruisers string their washing vertically from flag halyards.

A tip for securing clothespins is to catch the item on the sides vertically just under the clothesline, instead of parading a whole series of pins across the top. The holding power is much greater. A

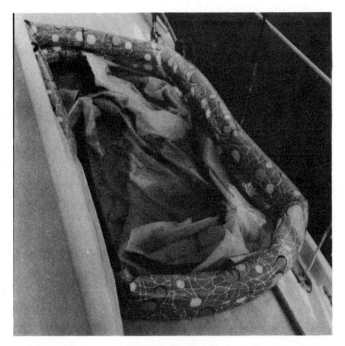

Sue Moesly's single-tub washing system. It got Sue, Don, and *Svea* around the world looking very smart.

gust of wind may whip the item around the line, but since it's being held underneath it won't tear loose.

Keep a copious supply of tea towels for galley use. Drying dishes washed in salt water makes towels grimy.

Buy the top-quality bath towel. The thicker the towel, the better it dries and the longer it holds up.

Use drip-dry sheets and pillowcases, with at least three sets per bunk. The stateroom bunks that can be left made up look attractive in matching print sheets and pillowcases. In cooler climates, add a cotton comforter with matching pillow shams. Thermal blankets are a good weight when a cover is needed. Sleeping bags are out of the question for tropical use, or even for long-term use in colder places.

For the cruiser who likes to sew, there's no reason not to take a sewing machine. Make it a model that can handle sail repair as well, and also make sure it has a hand-crank option so it can be used either manually or with power. Patterns are hard to find in most places, so take your own.

Buying clothes along the way can be difficult. Australia, the U.S., and South Africa were the best countries we found for buying clothes. New Zealand, although an industrialized country, has very expensive clothing. Paying $10 for a pair of rubber thongs stretches most cruisers' budgets too far. Bali, with its batik clothing, is a bargain hunter's dream. Cruisers there dressed very well in $2 hand-painted shirts and $3 dresses.

When you start traveling through the South Pacific, plan on taking with you as much as you can of what you need. Grandparents sending clothes to our children along the way helped us out, for children's clothes in many of the places we visited weren't the style or type we are used to. For instance, in Fiji all we could find in little girl's dresses were very frilly, ornate ones, not appropriate for cruising life.

Haircuts are a must for good grooming. It needn't be kept short, but hair should be shaped and trimmed. Get a good pair of barber shears and learn to use them. Most women want a simple hairstyle for cruising—either long so it can be worn back and up for coolness, or short, which with a daily shampoo and brushing keeps looking neat and cool.

Women should protect their hair from too much sun by wearing hats and scarves. The visor-type hat is most practical, as it stays put in a breeze. Take a good conditioner. Salt, wind, and sun are very hard on hair.

Cosmetics are universally available, as are toilet articles. Take along a bottle of your favorite perfume or cologne or a box of perfumed dusting powder for a morale booster. Or you may want to pick some up in a duty-free port.

62. Children's Schooling

One of the questions cruising families ask most often is what to do about the children's schooling? And rightly so. Although children pick up a lot of information through their traveling and sailing

Small children are easier to raise aboard than on land. You don't have to worry about their playing in traffic, and there is much less mischief they can get into. (S. A. Dashew)

experiences, they will be severely handicapped when they get back ashore if you haven't kept up their formal schooling while they're away. The added responsibility this imposes on cruising parents (usually the mother) is not that onerous, and the results are well worth the trouble.

The options are to carry correspondance courses or to devise a program of your own, getting supplies and books from your local school before you go. If you're going for a short cruise it's possible to improvise this way, but in general it's easier to carry correspondence courses. The most popular courses among cruising families are offered by the Calvert School in Baltimore, Maryland. This is a program that covers kindergarten through grade 8. It's designed to be taught by nonteachers (parents), and provides detailed daily lesson plans. For basic reading, writing, arithmetic, history, spelling, and science, with some art appreciation, poetry, and mythology, we found it adequate. Some parents are lucky and have self-motivated children who will sit down and work alone, but most children need guidance. It takes two to four hours a day to complete a lesson, depending on the grade level. The older the children, the more work and time necessary. Calvert understands that cruising parents are busy, so they plan a two-year period in which to complete two semesters of work. It took us 12 to 14 months to complete a 9-month course. We found it best to establish a definite time of day for schoolwork, usually right after breakfast. But this wasn't always possible, especially when underway so schooling at sea requires flexibility.

The basic syllabus can be supplemented by special projects involving the area you're visiting, studying the history, customs, flora, and fauna of each. Sightseeing trips ashore are good subjects for notebooks or art projects. Elyse and Sarah, for instance, did reports on the copper mine at Kieta, New Guinea, wild animals in the game parks of South Africa, and Columbus's first trip to the New World, all based on their firsthand experiences. Math can be supplemented by doing simple navigation problems and by working on recipes in the galley.

You'll find that your children will read more away from television. Take along an extensive children's library. Talk to your child's teacher before leaving for suggested titles. Elyse's second-grade teacher suggested that we take an anthology called *The Illustrated Treasury of Children's Literature,* edited by Margaret E. Martignole (New York: Grosset & Dunlap), and we added the *Anthology of Children's Literature* by Johnson, Sickles, and Sayers (Boston: Houghton Mifflin). The classics are always good, and if your child's too young to read *Wind in the Willows, Charlotte's Web,* or the *Secret Garden,* have reading-aloud sessions with the whole family. You'll all enjoy them. As you finish books, look for other cruising families to trade with. You can also exchange your books at used-book stores along the way. We found them in most major English-speaking centers.

High School courses are available through the University of Nebraska. College Entrance Exams can be taken through various American consulates.

Bruce and Liz MacDonald were both teachers before setting off on their circumnavigation, so when it came to teaching their son Jeff, who was 8 when they left and 11 when they returned, they outlined

Whistling out a hermit crab. Sarah masters an advanced technique in animal training, at Champagne Beach, Espiritu Santo Island, New Hebrides. (S. A. Dashew)

a program for him using materials they brought from home and some they picked up from a school in Panama along the way. They supplemented the material by doing library work ashore when possible. And when they spent six months in New Zealand, they enrolled Jeff in a local school. He also attended classes in Durban, South Africa, the month before the schools broke for their summer holiday.

Vickie and Sy Carkhuff were gone five years on their circumnavigation, and taught their son David through grade five. When they returned to Florida, David went right into the sixth grade with his age group. It was his first formal classroom experience, and the only skill he lacked was on the football field. (Of course the other boys couldn't scuba dive or handle a dinghy.)

When we returned to the States after 3½ years, Elyse and Sarah tested well and went right in with their age groups in school. In

Sarah's case the last nine weeks of second grade were her first formal schooling experience, but she had no problems. (She had more trouble learning to roller skate and ride a bike.)

Most educators are thrilled at what you've given your children by traveling with them in this way *as long as* you've made sure they are good readers, know their basic math skills, and can write.

Those living in New Zealand and Australia are lucky in that their governments offer correspondence school services for free. These countries have many families living in isolated circumstances, and so are set up with correspondence school services on a national basis.

If you decide to take correspondence school along with you, be sure to order it well in advance. Calvert sends a complete year's work at once; domestically, delivery time is no problem, but when they ship it overseas to catch up with you enroute, it goes by ship and can take up to three or four months to reach you.

We took the first year's work with us, had the second year's kit sent to Honiara in the Solomon Islands, and the third year's to Darwin, Australia. If you're expecting a large shipment like that, write to the postmaster in the port of delivery, advising him to expect it, and when you expect to make port.

63. The Cost of Cruising

One of the joys of cruising is that it's cheap. Once your yacht is paid for there is simply no other lifestyle that offers as many rewards for as little cash as cruising. Most people planning long trips budget more than is necessary to maintain themselves in reasonable style. As a result, many of them put off going cruising longer than they need to.

Our experience was no exception. We carefully evaluated what we thought the various aspects of our adventure would cost. We talked at length with Skip's dad about what he had experienced on his 24-month cruise in the late 1940s, as well as with others who had been to Polynesia for a year. Based on this research we budgeted $1500 per month (this was in 1976).

In Mexico we found food cheap, and besides that and a little diesel oil there wasn't much to spend money on. By the time we reached the Marquesas Islands, we had averaged less than $150 per month, total expenses. In the Marquesas, our spending picked up a bit, but we were fortunate in having stocked *Intermezzo* to the gunnels with food and supplies, so except for an occasional night out, a ride through the mountains, and a drum of diesel, we had few new expenses. By the time we had left American Samoa, with *Intermezzo* completely restocked, we were averaging less than $7500 per year.

The more recent experience of two cruising friends who left in 1979, when inflation had diminished the purchasing power of most currencies, is typical. They ate well, beautifully maintained their 30-year-old, 40-foot wooden ketch, ate out occasionally, entertained aboard and ashore, and spent $6700 during the year. Their costs broke down this way: groceries, $1531; postage, $127; fuel, $321; gifts, $80; Customs fees, light fees (a sort of user tax charged by some countries to help pay for lighthouses—which almost never work anyway), and such, $253; entertainment and miscellaneous, $2248. Outside services such as hauling, parts and labor for maintenance, etc., ran $1026. General supplies for upkeep were another $1120.

The cost of keeping an older vessel, especially wood, is a lot higher than for a new, low-maintenance yacht. Another couple we have shared many anchorages with has a three-year-old fiberglass yacht. In 1978–1979 their expenses ran $5400. The breakdown is one-third for food, one-third miscellaneous, and one-third maintenance. As you can see, there's a big difference in the maintenance costs of the two vessels, both of which are kept in Bristol fashion.

On a 54-foot schooner, other friends' expenses have run $7200 in the same time frame, including feeding three teenagers. This couple feel that they are shaving things too close, however, and would like to spend another $200 per month. The bigger boat and extra mouths to feed make sticking to this figure tough—all but essential items are left out. But they are out cruising!

Other friends in smaller boats average around $4000 per year. If you really watch the nonessentials you can cut down to $3000 per year for a couple, before yacht expenses.

None of these examples contains an allowance for disasters. A

One of the traits the author's father failed to pass along was a knack for fishing. We averaged one fish per 2000 miles, at a cost in gear of $6 per pound! The author's father is shown here off the coast of Panama in 1949.

major engine overhaul, dismasting, new sail inventory would all be on top.

And as time and inflation march on, cruising costs keep pace.

We have discovered that bigger yachts, if properly found, don't cost that much more. Aboard *Intermezzo* working on a $7500-per-year figure, we found that as inflation cut into our purchasing power, we got to be smarter shoppers. Neither our lifestyle nor maintenance suffered. We ate well, maintained the vessel, spent a lot on postage and photos, went out several times a month, rented cars for sightseeing, and bought a lot of gifts. Granted, our two young daughters didn't eat much; but the difference between what we spent aboard *Intermezzo* and what it would have cost to live at home is amazing.

We both feel that the most additional money we could spend within the constraints of life aboard a small boat would be another $200 a month. In the really good cruising grounds this would entail a lot of entertaining ashore, perhaps more sightseeing; in towns it would mean buying more expensive clothes, gifts, and souvenirs, and going out to dinner more often.

These examples are typical of most of the yachts we have met cruising. One feature they all have in common is that they spend two-thirds of their time in the outer cruising areas, with the occasional trip back to civilization for supplies, mail, and a night on the town. Obviously, it costs much more staying in marinas in the West Indies or in Europe than in the lagoons of Polynesia.

How do we all do it? As with most things in cruising, there's a lot to learn as you go. Many folks leave home loaded down with spares, clothing, and miscellaneous junk that will never see action. That space and money, if put to essentials, extends cruising time. Aboard *Intermezzo* our motto became "when in doubt, don't."

The biggest trap for your dollar is that first week in civilization after months in the wilds. Our stop in Papeete, Tahiti, was an example. After three months in the Marquesas and Tuamotus, where we spent less than $100 per month, we blew almost $100 a day in Papeete. Store windows were full of things we hadn't seen since California. The urge to spend was irresistible.

Fiji was another trap. Ostensibly a duty-free port, the windows of 75 percent of the shops are lined with an incredible array of electronic gadgets and goodies of every sort. Some Australian friends of ours, cruising on a fixed-income monthly budget, had been assiduously saving in the outer islands and big cities. (They even escaped Papeete.) Ten days in Suva and they had the biggest collection of calculators, watches, and radios you can imagine.

The general pattern of saving in the country and spending in the cities is unavoidable. Once in a while you want to see a movie, eat ice cream, go out to dinner. However, for the first week in town, hold onto your wallet. The consumer urge will die down and you'll find which stores have the best buys.

Food is usually the biggest item on everyone's budget. If you like to eat well, a little planning can reduce costs considerably. In each cruising area there will be ports or islands where certain items are very inexpensive. A good example was New Zealand. Meat, dairy products, and fresh fruit and vegetables were about a third of U.S. prices in 1978. A good-size freezer can keep you eating well for half a year after you leave. If you have no freezer, you really ought to learn how to can food aboard.

In the Marquesas Islands, anything from civilization costs several times what you'd pay at home. The trick is to stock up on canned goods at home, then buy or trade for fruit, local meat, and vegetables, which are inexpensive, as you go.

Throughout the Pacific Basin and the Indian Ocean areas we have visited, we have generally found plenty of garden vegetables and fruit available from the locals in out-of-the-way spots. Most big ports have native markets where the produce is fresh and very inexpensive. Meat can be quite high if flown in; but many copra plantations these days run cattle to keep down the undergrowth, and maintain butcheries. They can resupply your larder with very tasty beef at low prices. In the Russel group in the Solomon Islands, we put 125 lbs. of steaks, roasts, and hamburger in equal portions into our freezer for $65.

As you extend your cruise, charts and navigational materials become expensive. There is no substitute for the right charts. But a roll of good-quality transparent paper and sharp drafting pencils give you the means to get a lot of free information from other yachts and commercial vessels. Another approach is the copy machine. We frequently trade charts with people going in the opposite direction. The exchange process also provides you with informed opinions of upcoming anchorages, places to buy and where to avoid.

Yacht maintenance is an area where ingenuity can go a long way

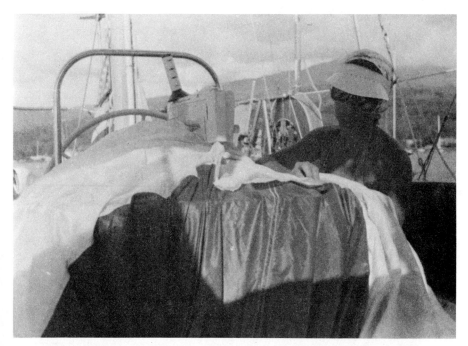

Linda restitches part of *Intermezzo*'s spinnaker with her Sears sewing machine while anchored in Bora Bora. The machine was later successful in repairs to our mainsail, working through up to five layers of 8-oz. sailcloth.

toward keeping costs down. In many parts of the world there is a substantial tidal range, and having to haul a boat for a bottom job or through-hull work is just about unheard of. After years of worrying about the boat's falling off shipyard cradles, our first experience with careening piles in New Zealand was an eye-opener. On the high tide we sailed up and tied alongside some pilings set in the sand. The tide receded; then we scrubbed the bottom, painted, and waited for the water to come back. It took us 4 hours to clean and paint and 12 hours later we were afloat again. When I think of all the yard bills I've paid. . . .

We found that by making sure we run electronic and mechanical gear weekly, keep mechanical and electrical gear dry and lubricated, and stay ahead of chafe on plumbing, wiring, and rigging, the need for outside help and parts is kept to a minimum.

On deck, sails should remain in good condition for up to 10 years if they are properly taken care of. The biggest contributor to sail deterioration is sunlight. It will do more to harm fabric than all the sailing wear and tear you give it. So when in port, bag and cover all sails even if you're going to sea again in a couple of days.

Modern standing rigging and aluminum spars require almost no expense to maintain. If running rigging is led so that chafe is minimized and if you catch the little problems in the sails before they magnify, your above-decks maintenance will be substantially reduced.

We met only one yacht in the last couple of years that carries insurance. The rest have found it too costly. Almost everyone cruising on a long-term basis has paid for their boat, so that monthly bank payments aren't a factor. A disaster kitty is a good concept, but a third of the people we have talked with don't have one. Medical insurance is another cost most people avoid. Outside the U.S., health care is much cheaper, although on a more basic level.

We were unpleasantly surprised by our ongoing expenses back home. Unlike many, we didn't cut all our land ties; if we had, three years later we would have had another year's free cruising ahead of us.

Insulating yourself against the effects of inflation is a good idea, if you can swing it. Many of the cruisers we have met have been severely hurt by the erosion in the purchasing power of their hard-earned freedom chips. If you don't have a source of income that is pegged to inflation and are working off savings, the best idea we have seen is a bank account based on a basket of world currencies or SDR's. The interest usually isn't more than a couple of percent, but it will cover most of the expected loss against the erosion in one currency by the offsetting increases in others. Many of the overseas banks offer this type of savings instrument.

Aside from disciplining your consumer instincts, there are some easy ways of saving money on cruising gear. First comes equipment for upgrading or maintaining the boat, which you will be buying continually. In the U.S. there are half a dozen discount catalog marine stores, which frequently sell to the retail buyer at lower prices than dealers or shipyards in a foreign country offer. In mid-1980 it was possible to purchase a Par pressure pump from one of these firms for $70. In Cape Town, South Africa, six months earlier, the dealer I went to was paying his distributor $150 for the item, and he wanted $210 from us. Keep on the mailing lists and order material enough ahead that you can have it sent via sea to your next major stop.

We have already talked about obtaining trade discounts as a means of saving, but researching costs in foreign parts can also be helpful. Just as in the stores you left at home, there can be wide variations among merchant prices and discounts. A little research goes a long way toward shaving costs.

What about earning money once you're "out there"? As a general rule it's possible to work four months of the year and earn enough to keep going for the remaining months.

Yachtsmen have a reputation for being good workers, especially in the island communities where there is a slower pace and local help sometimes takes the mañana outlook. Your services are generally in demand. There are restrictive hiring practices, however. Almost everywhere in the world you have to have a work permit to work legally. Work permits can be difficult or impossible to obtain, and the process at best is time-consuming. As a result, most yachtsmen "moonlight" at their work and are paid in cash. This happens everywhere, and only once, in New Guinea, did we hear of someone getting into trouble and being asked to leave the country.

The skilled trades are most in demand. Mechanics, refrigeration engineers, carpenters, electricians, or heavy equipment drivers can find work anywhere in the world. Skills of the brain are harder to sell than mechanical ones. Frequently the jobs are there, but they are of longer duration and are more likely to require work permits.

We have seen doctors and executives putting roofs on homes in Tahiti, and former white-collar workers scrubbing bottoms in the local shipyard.

If I were tight on cash and thinking about leaving on a cruise, I would take the time to attend trade-school courses in several subjects. Diesel engines and refrigeration knowledge would be helpful aboard the vessel, and easy to sell ashore.

Some people eke out their income with occasional charters, but this is usually a matter of luck, and can't be counted on. It is possible, though, if you are willing to stop for a while, to make an arrangement with a tourist hotel for day charters. I think this is a good scheme, since it can be lucrative, and yet leaves you with your home and privacy in the evening.

Writing for magazines is a very iffy proposition. Everyone does it, the competition is tremendous, and yachting magazine editors have hundreds of manuscripts to read monthly with only a few slots to put them into. But nothing ventured, nothing gained.

If you are willing to cut back to essentials in the way of your vessel, sightseeing, and personal luxuries, it is certainly possible to support yourself by working as you go, on an itinerant basis. But if you want to do it in comfort, then itinerant work will at best supplement the kitty.

A last resort to consider is returning home for a stint in the mill now and then. Once you discover how inexpensively you can live abroad, an income you thought modest at home can generate savings very quickly to keep you going for long periods when cruising.

64. The Business Side of Cruising

Most people go cruising to get away from the hassle and complexities of the everyday world back home. As your cruising time lengthens, however, you'll probably find that some communication and commerce with home become unavoidable. Many people find this a frustrating annoyance at first.

The first major problem is mail. In each port the best place to have mail sent and held varies, but generally a local yacht club will hold mail, and we have found this quite convenient in many areas. In some places mail will best find you if addressed in care of the port captain. General delivery, or *poste restante* in French-speaking areas, is another good bet. If your bank at home has a correspondent bank in a major city and you are doing business with the correspondent, they will often hold and/or forward mail. Be sure to have the mail addressed in your name along with your yacht's name, and noted "Hold for Arrival" as well.

Airmail in most parts of the world will arrive in a week or 10 days.

The longest time we experienced was three weeks, in the Marquesas Islands. Surface mail will generally take two to three months— sometimes five.

Often, of course, mail will arrive after you leave for another port. Most cruisers find it best to have a shore buddy or another yachts- man send on their late-arriving mail (have the mail readdressed and sent airmail; post offices forward mail by surface).

It is generally best to leave an itinerary of major stops, where you expect to be for a month or more, with the folks back home. Some people try to have all mail sent to one Stateside address and then forwarded. This is good in theory, but our experience has been that our friends like to write directly to us at some exotic location. You'll get much more mail if people can write to you direct.

It is important to drop a note to your next mailing address, advis- ing them of your ETA and asking that mail be held for you. Many post offices will hold unclaimed general delivery mail for only a few weeks if arrangements haven't been made in advance. If we find we're running late, we send a follow-up card.

Urgent messages can be wired in care of the port captain or yacht club where you are staying. If you have high-seas radio capability, KMI, WOM, or WOO in the U.S. will hold a call from home for 24 hours, giving you a call in the traffic listings every six hours. Gener- ally the call has to be replaced after 24 hours. If you have a ham radio aboard, a regular schedule with someone at home is great; or one of the maritime networks of hams can list the traffic for you. In most cruising spots these days there are always some yachts with ham gear aboard, and a general call for your yacht will usually be relayed.

The financial side of foreign cruising can be simple if handled properly. To begin with, travelers checks are universally accepted in the most primitive parts of the world. You generally get a 1.5 to 3 percent better conversion rate to local currency to boot, as the local banks don't like to handle cash. Once your initial supply runs out things become more complicated, unless you have a credit card that gives you cash-drawing privileges. Cashiers checks drawn on a major U.S. bank are easy to cash and avoid the cost of a transfer by wire. However, most foreign banks in out-of-the-way places will wait for the check to clear before advancing funds, although you may be able to draw a percentage before clearance. Wire transfers we found to be the best, and that's what most of the cruisers we have met use.

Get a list of correspondent banks from your home bank. You can then easily instruct them from one port to wire funds to the next.

Wires generally take from 4 to 10 days in and out of most cruising areas. Have your home bank purchase foreign currency and wire the foreign funds, if you are planning on staying in one country for a while. Almost all foreign banks take a straddle position in currency and make handsome profits buying and selling money. U.S. banks as a rule do not, but will go into the foreign-exchange market and purchase funds for you on a spot basis. You can save as much as 3 percent this way.

Another thing to check before having U.S. funds wired to you is the conversion regulations. Certain banks automatically convert to local currency. If funds are wired to you to cover the next few countries, this means you'll have to reconvert to the next currency. Each time you convert, you'll pay a handling charge. Check with the local bank in advance.

In exchanging currency you will find that rates vary on the same day from bank to bank. Banks are generally 5 to 10 percent better than the local merchants on exchange. The only place we found this not to be true was in Mauritius, where the moneychangers gave a better rate. But be careful not to run afoul of the currency regulations in the smaller countries.

An American Express card is perhaps the best system we have found for getting funds. With a standard Amex card you can cash personal checks at their offices around the world for up to $1000 every three weeks. With a gold card the amount is $3000. The only fee involved is the 1 percent charge for the travelers checks, and these are issued in whatever currency you desire. After spending a lot more than this on wire transfers and long-distance phone calls, we finally arranged for a card.

VISA and MasterCard cards in some areas are good for modest cash advances, and we'd recommend carrying one or the other as a form of insurance in case you get caught short.

If you are planning to spend a season in one country, waiting out the cyclone season in New Zealand for example, it is generally a good idea to open a local bank account. This saves the costs of travelers checks and allows your money to earn a little interest.

As we noted earlier, buying spares, replacements, or new goodies from home can be greatly facilitated by having a good collection of catalogs. If you do have to order via friends back home, be sure to give them the serial number of the unit you have aboard and the part number you want. Even if it's something simple, the description must be as complete as possible.

Most people start off ordering things from home without really checking out the local sources. After you spend more time cruising you find that if a port has the transportation facilities to get your goodies from home to you expeditiously, the chances are that what you need will be on the shelves of some local merchant.

When having parts sent to you, be sure they are addressed to your yacht with the notation "yacht in transit." Invoices should be packed on the outside of the box in a separate envelope. Most Customs officials will allow spare parts in duty free if they are for a yacht in transit. Occasionally it may be necessary to post a bond for duty, which is refundable upon your departure, or to put the gear in question in a Customs warehouse until you leave, at which time the clearing officers will bring it aboard. If the items are of any value, it is best to check in advance. You may want to hold off and have them sent to you at the next stop.

Taxes are a consideration if you are gone any period of time. First is the property tax (if your state has one) on your yacht. In some areas, such as Los Angeles County, California, you will be assessed property tax as a migratory asset even though you are not in your home port for several years. Don't forget the income tax. In many countries the revenue service likes to hear from you annually even when you're offshore, unless the proper extension forms are filed.

Most of us have some commitments at home that require regular payment of bills—a house or valuables in storage, perhaps. We have found it best to negotiate to pay a year in advance and get a discount for doing this to cover the interest lost on the funds.

If you appoint a friend, associate, or relative to take care of business that must be handled locally, be realistic about what's involved. Often what appears to you to be a simple chore or two when you are familiar with the details is something else to an inexperienced friend. There is absolutely nothing more frustrating while cruising than to be beset by business problems at home that are not being handled properly in your absence.

It's a good idea to leave either a general or specific power-of-attorney with someone you trust to execute necessary financial dealings. If you don't leave the papers at home, then take several power-of-attorney forms with you. They can then be filled out and sent home if needed. But be sure to have them notarized before you leave. It is very difficult to have a foreign notary validated in the U.S. We learned this the hard way when we were in Papeete.

My brother, an attorney, had properly prepared us with the right power-of-attorney forms. While in French Polynesia we decided to sell a house we owned rather than cope with the hassle of being long-distance landlords. The house was sold in due course, and one day we received a call informing us that the title insurance company wanted our signatures on a certain form. This form had to be notarized. That was simple enough, but when the papers were received back in Los Angeles, it turned out they wanted a notary registered in the U.S. We finally got around the problem, but not before a lot of hair pulling and long-distance phone calls were made. A week later, to my surprise, I found out that Doris, a good friend sitting on her ketch in Moorea, was a U.S. notary; subsequently we have met several more in anchorages around the world. (Consuls are usually able to certify documents where necessary; but there was no U.S. consul in Papeete.)

You will have to make arrangements to keep your yacht's registration current while offshore. State and national regulations vary. The U.S. Coast Guard, for example, will hold your document open as long as you write to the home-port office and inform them you are out of the country.

Basically, as with all other aspects of life aboard a long-distance cruiser, you are better off if you can be totally self-reliant. A little planning and forethought on the business side of cruising will go a long way toward easing the frustration of keeping things going smoothly back on the home front.

7
The Boat

The first thing to think about in choosing a suitable cruising boat is money. Once you've established your budget, the field is narrowed substantially. (And don't forget that an important adjunct of a boat's cost is its eventual resale value.) When you have fixed your financial parameters, remember the first general rule about cruising boats: the bigger, the better. Bigger boats are usually easier to handle in heavy weather, take little extra maintenance if properly set up, and are more comfortable in port or at sea. With modern gear and moderate-displacement designs, an average couple can easily handle a boat in the 50-foot range, if they can afford it. Also, be aware that the initial cost of a new boat is merely the first drop in the bucket. The list of gear necessary to make a new sail-away vessel really cruiseworthy is staggering.

Without doubt the best bet is to find a good used boat in sound structural condition that has been set up for cruising or racing. My preference runs to old racing boats that have been thoroughly tested. Their gear will be extensive and they depreciate quickly, leaving you with a fast, generally roomy, proven vessel. Racing boats built to the old CCA rule, such as *Intermezzo,* are ideal. Early IOR boats are also excellent cruising choices. (But we are definitely *not* talking about modern lightweight IOR racers.) If the boat has been raced or cruised hard, it is easy to see if she has any structural flaws. A thorough examination will almost always reveal the state of a used

The moderate-displacement Cal-40 is a prime example of a successful racing hull converted to cruising. Doug and Kristie Hotchkiss have lived aboard *Gypsy* for 10 years. She has been all through the Pacific Basin, and was in Fiji preparing for a trip to New Zealand when this photo was taken.

vessel's structural integrity. (A new boat that hasn't been tested, on the other hand, is an unknown quantity.)

When we first looked at *Intermezzo* she fulfilled these criteria. A careful examination of all her structural bulkheads, her chain plates, and her hull-to-deck connection showed a vessel in perfect condition. She was in such good shape that I couldn't believe she had been raced hard. I talked to people who had known her in her racing days and they confirmed that she had indeed been pushed to the limit. A boat tested in such a manner that shows no signs of stress has been extremely well built. With a used, well-equipped racing boat, you have let someone else take the big depreciation on the initial investment. Rarely will it be possible to recover more than 30 to 40 percent of the cost of the accessories purchased. If someone else has bought them for you, so much the better.

Another approach is to go against current market trends. Small steel yachts in the U.S., for instance, generally have a very low price in the used-boat market. Yet many feel that steel is the ultimate material for cost and security. In Europe, steel is looked on with favor and can cost as much as or more than fiberglass. If you find one with a low price tag, you may be able to get a lot of boat for a modest investment.

Don't worry about cosmetics. A dirty boat with paint in poor condition and generally a mess below is going to go for a lot less than a boat that sparkles. Yet what we are concerned with are size, seaworthiness, and gear. Paint and polish come cheap.

In many cruising areas labor is a fraction of its cost in the developed countries. Taking a sound vessel which needs cosmetic work to one of these areas is an easy way to build equity in your new investment.

The last thing anyone going cruising for the first time should do is build a boat. No matter what you build, or how many ideas you fit in, you will wish it were different when you have a year of cruising under your belt. The average time for inexperienced people to build a boat (that is, for the small percentage who finally finish and get away) is five years. If funds are short and you are trying to stretch your boat size by building it yourself, don't. Buy a good used smaller boat, go and get some experience on the ocean, and then come back and build your dream boat.

As to what constitutes the proper design to go to sea in there is, of course, endless debate. Those of less experience tend to take comfort in the apparent conservatism of the older, heavily built, full-keeled designs of yesteryear. Since a majority of people cruising today are neophytes, there are a lot of these boats in anchorages around the world. But the 5 percent or so of sailors who have had real bluewater experience before they go cruising will invariably be in boats of moderate displacement that have higher performance than those of their tyro comrades. These boats will be faster, easier to sail, much safer in heavy going, and in the main, more comfortable.

It is rare to find a cruiser who has been out for more than a year in a full-keeled, heavy-displacement vessel who would choose the design again.

65. Crew Size

Next to budgeting, crew size is the most important decision to be made before actually looking at boats to buy. If you're gregarious, or have a large family, you'll be forced to look at larger boats. If you like privacy, prefer a little solitude now and then, and have a reasonable amount of confidence in your abilities, you'll have more options in terms of size.

Certain harbors in the cruising world are famous for their unhappy crew stories, probably none more so than Papeete, Tahiti. It's the first big port after thousands of westbound miles of ocean sailing and primitive island hopping. Frustrations are easy to vent, and it's rare that a crewed boat leaves Papeete with the same individuals aboard with which it arrived.

When planning a cruise you will be subject to all sorts of outside pressures, subtle and otherwise, on this question. What do you do with the boat in heavy weather? What happens if someone is sick? How about man-overboard situations? These questions, which lead one to consider extra crew beyond the basic family unit, are difficult to answer. The other side of the coin involves the friction of life aboard a small vessel, the lack of privacy, the ease of handling modern vessels—and these matters are not easily assessed without actual experience.

Linda and I were no exceptions. Friends, parents, and even sailing buddies suggested we take crew. Thoughts of heavy weather and illness filtered back and forth through our minds. Knowing something of the sea and life aboard a small vessel, we carefully went through our list of acquaintances, looking for those who would be compatible not only with us but also with the children. It came down to three good friends. Unfortunately, at the time none of these could get away from home. We didn't advertise for crew, though many do so successfully. So we went alone, and stayed that way.

It was in Taiohaie Baie, in the Marquesas Islands, that we first started picking up on the crew problems people were having. Linda, the sympathetic listener, heard it from disgruntled crews. I got the other side from the skippers. Few of the crewed boats we encountered were happy ships. It's very difficult to change crews in the Marquesas, which are not major government headquarters, and yet are usually the port of entry for boats crossing from North America. French immigration policy is very strict, so unharmonious crews had to put up with each other until they reached Papeete, the French Polynesian capital, to sort themselves out. After their initial experience, the vast majority of skippers of moderate-size vessels leaving Papeete Harbor did so with basic family aboard and no outside crew members.

Modern boats are much easier to sail than earlier cruising vessels. With low-wetted-surface hulls, moderate displacement, reliable self-steering, Dacron sails, self-tailing winches, and roller furling, fewer hands are needed. A 50-footer of today is simpler to handle than a 30-footer of 25 years ago.

In examining the various activities that have to be performed at sea, in every instance there is an answer available to a two-man crew. And don't forget that on the average only 1 in 10 days is spent at sea. This is important. On *Intermezzo* we spent an average of 1 day at sea for every 12 days in port on our trip.

Emergency situations are one area where an argument can be made for extra personnel. But the extra crew's presence in a crisis presupposes that he will be a bonus and not a liability. This means possessing a clear head, previous experience, and training in the particular problem that has occurred. Will he be an asset or a hindrance?

How big can you really go? This depends on many factors, but assuming that you're looking over your shoulder for potential problems all the while, here is a list of factors that affect a given size vessel:

1. Docking.   Without a doubt this is the activity that takes the most hands, and whose difficulty is directly related to size. A good-size engine, efficient propeller (especially in reverse), and a rub rail sturdily constructed and easily repaired mitigate damage to the vessel (not to others). If you are going foreign, then most of your time will be spent hanging on the hook, so the problem becomes less of a daily concern than if you were stopping at marinas along the way. The Mediterranean is another story, since you have to moor bow- or stern-to in most harbors.

2. Anchoring.   With a powerful electric or hydraulic windlass, size has little to do with anchoring. A backup system to get the anchor and chain back aboard must be available, and if it's by hand-cranking, that's related to stamina and physical strength. Another aspect is freeing fouled anchors. They happen. Our average has been about three per year. Scuba diving is an easy way to rectify the situation, but it is frequently necessary to exert force on the bottom to move an anchor one way or the other. A 75-lb. anchor can be slid from under a coral head by a middle-aged cruiser in reasonable condition. Anything larger may take extra help, or power from above.

3. Sail Handling.   Modern fabrics, roller furling, self-tailing winches, and new sail-cutting techniques have completely changed the size parameters for shorthanded sail handling. Aboard *Intermezzo* the biggest job in sailing was hoisting the mainsail (and later furling and covering it). Her main was 425 square feet of 8½-oz., heavily resinated racing cloth (softened a bit by age). In planning the main on our new boat, I set a limit of 540 square feet as what I was willing to deal with on a daily basis. Not that a larger sail couldn't be handled, but it was just too much work.

Headsail handling essentially involves raising, lowering, and bagging. Once the sail is up, even a child can trim a large genoa if he has the time and a powerful enough winch. Weight is the question, size times cloth weight. On *Intermezzo* our light #1 genoa, 780 square feet of 3½-oz. Dacron, was a snap to handle. It could have been 1000 square feet and still have been easy. Our #2 genoa, just 580 square feet, but 8-oz., was much more difficult. We didn't even take the #1 heavy. It was too big and cumbersome, period.

Changing headsails at sea can be wet, time-consuming, and laborious. Aside from mishaps, such as a seam starting to go, it is weather that forces a change. On smaller boats there is no choice. The speed range is limited to begin with and they usually carry all the sail possible. Having less stability, they are forced to change headsails or reef quickly as the wind increases. A large boat can hang onto her sail longer, or can start with smaller sails and still have a reasonable turn of speed.

Roller furling can make even the largest sail a snap, *if* everything is working. But in the back of your mind when looking at roller furling vs. vessel size you must be aware of the possibility that something may go wrong. (See Chapter 70 for more discussion about roller furling headsails.)

As a point of reference, during the 3½ years of our circumnavigation, weather conditions forced us to change headsails at sea only three times. Twin jib stays spaced fore and aft of each other almost eliminated the need to unhank sails. On another seven occasions maintenance caused sail changes (her sails were eight years old when we left). If she had been a 40-footer instead of a 50-footer, we would have had to change three or four times as often.

4. Maintenance. Some aspects of maintenance are common to vessels of all sizes. Lubricating the steering gear, maintaining the windvane or autopilot, keeping the freshwater system operational, checking through-hull fittings, servicing the toilet—all fit into this category. Painting topsides or bottoms, reworking sails, or overhauling running rigging are proportional to size. A fiberglass 50-footer in good condition at the beginning of the journey will require less maintenance than a 35- or 40-footer in steel or wood. Assuming you can afford the extra maintenance materials, and that you do most of the work yourself, it's not too much to expect a single man to keep up a 60-footer of low maintenance materials with 10 hours of work per week at the most.

5. At Sea. Standing watches can be interesting, exhilarating, or a colossal bore. But near land or in shipping lanes it's a necessity. In the middle of the ocean its necessity is subject to debate. With two people at three hours on and three off or four on and four off, a routine soon settles in and the nights do pass. Self-steering is an absolute must if you're shorthanded. For that matter, I simply would not go if I didn't have self-steering, regardless of crew size. From a watchkeeping standpoint, there is radar and the new radar warning alarms. Most of these collision-alert devices are less than $1000 installed, and well worth the funds if you can afford it.

6. Emergencies. There is no substitute for help in an emergency.

The worst situation is going overboard. In this case the bigger the vessel, the less likely it can be turned around properly. On the other hand larger vessels are less likely to pitch their crews overboard. Linda and I make it a habit always to wear a harness on deck.

So much for variables. Let's look at absolutes. The largest two-person crew we have seen cruising was on a 70-footer. These friends of ours managed 130,000 lbs. of Sparkman and Stephens ketch with the aid of roller furling, even on the main, power windlasses, and all the electronic aids one could imagine.

Down toward the more moderate end of the curve, most of the larger boat couples we have met are in the 48- to 52-foot range. Nobody has reported having problems yet, and several of the couples were in their late 50s or early 60s. Of those sailing 40-footers, virtually every person we've met would like to have a bigger boat, if they could afford it.

Single-handers present another story altogether. There are more of these people out cruising than one would suppose. Many just haven't found the right crew and think it's easier to do by themselves. Their gear will run about the same as their crewed counterparts, with a tendency to be just a bit simpler. Forty feet seems to be the median size, but two single-handling friends are planning 50-footers when they return home. At the end of the spectrum was the late Tom Blackwell and his *Islander*. We first met Tom, a wiry 70 years old, in Port Louis, Mauritius, in 1979. *Islander* is a classic Scottish cruising design, 56 feet overall and 35 tons—a lot of boat for one man. Yet Tom was on his third circumnavigation in her. With wooden spars and running backstays, she would be a handful for a full crew. Tom's solution was to take his time. He wasn't in a hurry, kept her shortened down, and did just fine.

66. Designs

A number of major factors must be carefully evaluated before you decide on a general type of hull shape or overall design. You have to have an idea of the kind of cruising you're going to do, and see which factors should be given priority among the multitude that go into the composite known as a proper cruising vessel.

Let's first consider draft. From a strict speed standpoint, a deep-draft boat is going to be faster to windward than a shallow-draft design. But it's possible to get a boat with moderate draft that performs well to windward; and the question of draft goes way beyond speed uphill. Accessibility to shallow cruising grounds is a major concern—like the Bahama Banks, for instance, or areas on the Inland Waterway, or the Chesapeake. On the other hand, besides the U.S. East Coast and western Caribbean, the rest of the cruising world isn't that shallow. *Intermezzo* drew just under seven feet when fully loaded, and only once, in a lagoon on Moorea, were we denied an anchorage we would have liked. So strictly from a cruising standpoint, the great preponderance of good spots around the world have plenty of water.

Another aspect that must be carefully considered, though, is hurricane holes. In many parts of the world the best protection from cyclones or hurricanes is up a river or deep in a mangrove swamp. Here draft becomes critical. Guam, in the Central Pacific, is a classic example. It can and does get cyclones virtually anytime during the year. There are some excellent rivers which give protection, but 6½ feet is the draft limit.

Another aspect of draft has to do with underwater obstructions. There is a direct relationship between draft and the possibility of hitting or just missing a given coral head or shoal patch.

Undeniably, draft does contribute to weatherliness in cruising; however, we are not concerned with ultimate speed, but rather the ability to work our way to weather in adverse conditions. In this case draft alone isn't the critical factor, but rather the hull shape combined with the keel. It is possible for a modern light-displacement boat of moderate draft with a good hull-to-keel transition and well-proportioned fin to outperform a heavier, older shape with poorly defined keel and substantially more draft.

There's no doubt that weatherliness is desirable on a cruising boat. From a safety standpoint, one has to be able to go uphill in bad conditions. The worst of situations won't be found offshore, but close to land. A shift in weather may make it necessary to quit an anchorage that has become a lee shore. A vessel may be faced with steep seas, have a difficult time getting room to accelerate, and be bucking 50 or 60 knots of wind. It may be unsafe to run the engine to help

This Vancouver 27 had cruised from California to New Zealand, and then back to Fiji under new owners. Her displacement/length ratio is on the heavy side, but that's a necessity in a yacht this size expected to do serious cruising.

out if you're heeling sharply or pitching madly. I recall trading stories with some friends on a large, unwieldy schooner after passaging the Torres Straits between northern Australia and New Guinea. They had been set by current into the mouth of the Fly River, and when they discovered their error, it was necessary to turn back and beat into 30-knot trade winds and steep waves stacked up by the shallow bottom. Being schooner rigged and of very heavy displacement, she had difficulty getting herself uphill in the best of conditions. There, in the mouth of the Fly River, they were forced to rely

The 76′ *Constellation* in her prime was considered an "ultimate" cruiser, with a full keel, attached rudder, and 80-ton displacement. In the 1930s to 1950s era she was a queen. Today, the rig, hull shape, and displacement evoke fond memories, but the four experienced crewmen necessary to sail her are hard to find. (S. A. Dashew)

on their diesel to make progress. The prop would come out of the water, allowing the engine to race, every second wave. For hours they crept forward with the engine going full speed, making perhaps one knot against the prevailing conditions. Had their diesel failed. . . .

It's true that cruisers tend to avoid going to weather. I know we certainly do, and *Intermezzo* is one of the fastest cruising boats uphill. But sometimes you have no choice; at other times there is a

Intermezzo's minimum-wetted-surface underbody and fin keel were at their best in light airs.

beautiful anchorage at the end of a wet beat. It's nice to have your options open. During our "downwind" circumnavigation we spent roughly 20 percent of the time on the wind. If you are out for a two-week vacation, weatherliness becomes even more important. A business commitment at home precludes waiting out bad weather.

Heavy-weather characteristics are another aspect to analyze carefully. It is rare to find truly heavy-weather cruising if you follow the seasons. But it happens, even in the trade-wind belts. We found a 60-knotter feeding out of a trough of high pressure in the Central Pacific during trade-wind season. If you plan on visiting New Zealand or Australia, are going around the Cape of Good Hope, or doing the Mediterranean, for sure you're going to find heavy weather.

Speed under sail is an essential ingredient to comfort and safety at sea. The ability to make fast passages reduces the time you're exposed to potentially bad weather or in the grip of an adverse current. It also means making an anchorage on an unfamiliar coast before dark, perhaps saving an anxious night of watching. It's not difficult to tell if a vessel will be a handy sailor. If she has a clean hull, moderate windage, and a good sail-area/wetted-surface ratio, it's pretty certain she will move, at least downhill in the trades. If you study the sail-area/wetted-surface ratios of known performers, you can set that up as an objective criterion at which to aim. With a moderate-displacement vessel, in the 40-foot range, a good rule of thumb is 2¼ square feet of measured sail (main and forward triangle) for every foot of wetted surface. In light airs with her staysails and spinnaker flying, *Intermezzo* could set over 6 square feet of sail for each foot of hull area.

Displacement/length ratio is another critical factor to look at. Expressed as the result of a formula in which weight in long tons is divided by the waterline cubed, times 0.001, it is an indicator of the relative weight of boats for their length. Basically, boats with low DLRs will move faster in a breeze, especially downwind, than their heavier cousins. They have a quicker motion, but that motion generally is endured for a shorter period of time.

In the olden days (not so long ago really) most cruisers had a DLR in the 450 to 500 range. The Tahiti ketches and Colin Archer designs were among these. Their inability to do anything but make big waves is legendary. Today, most modern cruisers fall into the 250 to 300 range. Generally, as a boat gets larger her DLR drops. I am a fan of light displacement. Since you basically buy a boat by the pound, you get more boat for the money. And a 50-foot boat of 25,000 lbs. is faster, roomier, and more comfortable than a 40-foot 25,000-lb. vessel.

However, the undeniable advantages of light displacement become less pronounced with smaller vessels. In light-displacement boats of less than 35 to 40 feet, the motion becomes too quick and they cannot carry a proper cruising payload. At that point light displacement becomes impractical for a long-distance cruising vessel.

Freeboard involves a lot of trade-offs in design evaluation. Windage at sea and at anchor are lined up against ultimate stability and interior space. Another important consideration is the ability to get back aboard if you have fallen over. I remember my first time aboard a modern IOR boat at Catalina Island. It felt as if I were on a stepladder looking down at the water. At that point I said I would never go to sea in a boat that I couldn't climb back aboard unaided. But transom steps and well-rigged (permanent) boarding ladders take the curse off this aspect of high freeboard, and on balance it works out to be an acceptable compromise.

High freeboard generally makes a boat drier and increases her ultimate stability. Furthermore, it makes a world of difference down below. In a moderate-displacement hull with shallow bilges, to get the headroom the topsides must go up. As long as this height is in proportion to the overall boat and you have the ability to get uphill against the windage, you're okay.

This leads directly to the question of trunk cabin versus flush deck. Without a doubt the flush-deck vessel is cheaper to build, safer at sea, and gives a huge amount of room inside. A trunk cabin or doghouse can allow more light inside and has the supposed advantage of letting people in the raised area see out. In many cases it looks more traditional.

The best thing to do is to look at boats in the size range you are considering. My eyes were opened when we met Beth and Al Liggett. After their first circumnavigation they had commissioned Robert Perry to design for them what was essentially a flush-deck version of the Valiant 40, with a very small doghouse. *Sunflower,* at one foot longer in length, appeared to have twice the interior volume of the standard Valiant. The difference was in the visual space achieved by allowing the eye to travel unobstructed to the edges of the hull.

A flush-deck vessel's hull is much stiffer than her trunk-cabin counterpart. The deck forms a continuous web between the gunnels, helping prevent the hull from bending and twisting. If you open a huge hole in that web for the trunk cabin, the hull is going to work more freely. At sea in heavy weather, not having to worry about stoving in a cabin side is a comfort.

If you detect a bias here in favor of flush-deckers, you're right. Over 40 feet they are definitely the way to go. Smaller vessels don't have the option and must stay with the trunk cabin.

Stability is also to be considered carefully. One has to look at a boat's sailing stability generally, close-reaching or beating. On an absolute basis, stiff boats are generally more comfortable cruisers than tender ones. True, their motion will be quicker, but it's so much easier to work and get about on a vessel which doesn't lie down on her ear. Modern designs are all substantially stiffer than the yachts of even a few years ago. Higher ballast ratios and stiffer hull forms both contribute. A stiff boat will stand up to her rig better, and in the end will make a much swifter passage than a tenderer cousin.

The question of range of stability must also be examined. This is the point at which the boat, lying with the mast under the water, will keep going right on over. Modern racing boats have very little ultimate stability and roll over rather easily—at about 100 to 110 degrees. Older racers can go as far as 160 degrees underwater before losing ultimate stability. A compromise for the less highly ballasted cruiser is an ultimate stability point in the rage of 125 to 140 degrees.

There are many combinations by which to achieve good ultimate stability. A lot of deep ballast in and of itself doesn't guarantee success. A wide, light boat, for example, with good freeboard and moderate ballast placed low, can have better ultimate stability than a more heavily ballasted but narrow and low-freeboard yacht.

The IOR racing rule has contributed more to cruising-boat evolution than anything that has come along in years. It has taught yacht designers that beamy hulls with short overhangs and an extra bit of freeboard can be moved through the water swiftly. From the cruising standpoint, the IOR reached its peak in the early 1970s. These boats were of moderate displacement, heavily built, with huge quantities of room inside. Obviously they are quick and easily driven. To get reasonable cruising passages shorthanded, it isn't necessary to put all the high horsepower of their lofty rigs to work. Small headsails in a cruising environment are sufficient to move them quickly.

Leading up to the IOR boats were the CCA boats at the end of the 1960s. William Tripp's designs have the traditional, albeit somewhat less practical lines, with graceful shears and moderate overhangs. Beauty is certainly a factor to consider, and with some it outweighs performance. Tripp's boats are sea kindly, move very well in light airs, and move with an easy motion in really heavy going. Bill Lapworth ushered in the era of the light-displacement cruising boat with the Cal-40. While her lines took getting used to, the short ends, straightish shear, and high freeboard spelled boat speed and room inside. She may jump around a bit, but if you compare her on a displacement basis with a 35-footer of equal weight, she will have the smoother ride.

At the other end of the spectrum are the "traditional" boats and their modern copies. Probably no vessel was less suited for long-distance cruising than Slocum's *Spray* (unless it was Hannah's Tahiti ketch). That he made his remarkable voyage at all is a tribute to the man, certainly not the boat. I doubt if Robin Knox Johnson would have sailed a Swahili if he could have afforded a more modern design.

The old-line, heavy-displacement boats of yesteryear are wet; they roll their guts out downwind, have a hard time getting uphill, jump around on their anchors like modern designs, and are a hell of a lot of work. Why do they sell? Advertising.

There is nothing that says you cannot combine traditional and lines with a modern underbody. Robert Perry (designer of the Valiant 40 and others) does this, and while some feel his "Valiant" stern is a marketing gimmick, his boats appeal to many as having that link with the past. With their modern underbodies, they are seaworthy and reasonably quick.

Equally important is the keel shape. One hears a lot about the advantages of the full keel in a cruising boat. They take the ground better, self-steer better, are safer . . . and on and on.

Well, that's a lot of baloney. Boats with a *moderate* fin and with spade or skeg rudder will self-steer better than any full-keeled vessel ever built. When the time comes to beat out of a harbor or maneuver under power, they will be far handier. The downwind antics of modern racing boats are usually cited as an indictment of the fin-keel conception; watching them broach left, right, and center, and do their death rolls as they head for the leeward mark, the full-keel advocate smirks in self-satisfaction. But remember that those racers are carrying gigantic rigs, including huge spinnakers in substantial quantities of wind to get the last tenth of a point of speed. Those same boats with moderate cruising rigs would be under control until well beyond the time the full-keelers were dragging warps.

From a standpoint of taking the ground, gridding to do one's bottom, or hauling in out-of-the-way places, a *moderate* fin presents no more problem than any other design if the yacht is properly balanced. Coupled with a moderate displacement and hard underwater sections in the area of the keel, the increased ability to weather ensures acceptable performance while allowing for a substantial reduction in keel depth.

In self-steering, hull shape and rig configuration are more important than keel shape. Well-distributed volumes, moderate to short overhangs, and reasonable rigs all help immensely. It was interesting to note the comments of the people who had crossed the Indian Ocean with us when we all met up in Gran Baie, Mauritius. We had each done 2300-plus miles of heavy reaching and running. Guess which boats had the best times and the least trouble with their self-steering gear?

Heinz Milner, a single-hander in a Sparkman and Stephens half-tonner with a sharp fin, had lost his self-steering vane just a few days out of Cocos Keeling. Using a sheet-to-tiller steering rigs he made the rest of the trip averaging the same time as several long-keeled, crewed 40-footers with steering vanes intact.

All the long-keeled older designed yachts had had to shorten sail to maintain a reasonable course in the boisterous conditions of the central Indian Ocean. They were all uncomfortable due to the increased motion that resulted from their being undercanvased.

Centerboards are great in dinghies. In cruising boats they bang, rattle, and jam with coral. They also make trouble with their winches and pendants. But moderate-displacement boats that need shallow draft and still want to go to weather need centerboards. It's interesting to note, however, that most cruising boats with centerboards rarely use them.

Rusty and Lorraine Johnson on *Aventura* are a good example. With a Hinkley Bermuda 40, a fairly deep board, and very little keel to hold the boat, they still rarely find it necessary to use the centerboard. Of course, when going to weather it can cost them as much as 15 percent in boat speed to have it up.

Carl and Jean Moesly on *Rigadoon* have a more modern hull shape. With a long waterline, *Rigadoon* has a stump keel about two feet deep in which her centerboard is housed. She does well uphill without it, and I wonder if it's really worth the extra expense and maintenance. A modern, short-overhang, moderate-displacement cruiser should be able to get by without. On the other hand if you have to do a lot of uphill work, it's good insurance. One thing is for sure: it's easy to plug up the slot if you get tired of the board's bouncing around.

There is some question in regard to the seaworthiness of double-enders. If you're planning on backing into the seas under power, as the lifeboats in the North Sea do, it's a good idea. If you're going to be sailing with the waves, the pointy stern doesn't rate too highly.

From a strictly practical standpoint, a double-ender has a heck of a lot less room in the hind quarters. It's difficult if not impossible to get any stowage aft. They hobby horse more going to weather.

On the plus side, proponents claim they part the seas that are overtaking them when going downhill and make less wake to disturb the crests behind. Maybe this is true for older boats of very heavy displacement, but a modern moderate-displacement cruiser with a long waterline plane makes much less quarter wave than a traditional design double-ender. With a hull, keel, and rudder combination that gives good control, you'll be surfing in front of wave crests with enough speed so they don't bother you when they do rumble aboard. In short, modern transomed boats with a good clean run aft are much safer at speed before big seas than the low-buoyancy double-enders.

The debate over inside vs. outside ballast has raged for centuries. Both sides have strong arguments. Inside ballast is easier on mainte-nance, has no keel bolts to leak, and if properly encapsulated and reinforced at the upper edges where the keel joins the hull, it makes a stronger installation than outside ballast for the same cost.

On the other hand, outside ballast, if it is lead, will absorb the shock of a hard grounding. Another advantage is the possibility of jettisoning outside ballast in case of severe grounding.

This last feature isn't to be dismissed lightly. If the keel bolts are run from the inside out, to nut plates molded into the *top* of the ballast, it is possible to withdraw the keel bolts from inside the hull. If you're hard aground, so that it's not possible to get your boat afloat as she lies, the keel can be removed, allowing her to float free or be dragged off. In the *Deerfoot* series of large cruising yachts which I helped design, the keels are all attached in this manner. Also incor-porated is a molded-in plate to which can be attached a lifting ring, so that the keel can be recovered once the vessel has floated free.

Intermezzo, however, has inside ballast, and I think that on bal-ance I prefer it. On three occasions she had severe run-ins with rock or coral. The bottom of her fiberglass keel looked more like a cheese grater than a racing yacht, but aside from some abrasion, she seems not to have suffered unduly, and she has never leaked.

Finally, we get to another matter of much argument and equal importance: rudder design.

Before departing South African waters for the final leg of our circumnavigation, *Intermezzo* was hauled for a touch-up job on her bottom paint. The surprise evident when her spade rudder hove into view was typical: "You'd take your wife and children to sea with a spade rudder?"

The question of steering systems really starts with an analysis of the risks one must face when cruising offshore. There are three sets of problems you can get into with a rudder. The first is grounding,

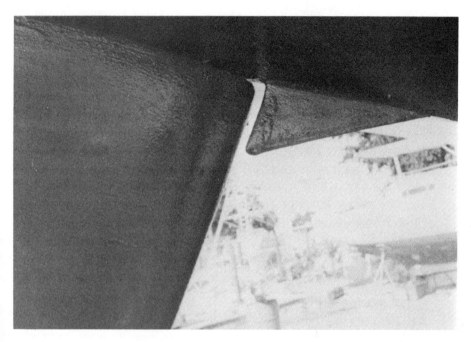

A closeup of the spade rudder and its weed deflector aboard *Intermezzo*.

an obvious hazard. The spade rudder is perceived as the most vulnerable in this situation. Structurally, however, a spade rudder can be made as strong as most skeg/rudder combinations without a weight premium. One simply has to decide what sort of cruising loads to engineer for and then design a rudder shaft to carry the loads.

One of the advantages of a counterbalanced spade rudder is that the rudder shaft normally exits the top of the rudder at its thickest point. This means that a maximum diameter is available structurally. Since bending strength goes up with the *cube* of the diameter of a structure, a little increase in shaft diameter goes a long way structurally. Compare this to the skeg, with its thinner sections, and you will see that with a little thought and weight a spade rudder can be made quite strong.

In a severe grounding situation vessels with skeg or keel-hung rudders are also subject to damage to their bottom attachment points. When this occurs there generally is no way to correct the problem short of hauling out. Two of our cruising friends in the Louisidad Archipelago of New Guinea had run-ins with reefs. In both cases the skegs were damaged and they were unable to continue without outside aid. On the other hand two other friends with spade rudders who hit reefs were able to continue after freeing themselves, albeit with minor steering problems.

The second potential threat for a rudder is a collision at sea. Flotsam, perhaps a whale, or hard backing when hove-to all can exert tremendous strains. While these risks are minimal, and although none of our cruising friends has ever reported firsthand such troubles, we must still be concerned with the possibility. Usually the keel will deflect whatever object is hit. If the rudder *is* hit and the load is substantial enough to damage it, a spade rudder offers a repair option that can be exercised at sea. Assuming the rudder shaft is bent so that the blade is jammed up against the hull, the jam can be freed by easing the shaft down a bit, that is, submerging the rudder more. Alternatively, a damaged trailing edge section can be removed with a saw.

The bottom line offshore, psychologically and practically, is severe weather. Under heavy conditions the safety of your vessel will depend on its ability to cope with the steering loads efficiently with a minimum of expended energy. Actual loss of control or fear of its occurrence can be more damaging than any of the other risks. And it is in these circumstances that a spade rudder really is at its best.

I clearly remember when a group of world-girdling yachts flying the national flags of a dozen countries were rafted together at the Point Yacht Club in Durban, South Africa. Bent lifeline stanchions, broken deck gear, missing spars, and storm shuttered ports on the new arrivals offered testimony to the fury of the southwestern Indian Ocean where the Aghulas Current, the 100-fathom line, and black southwesterly gales come together.

These yachts had just come through what might be considered an ultimate storm. One rollover and two severe knockdowns head the list of sea stories.

A single fact emerged from the comments of those aboard the newly arrived yachts. Good steering control is of paramount importance.

Intermezzo came through the blow unscathed. With reasonable lateral plane and excellent directional control from her powerful

Aries windvane, she was able to beat slowly to windward, taking the breaking waves on her bow.

The violence of the seas required large steering corrections on a continuous basis. Coupled with her slow progress through the water, averaging less than three knots, only the most efficient rudder systems could have enabled *Intermezzo* to adopt the tactics employed in a safe, seamanlike basis.

By virtue of the fact that a spade rudder is partially counterbalanced and highly efficient, steering loads are reduced while actual control is improved. Coupled to an efficient self-steering system, whether windvane or pilot, it means that the range of conditions in which you can trust your yacht to its self-steering is increased dramatically. Less exposure for you, less battery drain, better boat speed, and more safety are all benefits.

When sea conditions reach the point where you feel that it's time to take over directly, your trick at the helm will be less tiresome. With very high speeds, which may be necessary to keep the seas off your back when running, you have better downhill control. At the opposite end of the spectrum, if you're trying to slow down the spade rudder will yield the most boat control for the least boat speed.

That the performance of the spade is superior in terms of control is borne out by the fact that all of today's hot racing boats use this type of rudder. And while their parameters are different from those of the offshore cruiser, the end result is the same: most control for least effort.

The well-publicized recent structural failures on the rudders of some of our racing cousins should not dim your enthusiasm for this form of steering. Today's racing boats use extremely high-aspect-ratio rudders of light construction, with very thin sections. Each of these characteristics reduces the structural integrity of the rudder—sometimes to the point where the search for speed goes too far.

When cruising, however, we are most concerned with safety. A fatter rudder airfoil allows a thicker rudder stock (remember that cube function of strength) at very small cost in boat speed. The bottom of the rudder itself can be made frangeable, or weaker than the stock, so that in the case of a severe grounding you might lose some of the blade but will keep the basic steering system intact.

When all the factors are weighed carefully, the answer will turn out "cruising in spades."

67. Multihulls

Nowhere does internecine warfare in the cruising community rage as fiercely as between mono- and multihull cruisers. The spectre of lead-filled bubbles bursting their seams and going to the bottom like a rock is held up by one group, and the nightmare of floating upside-down in the middle of the Atlantic or off the Cape of Good Hope is raised by the other.

Well, I'm here to tell you that multihulls have some good points and some bad points, but that if you're going to consider them at all, you must consider *all the aspects carefully* in reference to your own skills and your proposed cruising area.

Before I jump into this discussion, let me give you a little of my own background. I started sailing catamarans in 1958. One day, sailing in a One-of-a-Kind Regatta on Newport Bay in California, I saw an ugly monstrosity with a bird-like sail whip the tar out of my beloved 17-foot Thistle, *Clish Ma Claver,* in light airs and to weather no less. Repulsed by the ugliness of this "thing," I was nonetheless overcome with curiosity about its origins (lower regions, no doubt). I wandered over to the beach where the boats were hauled between races and met Dan Sanderson and Roy Hicok, the builders and sailors of *Wildcat.* They offered her to me for a sail. "No thanks," I said. "I just wanted to look at 'it.'"

But curiosity soon got the better of me and it wasn't long before I was screaming around the bay in *Wildcat,* out of my mind with enthusiasm. I put the boat back in Dan's and Roy's hands, ordered one, and never looked at my Thistle again.

For many years after that I raced, then designed and built a series of catamarans. Along the way we won a few races, set a record here and there, and generally had a good time. My dad got the bug and built a luxurious 58-foot cruiser.

Our boats were lightweight, high strung, and their sheets were never cleated, even day-sailing in light airs. It was our last boat, *Beowulf VI,* a 37-footer with a small cabin, that gave Linda and me the idea to really go cruising.

As a designer, the problem I continually saw with *cruising* mul-

Beowulf V, the authors' D-class 32′ catamaran at speed. In 1971 she set a world record for speed under sail of 35.38 miles per hour. (S. A. **Dashew**)

tihulls was weight. They wouldn't carry a big enough payload to cruise at speed. And speed, after all, is the name of the game. Their other problem is lack of ultimate stability and its risk. Multihulls have high initial stability, but once one hull is out of the water, very little besides quick reflexes separates you from getting wet. I couldn't see exposing my family to a potential capsize situation, brought on by a lapse in clear thinking. We wanted to sail by ourselves, and the boat would have to take care of herself from time to time.

As a result we bought a "leadmine," and while *Intermezzo* was faster than most cruisers, her top sustainable speed in the 8-knot range didn't begin to compare with the steady 28 to 30 knots *Beowulf*

A conservatively designed Jim Brown trimaran. We met tri's of this design in many parts of the world.

VI was capable of doing in the open ocean (sea conditions permitting).

After the first half of our shakedown cruise in *Intermezzo,* I was ready to bring her back, sell her, and start on a 55-foot, high-performance multihull cruiser. This would be a boat with an interior similar to perhaps a 30-foot monohull, light on her feet, that would fly. Sailing downwind at 6 knots in 10 knots of wind when I could have been moving at 14 or 15 was just too much to take.

On our way back home we stopped off at Cedros Island, just off the Baja California coast. We were anchored off the northern end in a small open bight close to the beach. The seals and sea lions made inquisitive forays into our territory, and we exchanged pleasantries with some fishermen anchored to the north of us.

It was a clear night and the barometer was high, good conditions for a northeasterly gale to develop. When the glass started moving up and the stars began to twinkle, I set an anchor watch. Then we saw the fishing boats begin to head out to sea. An hour later a swell from the northeast began to roll in. There was no doubt—a northeaster was about to hit us. We hurriedly got the hook up and worked our way off what would soon become an extremely dangerous lee shore.

It wasn't long before 60 knots of wind was blowing across the deck. I decided it was foolish to try to go uphill in these conditions, so we turned *Intermezzo* around and ran off before the storm toward Bahía Sur on the southern end of the island, where we would find shelter from the sea. By the time the sun was up the true wind was steady in the 60s and *Intermezzo,* under her double-reefed main and storm staysail, was wildly surfing down the short seas that had built up.

Nearing the southeast corner of the island I realized that the shape

The catamaran *Sonadora* in Gran Baie, Mauritius, after crossing the Indian Ocean from Perth, Australia. She averaged a respectable, but unspectacular 150 miles per day for her trip.

The Piver trimaran *Wind Rose* in Gran Baie, Mauritius, preparing for her crossing to Durban, South Africa. *Wind Rose* eventually carried John, Sallie, and Vinaka Wishovich safely around the world.

of the land would create a downslope condition and that we would get some pretty good gusts. We pulled the main down to the third reef, put both kids in the pilot berths below with their leeboards up, and put in and locked the companionway slides.

The main was jibed to port and we were ready to turn the corner. All during this procedure I had been thinking how it would be to be out here in the new multihull now forming in my mind's eye. I figured we would be having one heck of a ride, but that it would be safe.

As I eased the wheel up on *Intermezzo* and allowed her to come under the land, we could see the first gusts heading toward us. The water was absolutely white and spray was everywhere, although the sea was essentially calm in the lee. As the first gust hit *Intermezzo*, it heeled her down till her spreaders were in the water, and held her there. Had we been in my multihull . . . ! *Intermezzo* of course put her seven tons of lead to work and came back; we continued on, and were flattened once more before we were able to beat our way slowly into some protection in Bahía Sur.

A week later we were beating up the coast toward Ensenada in the teeth of a northwesterly gale, common at that time of year. The crew was a bit under the weather, but with a short rig, *Intermezzo* was driving herself easily uphill. Occasionally a squall would bring gusts in the low 50s, and she would be momentarily overpowered. By this time I was worn out, and I let her fend for herself. I never could have done that in a multihull.

As a result of these two experiences we kept *Intermezzo*. I came to realize very quickly that in spite of all my previous experience in multihulls, if we were to go offshore in one I would have to stay continually alert and could not afford a mistake like turning the corner of Cedros Island.

Four years later, sitting in beautiful Gran Baie on the island of Mauritius in the Indian Ocean, I was discussing just these experiences with Sally and John Wishovich on their Piver trimaran *Windrose*. Sally had kept track of multihull disasters during the four years they had been cruising. It appeared that 8 percent of the multihulls they were aware of had flipped or been reported missing during their journeys in the Pacific Basin. They thought it might be a leadmine for them the next time.

But there is another side of the story. Multihulls do offer several real advantages. The first, of course, is that they are unsinkable. And while I think that the chances of sinking are remote in a monohull if she has a collision bulkhead, good pumps, and keeps a reasonable lookout, it remains a factor to consider. Gerry Eaton, an old sailing buddy of mine from way back, related an experience he had had setting out in a trimaran from Puerto Vallarta for the Marquesas. Several days out from the coast they spotted a school of killer whales.

As the whales played around their 40-foot tri, Gerry and his friends tried to communicate by whistling. Apparently they hit the wrong note, because the next thing they knew one of their black-and-white friends had poked his head up through the main hull, leaving a gaping hole which rapidly filled with water. They were supported by their amas until a patch could be made and the main hull bailed out. They returned promptly to Mexico somewhat the worse for the experience, but still around.

Another aspect of a multihull's advantage is in draft. The shallow draft has a major safety side to it. On the average, 1 in 12 boats that spends more than two years on the Pacific Basin ends up on a reef permanently. I know of three instances in which multihulls hit reefs and escaped with scratches. On each occasion a monohull would have been a total loss. While this is not usually a life-or-death situation, it is still a major factor to consider. Our friends the Sandstroms, on their 40-foot Brown-designed tri *Andural,* for instance, found the Wallis Islands the hard way, by running into the fringing reef. They bounced over the edge and sat, just out of reach of the breaking sea. As the tide came up, minus most of their rudder they made their way into the lagoon. Still in one piece, they eventually completed the circumnavigation via the Suez Canal.

Multihulls offer unsinkability, shallow draft, and comfort at sea. But they can and do flip over. They have to be watched carefully, all the time.

Now let's look beyond the basic points. Contrary to what some people say, multihulls are relatively expensive for the amount of interior room and payload they will carry. They take more time to build, and require higher skills to be successfully completed than comparable home-built monohulls. Their resale value is lower for a given level of workmanship and investment in material. In short, they don't make much financial sense.

Speed? Those dreams of dashing here and there are hard to come by. I have seen only one cruising multihull of any size that was remotely capable of keeping up with *Intermezzo* on a passage-by-passage basis. This was the beautifully executed 42-foot cat *Ned Kelly,* and her Australian crew watched weight like a hawk. But even her times were, at best, equal to ours, and usually a few miles a day less. The average multihull found cruising is slower on trade-wind passages than a comparable-size monohull.

The camataran or trimaran debate, I must confess, baffles me. Of course I'm a bit biased, having owned eight cats, but I can't see why tri's are so popular. They are slower than cats, more expensive to build, and no more seaworthy. But there must be something to them, as they are numerous.

If after all my words of wisdom you are still hot for a multihull, there is one last thing you should do. Buy a copy of Adlard Cole's *Heavy Weather Sailing* and study the photographs carefully. Then consider if you want to be out in these sorts of conditions with your multihull. Keep in mind that 95 percent of the damage inflicted on cruising yachts comes from the sea, and not the wind. You can deal with the wind, but when the right sea catches you at the wrong angle, no amount of seamanship or alertness can prevent disaster in a multihull.

Multihulls, to take advantage of their design, must be light. There really is no way to keep a reasonable-size multihull from getting too heavy when it's fitted out with all the gear you need for long-distance cruising, unless you're willing to put up with a totally spartan life-style. (Long-distance racing multis are a different story, of course. They go extremely light and extremely fast.)

If you're *still* game, I would advise the following. First, be sure that your total all-up weight doesn't exceed a displacement/length ratio of 60. Second, don't have more sail than can be safely handled with a beam/length ratio of 2 to 1. Next, make sure your rudders are strong, deep, and capable of handling your multihull at a speed/length ratio of at least 4 without ventilating. The hull should have a collision bulkhead as far forward as possible, with a watertight bulkhead just aft of that. The remainder of the hulls should be segmented into compartments so that a puncture in any one of them will not disable you with water. Your sheet loads and winch set-up must be such that you can quickly cast off any sails if you start raising a hull. Provision must be made for access to your vessel if she is upside-down so that food, water, and shelter will be available. If possible, the hulls should each have solid foam in their bottoms up to their load waterlines, so that if you are holed, the watertight section that is breached will not hold a significant volume of water.

Finally, don't take chances with the hurricane season, try to avoid sailing in regions such as the Tasman Sea or off the bottom of Africa —and always have a hand on the sheets.

68. Materials

Fiberglass is by far the most popular material in today's cruising fleets. It is relatively inexpensive, easy to maintain, and generally makes for good resale value at the end of the voyage.

Mass production has substantially reduced the cost of modern cruising boats. Part of this has been achieved through increased efficiency and part through skinning down their scantlings. A majority of boats rarely leave the marinas for very long, and are seldom subjected to heavy loads at sea. As a result, it is unusual to find a heavily built, modern mass-produced boat. For this reason, it is usually better to look for an older fiberglass boat, built, say, before 1973. That is the year that resin prices first shot up. Before that, with resin going for under 20¢ a pound, manufacturers could afford to throw in extra laminate here and there.

When I worry about the scantlings of a vessel, it's not the sea that concerns me. The loads of heavy weather can be substantial, but hull failures under sea loads are rare even in the skinned-out racing boats of today. It's when the boat meets the ground that problems arise. A lightly built hull, with hard spots at poorly bonded bulkheads, will last a fraction of the time of a heavily built hull when lying on a reef. And if you are going to cruise, you must assume that sooner or later you'll find yourself pounding on a shoal or reef.

Some fiberglass boats are built with sandwich construction. Most commonly, end-grain balsa wood or PVC foam is used as a sandwich material. These materials have the advantage of insulating the hull, dampening noise, and increasing stiffness while reducing weight.

In deck structures, even on an all-out cruising boat, either material can add substantially to weight reduction of the overall boat and contribute to lowering the center of gravity, which in turn means a stiffer, more comfortable and weatherly vessel.

The sandwich construction in the hull on a cruising boat is somewhat suspect in my mind, but not for the usual reasons. Both Airex PVC foam and balsa cores will give excellent long-lasting results when used in the hulls. If the lamination is done by skilled people with experience in this form of glasswork, problems of rot, moisture, and delaminations are rare.

Once again I'm thinking about when a vessel is sitting aground. The purpose of using cores is to reduce the amount of fiberglass in a given laminate, thereby saving weight. But if you don't get off a reef promptly, the vessel's survival depends on whether she has enough material in her bilges to resist the abrasion of the reef. A cored boat has that much less material to resist the reef.

When examining a fiberglass hull, look carefully at the bonding of bulkheads and the extra glass at the hull-to-deck joint. If the boat has had some hard sailing, you'll be able to see if she's working. If you can't see all the structural joints, because permanent cabinetry is in the way, or if the hull-to-deck joint is hidden, stay away from the boat.

Steel is the next most common material for cruising boats, and perhaps the best material for the money available for small-boat construction today. It is strong, easy to work with, and virtually indestructable on a reef. If you collide with a log or another small boat, there is no question who is going to come out second best. Over 40 feet, a steel boat can be of moderate displacement. The negatives come in maintenance and resale. For some reason steel boats are not in favor in the U.S. It is frequently possible to pick up good steel boats for half the price of their fiberglass counterparts.

Without question steel presents maintenance problems, especially from a cosmetic standpoint. But with modern materials, properly applied, these are not insurmountable. The only way you can be sure of a good finish is to take a hull down to bare metal, sandblast it well, and build back up with a good epoxy or polyeurethane paint system. Inside, the hull should be well painted too. Most steel boats are foamed on the inside to help protect the skin, prevent condensation, and reduce noise.

There is a family of rust-resistant steel known as Corten that is the best material for boats. While it does rust initially, it won't continue to rust once an initial surface corrosion has developed. It's a little more costly as a raw material, and more difficult to weld and shape, but if you are starting from scratch, it's well worth the cost.

If you buy a used vessel in steel you need a qualified marine surveyor. Electronic gauging equipment to verify plate integrity should be used. The advantages of steel, including built-in tankage, watertight bulkheads, and the ability to weld fittings to the decks (thus eliminating possible leaks), make powerful arguments in its favor.

Aluminum is the ultimate sea-going material. It has the strength of steel without the drawbacks of rust. Its light weight makes it possible to reduce displacement, rig size, and/or draft to give a much higher performing cruising vessel than with any of the other materials.

It is important to watch dissimilar metals, as even stainless steel in contact with aluminum will start to corrode and ruin any nearby paint. These junctures require close maintenance. You also have to be careful about electrolysis: the ship must be properly wired and plumbed, something that is easy to verify. Modern, inexpensive gear exists for keeping an eye on galvanic corrosion.

Aluminum and steel pose a larger problem when you come into a marina. With powerlines dipping into the water and heavily wired powerboats nearby, you can have serious electrolysis problems. In this case it's a good idea to have extra protection in the form of zincs that are hung over the side or one of the new impressed current systems.

The cost today of a *custom* yacht in aluminum need not be any higher than with other materials. If increased resale value is taken into account, it makes a good investment. More and more wooden boat builders are switching to aluminum. Some feel that the day will come when aluminum production boats will be cheaper than fiberglass. As with steel, aluminum finds much greater acceptance in Europe than in the U.S.

Until *Intermezzo,* I owned exclusively wooden boats. I loved the feel of the wood, the smell of it, and the sense of communion with nature that it gave. But cruising is different from keeping a boat stored in a marina and using it occasionally. It entails running aground and going for months without hauling. There are lots of maintenance chores to perform beyond problems with the hull. Older wooden boats are cheap to buy because they are maintenance headaches. If you want to get a lot of boat for the money, buy a woody. But it will be heard to recover the funds that you invest in rigging her for cruising. Once underway, a disproportionate amount of your time will be spent on maintenance. If you are good with your hands and enjoy working with wood, okay. But if you're going to need others to help out, the initial cost advantage of an older wooden boat will rapidly evaporate in shipyard bills. Wood has its problems in the tropics, between opening up from the heat and being attacked from within by dry rot. When it comes to a reef, there is little chance of getting off. Where fiberglass or metal will slide reasonably well over coral, wood is too soft to resist the abrasion.

Lest you think I have only one prejudice, let's go on to stone boats (ferrocement). Of all the materials we have seen, it is the most unsuitable. Chosen by neophytes because of its supposed ease of construction, it was at one time considered the "people's" material. A little experience has convinced most insurance underwriters not to touch concrete. That should tell you something.

There are two major problems with this material. The first is resale. You might save 10 percent on the overall cost of a cement vessel compared to metal or fiberglass. But when it comes to selling the boat, your materials and labor have been invested in something that doesn't have a ready market. Even if she's beautifully fair, a comparable boat in another material will bring a much higher price. Second is those old reefs. Concrete does not have the impact resistance of other materials, and when the reefs get at ferroconcrete hulls, they go so quickly it's unbelieveable.

John Nichols and his beautiful *Heart of Edna* is a good example. *Heart of Edna* was meticulously crafted to extremely heavy scantlings. One late afternoon in the Louisidad Archipelago in southern New Guinea, John was faced with a no-win situation. With a low sun angle, he was forced to try to find his way into the lagoon. To stand offshore until the next day would have been equally dangerous in those treacherous waters. He missed, and *Heart of Edna* went fast aground on the fringing reef. Unable to free her right away, they left her for the evening and joined two other yachts inside the lagoon. They returned at first light to try to pull her off on the rising tide. They found three gaping holes in her bow section, and there hadn't been much of a sea running during the evening. John's new boat is aluminum.

Near Kieta, on Bougainville Island, also in New Guinea, lies what's left of a beautiful, heavily built ferrocement junk. Caught on a lee shore in a severe northwesterly blow with a very short fetch, she was driven ashore. The beach was mainly sand with an occasional rock. The short fetch prevented much of a buildup of sea. Yet within hours the boat had started to disintegrate.

Everywhere one cruises, stories abound of ferro boats not standing up to groundings that even a wooden boat would have survived.

What do you do if you already have a ferro boat? Be damned careful!

69. Positive Buoyancy

Surprisingly, there is no reason a boat with a displacement/length ratio under 275 cannot be built with positive buoyancy. If one is willing to go to the expense and effort of filling the bilges and some of the lower storage areas with foam, and build in watertight bulkheads, this goal is relatively easy to achieve.

Consider the advantages for a moment. At sea there is the obvious security and mental comfort that comes from knowing that your own vessel is its own best liferaft. If you happen to be caught on a reef and the reef chews through the side of the bilge, the rush of water and debris will be met by a barrier of foam that will give additional time to try to float free.

It isn't feasable to work toward positive buoyancy unless you are building. If you are, you must figure the weight that must be supported by buoyancy. This depends first on the building materials. Wood is self-supporting in the water. Fiberglass will support 70 percent of its weight, so only 30 percent is left for the flotation to carry. Aluminum will support about 30 percent; steel is a surprising 15 percent. At the bottom end of the scale is lead, which needs a 95 percent crutch. When the different weights are analyzed, you then take what is left in weight that needs support and divide that figure by 64 lbs. (or the weight of one cubic foot of salt water). This will give the answer in cubic feet of foam required to do the job.

The next question is where the buoyancy can be installed versus where the weight is that needs to be supported. The moments of relative balances have to even out or you may end up floating with one end of the boat pointing up.

Another way to assist the flotation is to compartmentalize the vessel. The foc's'l should be ahead of a watertight bulkhead. This will prevent the rest of the boat from flooding in the event of a collision, and provide extra buoyancy if the center of the boat is holed. If you have a beamy stern with good volume, try to work out a watertight compartment aft as well. The idea would be to have the two ends float the vessel by themselves with the foam in between as a backup.

Virtually any existing boat can have either a full or partial watertight bulkhead worked in forward. To do so is relatively easy, and could save your boat if you connect with something at sea that shouldn't be there. Normally, if you plug the drain holes, install a good bilge pump, and seal the bulkhead to the hull, you're in business. If you need access through the bulkhead for storing spare anchor rodes or sails, Bomar makes a cast, watertight door that does an excellent job.

70. The Rig

The best rig for a given cruising vessel depends on a variety of elements. First is the crew—its number, age, physical capabilities, and experience. Next comes the physical size of the vessel and the sail area required for adequate performance. The area in which you'll sail also plays an important part. What kind of performance you are looking for in light airs and heavy airs is a major ingredient, and the form of reefing system to be adopted is the final determinant.

Before getting into the different sail plans available, let's look at each of the factors to be considered in some detail. Then we can apply them to various types of rigs.

To begin with there is one absolute truth. Under poor conditions, in heavy weather, shorthanded, you *must* be able to handle the vessel. Any form of modern convenience such as roller furling or roller reefing is just that, a convenience. You must face the fact that it may not be functional when the chips are down.

Intermezzo anchored in Whangaroa Harbour, New Zealand. She carries her #3 and #1 jibs in the forward triangle. The full battened mizzen works well as a riding sail.

The size of a rig per se is not a major factor. Small sails can always be used on large rigs. Assuming that your vessel has a reasonable underwater shape, moderate to low wetted surface, and that the rig is efficient, small working sails if properly cut will give a reasonable turn of speed, even in light airs.

So much has to do with the region in which you are cruising. Trade-wind areas rarely surprise you with violent squalls or aberrant long-term weather systems. And while you may encounter some really good blows in trade-wind areas, even during the docile months, they come on relatively slowly; you generally have time to change down in sails if you feel something is coming.

Sailing in the higher latitudes is another case entirely. Virtually every high-latitude region has its "bad spots": Cape Hatteras with its infamous storms that materialize without warning, the Tasman Sea, even the west coast of California in winter. When sailing in these areas you have to use a different approach to your rig and the sails you carry.

The same philosophy applies to any type of rig: cutter, ketch, schooner, or whatever. You want to be able to carry a good press of sail in the pleasant sailing areas of the world, and still shorten down quickly when necessary.

As to absolute areas, one has to look at weight of sailcloth vs. size of the overall sail. Hoisting or sheeting a sail is not the problem; hanking it on and taking it off the headstay is what causes problems for shorthanded crews.

Factoring in your own experience, physical condition, and inclination is a difficult equation. If you don't have the experience to evaluate the situation, you're at the mercy of the "experts." My advice is to remember that you can always use the small sails. Be sure the rig will accept good-size sails, and then as your experience and self-confidence increase, more of the sail area can be used.

A point to consider in rigs is their relative efficiency. The amount of horsepower output per square foot of sail area varies tremendously from one type of rig to another. With an efficient rig, you may get away with carrying as much as a third less area to produce a given speed than a neighbor with something less desirable. Efficiency becomes really important on the wind, and also as the velocity of the wind increases. We must calculate not only the lift a given sail produces, but also its drag. Once the breeze starts to increase and you are at your normal heel angle, drag becomes the overall concern. A boat with a high-drag rig will heel quickly, load its keel, sideslip more, and require shortening down much sooner in gusty weather.

In absolute terms you can't do better than a solid airfoil such as is used on some of the C-class catamarans. Next come single-sail rigs as seen on many dinghies and small cats. A unirig of this nature will generate as much as 30 percent more horsepower and/or less drag for a given area than a conventional fore-and-aft rig. In other words, the more sails there are, the less efficient they become.

Rigging and spars contribute enormously to the depowering of sails and the increase in drag. Again, comparing a rotating mast or sock sail on a small boat to a fully rigged fixed spar, there can be 15 to 20 percent difference in drag. Even if you're not that interested in speed, we are now talking about comfort as well, when going uphill or reaching. This again relates directly to how many spars, and how much rigging (and, heaven forbid, baggy wrinkle) is involved.

What the maximum IOR racers have found is interesting. The split rigs originally found on such big vessels as *Kialoa, Ondine,* and *Windward Passage* got big rating credits for the supposed inefficiency of their mizzen masts. The mizzen area was only rated at 30 percent of the normal, and they were allowed to carry gigantic mizzen staysails and spinnakers for free. Yet today, every one of those boats is a sloop. They found that even with all that "free" area they were better off as a single-sticker.

And it's not only aerodynamics we have to think about. The weight aloft of a second stick is also a drawback. A mizzen mast reduces stability considerably, which in turn makes it necessary to reduce sail sooner or sail farther over on your ear.

Reefing and furling systems have changed greatly in modern cruising boats. We've come a long way from the old days of carefully and laboriously tied reefs to today's rigs that furl with the pull of a line or the push of a button. For marina sailing or an occasional cruise, I think these modern systems are great. But for extended offshore work they have to be carefully evaluated.

Let's look at the extruded-red headstay systems first. These were pioneered on racing boats and quickly gained acceptance due to their higher aerodynamic efficiency and speed of sail changing. On both scores you can't deny their worth. But you aren't going to have a full crew aboard; wrestling with a headsail on the foredeck in a good breeze on all but the smallest boats is a hard job, even with hanks. Trying to hang on with one hand and feed a new sail into a luff groove with the other under bad conditions is virtually impossible.

As the wind increases into the gale range, your capability deteriorates with the square of the increase in wind velocity, until getting the sail down safely becomes the first concern. So, if using roller furling on rods, you need a system that allows a choice of headsails, to fit the conditions you expect to meet, without having to change to a new sail. We have seen combinations of one roller-furling rod and one normal headstay set abaft the rod and carrying hanked-on jibs that worked well.

Note that I haven't used the word "roller reefing." In spite of all

The 68′ cutter *Deerfoot* close-reaching in Auckland Harbour, New Zealand. Her sails are so large that to be a practical boat for shorthanded cruising she must use roller-furling gear. The main, Yankee, and staysail all furl on Stearns rods. (S. A. Dashew)

Closeup of *Deerfoot*'s furled main. (S. A. Dashew)

the advertising to the contrary, there is simply no such thing as a roller-reefing headstay. Those great-looking photos are always taken in light airs with the boats going downwind. Ask for a photo or a demonstration going upwind in a good breeze and see what happens. The problem is this. As the wind increases, you want not only smaller sails, but flatter ones as well. If the sail is too full for the conditions, it will generate too much heeling moment and the boat will lie down and go sideways. When you roller-furl the headsail there is no way to adjust the draft or maintain a decent tension on the luff, and as a result you end up with a small bag. Thus rolling up the sail partially to reduce area makes it smaller, but also fuller. The boat is still lying on its ear. So the answer really is that you have to use that roller-furling headsail full size or not at all.

Roller furling has come more and more to be used on mains and even mizzens these days. Undeniably it is a convenience, but the same complaints about reefability apply here. In addition there is another problem. All headstays have a certain amount of sag, even

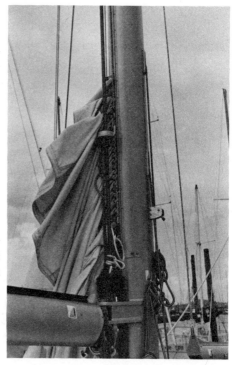

When passaging offshore *Deerfoot* frequently flew a Swedish main hanked on in a conventional manner to a track on the mast. (S. A. Dashew)

though they are powerfully opposed by the backstay. The sailmaker, if he knows his business, allows for this in the cut of the sail. On the main, however, you don't have the ability to really tighten up on the roller-furling stay. The eccentric compression load of the rod greatly reduces the load-carrying ability of the spar if too much pressure is put on. So you are left with poor sail shape due to spar sag or you are forced to go to a heavier and less efficient spar section. Thus you end up with lots of sag and a baggy sail or extra weight aloft, both of which, again, mean that you heel over too far. Or if the sailmaker hollows out the luff to allow for this, you have a flat board of a sail in light airs or downwind, when it should be nice and full. My guess is that a roller-furling main at best would be 30 percent less efficient than a normal main-spar combination. Of course, they are fantastically convenient, and if you have to have much over 550 square feet of sail area in the main, you may have no choice. Also, as one's age goes up these systems become more attractive.

If inclination, size, or physics push you in this direction, be sure to have a track on the outside of the spar, with a Swedish or storm main hanked on, reefable to trysail size. A Swedish main is a narrow sail with a hollow leech, no battens, and a shorter luff. It's good for moderate going on long offshore passages, and is a backup if something happens to the roller-furling gear.

REEFING

The strength of Dacron sailcloth makes possible the use of the slab-reefing system. In this rig a line is passed from the boom up through a reefing cringle on the leech of the sail, back down to the boom, and then forward to a winch at the mast or back again to one in the cockpit. To reef, you ease off the halyard to a predetermined point, pull down and tie off or hook the new tack cringle to the boom, and winch down the flapping clew. After the boat is moving again the reef cringles along the sail can be tied in to neaten things up. It's simple, efficient, and easy to use, and that's the system we used on *Intermezzo*. I found that it took me about three minutes on my own to crank in a reef. If Linda was up and the two of us worked together it was faster.

Boom roller-reefing systems used to be popular. But they are less efficient, since the man rolling has to be forward longer and since someone has to keep the leech of the sail stretched neatly along the boom. Furthermore, roller reefing requires that nothing be attached to the boom between the clew and the gooseneck. In the 1950s and early 1960s some of the ocean racers I sailed on used this system, but I feel it belongs in the Smithsonian Institution today.

Another way of reefing is with a bendy-mast rig. Just as a sagging headstay will put draft into a sail, a mast that is bent forward in a fair curve will take draft out. To utilize a bendy rig doesn't mean you have to go to featherweight spars as seen on today's ocean racers. Bendy rigs on boats 40 feet and down can be accomplished with conservative spar sections and good safety factors. It is a lot easier to crank in a mast bend than pull down a reef. And it enables you to have a full, powerful sail when going off the wind. This in turn reduces the number of headsails necessary for a given amount of boat speed.

ASPECT RATIO

Aspect ratio is another area to consider in looking at rigs. Up to a point, a high-aspect-ratio sail will perform better upwind than a low-aspect sail. Downwind, the roles are reversed. The extremely narrow, high-aspect-ratio sails seen in current IOR boats are designed in some cases to serve the rule rather than to produce speed. Furthermore, they put very high loads on the mainsail leech, which requires heavier cloth and makes trimming the sail more difficult. A low-aspect main can be lighter in weight and is more easily sheeted. When broad-reaching or running, its advantage in speed and ease of handling will outweigh whatever gain the high-aspect-ratio sail provides. A 3 to 1 luff/foot ratio is about as extreme as you want to have in a cruising boat.

RIGS

By far the best offshore cruising rig, size permitting, is the cutter. Properly set up, a cutter will have the sail distribution capability of a ketch without the attendant cost, complexity, or aerodynamic inefficiency. A good-size mainsail that can be used when set full with a staysail, jib, or with both headsails at once makes a powerful, easily handled rig. Additionally, a cutter should be able to sail under her staysail even when going to weather. Add to this a storm trysail and you can take just about anything without ever changing the headsails on their stays.

A cutter rigged with twin headstays can use either of two sizes of jibs (or both, when broad-reaching or running), and then shorten down to one jib and a staysail, and then to a staysail alone. The staysail, in fact, can do triple duty if it is reefable: (1) with a jib, (2) with the reefed main, and (3) on its own in really bad weather. The inner stay, or forestay, is ideal for carrying a storm headsail—it's easier to work around, being placed well abaft the stemhead, and if you're going upwind its sail is less likely to blow the bow off in heavier conditions or when you're cresting the tops of high seas.

Another advantage of the cutter is in her spars. The size of a yacht's spar is determined by the compression load, and this is a direct function of, among other things, shroud angle. Since the spar is farther aft than on other rigs the shroud angles are not so extreme, and as a result rigging and spar sections can be lighter for a given righting moment. This saves weight (and money), which in turn makes the vessel stiffer.

The cutter rig also allows you to go farther up in size without having to rely on roller-furling headsails. The double-head rig breaks up the size of the working headsails into manageable proportions. Take *Intermezzo II,* for example. Her working rig consists of a 600-square-foot Yankee (or #1) jib top and a 400-square-foot staysail. Going to windward this area is equal to about 900 square feet of more efficient genoa in the lighter wind ranges. That's not much penalty to pay. Reaching, it's probably superior. But a 900-square-foot 8-oz. genoa would be impossible for me to handle, so there's really no choice short of being forced to go to roller furling. I'd rather have two manageable sails.

The most popular rig, in terms of numbers, is the sloop. It is initially cheaper, because it eliminates the running backstays, forestay, and related chain plates necessary on the cutter. But it can carry only one headsail at a time, and under extreme conditions a small jib on the bow must be balanced by a storm trysail. Downwind, with their larger mains and single large headsails, sloops are faster than any of the other rigs. Sloops often set a staysail under a spinnaker or even with a jib in moderate conditions, without using running backstays. But this is only a way of developing more sail area, and is not to be attempted when the going gets rough.

If you are buying a used boat, you'll find more sloops available than anything else. Then you might consider adding a forestay and running backstays to increase versatility and heavy-weather capability.

In smaller sloops, fractional rigs also have a lot to offer. They provide the flexibility of mainsail draft control available with the "bendy" spar inherent in this rig, and also mean smaller headsails that are easier to handle.

I can't think of much good to say about yawls. They are aesthetic. The mizzen is great to rig an awning, makes a wonderful handhold and backrest, and is an excellent radar platform. Some people tout the yawl's mizzen as a steering rudder when maneuvering under sail in crowded conditions. *But . . .*

The ketch rig at least has sensible proportions, and the mizzen can provide some drive when reaching. But running it's a useless sail, and going to weather in conjunction with the main it's so badly back-winded that its drag is much higher than any beneficial lift it may create.

We did find on *Intermezzo* that she sailed exceptionally well under mizzen and headsail, with the main furled. Other friends with split rigs have reported this same result. But in our entire circumnavigation, we did this only once. There are a number of practical nonsailing benefits which accrue to the mizzen on a ketch. It allows the rigging of a sailing awning under its boom which also works as an efficient rain catcher at sea. There is a certain amount of security from having a second stick, independently stayed, of course. All things considered, though, a split rig of this sort on any vessel under 50 feet doesn't make sense. Over this size ketches begin to show to advantage, despite their increased cost and complexity.

We started by saying that a single sail was the most efficient way to get horsepower from a given amount of sail area. Well, you can imagine how we feel about schooners—two expensive spars and sets of rigging, and a whole bunch of postage-stamp-size sails. They look great, and if a spinnaker and gollywobbler are used they go like hell on a broad reach. But we are cruising shorthanded, and no short-handed schooner sailor I know ever uses his gollywobbler (which is the whole raison d'être for schooners); so why bother? Tradition, aesthetics . . . if that's your bag and you're willing to pay for it in boat speed, dollars, and difficulty in working your way off a lee shore, okay. But as a sensible rig on boats under 75 feet it doesn't make any sense.

The junk rig has always intrigued me. The simplicity (not to mention low cost) of the unstayed spars and apparent ease of handling are all cited as advantages. Tom Colvin has been an exponent of the junk for years. We have on several occasions met junk-rigged vessels cruising, the last of which was Peter Crowther on *Galaway Blazer* in Cape Town, South Africa. He had been rolled three times and dismasted in the South Atlantic at about 50 degrees south latitude and was in for repairs.

Peter said he had been lying a-hull at the time of his rollovers and felt that if he had had sail up and could have kept moving downwind, he would have been alright. At the time his foresail was damaged and couldn't be used. The first panel in his main was too large for the conditions. Hence, he was lying a-hull. One of the key factors in a good cruising rig is versatility under adverse conditions. Obviously this was lacking. And yet some amazing journeys have been made with the junk rig in high latitudes. Its other drawback is light-air performance. It's difficult to get a good shape to the sail, and this is the most important aspect of light-air sailing.

The sock-sail rig as used on the Freedom boats designed by Gary Hoyt is another interesting development, though still in its infancy. It generates very high horsepower per square foot of area with low drag coefficients sailing upwind due to its clean forward entry and lack of rigging. And obviously, with no standing rigging it's a cheap rig to build.

The jury is still out, however, on its suitability to high-latitude sailing. No one I have talked with in the West Indies has felt the reefing systems have been as yet worked out to deal with heavy air. Gary says he's close to solving the problem; we'll wait and see.

STANDING RIGGING

Now let's look at some of the details in rigging. The first thing to do is to establish a basis for the size of the various elements in the rigging system. To do this you have to look at working loads, ultimate loadings, and cyclical loadings. Like so many things in sailing, the hard engineering is based on experience rather than pure numbers. Miles at sea, reverse cycle loadings, temperature, and even variations in salinity play a part in determining these figures.

One hears a lot about safety factors in advertising literature. But how they are determined can vary tremendously from one firm to another. As a general rule, most naval architects develop their safety criteria for a boat's spars and rig at a stability figure based on a vessel carrying half her intended payload. Cruising boats always carry their full payload, and then some. The result is a reduced factor of safety, if that extra load is stowed where it will contribute to stability, because more stability means the rig will be subjected to more strain. Normal practice among naval architects is to use a factor of safety of between 2.5 and 2.75 to 1 on standing rigging. Our experience has indicated that this is fine if the boat isn't too heavily loaded. Another factor to look at, however, is what is actually required in wire size to meet these loads. If the design specifications call for 14,000-lb. wire, for instance, you'll be forced to use ⅜" diameter. That is the closest size up, and its breaking strain is about 17,500 lbs. So you actually have a much higher safety factor.

Aside from straight loads on rigging, the next thing you have to look at is what is called reverse cycle loading. This is where you have an off-again, on-again load, and is potentially much more fatiguing to the rigging elements than the basic sailing loads. It is particularly relevant to lower shrouds which are usually left looser than the cap or intermediate shrouds. The lee rigging, slatting back and forth, is a major problem in this regard. But that is where experience and the factors of safety come into play.

How does all this apply to a cruising rig? First, in order to be sure that the entire system is working together, the wire, turnbuckles, toggles, hull tangs, and mast tangs must all be sized to carry the full breaking strain intended. One thing to examine carefully is the bearing and shear on mast chain plates. If you see a gigantic chain plate at the gunnel and a featherweight on the mast on the same wire, you know something is out of balance.

Another danger to watch out for is stress risers. Any sharp edge, corner, or change in direction structurally is a potential stress riser, and if located where load can occur, will usually concentrate and increase local stress as much as much as 300 to 500 percent. An example of this could be a chain plate bent at an angle, with a hole right through the bend. Around the edges of that hole will be five times the stress the rest of the chain plate is taking. If it's going to break, guess where the failure will occur?

Always make sure the lead from the chain plate through the turnbuckle and up the wire is fair—no kinks, bends, or hard spots. If there are fore and aft lowers hanging on a common tang on the mast, be sure that all the pins rotate freely so that when the mast moves its load from the forward to the aft lower, the pins can rotate, and the swages aren't bent back and forth.

If you want to check up on the spars and chain plates, have a look at Skene's *Elements of Yacht Design*. There are some tables and short-form methods for working out loads that will give you a good idea where you stand.

Virtually every vessel we've seen cruising uses stainless-steel wire for standing rigging and where wire is called for in halyards. Galvanized plow steel is cheaper, but the toll in chafe from its rough texture far outweighs any cost advantage. Some claim a longevity advantage, but I don't believe it.

There is lots of controversy on end fittings. Swages, if properly done, are excellent and will give a reasonable service. But as with anything in the primary structure chain, you must keep an eye on them. Rarely will they ever fail without first giving ample warning of a potential problem. We met only one boat on our circumnavigation that ever had a *complete* failure underway with a swage fitting. On the negative side, some people feel that in the tropics they deteriorate rapidly due to salt water corrosion. *Intermezzo*'s rigging, for the most part, was eight years old when we left, and had seen quite a few miles. With the exception of one lower shroud which started to strand, we never had a problem in 30,000 miles.

The other approach is the Sta-lok/Norsemen type of terminal. They work well and have the added advantage of being reusable, if you carry spare cones. But they're very expensive. A good compromise is to use swages on the mast end of stays and shrouds and the Sta-lok fittings on deck, where they are subjected to more stress and corrosion.

Stainless is almost universally used for mast tangs. Clevis pin holes should be watched for wear, but one of the nice things about stainless is that if it's working too hard it gets stronger and stronger, for a while. This is called work hardening. Eventually, if the tangs are on the light side the clevis pin will start to eat its way through the stainless. This doesn't mean a catastrophe is on its way as long as there is sufficient meat around the hole to do the job intended. An easy cure or a double-check is to have bearing washers welded around the offending holes. However, if you have aluminum tangs, perhaps for a headstay or backstay, and see the hole working, that's an entirely different kettle of fish. Extrusion-grade alloys, such as used on masts, generally start to yield only 10 percent before they fail. If you see a pin hole widening in an aluminum tang, disaster is but a hair's breadth away.

Before we leave this topic, let's talk about stainless steel for a moment. There are stainless steels and there are stain-even-less steels. Type 316 is by far the best, but in the U.S. most wire and swage fittings are made of type 304. It is more subject to staining and stress corrosion than type 316. Wire and swedge fittings of type 316 are available if you hunt around. Generally they're about 20 percent more expensive, and if you're rerigging, they're the way to go.

SPARS

Modern spars are generally made of aluminum. For the purpose it's as close to being a miracle metal as anything. Light, strong, maintenance free, aluminum spars with a little care will outlive a vessel's owners. They will take substantial amounts of punishment as well. If you ever wonder what your spar will really take, go have a look at modern IOR racers 10 or 15 percent shorter than your cruiser; in spite of their shorter length, they'll have about the same initial stability due to a lower center of gravity and more ballast. Then compare staying base and rig height. You'll see they have extremely narrow shroud staying angles and very tall rigs. After this, look at the mast section. When you consider that stiffness, or section modulus as it is known among the engineers, increases with the cube of the increase in spar diameter, you'll understand that you are probably very conservatively sparred.

Wood spars are more expensive than alloy nowadays (unless you make them yourself), and are difficult to maintain, especially in the tropics. If you have them already, be especially careful of hardware attachment points. Dry rot is a major problem in these areas and a careful vigil is necessary.

Wood and aluminum spreaders are seen frequently on aluminum spars. Wood is generally lighter, but again it suffers from dry rot at the base and cap. In spite of our best efforts, we lost two of *Intermezzo*'s beautiful spruce spreaders to rot, and in New Zealand we replaced them with a pair of aluminum clubs. The attachment point of spreaders to the mast is also worthy of careful consideration. Normal sailing loads on the windward spreaders are very light with the spreaders in compression. But its poor cousin to leeward is having a devil of a time. First, it flops around fore and aft, with the weight of the slack lee rigging trying to wrench it off the mast. Then

Twin headstays on *Tina*, photographed in Pompano Beach, Florida, after her circumnavigation. Note the spacer bar between the upper jaws of the turnbuckles.

when sailing free, in spite of your best efforts and a vang, the mainsail is pushing steadily against it, exerting tremendous forward loads.

One solution is to use single-point attachments, which allow the spreader to rotate freely. This relieves both of the problems mentioned above. However, I don't care for it because if you have an extreme knockdown or rollover, the spreaders can be rotated out of column by the water pressure, which will lead to rig failure. A better idea is a heavy-duty base on the spreaders that takes the load in stride.

There are many kinds of turnbuckles on the market today. Those with a double-acting clevis pin are best. Only open-body turnbuckles should be used on an offshore boat. If there is a choice of bronze or stainless, bronze is better as it is less subject to fatigue failure than stainless, although I have never heard of a *properly led* turnbuckle failing.

Twin side-by-side headstays offer some advantages. With them you can set twin jibs downhill, and of more significance to me, you can have two different-size headsails hanked on and ready to go. To be successful they must be on a structurally stiff boat, with the fore and aft stays set up tight. Otherwise the weather stay, if it is working, will sag onto the leeward stay and the hanks will interconnect. Naturally, it will happen to a hank halfway up the stay, which will then jam on the way down. Another problem arises not infrequently when you're sailing free with the headsail hanked on the weather stay: the luff of the sail rubs against the leeward wire and causes serious chafe.

The other approach is to use two headstays, one abaft the other as we did on *Intermezzo,* with the outer stay being a roller furler and carrying the light headsail. This necessitates rolling up the outer sail for tacking or jibing, but that isn't too big a price to pay. The distance apart can vary from one foot to several, depending on your rig, sail size, etc.

Twin backstays, one to each quarter, are frequently seen on cruising boats. If you have twin side-by-side headstays, then they are necessary to help counteract any eccentric load that may be put into the masthead crane by the off-center headstays. With a single headstay they make little sense. If you're worried about strength, go up a size in diameter. It's lighter, cheaper, and less windage.

Keel-stepped masts are much more efficient structurally than a deck-stepped spar. The bond-beam action formed by the keel step and deck makes it possible to reduce spar weight by as much as 10 percent. In addition, if you're dismasted through the loss of a backstay or lowers, you will normally be left with a stump perhaps a third of the distance to the lower spreaders to which you can attach a jury spar.

Furthermore, a deck-stepped spar will not stand structural abuse as well as one stepped on the keel. Rigging failures that could be tolerated with good seamanship on the keel-stepped unit lead to immediate and complete dismasting with a deck-stepped spar. One exception is the deck-stepped mast placed in a structural tabernacle (this is normally possible only on metal boats). The tabernacle forms its own bond beam, and approximates the keel/deck connection. However, it is cumbersome, heavy, and expensive; unless you're planning to drop the spars for lots of bridge or canal work this is not worth the cost and complexity.

SAIL INVENTORY

There are numerous considerations to be weighed and compromises to be made when deciding on the proper sail inventory, including versatility, ease of handling, good light-air performance, heavy weather, storage, and longevity.

Let's begin by evaluating the various characteristics we have to work with. The most basic is storage. As mundane as that may seem, you have to decide how much space will be devoted below to sails and what sails will be stored on deck. You can assume that the working sails can be left on their stays, in sail bags to protect them from the sun; but the rest of the inventory will need a home below, at least at sea.

We have shared more than one anchorage with friends who remove their sails from the forepeak when they are in port, storing them on deck while the hook is down. We prefer to keep our decks clear, but then we have always had a good sail locker.

Heavy-weather sails are small, relatively inexpensive, and compact. Generally, if you have a trysail aboard, it will be stored on the mast on its own track. That leaves the heavy-weather headsails to worry about. On *Intermezzo* these took maybe 10 percent of our total sail storage area.

Assuming you have limited space and a limited budget, what do you do to make the most of what's available? Here you have the trade-off between weight and performance. Heavier sails last longer, will work well into higher wind ranges, and offer more versatility. On the other hand they are more cumbersome to handle and store, and don't set as well in light air. We have found over the years that going one weight in cloth above what is considered right for a wide-range racing sail is generally best for cruising.

Versatility can be improved somewhat by sail design features such as stretchy luffs. By using a combination of Dacron tape and rope instead of wire in the luff, the draft in a given sail can be varied over a moderate range of wind by tightening or easing the halyard. The disadvantage is that stretchy-luff sails don't last as long as ones of fixed-luff construction, and can't be abused as much by carrying them into higher wind ranges than those for which they were designed. Another factor to consider is that stretchy-luff sails work better with bolt-rope systems than with hanks or slides as they don't scallop when the tension is eased.

On smaller boats it's better to go with a little heavier mainsail cloth than normal. The extra weight and bulk don't present a handling problem and the extra longevity to be gained is well worth the small increase in cost. Additionally, an extra row of reefs can be added for carrying the sail into higher wind ranges where one would be forced to set a trysail on a larger craft.

As sail area approaches 400 square feet, furling and hoisting become considerations to be carefully weighed. At this stage I prefer to start looking at lighter weights, with the basic assumption that a trysail or Swedish main will be carried once the wind gets beyond first or second reef strength. This involves the step of setting an extra sail, but offshore it doesn't happen that often, and will substantially increase the life of the basic working main. Battens along the leech are definitely a pain from a maintenance standpoint, but the alternatives are not worth considering. Without battens, the sail's leech has to be hollowed and the sailmaker loses control of his shaping tools. The result is a sail that will only set well within narrow parameters. The rest of the time it will look like a dead horse, and you won't move.

To alleviate some of the problems caused by battens, and ease the sailmaker's job, consider using extra-length battens. Batten lengths are fixed by racing rules, not practical necessity, and if they are made 50 percent longer, the stress they have to work against is distributed more evenly. Trap-style pockets are the best, and the battens should be seized in place. The pockets should be double-reinforced, with extra care taken at the forward end. For cost, availability, and serviceability, I have found that PVC tubing, flattened at the ends after being heated over our propane stove, makes the best batten material.

Intermezzo has eaten eight battens during our time aboard. In every case this occurred during taking in a reef that was delayed too long. Only once, at the end of our trip, was it necessary to repair a batten pocket.

Mizzen battens are another problem. We experimented with full battens, as I mentioned earlier, to keep the sail quiet when it was in use at anchor. However, we found that the full battens also improved the performance of the sail going to weather and close-reaching. The leading edge was not as quick to cave in because of backwind from the main, and the drag angles didn't deteriorate as quickly. It also made the sail a lot easier to handle in heavier air when reefing.

A working jib has several functions. First, it is an intermediate-wind-range sail on all points of sail. Second, you may want to use it sailing in and out of harbors for fun or necessity. The short-overlap and quick-sheeting aspects make it ideal for maneuvering. In combination with light headsails running or broad-reaching, it can be flown to weather on the spinnaker pole. The clew should be high enough to provide good visibility, and to keep it out of the water when reaching. Another consideration is the lead. If possible, work the clew angle out so the sheet can be led through the end of the boom when reaching. This helps the shape of the sail tremendously.

Light headsails offer a lot more possibilities to be creative. When we bought *Intermezzo,* she carried a light #1 jib topsail along with heavier headsails. We elected to keep the light #1, for although it was 780 square feet, its 3.5-oz. construction made it easy to handle and stow. With the apparent wind at 50 degrees it could be carried until *Intermezzo* was overpowered. Beam-reaching and running, poled out or to leeward, it was a powerhouse. Upwind, it had to come off in 10 knots apparent. But for our trip, it was the workhorse of our inventory. In spite of its advanced age, it made it all the way to the mid-Atlantic before giving up the ghost, and even then it went only because I pulled a substantial blunder.

A light headsail, to do the same work on a smaller boat, say, a 35-footer, could still be built from 3½-oz. cloth and do well, and of course would have a greater wind range. Light sails of this nature benefit from stretchy-luff construction.

In between the light #1 and a working jib comes a #2, generally splitting the difference on size. On *Intermezzo* our heavy #2 was 580 square feet and 8-oz. cloth. When we had upwind work, or in the breezier parts of the Indian Ocean, we went to this sail. Its heavy construction made it a lot of work on the foredeck, but it was in effect bulletproof, and downwind we carried it up through 45 knots apparent on occasion.

An inexpensive, easy-to-store, and versatile light-air sail is a drifter. Generally built of ¾- to 1½-oz. nylon, with a wire luff, it works well reaching in light airs, and can be dynamite when flown to leeward with another jib to weather. *Intermezzo* carried a ¾-oz. drifter and it saw duty on virtually every long trade-wind passage.

My favorite of the cruising inventory is the spinnaker. *Intermezzo*'s was in use on 30 percent of the days we were at sea. Spinnakers take up a small amount of space for their usefulness, and greatly improve the performance downhill. (Remember, most trade-wind sailing is in light airs.) We have found that the spinnaker is easier to fly and requires less adjustment than twin jibs. From a design standpoint, an old-fashioned CCA crosscut cannot be beat. They go well downwind, are stable, and are cheap to build (see Chapter 38).

In heavier air the forestaysail comes into its own. Balanced against a close-reefed main or with a mizzen, it provides a good way to handle the intermediate wind ranges. As the starts to howl and sails have to get heavier and smaller, the staysail becomes the best weapon aboard for heavy work.

The mizzen staysail is the only thing that makes a ketch or yawl rig worthwhile. The sail does very well in light airs, and on those occasions when the air is too light for the sea that is running, can help power the boat along when the main is furled due to the sloppy conditions. It's not unusual for a moderate-aspect-ratio ketch or yawl to have a mizzen staysail as large as the main itself. Properly used, it can add substantially to boat speed. *Intermezzo*'s light mizzen staysail was ¾-oz. nylon. At 418 square feet, it was almost identical in size to her main. On a broad reach, if the true wind was 10 knots, the steam gauge would jump half to three-quarters of a knot when it was sheeted home. Once the apparent wind goes aft of 145 degrees, though, the sail is no longer of value. On the other hand if you have a flat mizzen staysail, it can be carried up to about 55 degrees apparent wind angle with some success. But as the wind picks up, the thrust that the staysail exerts aft combines with natural weather helm to overpower the self-steering, so these are definitely light-air sails.

The subject of storm sails could take a book in itself. You must have *a selection* of storm canvas ranging from what we call a survival sail, for ultimate conditions (just before running under bare poles), up to a more orthodox storm jib. Remember that you have to be able to match the speed of the boat to the sea conditions, and that the sails have to be able to balance the boat so she will go uphill if need be. This means a staysail that is large enough to overcome windage going to weather when set alone if you have a cutter rig, or a storm jib and trysail (or reefed mizzen) combination on other rigs. To repeat what we said earlier, storm sails are generally inexpensive and take little space; but when they are necessary, *there is no substitute.*

Reefing headsails are seen more and more these days. On a limited-inventory cruising boat, for short-term sailing, they are an excellent answer, but for a long-term cruise I'm not so sure. Harry Ellens, the manager of Ellens and Hudson Sail Loft in Durban, South Africa, probably has more experience with storm sails and lousy weather than anyone I know. The sailing conditions along the coast of South Africa are so bad as to defy description. But yachting, and even racing, flourish there. Aside from building and repairing these sails, Harry does a lot of work on the round-the-world cruisers that call in at Durban every November. He feels that the reinforcement patches required on the leech of a reefable headsail cause more problems with maintenance than they are worth. In heavy weather they often cause the sail to flog, ruining the fabric and stitching.

RUNNING BACKSTAYS

If you're sailing a cutter or a double-headsail rig of any sort, you'll need running backstays. They're a nuisance, but rigging them properly can make life a bit easier. To begin with, rope tails, directly from the 1 × 19 backstay wire to a winch in the cockpit area is the easiest way to control them. Usually a 2- or 3-to-1 tackle is used. Remember that the blocks and their attachment points must have a breaking strength equal to the 1 × 19 wire. For pulling and holding the unused backstay forward, I use a piece of ¼" braid run through a block positioned on deck so the retrieving line will hold the wire just clear of the aft side of the lower spreader. The line is led aft to a jam or cam cleat in a convenient spot.

Aside from supporting the mast, running backstays have several other advantages. If you are running free and have to turn the boat quickly with a jibe, the main boom will fetch up on the set runner and drive the boat quickly into the wind, stopping way almost instantaneously.

Runners also are great as a midpoint attachment for deck awnings, especially if you have a single-sticker. And, of course, they make a nice handhold.

If you are dead set against the hassle of running backstays but still want or need an intermediate forestay, there are some other approaches. The first is to locate jumper struts at the intersection point of the forestay and mast. Shrouds are run over the jumpers above and below, and keep the mast in column when a load is placed on the inner forestay. Or you can use standing lower backstays. In this system a chain plate is placed a little way aft of the after lower shroud, but it requires a much heavier wire and adds considerably to compression load. We have also seen boats with a double-spreader rig whose lower spreaders are swept aft. They lead the intermediate shroud on an aft angle, thus helping to counteract the forestay load. None of these three systems will yield a really tight inner forestay. If you expect to go to weather in much of a breeze, and want everything going for you, runners are the best bet.

DOUBLE SPREADERS

Double-spreader rigs are inherently more seaworthy than single-spreader supported masts. Assuming that the structural loads are equally spread, the double-spreader rig offers more of a chance of saving the spar in the event of a rigging failure. With a single-spreader rig, if you lose a shroud it's almost certain the spar will be lost.

A double-spreader set-up requires two upper shrouds, a cap, and an intermediate. On racing boats these two are usually joined at a toggle just above the lower spreader. There is a turnbuckle at the deck and another at the upper or lower end of the intermediate section for adjustment. This rig offers less weight aloft and less windage than two separate wires. With a little forethought, you can also use one piece of wire to replace any of the side shrouds. If the cumulative effect of the loads doesn't force you into an extra-expensive turnbuckle and wire size, I think this system is the best way to go, due to the replacement aspects. Its negative side, of course, is that if the single lower section goes, the mast goes with it. Many people we know feel that a separate intermediate and cap shroud is a safer approach, and they carry more wire aboard for emergencies.

LOWER SHROUDS

Many racing boats are rigged with a single lower shroud, usually led slightly aft of the cap shroud chain plate. A baby or midstay supports the mast in a fore-and-aft direction. The other approach is to use fore and aft lowers, as is seen on most cruising boats. This latter rig has two advantages. First, if one of the lowers carries away, you still have the other. Second, they make the best possible place for wood or rope steps necessary for going aloft to view coral or to get a better idea of what's on the horizon.

BOOM VANGS

Boom vangs are an absolute necessity for controlling sail shape downwind. The vang has to be powerful enough to keep twist out of the leech and the main off the lee rigging. It should be weaker, however, than the boom it is attached to. If you end up rolling the boom under when reaching in strong breezes, something may give, and it's best if it's the vang. We found that by taking our vang to the lee rail instead of the mast base when running or broad-reaching, it

Intermezzo II uses a compression strut in lieu of a topping lift.

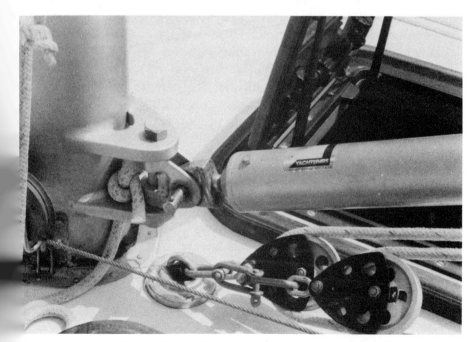

The forward end of a similar strut aboard *Deerfoot*.

did double duty as a preventer. On several occasions it was tested when *Intermezzo* decided to jibe herself in heavy going, and it worked well every time.

TOPPING LIFTS AND GALLOWS FRAMES

Topping lifts are the most cantankerous piece of running rigging aboard. They love to wrap themselves around backstay insulators and chafe on the leech of the mainsail. The only solution is to use a long, heavy piece of shockcord to keep them tight when the boom lifts. They should be heavy 7×19 stainless-steel wire, plastic covered to minimize chafe, with a rope tail.

After the topping lift comes the boom gallows. I don't like them, but if the boom overhangs the cockpit, some people think they are a necessary safety feature. Dr. Emory Moore told Linda and me one day when we were having drinks together in Rabaul, New Guinea, of three people he knew whose heads had been cracked open by booms when the topping lifts had failed. Some seamen also swear by the gallows frame as a secure leaning post, especially when taking sights. But we feel they don't belong on modern yachts.

A way to avoid both topping lift and gallows frame is the compression strut used on the *Deerfoot* class yachts. This is a simple, nonhydraulic tube within a tube, fitted from low on the mast up to the boom, that prevents the boom from dropping but does not restrict its upward movement. With it is rigged a separate boom vang running below the strut from mast to boom, with several parts that end up back in the cockpit.

WINCHES

Today there are so many types of winches available it's hard to know where to begin. The Cadillac of winches, from a construction standpoint, is certainly Barient. Their stainless bearings and bearing cages

The "jammer" is one of the best inventions of our
era for cruising.

along with their machining in general are a notch above the others.
There is certainly nothing wrong with the other brands, however.
Self-tailing winches are a fantastic invention; if you can afford them,
they are a boon on the primaries, main sheet, and perhaps main
halyard, and certainly the slab-reefing winches.

Reel halyard winches should be outlawed. More people have been
injured on yachts by these devilish machines than anything else. If
the winch-handle operator is constantly attentive, everything will go
fine; but if he's careless for an instant, watch out!

JAMMERS

Sheet jammers are an interesting throw-off from the racing fraternity. In certain applications they can save time and the expense of
an extra winch. But they do chew up line, and if they are used on

one that is heavily loaded it will need to be replaced before long. For an offshore cruiser that is going to do a lot of miles, they have a limited value if in constant use.

HALYARDS

I have tried for years to convince myself to try prestretched or low-stretch rope for halyards. What a convenience! But every time I have been aboard a boat of 40 feet or more with rope halyards I find that, if the wind is blowing, the sails can't be kept tight enough on their luffs for a decent shape. Wire with a rope tail is a good compromise. Virtually any size of rope tail can be spliced to wire, and if you go up a size or two from what's recommended, the rope-to-wire splice will be by far the strongest part of the system.

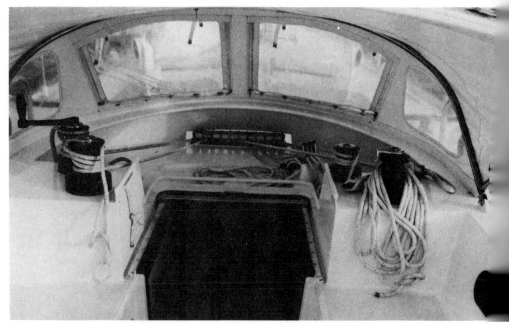

Eight lines lead under the cozy dodger and are serviced by four self-tailing winches. The spinnaker halyard and four reefing lines share a winch and a triple jammer. At sea, rope tails are usually coiled and flaked in the forward section of the combing.

Intermezzo II's flush-deck layout allowed us to bring the reefing lines, main halyard, main sreet, vang, and spinnaker halyard aft. The full-width traveler, with four ball-bearing cars, make it possible to sail her like a big dinghy. The main street is used for leech tension while angle of attack is controlled by the traveler. The vang is only used to the rail when running or broad-reaching. (Harrill House)

Thus you can have the handling of rope and the low stretch of wire. Wire halyard sheaves should be at least 25 times the diameter of the wire, if you expect the halyard to last.

Aluminum winch drums are the most popular because of their low cost and weight. But if you intend to put wire on the drums, they must be bronze or stainless. It's positively amazing how fast a piece of 7×19 stainless wire will eat its way through aluminum.

I am a great fan of leading some of the halyards and reefing lines to the cockpit area if it doesn't create a rat's nest. Being able to handle a vessel from the security of the cockpit, especially on smaller boats, is a real blessing. But people often try to do too much in this regard, and the result is chaos, with lines and coils in a frightful tangle. If you can lead the main halyard, the spinnaker halyard, foreguy and topping lift, and the slab-reefing lines aft, you have covered 90 percent of your needs. (When lowering or breaking out headsails, you'll probably have to go forward anyway.) Obviously, flush-deck vessels make this approach easier.

SHEETS

There are numerous brands and grades of rope available, but for running rigging the double-braids are best. When deciding on size, remember that, just as with sailcloth, a little increase in size will yield tremendous benefits in longevity. Heavier line will stretch less under load and chafe less as a result. If chafe does occur, it can go a long way before you have to end-for-end it or replace the section in question. If you're buying in small quantities, consider color and texture coding. Most rope manufacturers make several finishes, and at night these can easily be differentiated by feel.

SPINNAKER POLES

Twin spinnaker poles used for winging out jibs for downwind sailing should be stored on the mast for ease of handling; but you also ought to be able to secure them on deck when the going gets rough, or when you expect to be heading uphill for a long period.

There are several ways to rig them. The cheapest is to use a fixed pivot point on the mast at the upper end of the pole; the lower, outer end is then hoisted up to sail-clew height by the pole topping lift. The disadvantages here are that the pole cannot be brought down to deck for storage, and that the clew of the headsail to which the pole is attached must be very high, since the pole's inner end can't be adjusted. The next scheme is to pivot the bottom end of the pole at about shoulder or working height on the mast. When stored, the outboard end of the pole is topped up into a chock aloft. The problem here comes in properly securing the pole when it's aloft. If you are pounding into a headsea, or rolling around in light airs, it's virtually impossible to stop completely the rattling of the poles aloft. Furthermore, as before, you can't adjust the inner end of the pole to keep it horizontal when in use. The most versatile approach is to have a track that runs up the mast to a height that allows storage of the pole while on the mast. In use, the pole is attached to the headsail sheet and the outer end is lifted slightly. The inboard end of the pole is then pulled down the track until the pole height is even at both ends.

When placing the deck storage hardware, put the forward pole chock in such a position that the pole can be rested on it while it is still attached to the mast. Then when you release the pole from the mast, the forward end will take care of itself and you will then only have to worry about the after end.

Spinnaker pole size should be conservative. We have frequently seen small-diameter poles sold for use with a jib only as whisker poles. They work fine in bay waters, but offshore, when you're running before a good-size sea or carrying a jib at close apparent wind angles, the failure rate can be high. Even if you don't intend to carry a spinnaker, the pole should still be sized for these loads. It should be at least as long as the base of your forward triangle.

The pole should be as light as possible. A large-diameter pole with thin walls will be stronger than a skinnier, thicker-walled pole of the same weight (for instance, aluminum). *Intermezzo*'s spinnaker poles were six inches in diameter, and sitting on the deck looked as if they weighed a ton. But in reality they were thin-wall tube that had been chemically milled even thinner. As a result of their substantial diameter they were extremely strong but very light. I could pick them up and maneuver single-handed with one in a seaway.

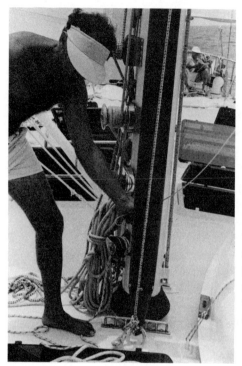

The 24' spinnaker pole aboard *Intermezzo II* is stowed vertically on the mainmast when running in moderate conditions. When reaching or going to windward it's stowed on deck. (S. A. Dashew)

To use the spinnaker pole properly, first the topping lift is attached, a load taken on the winch, and the pole lifted outboard of the lifelines. The sheet of the headsail or spinnaker is then led through the pole end. The mast (inboard) end of the pole is then winched down and the topping lift evened out so the pole is horizontal at a predetermined height. Next, a temporary afterguy (shown here) is rigged aft to the toe rail. (S. A. Dashew)

Finally, the headsail is hoisted and sheeted out. After the sheet is set, the afterguy is removed and taken forward and used as a foreguy. (S. A. Dashew)

There are all sorts of end fittings available today. The simple piston ends and mast cars with rings are the least expensive and work well, up through 45- or 50-foot boats. Above that, it's wise to investigate the articulated cup or male and female inboard end arrangements. When reaching with the spinnaker, the inboard end of the pole is in straight compression, but when running with either the chute or a job you have the compression load as well as a bending moment on the mast fitting to contend with. To carry this load, the mast fitting and the track have to be stoutly made and attached. The track should be through-bolted if possible. Avoid rivets unless they are monel, and even then use them as a last resort. If the spinnaker car track loads were in plain shear, or sideways load, rivets would be fine. But there is the possibility of a combination of shear and a lifting type of load as the car tries to rotate the track off the mast. A machine screw, tapped into the mast wall, is a better bet if you can't reach to through-bolt.

71. Steering Systems

The best and simplest steering system ever invented is the tiller, if you can hang onto it. It has good feel, is inexpensive, and is virtually foolproof. It even lends itself to simple autopilot installations. But above 35 feet in boat length, the tiller becomes hard to handle, especially in a blow. There are a number of good wheel-steering systems on the market today that use cables. The combination of needle bearings, large-diameter sheaves, and large steering wheels that yield almost the same feel as a tiller. Since the cruising yacht will rarely be hand-steered, however, we are more concerned with reliability than feel.

In this respect there are two important aspects to consider. One is sheave diameter. Using 7×19 stainless-steel wire for controlling the quadrant, a sheave of 40 times the wire diameter should be employed. This will ensure that the breakdown of the stainless-steel wire where it passes over the sheave will be delayed for the longest possible time. Second, the sheave should be deep enough so that if some play begins to work into the system, there is no chance for the wire to jump out. Observe the action of the wire as it leads from the sheaves to the quadrant when the quadrant goes through a full arc from hard port to hard starboard and be sure that the lead is fair all the way through the length of travel.

If you install an automatic pilot with cable steering, try to set up the pilot system so that it leads directly to the rudder shaft with its own tiller arm or quadrant and cables. With this rig the pilot can be

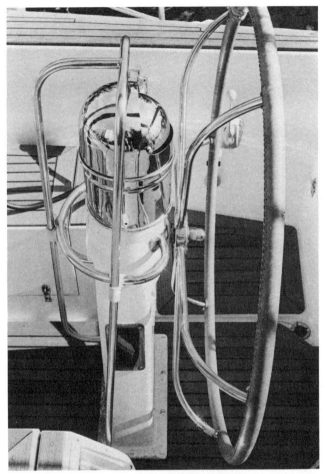

Steering pedestal on the world-girdling Swan 65, *ADC Accutrac*. Note the inspection port to view the steering chain and the sturdy handrail/compass guard.

engaged to steer the vessel, should the main steering be lost at an inopportune moment.

Worm-gear steering used to be popular and had what some people felt was an advantage in limiting feedback. However, it is rare to see it on a modern vessel, because of its weight, expense, and lack of "feel."

Hydraulic steering, if assembled with the best materials, can give good results. The space occupied by the quadrant is eliminated and there is more freedom in placing the wheel. One big negative here is lack of a king spoke. Because of inevitable internal leakage in all systems, there is no sure guarantee that the rudder and steering wheel position will always correspond. If you have hydraulic steering and want to set up an inside steering station, it is simply done with the addition of another wheel and pump that tie into the same lines and cylinder as the master unit.

Hydraulic systems such as those sold by Wagner Engineering have been in use by commercial fishing boats in the Pacific Northwest of the U.S. and Canada for years. As with any gear aboard, you must be capable of maintaining it. In this case that means spare seals and the know-how to change them. Hydraulic seals, when they start to go, generally give warning by telltale leaks.

Every vessel must have the means of fitting an *easy-to-use* emergency tiller. When evaluating this piece of vital gear, imagine how a sheet-to-tiller arrangement would be devised for self-steering. Be sure the emergency tiller can be rigged on short notice. Some set-ups require the removal of the binnacle before the emergency tiller can be shipped. Consider its strength as well. Emergency tillers are frequently too weak for the high loads they must withstand.

72. Interiors

Interior requirements for the long-range cruising boat vary dramatically from what would be acceptable on a vessel used primarily for weekends. Perhaps the biggest difference is this: on a cruise your vessel is going to be your home, and she will have to provide you with the storage space and amenities that allow a comfortable, enjoyable existence.

Once the sheer joy of getting away from it all wears off and the initial excitement is over, the camping-out aspect also starts to wear thin. If you and your crew are to gain the fullest enjoyment from cruising, it must take place in reasonable surroundings.

A very important aspect of a good cruiser's interior is its *apparent* roominess. This can be achieved two ways: with color and with *unbroken* space.

Light colors and textures help develop a feeling of open space. Dark finishes and heavy patterns close in on space. Many of the production yachts on the market boast teak veneer bulkheads, which are supposed to be traditional, expensive, and practical. In reality, a boat that is finished off in dark woods shrinks considerably in apparent size. Boat builders like dark veneers because they are cheap to install. A veneer that has three coats of matte-finish varnish, or oil, can be passed off as quality. But if a builder were to paint that same panel, it would take many coats of primer and paint before an acceptable finish was achieved. And teak veneers are not traditional. A majority of older, wooden vessels were finished in light-painted paneling or light-wood paneling with darker wood trims. It's all a

A combination of light Formica and vinyl, with some natural woods and a lot of window area, creates a very warm yet open saloon aboard *Deerfoot.* (S. A. Dashew)

matter of personal preference. If you like the look of wood below, use it in the trim.

If your eye is allowed to roam unobstructed from one end of an area to the other, it will perceive a much greater open feeling than if an object interrupts the flow of vision. An example of this would be a hanging locker placed in the galley, between the saloon and after end of the boat. Such an obstruction would, in effect, cut the interior in half. I was amazed when we rebuilt *Intermezzo*'s refrigeration system and removed the vertical handholds from the galley. These columns, only 2½ inches around, had cut down substantially on our apparent space.

As to the actual physical space below, you start right off with a severe compromise. At least 90 percent of your time will be spent in port or at anchor, and obviously you want comfort and privacy during this period. But that 10 percent of the time you spend at sea has a substantial multiplier effect if it isn't comfortable aboard. Then aside from the in-port/at-sea trade-offs, you must consider ventilation and staying dry. The ability to stay dry and move about safely under rough sea conditions is crucial.

Let's start with general layouts. Aft-cabin/center-cockpit arrangements have been very popular for a few years. On a short-term cruiser with several couples aboard, this makes sense. Everyone has privacy, and there's a nice bulkhead, not to mention a hunk of engine, isolating the vessel's ends. But the vast majority of long-term cruising people end up aboard by themselves, with occasional guests visiting for a week or two now and then.

And for a couple cruising long distance, there are two objections to the aft-cabin/center-cockpit layout. First, the roomiest, most comfortable part of the interior is given over to the cockpit and engine room. Second, the interior is broken up into small sections. Consider what could be done with that space by moving the cockpit aft and putting the engine under the cabin sole. Center cockpits are much wetter going to weather; running downwind, if the vessel decides it wants to roll a bit, the increased height of the center-cockpit seats will give you a more uncomfortable ride.

The aft-cockpit layout has the advantage of providing a continuous unbroken interior to work with. It is still possible to develop an aft cabin if the vessel has the beam aft to accommodate this type of approach.

An excellent example of the aft-cockpit/aft-cabin layout can be seen in Bill Lapworth's Cal-48. Designed in the early 1960s as a big brother to the Cal-40, she has a powerful stern, carrying her beam well aft. Even with moderate displacement, she is able to accommodate a large aft cabin.

The layout on Caroline and Bob Osborne's *Decision* is also a good example. Coming below from their large aft cockpit, you enter the owner's cabin with a nice double bunk to starboard and a single to port. Ahead of the single is a modest head compartment. On the starboard side, opposite the head and in front of the bunk, is the navigating station. This layout gave them privacy in port and allowed Bob to sleep close by the cockpit when at sea.

The rest of the boat was devoted to galley, saloon, and forepeak with twin berths. There was a second entrance through the coach roof and into the saloon for use in port, if the aft cabin was occupied.

The actual amount of deck space devoted to the cockpit has been shortened in recent years, and this is a good trend. *Intermezzo* was an example of the old-style weekend cruiser/racer. She had a very long cockpit, set ahead of a lazarette, and as a result lost almost a third of her potential interior volume. Before correcting this in New Zealand, Linda and I frequently looked longingly at that space, dreaming about what a nice additional cabin it would make. The cockpit needs only to be big enough to hold you and a few occasional guests. The smaller it is, within those parameters, the safer it is at sea for the vessel and her crew.

SLEEPING ACCOMMODATIONS

Sleeping arrangements are perhaps the most important aspect of an interior. If you can't get a comfortable bunk to sleep in when at sea, you aren't going to be doing much voyaging. "Comfortable" means a bunk that isn't too big, that is ventilated with a flow of fresh air, and that is *dry*. The optimum location varies depending on conditions. Generally speaking, midship pilot or settee berths are most comfortable except when the boat is oscillating downwind. In this case, the pilot berth being high and at the extreme edge of the beam subjects the sleeper to a good deal of motion. Bunks in the forward

Looking into *Intermezzo*'s saloon from the galley/navigation area.

part of the boat are generally used only under ideal conditions, unless there are children aboard: they don't know any better. Among most of our friends cruising as couples, the main saloon area is the only part of the interior that is used at sea. Quarterberths set aft by the companionway are perhaps the best in terms of motion, but they pick up noise from outside via the companionway opening, and are known on most boats at some point as quarter*baths.* If an aft-cabin arrangement is employed, these bunks, except for occasional noise problems, are excellent.

In-port living requires different answers. First, a good snug bunk that keeps you from rolling too much at sea is too tight to be comfortable in port, especially in the tropics. I opt for maximum comfort in port, and if necessary, throw in a pillow or two offshore when the going gets rough to prevent excess body movement. Next, most offshore crews, being couples, are going to want a double bunk, at least for in-port sleeping. One end or other of the vessel is usually the best place for a private double bunk. Doubles in the main saloon are less desirable since they are in the middle of your living room; you have to make and unmake the bunk every day. This is not conducive to spontaneous sleeping situations.

For a single bunk, dimensions of 2 feet by 6½ feet work well. The width can taper down six inches or so at the feet if necessary. A minimum-size double bunk in the tropics is 44 inches wide at the head. In cooler climates you can get away with a substantially narrower bunk. But overall, the goal of enjoying companionship favors a good-size double bunk.

Where, you may ask, am I going to fit in a double bunk that is serviceable without going into the main saloon? Consider an athwartships bunk up forward. Most modern boats are full enough in their bow sections to rearrange two single bunks running fore and aft into a double that runs athwartships. We did this aboard *Intermezzo* and she was fairly narrow forward. It resulted in a bunk that was 7 feet long on the outside (aft) where I slept, and a hair under 6 feet at the very inside (forward) edge, where Linda slept. At sea going downwind, this was fine for sleeping, and on the hook in a rolly anchorage it was definitely preferable to fore-and-aft sleeping.

When you look at the bunks, consider also how difficult it will be to make them up each day. Most cruisers find that after a short while sleeping bags are put aside in favor of sheets, pillows with nice casings, and blankets, just like at home. (In the tropics, matching print sheets and pillowcases look neat and cool, and in colder climates, matching quilts and pillow shams are an easy way to dress up a bunk.)

GALLEYS

After sleeping accommodations, the galley ranks as the most important part of the boat. Without exception, modern designs locate the galley so as to provide direct access to the cockpit. This provides good air flow from the companionway, easy access for taking food on deck, and less motion for the cook. But the major advantage cited in some sales literature, i.e., that the cook becomes part of the party, doesn't count when you're cruising for long periods. Remember, your party goes on, perhaps for years. On some boats a good place for the galley in terms of space and layout is farther forward, by the mainmast. The steep angles of the topsides minimize sole area but

Fitted rails on the athwartship-mounted stove of *Intermezzo II*.

Our compact and efficient galley aboard *Intermezzo*. The sink is to port and the reefer to starboard.

Galley sink covers also serve as chopping boards. Note the dish storage behind the sink. (S. A. Dashew)

Rigadoon's very seamanlike sink. Note especially the high fiddles and angled sink boards for good drainage.

allow for good counter space and related storage. Motion is greater, but many modern boats would benefit from this arrangement as long as they're well ventilated.

The galley must have storage space for a variety of pots and pans, including such items as large and small frying pans, a large kettle for boiling lobsters and crabs, a tea kettle, two or three medium saucepans, including a double boiler, and a small saucepan. There should be good counter space that doesn't block other storage areas. You may also want to provide for space for a few small electrical appliances.

Consider allowing space for a microwave oven, if you have room in the engine room to fit a small AC generator on the main engine or a compact 12-/110-volt inverter. Fast and efficient, microwaves are fantastically helpful when at sea.

Marine sinks are on the small side, but in most cases this is fine as they will conserve dishwashing water, and space is limited in any event. But they must be deep. About nine inches is best for a small craft, although a larger, stiffer vessel can get by with a seven-inch depth. If the sinks are located off the centerline, chances are that unless the boat is of very light displacement and high freeboard the sinks won't drain when the boat it is heeled. In this case, it's necessary to fit a hand pump for pumping used water overboard.

Floor areas should be contrived so that there is always a good place to brace yourself in the galley when at sea. Safety straps with sturdy pad eyes will have to be worked in. If possible, the stove should be mounted athwartships, facing forward or aft, as opposed to being mounted on the side of the hull. This athwartships orientation means that a sudden roll will not throw the cook into the stove or the stove's utensils into the cook. Gimbals are not necessary if deep pans are used and good pot restrainers are mounted on the stove top. But one gimballed work area while at sea is handy for keeping ingredients and prepared food in place. If the stove is placed outboard, then most people gimbal them. Have a locking hook handy for severe weather.

Insulating the area around the stove with fiberglass wool helps the oven tremendously. If space permits, an overhead hood with an exhaust fan works wonders in the tropics. Without an exhaust hood it isn't unusual for an evening meal to warm the interior of a small boat 10 degrees Fahrenheit or more (another plus for the microwave).

Rigadoon's stove was gimballed athwartships. A heavy bearing was mounted on the engine room bulkhead and the stove bolted to it, allowing it to swing when at sea. If anything went flying, it wasn't going to hit the cook.

Stowage for dishes, glasses, pots and pans, etc., must be designed so they'll stay in place when at sea. And anyway, one of the things you'll have to do during the first day or two of a new passage is track down and eliminate rattles and squeaks in the galley.

Countertops obviously need fiddles. They should be at right angles to the horizontal surface, be at least 1½ inches high, and if possible, be rounded in their intersecting corners. There is some debate between the open-corner school (cheaper to build and easier to clean) and the closed-corner school (retains the spills until you have a chance to mop up).

There are really only two stove fuel options for cooking on a long-distance cruiser: kerosene and propane. Kerosene, less popular by far, is cheap and very safe. But it's less convenient to use than propane, very messy, and takes an inordinate amount of maintenance. If the stove valves and related gear aren't cleaned and adjusted on a weekly basis, then the burners won't properly utilize their fuel. The result is a layer of soot all over the headliner. Even with

A well-executed can locker in the galley of a 55′ Palmer Johnson / Sparkman and Stephens effort.

Sliding trays in the galley are easy to build and very convenient.

Effective storage aboard *Tina:* cups, dishes, liquor, and a top-opening fridge all in one small locker.

A proper galley fiddle rail, 2½″ above the galley counter.

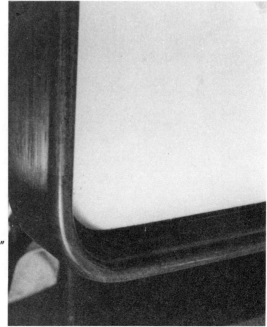

good burner maintenance, the headliners get dirty. When it's time to start up the stove, alcohol must first be burned to heat up the kerosene. The smell of burning alcohol is very offensive to some people, and on a rolling vessel. . . .

I don't like the dangerous aspects of propane on a boat, but it's the best compromise. It is essential to have an electromagnetic solenoid valve at the tank that shuts off when the stove is not in use. By making sure the line from the tank to the stove has no couplings and is insulated where it passes through a bulkhead or support point so it can't chafe over the years, and by keeping the tanks on deck or in a vented, isolated locker, you minimize the chance of an explosion. An accessory to consider is an inexpensive explosive atmosphere meter. These are available from $75 to $150. Some models have controls that automatically shut off the solenoid valve at the tank if a leak is detected. However, never depend on these devices to do any checking you might do without them.

Worthington Manufacturing makes aluminum propane tanks that are excellent in a saltwater environment. They are less than half the weight of the steel tanks, and eliminate untold hours of chipping rust.

Propane is available all over the world and is the primary cooking fuel in such far-off spots as Rodriguez Island in the Indian Ocean, the Solomons in the Pacific, and Saint Helena in the Atlantic. We never had a problem finding it. Occasionally, we had to go to the main station rather than a neighborhood store, but our tanks have always been filled.

In American Samoa, we learned one useful trick: If you want to go from a large tank (perhaps at a restaurant) to a smaller one, open the bleeder valve on the top of the small tank after the two tanks have been connected. Then place the small tank you are filling below the big one. The *liquid* gas will flow between the two, just like water, albeit somewhat more slowly, and eventually you will be rewarded with a small stream of liquid propane at the bleeder valve on the lower tank. When this occurs, your tank is filled.

Alcohol doesn't deserve mention except as a priming fluid for kerosene. It is unbelievably expensive and hard to come by in other parts of the world. Those people we know with kerosene stoves all say the alcohol used for starting purposes costs them as much as the kerosene they use when cooking.

Diesel stoves are fine, for high-latitude sailing. They are cheap to

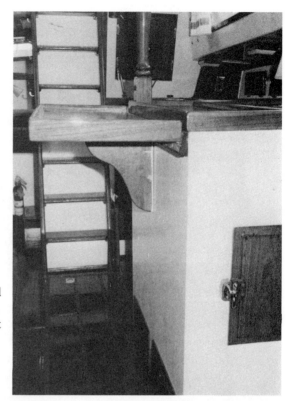

This lift-up sideboard increased galley space aboard *Intermezzo.* When there was a baking project going, this was always in use.

Bottle "socks" reduce noise when rolling downwind.

An interesting innovation aboard a Lavranos 47 in Cape Town, South Africa. The rack attached to the stove swings with the stove, keeping mugs and dishes level when heeled.

run, and since they are very hot, they can heat the rest of the vessel, as well as provide hot water. But in the tropics it's impossible to cook with diesel. It heats up the interior too much.

Electric cooking, combined with one of the other systems, is a good bet. On its own electric cooking leaves you dependent on machinery, which in turn makes it necessary to carry an extra generator as a backup. The daily noise is hard on your neighbors. Microwave ovens, toasters, electric frying pans, etc., can all be used with large inverters or small AC generators mounted on the main propulsion engine. You will probably be running the engine half an hour to an hour a day for refrigeration and batteries anyway, so you might as well make some AC with it and put that to work in the galley along with the gas or kerosene stove.

Trash storage is always a difficult problem. Rarely does a good trash storage area get designed into a new boat. Without it you're left

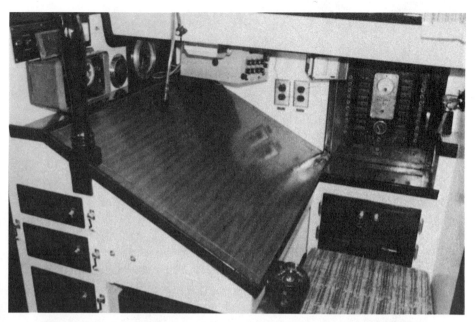

The angled chart table aboard *Intermezzo* was great at sea, but didn't do well as a desk in port.

to catch as catch can. If you're building, allow for at least a five-gallon container.

You should also have a ready locker or two for everyday canned and dry goods. Even if the galley lockers are small, keep one or two for your immediate requirements. These can be replenished on weekly forays under the seats or into the bilge.

NAVIGATORIUM

The navigating area on the proper cruising vessel can vary from the reefer top or saloon table to a luxurious chart table navigatorium. From a strictly navigation standpoint very little specialized space is required. Storage for charts, sight-reduction tables, the current pilot, light and radio aids list, and a few instruments is all you really need. If you use electronic navigation aids, you'll want a nice home for them.

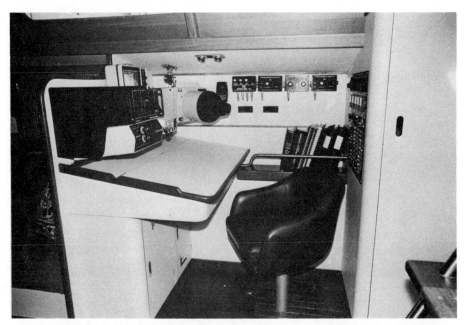

A compact chart table with moderate slope makes it possible to use it as a ship's office. (S. A. Dashew)

The navigation station aboard the Swan 47 *Vemon,* in Cape Town, South Africa, is used standing up. It's possible to use otherwise inefficient space for a good chart table if you're willing to give up your seat. *Vemon* was ready for the last leg of her circumnavigation when this photo was taken.

Overhead chart stowage on *Tina*. She was ready for her Durban to Cape Town, South Africa, passage and the required charts are right at hand.

Aboard *Intermezzo* the navigating area was used more as a desk/work area than for pure navigation. And since the area was handy to the companionway, with a comfortable seat in which we could brace ourselves on either tack, we found we spent most watches reading at the chart table with a trip topside to scan the horizon every 15 minutes.

The chart table itself, if there is one, should be large enough to handle U.S. charts folded in half. A pencil sharpener should be close at hand, and a rack or drawer for dividers, parallel rules, and pencils. The chart table top should lift up and allow for storage of at least a dozen charts. The rest of the inventory will find its way under bunks or be rolled up in lockers. It is rare, even in a 50-footer, to have enough space for proper chart storage.

HEADS

Following the recent trends in new home construction, it appears that the heads on production boats are getting larger and larger. On a vessel with already severe limitations on its interior volume, this allocation of space to an area that is used so little is puzzling. Further, a good head at sea *has* to be compact. There are certain times when you must have one or both hands free. If the vessel is bouncing around, the tighter the quarters are, the better off you will be. If possible, the toilet itself should be placed fore-and-aft, between the side of the hull and the sink, or the sink counter on larger craft. This way you are naturally braced when the boat is heeled on either tack. If the toilet is athwartships, then strategically placed handholds are necessary.

As for the toilet itself, most seem to work well if they are simply constructed and not abused. *Intermezzo* had an inexpensive Wilcox Crittenden "Headmate" that stood up well for 3½ years. It needed an overhaul of its rubber parts every nine months. One tip: Always keep the cover down when the head's not in use; otherwise, sooner or later something will fall into the bowl and crack the porcelain or choke the plumbing.

You should also be able to shower in the head at sea with the vessel pitching. Again, handholds are the solution.

Pressure fresh- and saltwater shower fittings should be included in the compartment. If you are on a freshwater diet, use the salt to lather up and rinse with, and then do a final rinse with fresh. You can shower completely in this manner, including washing your hair, for less than a quart of fresh water. On the other hand a straight freshwater shower, if you're careful, can be done for about two quarts, as long as the long-haired members of the crew refrain from shampoos.

SALOONS

The main saloon gets what's left over of the space. It will normally serve as entertainment center, dining room, library, and perhaps boudoir. In general the saloon has the most open floor area, so you

Tape storage aboard the Hinkley 48 *Sassy.*

must be sure that there are enough handholds so that you can get from one end to the other in a seaway without letting go completely. The table must be strong enough to resist the weight of a person flung at it by an errant sea, and it goes without saying that sharp corners must be replaced by radiuses for safety's sake.

There are many table designs. Since it occupies a large percentage of the available floor space, the table should be built with folding wings, if possible. The size of the table also must be considered in relation to its use on your cruises. Most of the time it will be serving just those aboard. On occasion you might have another couple or two below for meals. If space is tight, you may want to have a small table that is at maximum efficiency 90 percent of the time. When you are entertaining, meals can be taken buffet style.

As for shelf and counter area, remember that you will want to display various artifacts, shells, or knickknacks from home when you are in port. They dress up the boat and give you more of a feeling of permanence and belonging.

CUSHIONS

Cushion construction is a very important aspect of the proper cruising vessel. To begin with, four inches of firm foam is a must; on bunks, six is better if you have the room. There are numerous grades of foam available both as to quality and density. Remember that after a while the foam starts to break down and soften. The cushions in the saloon get a lot of wear and tear, so it's a good idea to choose higher density foam than your sailmaker/upholsterer might normally pick.

Why are the seats on boats always so uncomfortable? In Auckland, New Zealand, we ran into an *upholsterer* who also did yacht interiors (note the distinction—not a sailmaker doing upholsterer's work). Bruce Withers showed us a sample seating arrangement he had made up. First we sat down on four-inch foam placed on a chunk of solid plywood. Next we sat down on the same foam placed on rubber webbing. The difference was unbelievable. We immediately made plans to adapt our saloon seats to rubber webbing. (This also improves ventilation in the lockers beneath.)

The seatback cushion is equally important. If you have room, it should be 5 inches thick at the bottom and 2 inches at the top, with a height of 14 inches. This allows you to relax when sitting back rather than having to sit up straight as in a dining room chair. The width of the settee should be 24 inches, which will be reduced to 19 inches of sitting room when the wedge-shaped back is in place.

There are so many types of cushion fabric around that it's hard to make a choice. Aesthetics, practicality, and comfort all have to be considered. Light colors open up the space inside but show stains more readily. Plaids and herringbones are great at hiding dirt, but

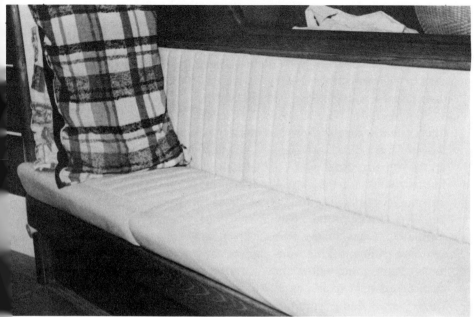

A quilted effect on vinyl upholstery is the most effective way to keep it looking neat over a period of time.

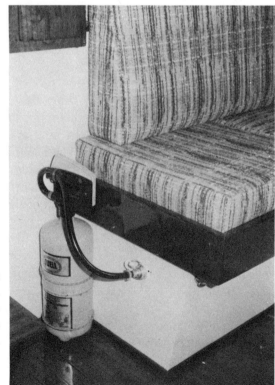

ɔoard *Intermezzo* we angled the ɑt back 15 degrees for comfort. ɔte the removable Halon fire ex-guisher which we fitted to the ɡine compartment in Darwin, ɩstralia.

are too busy, especially on smaller boats. Also, when you choose a new fabric, remember that in the tropics there will be a lot of bare skin aboard and that bare skin is oily.

Some people abhor vinyl in the tropics. We found that *textured* vinyl against bare skin was as comfortable as any heavily textured woven fabric. For sleeping, you will normally want to use a sheet, and if you add the convenience of a small bed pad, your body won't know what it's sleeping on. Vinyl has the advantage of being easy to clean, nonstaining, and allowing water to run off or be mopped up before it soaks into the cushion. This last aspect is not to be underestimated. Every boat has leaks from time to time, and nobody is immune from sneaking a hatch open now and then and having an errant wave come below. Salt water which finds its way into foam cushions is next to impossible to dry out. The salt is retained and keeps getting damp from moisture in the air. So a good compromise is to use vinyl on one side for practical purposes and when at sea, and a nice fabric on the other for entertaining or when you want a more formal look.

LIGHTING

The advent of fluorescent lights has done much to dispel the dungeon-like appearance of yacht interiors. Fluorescents are easy on batteries and usually are maintenance free. They should be carefully placed where needed in each living area with extra care taken in the galley to give the cook and dishwasher good light with which to work. The mirrors in the head should be backlit. Today most fluorescents are of the suppressed-noise type so they don't interfere with radio reception. If you hear a high-frequency noise or hum on a receiver, however, try switching off the fluorescents. That may cure the problem.

In addition to the general lighting provided by fluorescents, you also need reading lights. Here, individual reflector units are best, placed so they shine directly on what you're reading and don't disturb someone else in the area who is trying to sleep.

You'll also need night lights in the head, navigating area, and

A twin-tube 30-watt fluorescent aboard *Intermezzo II*. We used 11 of these throughout the boat to be sure we had good lighting. Note the small incandescent bulb nestled between the tubes; these were used for soft light.

A built-in dustpan aboard the Nicholson 38, *Wind Rose,* at Cocos Keeling Island.

galley. These should be either dual-switch light units which have a red night light as well as regular white light, or reading lights that have red-painted or red-filtered bulbs placed in them at sea. This is particularly important in the navigation area, when you don't want to disturb the off watch or are trying to preserve your night vision at sea.

WATCHKEEPING

Most of your watchkeeping time on a small boat does not have to be spent on deck. To make these hours more comfortable, it is important to set up one area below to be used as a watchkeeping station. From this spot you should be able to hear clearly the sounds of the ship above decks and the elements as they interrelate. A telltale compass is a good idea. The watch area must be comfortable on both tacks, and its reading lights must not bother other crew members who are trying to sleep. Normally you will need a separate reading light for each tack.

ENGINE ROOMS

Where do we put the engine? First, we have to order our priorities. An engine room on a vessel under 55 feet is a fantastic waste of space. It's nice for those few times when you have to battle with the iron monster, but for the other 95 percent of your cruising time the space is wasted. As a result, in most vessels the engines are under the cockpit floor, the cabin sole, or the companionway. The cockpit floor is fine if you can invent an absolutely watertight seal. If not, those occasional saltwater drips (or worse) will play havoc with the engine electrics. The companionway location is drier (though not completely), but normally the galley is to one side and the navigation area/quarterberth is on the other, making it difficult to find room to work on the engine.

Under the cabin sole works well if the boat has the hull depth to accommodate this arrangement, which in general won't work for boats of less than about 40 feet. Although it usually puts the engine under the floor of your most prized living space, it offers low center of gravity and thus contributes to stability. Also, engines installed here are easy to work on, even though they require that you do most of the work while lying on your stomach. The big disadvantage is in case of a leak or flooding. The engine is so low in the boat that it's the first thing to be wiped out by incoming water, and if your big mechanical bilge pump is hooked up to the engine, you may be in real trouble. If your engine is under the sole, the oil dipsticks (both engine block and fuel pump) and fuel-pump breather vent should be raised, along with the engine air intake, right to the bottom of the sole. This will give you a maximum amount of time after flooding begins before the engine must be shut down. Note that a diesel engine will start under water so long as the batteries are dry and the air intake isn't submerged. Salt water mixed in the oil while the engine is running, though, will make an incredible mess of the inside of the engine and requires partial disassembly for cleaning.

It is vitally important that the engine and other machinery be well insulated for sound. There are several good products for this purpose, usually a combination of lead, foam, and plastic. A modest investment in cash and time can yield tremendous rewards in reducing machinery noise. Special note should be paid to V-drives. If the transmission oil is water cooled, you may be able to make up a double-layer insulating system directly around the V-drive and transmission to get rid of characteristic gear whine.

STOWAGE

The decision on what type of stowage to build and what sort of gear to carry will involve many hours of soul searching.

The first priority is to inventory all your available stowage space. Since food will take up the most room, building "can" castles ("tin castles" for our non-American readers) in the lockers or bilges designated for this commodity will show you in short order what their

An extra hanging locker converted to more useful
storage with removable shelves.

capacities are. If you multiply the number of cans along the wall at
the end of a locker by how many cans long you can go, you will know
without having to fill in with cans what the locker will hold. Space
has to be allowed for cold-climate-clothing storage as well as what
will be worn in the tropics. Ship's spares take a small percentage of
the storage space, unless you are a pack rat. What is actually needed
for the engine, general maintenance, and special projects will rarely
take more than one section of a seat locker. Space must be allocated
for tools, and should be divided between those constantly in use and
specialty items.

Many vessels today are built with two or more heads. On an

offshore boat these extra heads usually end up full of sail bags and other odds and ends because the space is too valuable to waste. Consider putting removable shelves in the second head, as we did aboard *Intermezzo*. It turns that space into a fantastic pantry, and gives you a tremendous increase in easy-to-use stowage for a modest investment. When the time comes to sell the boat, if her new owners want the multihead arrangement, the shelves can easily be removed. Hanging lockers are another good candidate for this treatment. Shelved stowage space is usually the most sought-after accommodation on any boat, and these are easy ways to increase it.

Special consideration must be given to foodstuffs stowed in glass jars. We found that our converted hanging locker, with its five rows of deep shelves, was ideal. As the inventory on each of the shelves dwindled, we stored our towels in front of the glass goods, so they wouldn't roll around at sea.

Foul-weather gear storage is often made into a big deal, but in the tropics, at least, it's a waste of valuable space. Since foul-weather gear is so rarely worn in the low latitudes, it's best to devote that beautiful locker to better things. On *Intermezzo* we used it for our trash bucket, tools, and engine spares. Foul-weather gear was stowed under a bunk when not in use, and on hooks by the companionway when we needed it at the ready.

COCKPITS

Cockpit design is an art in itself. Drainage must be substantial. If the cockpit is well aft, see if drains through the transom or counter will work. They can be huge, and this eliminates two through-hull fittings. Next, be absolutely certain that the water will drain fully when you are heeled and when sailing downwind in heavy going, *with the vessel fully loaded.* There is nothing more annoying than having your feet continuously in sea water, even if it's only a small puddle.

The same goes for cockpit seats. They should be angled outboard as they run to the stern. If they are not, then inboard drains must

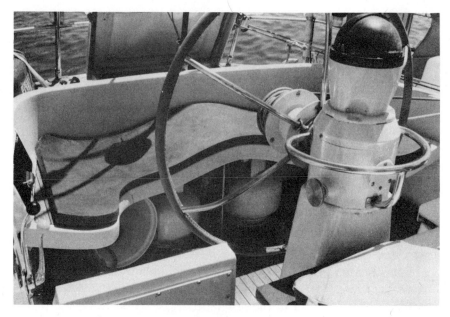

A contoured helmsman's seat on a Swan 47. Note the sturdy binnacle and safety harness attachment points.

In wet going offshore, Don and Sue Moesly rigged covers to protect their cockpit seats from direct spray. Photographed in Rabaul, Papua, New Guinea, the covers were also used to protect *Svea* from the sun.

be provided at the forward end or else water will puddle up to leeward with nowhere to drain when you're heeled. The width of the cockpit well should be such that you can sit to weather and brace your feet on the leeward seat edge.

Cockpit seats should be long enough to sleep on. The backrest should be 14 inches high and angled outboard 15 degrees. When you are mounting winches, try to position them so they can be worked without interference with people sitting in the cockpit area. Cockpit lockers should be eliminated if at all possible. If you can't avoid them, a large upstand with good angles and a positive rubber or foam seal *must* be used. In heavy going, despite all your precautions, a substantial quantity of water will find its way below through these openings.

The companionway hatch and slides obviously have to be heavily built. You must be able to lock them from inside and outside. If they aren't locked, and you suffer a severe knockdown or rollover, the odds are they will drop out or slide open and allow thousands of gallons below.

DODGERS

Dodgers, properly installed, are a tremendous boon to cruising. When conditions are wet or uncomfortable they provide excellent shelter. They can extend the cockpit's use greatly, even when anchored. The dodger should be long enough to cover both crew members sitting to leeward. The front and side windows should snap or zip open so that in moderate going you can have some air flow. Fitting an awning extension from the after end of the dodger to the mizzen shrouds or main backstay (with a batten) is also a good idea. Avoid dodgers with plastic fittings. Insist on good-quality, heavy-duty bronze or stainless. The framework will inevitably be used as a major handhold at sea and will be subjected to lots of abuse.

A heavily framed dodger aboard a Bowman-built yacht in Florida that has seen several Atlantic crossings. Its compact size will tend to keep one dry longer, and will withstand severe punishment.

A California-style dodger, with lots of windows, removable side curtains, and two light frames. When it's howling out, this dodger will have to be folded down. (S. A. Dashew)

73. Plumbing

There is no reason why plumbing should cause any major problems on modern yachts. With proper installation and the use of the right materials, plumbing fixtures should require no more attention than dutiful maintenance.

It is important that all your hose clamps are stainless steel and designed for marine use. If they are going to be in contact with salt water, clamps should be doubled up, as should the clamps on all through-hull fittings.

As for hoses, it is most important that they be protected from chafe when used on machinery that vibrates; chafe can ruin a hose as quickly as it eats through line. There are dozens of types of hoses on the market, but our experience has shown that nylon-reinforced PVC hose is best in terms of cost combined with fresh- and saltwater applications. Be sure that the hose used on the hot-water side of the freshwater system is designed for high-temperature operation, at a pressure in the range of 60 lbs. per square inch.

Hoses that carry water to and from the engine are generally best made from double rubber/canvas construction. This is far more expensive than PVC, but also more resistant to chafe.

A minimum of through-hull fittings should be tolerated on a serious cruising vessel. One saltwater intake with a large, easily viewed and cleaned strainer will service the entire vessel. If the cockpit drains can be lifted above the waterline, then the only other through-hull fittings are the head exhausts, and perhaps the galley sink.

Through-hull fittings close to the mainmast or main rigging can be dangerous for another reason. They are a convenient outlet for lightning. We know of two vessels that, in spite of grounded systems, have had holes blown through their sides as lightning exited via a through-hull fitting.

For shower, head sink, and icebox drains, it is best to use a sump with an overboard pump. The galley sink, unfortunately, must usually be drained overboard. If it goes into the sump, the buildup of food particles and grease creates an intolerable olfactory condition. On lighter displacement, high-freeboard designs, it is sometimes possible to drain head and galley sinks directly overboard with the hull penetrations above the at-rest waterline.

All through-hull fittings, of course, must have sea cocks. Plastic valves have been making an appearance recently, and they seem to work well. Their nonmetalic properties eliminate the worry of corrosion and electrolysis, and minimize maintenance. For heads, however, metal is still the best sea-cock material. The buildup of salts that occurs in the exhaust line of a well-used head will eventually lead to scarring of the ball and seat of plastic valves when they are cleaned, which renders them less than watertight.

There is no reason not to have pressure fresh water aboard a cruising boat. Consumption with pressure water will be the same in the heads, assuming you are diligent, and actually less in the galley, because it is easier and more efficient to use. Pressure water also makes taking showers easier.

The most popular pressure pumps are made by the Par division of ITT. These units are simple and easy to work on. The belt-driven models seem to be more reliable than those that have a direct-drive rocker-arm assembly to move their diaphrams. A single pump will take care of both cold and hot water; once the water leaves the pressure side of the pump it can go to the cold-water taps as well as to the hot-water system via a "T" in the line, a check valve, and the hot-water heater.

Many hot-water heaters on the market utilize both the engine's freshwater cooling system and 110-volt shore power. A freshwater-cooled 35-h.p. diesel engine will heat eight gallons of water in less than 20 minutes. The heaters come with one inch of fiberglass insulation inside the case. If you increase this by building around it a box of polyeurethane foam, with an average thickness of one inch, the hot water will last four times longer. The eight-gallon unit on *Intermezzo* without extra insulation would have water hot enough for a shower the morning after running the engine the night before. (For those who are skeptical of the concept of a hot-water shower, let us assure you that of all the luxuries aboard a cruising boat, this is by far the most important.)

With a pressure system you obviously need a backup system for getting fresh water out of the main tank should the electrical system fail. The best approach is to install a hand pump in the galley that can be used just in case.

The addition of a charcoal water filter will pay off in those locales where the water has a bit of local color (and taste) to it. There are even units on the market today that will eliminate bacteria that cause intestinal disorders. When fitting a water filter / purifying system, put it on a separate outlet in the galley. The capacity of the filter is limited and should be used only for drinking water.

Pressure salt water is also a good investment. It makes washing down the decks, anchor, and chain a snap, and is a boon in the galley. The pressure salt water should be led to the head(s) as well. Coupled with a showerhead alongside the freshwater unit, it will do yeoman service in keeping the crew smelling sweet when fresh water isn't abundant. Another advantage is when the toilet bowl gets heeled well to windward and won't fill with salt water for flushing. In this case the showerhead and pressure pump can be used as a backup.

Faucet fixtures of the spring type are favored by some because they are designed to save water. However, they require an extra hand to operate; because of this awkwardness they end up using more water than regular faucets.

The shower system should employ a mixer valve, with a second shutoff at the showerhead. This way, once the water temperature is set you don't have to move the temperature setting as you turn the water on and off, as you have to do to save water.

Freshwater tanks should be made of stainless steel as a first choice. There must be ample clean-out ports, and if at all possible the tanks should be removable. In many modern fiberglass boats, tanks are made from fiberglass as well, and use the hull as part of the tank. If the job is done properly this system is fine, but you're dependent on the laminators, and how they felt the day they were doing your boat.

By adding a couple of ounces of chlorine bleach per 50 gallons of water now and then, any algae that starts to grow can be kept in check.

Fuel tanks must have a clean-out sump built into the lowest part of the tank, with the fuel pickup just above or in another tank section.

If you buy fuel from bulk tanks it will usually be in good condition. We carried a three-stage portable filter that we used to prefilter all fuel that came aboard. Only once, when buying 30 gallons in 5-gallon containers in the Santa Cruz Islands, Solomons, did we pick up contaminants.

Bior JF or a similar fungicide should be added to the fuel tanks

at regular intervals just in case you buy fuel that has been con-
taminated with a fungus. It is rare, but when it happens, it usually
means a new fuel pump, once the fungus gets past the filters.

I have left the question of head effluent-treatment systems to the
last. As this is written, the U.S. is just beginning to enforce its
somewhat chaotic laws on marine heads. However, nowhere else in
the world have we seen a problem in this regard. For the present, the
best solution is to do nothing, or if cruising in the U.S., do the
absolute minimum necessary. In most cases this means "Y" valves
on the heads, with one end leading overboard and the other to a
holding tank. Be sure to have your own holding tank pump-out
capabilities; don't depend on being able to do it at a marina because
pump-out facilities in the U.S. are still few and far between. One
clever approach to this problem was worked out by John Nichols on
Heart of Edna. John did a lot of charter work and most of his clients
were divers. With six to eight guests aboard at a time, he wanted to
keep the immediate vicinity around his yacht as free of pollution as
possible. So he used a holding tank, which he cleared at sea using air
pressure from his scuba tanks.

74. Machinery

ENGINES

Many factors will affect your choice of a diesel engine: reliability,
parts availability, budget, fuel economy, not to mention the vessel's
requirements for power. As skill levels increase in ship handling, less
and less power is required. Another direct factor on engine require-

ments is the sailing characteristics of the vessel herself. A good sailing boat that a small crew can maneuver in tight quarters will not require the same propulsion machinery as a sea cow that can't sail her way out of large unobstructed anchorages.

On the assumption that you have a handy sea vessel, and that we are looking at the engine as an auxiliary—i.e., as a help in docking or anchoring, and for use when the wind is too light to sail—let's consider horsepower requirements.

To begin with, the two most important aspects are how fast you want to move and propeller efficiency. Without going into a lot of technical data, there is an approximate fixed amount of horsepower per ton of displacement required to move most vessels, at a given speed/length ratio. The speed/length ratio is the square root of waterline length divided into the speed. Once a SLR of 1 has been reached (i.e., 6 knots for a 36-foot-waterline vessel) the horsepower required to move her faster than an SLR of 1 goes up with the square of the increase in speed. This means that if you want to go 7 knots instead of 6 it will take 36 percent more horsepower and fuel.

What this adds up to is that cruising vessels intended for long-term offshore work, where there are no vacation deadlines to face at the end of a cruise, require much smaller engines than their shorebound counterparts.

Intermezzo is a classic example. She is powered by a 50-h.p. Isuzu diesel, considered by some to be light for her size and displacement. Yet we utilized an average of only 15 h.p. when under way during the major portion of our trip. Running a diesel at 25 percent power is not particularly good for it. The engine tends to carbon up more rapidly and foul its lubricating oil with unburned fuel. Instead of that large four-banger we would have been far better off in terms of weight, space, and engine longevity with a unit in the 30-h.p. range.

Many aspects affect horsepower requirements other than what is required to push the vessel through calm water. You have to consider the increased resistance from wind and wave if you're working your way against adverse elements. A 20-knot wind and three-foot chop will increase the horsepower requirement by a factor of 2, more if you have a high-windage clunker. The engine accessories such as alternators, reefer compressors, AC generators, and pumps all take horsepower. For this reason, if you follow our suggestions and go toward a smaller engine, there will be occasions when you will have to shut down all engine accessories to get full power for the vessel. This is a small price to pay for the economy and comfort of a smaller power plant.

If you have a V-drive, hydraulic drive, or a long propeller shaft with a number of bearings, you will lose additional horsepower. But the most important factor is propeller efficiency, or lack of it, which can force you to double your horsepower requirements (see the next section).

If you buy a boat with an engine already installed, the discussion is moot except insofar as determining her serviceability with the existing power plant. If, on the other hand, you are repowering or building, these factors need careful attention. The calculations shown in Skene's work well for most applications, but the best approach is to take a similar vessel out and measure what she requires, then interpolate for your weight, hull shape, and propeller efficiency. This can easily be done by measuring the amount of fuel consumed.

Surprisingly, almost all diesel engines range within a few percent of one another on consumption. If you figure $4/10$ lb. of fuel per horsepower per hour, you'll be very close to the actual consumption rate. This means that if the engine consumes 4 lbs. of fuel in an hour it is using 10 h.p. (one gallon of diesel fuel weighs approximately 7 lbs.).

An interesting corollary is that this factor applies more or less regardless of engine size or R.P.M./h.p. rating. An engine rated for 30 h.p. at 2500 R.P.M. that is using only 15 h.p. will consume only 15 h.p. worth of fuel, plus a little for engine friction at the higher R.P.M. This is because of the fuel-metering system employed in diesel engines. When the throttle is opened to a certain point, you are telling the engine to run at a fixed R.P.M. This R.P.M. is regulated by a governor, which senses engine speed and adjusts the fuel flow to keep it constant. If there is a light load on the engine, not much fuel is required to maintain the required setting, so the governor reduces the fuel supply accordingly.

Let's look at the engines themselves. First, virtually all marine engines are adapted from those found in trucks and cars. There is nothing wrong with this as long as the adaptation is well done. To convert an engine, the primary manufacturer or engine converter adds only a few items. Usually a heavier flywheel is attached to the back end to dampen vibration. The starter and alternator attached are engineered and sealed for a marine environment. For cooling, a jacketed exhaust manifold is put on which allows circulating salt water to cool off the exhaust. Last, a saltwater pump together with heat exchangers for the fresh water, and possibly engine/transmission oil, are added. Many small diesels employ direct saltwater cooling of the block.

It really is much simpler than it sounds, and there is no reason a person can't buy himself an engine from a wrecked truck or diesel-powered auto and make the conversion on his own.

The items on a diesel engine that usually give trouble are the starter, alternator, and saltwater pump. For this reason they should be inspected carefully, and spares should be carried. Alternators and water pumps are cheap, but the starter is another question. If a full spare starter isn't aboard, at the least brushes, a solenoid, and a few spare windings (stator) should be on hand. If the electrics are located low on the engine, as they usually are, you must be careful with moisture.

The starting capability of an engine also should be considered. Many diesel engines adapted from autos require glow-plug starting. The glow plugs heat a precombustion chamber; if the engine is cold it usually takes 10 to 20 seconds before the engine can be fired off. This delay can be a problem in an emergency. Indelibly etched in my memory is an occasion in Rabaul, Papua, New Guinea, after which I swore I would never have another glow-plug engine. I was listening to the radio in the main saloon when a vicious line squall bore down on the fleet anchored at the west end of Rabaul Harbor. I heard the squall strike, felt *Intermezzo* lean a bit, and then round up (I thought). In fact our anchor had broken free (one of two times on the circumnavigation) and we were drifting rapidly through a crowded anchorage. Linda and the kids were ashore, and since I was still listening to the radio, I didn't hear people yelling outside as I drifted by them. Finally someone from a nearby yacht dinghied over to try to do something. When he bumped as he came aboard I decided something was amiss. After a quick look around I realized we didn't have enough sea room for a second anchor to set itself before we would be among the smaller boats anchored astern of us. So I went for the engine. Those 20 seconds I had to hold that heater felt like 20 minutes. Some engines start cold without the aid of glow plugs. On *Intermezzo II* we went this route.

Most engines under 30 h.p. have provisions for hand-cranking should the starter system or batteries fail. If this is your case, be sure that the cranking system actually works; practice hand-starting before you need it.

For larger engines you can buy what is called a spring starter, made by the CAV division of the Lucas Company. Spring starters are generally employed on emergency backup generating plants at hospitals or similar installations. You simply wind up a very stiff spring, using a socket wrench, hit a trip lever, and over she goes. With a compression release or loose injectors and a mechanical gear box, some engines can be started by allowing the propeller to spin when sailing.

Don and Sue Moesly utilized a hydraulic starter on their engine for *Svea.* They also carried an electric starter motor in case their seals ever went out, which they did now and then.

Another thing to think about in the engine installation is changing the oil. If this is at all difficult, install a permanent, large-bore hand pump that is ready to go at a moment's notice. This reduces the mess and your resulting reluctance to tackle this necessary albeit onerous chore.

TRANSMISSIONS

There are numerous choices on the market for transmissions. Over the years the most popular has been the muscular Borg Warner CR 71. It has the advantage of having parts available all over the world, although I've never heard of a failure. Their disadvantage is that they are heavy and take a considerable amount of the engine's horsepower to overcome friction. The fact that they are rated for well over 100 h.p. yet utilized for 35-h.p. engines will tell you something.

Of late, the German Hurth Box has become popular. It is lighter, much more efficient on horsepower, and quiet, and at this writing most small-engine manufacturers have switched to it, without any complaints as yet from users.

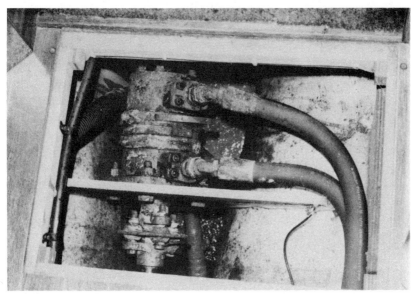

A hydraulic pump takes care of the prop shaft aboard *Wind Rose*. It is compact, lightweight, and allows the engine to be installed well aft, under the cockpit.

This brings us to the subject of reliability in general. Industrial diesel engines, such as those used on pumping systems or generating sets, usually are run at 75 percent of their maximum power on a continuous basis, 20 or more hours a day, every day. Engineers normally figure a minimum of 15,000 hours between major over-hauls. The average cruiser, if he uses his engine an hour a day for charging and refrigeration, for an occasional short hop, and to get in and out of harbors, will be lucky to put 500 hours on it per year. When viewed in this light, the question of high-R.P.M. engines vs. the presumed reliability of low-R.P.M. units, or high compression vs. low compression, loses some of its impact. In reality, an intermitently run yacht engine will have a shorter life than one run continuously at full bore. The yacht duty, while using less horsepower, is much more taxing because of the salt environment and the intermitent low-power use. But even if you figure 7500 hours instead of the 15,000, you can expect 15 years of use before a major tear-down.

Still, reliability and parts availability are major considerations. In this regard there are three standouts. The first is Perkins. The Per-

Intermezzo's trusty Ferris taffrail generator would keep up with the auto-pilot when we were moving at more than 6 knots.

kins 4-236 is probably the most popular marine engine of its size in the world. It's a good unit; but more important, there are industrialized engines of this variety on every island and in every country wherever you go. You can always buy, beg, or steal the necessary parts. The Ford four-cylinder diesels would be next. They, too, have a wide industrial dispersion. Be a little careful, however, of the marine version you purchase. Some of the overseas converted Ford engines are not up to U.S. or English standards. GM diesels run forever (almost) and are available all over the world, but not on such a widespread basis as the Perkins or Ford. Two-cycle diesels such as the Gimmies, though, are very noisy. This is a problem for those living with one, and for the neighbors.

There are many other makes of diesel engines around. All of them seem to give good service, and air freight is available almost everywhere one travels, should parts be required.

Gasoline engines, because of their inherent safety problems, have no place on a cruising yacht.

PROPELLERS

The propeller is the most important element in a sailboat's sailing efficiency. No matter what you do with hull shape, rig, or sails, if you have a fixed three-blade propeller your boat won't get out of its own way in less than a real blow. On the average vessel a fixed three-blade cruising prop will add 40 percent to the total drag. This especially hurts going to windward, where your rig provides a finite limit of sailing horsepower. Off the wind, in light airs, it can knock 40 percent of boat speed right off the top. As the wind increases you will be able to overcome the drag, but only by carrying more sail. If drag is increased by 40 percent, you will have to increase the load on rig and hull by an equivalent amount to make the boat move when the wind is blowing.

There are many other ways to go than the fixed prop: variable-pitch prop, which is featherable; full-feathering fixed-pitch props; or one of the folding props.

Before examining the various available units, consider the following. Propeller efficiency on an auxiliary sailboat depends on a whole series of conditions and will vary between 25 and 50 percent. This means that if the engine calculations show that you require 10 h.p. to move the boat at 7 knots and your prop has a 25 percent efficiency factor, you actually need 40 h.p. pulling to make your 7 knots! Should you improve that efficiency factor to 50 percent, it will cut in half the required power. It behooves you to do everything possible to maximize prop efficiency.

Among the related nonprop factors are shaft angle, water flow, and propeller location. A prop located in a cut-out between a long keel and its attached rudder will have the most disturbed water flow and therefore the worst efficiency rating.

A prop behind a well-faired keel will be much more efficient than if it is downstream of a keel that has a blunt trailing edge. Many modern cruising boats have very blunt trailing edges on their keels

A feathering Max Prop is the best cruising compromise we have found, with low sailing drag and full power ahead and in reverse. The pitch may be adjusted by changing the internal gear ratios.

because they are cheaper to laminate that way. Considering the deleterious effect this has on sailing and powering, it may be worth performing a fairing job.

Prop diameter and R.P.M. are next in line. Generally speaking, the slower the prop turns and the larger the diameter, the more efficient the set-up. Working against this is tip clearance. The propeller edge must be at least 15 percent of its diameter away from the underside of the hull or the resulting noise and inefficiency will be unacceptable.

The maximum reduction gears usually available for yachts are in the 3 to 1 range. So it isn't possible to go too far in this direction.

If you have an off-center propeller, be prepared to learn about close-in maneuvering.

The ultimate in prop efficiency is the variable-pitch, fully feathering unit such as those sold by Hundestadt and Sabb. A variable-pitch prop allows you to pick the ultimate propeller setting for motorsail-

A "racing" version of the folding prop has poor blade design and is the reason that folding props in general have a bad reputation.

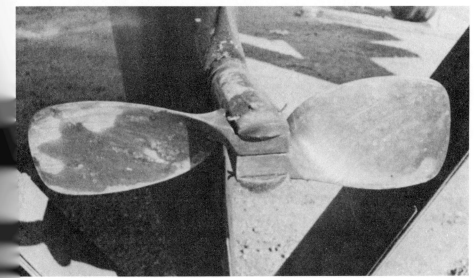

We used a Martec propeller with square-ended cruising blades aboard *Intermezzo.*

ing (where you want lots of pitch and low R.P.M.), or for fighting your way in the teeth of a gale into a harbor where higher R.P.M. and flat pitch are essential. Of the two, the Sabb unit is more suited to smaller yachts as it is more streamlined underwater and less costly. The Hundestadt is probably the most reliable unit in the world.

Next come the feathering props. There are a number of these on the market, among which are the units made by Paul Luke (the old Hyde wheel) and the Italian Max Prop. The latter allows you to change its pitch at the prop. In other words, you can vary the pitch on a semi permanent basis when you haul out.

A big consideration from a safety standpoint in both feathering and variable-pitch props is reverse power. The normal fixed prop is substantially less efficient when its rotation is reversed. Designed for optimum performance with the blades pitched in one direction, simply reversing the direction of rotation doesn't buy much in performance. With the variable pitch and feathering wheels, though, the blades themselves reverse, giving you the same thrust in reverse as in forward. If you are trying to back off a reef, shoal spot, or coral head, this can make a world of difference.

Folding props are the best for sailing, next to no prop at all. Contrary to popular opinion, most of these, if they have good blade area, work well pushing the boat forward. In reverse, however, the blades don't open out all the way, and as a result are very slow in stopping the boat. There is a big difference between the pointed-tip wheels used on the racers today and the square-edged large-blade-area units of yesteryear. The latter are much more efficient. *Intermezzo* has one of these aboard made by Martec. When we first purchased her, I had the Martec removed in favor of a three-blade prop (I was going cruising, right?). Several months later I decided to have the three blade repitched to improve our speed, and in the interim put back the Martec. You can imagine my surprise when our cruising speed maximum jumped from 6.75 to 7.25 knots with her CCA "racing prop." Of course, it must be admitted that in adverse conditions such as headwinds and seas the folding prop doesn't have the blade area to match the solid prop, but, then, you aren't supposed to be sailing in those conditions.

One thing we did which helped our fuel efficiency was to purchase a second set of blades. *Intermezzo*'s 20 × 13 prop was fine for powering when we needed good thrust, but for motorsailing, which

Buried behind a fat keel, this prop will deliver less than a third of the engine's power to the water.

This motorsailor's prop will make it impossible to sail in anything less than a gale.

Compare the blade area of a typical two-blade fixed prop with our folding Martec. The folding prop is actually better under power than the conventional design (except in reverse).

is what we did the most, a second set of blades with 15 inches of pitch was used. This substantially reduced engine revs and improved our motorsailing performance.

No matter which system you carry, a spare prop should be aboard. Sooner or later a line, a lobster pot, or a piece of flotsam will foul the prop. It's easy to change a propeller in the water if you have an adequate puller aboard.

One thing you'll have to decide is what engine R.P.M. you will use for cruising. Recalling our earlier discussion on fuel consumption vs. actual horsepower used, it's usually best to find the point where the engine generates maximum torque. This will correspond to the best point for fuel efficiency. If you allow yourself 30 to 40 percent horsepower leeway for use when the breeze kicks up, you'll have a combination of good fuel economy with a bit of reserve power.

Note that in the final analysis everybody, even the best designers, *experiment* to get the best propeller configuration. Considering the effect of improved efficiency on your cruising range and fuel costs, it's worth the time to find the best compromise.

POWERING RANGE

One hears a lot about range under power when looking at new or used boats. It is important to study the conditions in which you will be using the boat before you decide if her tankage is sufficient. Most of your engine time will be spent generating rather than propelling. In this mode, you can expect to use half a gallon an hour or less. If you forget about powering range, it means that a 100-gallon fuel capacity will give you a year's charging capacity.

In actual fact, due to cost, noise, and lack of a schedule, most long-term cruisers find that they use about 75 percent of their fuel for charging and 25 percent for powering the boat. At 6 to 6½ knots *Intermezzo* used about a gallon an hour. We generally topped her tanks up once every four months with 60 to 80 gallons of fuel. You'll find that your cruising speed will generally be in the range of .85 to 1.00 times the square root of your waterline length. This is usually the most efficient point in terms of miles per gallon, and results in relatively quiet going.

A 600- to 700-mile range would be an ideal minimum. That's enough to get you through any long light periods when crossing the variables in areas such as the Tasman Sea, southwestern Indian Ocean, or on your way to the Caribbean from the northeast part of the U.S. Even though we're all *sailors,* it's usually prudent to get through the variable belts, where severe frontal conditions can disrupt weather, and into the trades, or port, with a minimum of lost time. If you are becalmed, sitting and waiting for the breeze, you may get clobbered.

DC ALTERNATORS

Now let's look at some of the engine accessories. First in importance is the DC alternator. An alternator is essentially a simple animal. A permanent winding around the outside, called the stator, picks up the pulsations from the rotor, or field. The rotor is spun at high R.P.M. by the engine, and produces current in the stationary outer winding. The rotor gets its power via brushes (unless you have a brushless unit). The outer winding then takes its power, which is alternating current, and runs this through diodes. Diodes are a form of electronic check valve; they allow current to flow in only one direction. The result of the check-valve activity is to convert the alternating current to direct current that can be utilized by the batteries.

Alternators are easy to work on, and if kept dry should be trouble free for years. When they do give problems it is invariably either the brushes (which are easy to change) or the diodes (also easy to replace). It's a good idea to carry a spare alternator. An inexpensive, rebuilt automotive unit can be purchased in the U.S. for under $50. An even better bet, space permitting, is to take the second unit and mount it on the engine and put it to work. Observe the mounting brackets, adjustment arm, and belt alignment carefully. These should be sturdily made and properly aligned.

The regulator on the alternator controls the voltage output. It senses the voltage of the batteries, and via a circuit (normally a zener diode) controls the amount of electricity going to the alternator's field (rotor). As the batteries increase their voltage and level of charge, the regulator reduces voltage to the field. Never rely on an internally mounted regulator. These have a habit of packing up from time to time and are difficult to hot-wire. It's best to utilize an externally regulated unit, so that it can be hot-wired, putting electricity directly to the field, or adjusted via a rheostat.

While we're on this subject, the question of charge rates on batteries frequently arises. The battery manufacturers generally agree that temperature, not charge rate, constitutes the critical factor. Thus batteries located in the engine room, where they have a high ambient temperature have shorter lives and will take less of a charge; 125 degrees Fahrenheit is considered a maximum. Generally you can charge at a rate of 14 to 14¼ volts; if, however, you are powering for long periods, watch the battery temperature. In this situation batteries will pick up heat over a period of time and will have to be charged at closer to 13.5 volts.

The best alternators are made for diesel trucks. These units are much more heavily constructed than automobile models and have an output of two to three times their smaller cousins. Leece Neville and Electrodyne are the two leaders in the field. Electrodyne has a brushless unit, with extra-heavy-duty bearings, and carries a 250,000-mile warranty; it puts out a healthy 140 camps at 3500 R.P.M.

Alternator output is a function of its R.P.M. Most automotive alternators hit about 80 percent of their rated peak output at 3500 to 4000 R.P.M. Be sure you have the pulley ratio to give good output at your engine's idling speed.

AC ALTERNATORS

AC alternators come in a variety of forms, shapes, and sizes. There are compact units and not so compact units. If you are using a 120-220-volt unit for casual cooking and appliances, as advocated herein, then a 3600-R.P.M. two-bearing unit will do fine. For those contemplating all-electric cooking and perhaps air conditioning, the 1800-R.P.M. units are much longer lived.

Remember that the alternator must run at a fixed R.P.M. to generate the proper voltage and frequency. A deviation of perhaps 10 percent is tolerable for most appliances. However, a high-speed alternator will rarely be able to go much over its maximum R.P.M. limit. The centrifugal force can damage the windings of the rotor if it is spun too rapidly. There are variable-R.P.M. units such as the Auto-Gen on the market, but I've never talked with anyone who has actually used such a unit over a long period.

Another approach to engine-generated alternating current is to do the job electronically via a Dynamote invertor. This unit taps into the alternator and pulls out 60 volts AC rather than 12 volts DC. It then takes this AC and steps it up and controls the frequency till you have 110 volts AC at 60 cycles. What's amazing is that the Dynamote will do this within a wide R.P.M. range, the limiting factor on R.P.M. being output power, not voltage.

COMPRESSORS

Refrigeration compressors are a subject in themselves and are more fully covered elsewhere in this book (see Chapter 7). As with all other accessories, they should be well mounted. Consideration should be given in the case of the compressor to a separate rubber mount.

MECHANICAL BILGE PUMPS

Mechanical bilge pumps, either impeller type or centrifugal design, will pump between 40 and 240 gallons per minute, and for damage control are essential. You have a choice of electric or manual clutch; the manual is more reliable, but the electric is easier to use. With a rubber impeller pump you should consider a vacuum shutoff switch to stop the unit in case it runs dry. Dry running will burn out the rubber impeller, and if you're using the unit in an emergency situation with many other things on your mind, you may forget about this aspect.

On the same subject, remember that in order for a powered pump to be of use, the engine must be able to run with the boat flooding. If the engine is located low in the bilge, consider a pump with its own motor, perhaps even a small gas engine, for emergency use.

EXHAUST SYSTEMS

No other item in the engine room is as prone to failure and chronic problems as the exhaust system. A combination of high operating temperature and saltwater corrosion make it an engineer's nightmare. The advent of the aqualift water-lock muffler and rubber hose has gone a long way toward solving these problems. The main thing to guard against is letting water enter the engine because of a failure in your exhaust system.

Be especially careful of jacketed exhaust systems. It's not always possible to eliminate the risk completely, but if a gate valve is placed strategically between the first entry point for water and the engine manifold, then the gate valve can be shut at the end of each running period if anything is suspect. Another valve should be placed at the hull where the exhaust line exits so that it can easily be shut off when running in heavy seas. It is not unknown for a large boarding wave to force water clear up and through the exhaust riser, allowing sea water to flow into the engine.

In some cases, where engines are mounted amidships, there is a temptation to let the exhaust out at the side of the vessel. This should be avoided where possible. Invariably you will end up with filthy topsides and a cleaning job after every passage. Running exhaust lines through the stern may be a bit more of a headache, but it's well worth the extra work. With two-cycle engines (GM diesels), though, you have to be careful of back pressure. With these engines you may be forced to take the shortest run for the exhaust line.

AIR CONDITIONING

Standard marine air-conditioning systems find little use aboard long-range cruisers. Without shore power they take too much engine time to be effective. However, if you already have a unit aboard, and if it's reliable, it can be used during the hour or so a day you run the engine for generating. If this is coordinated with cooking, which it usually is, the air conditioner can remove some of the heat aboard from the stove. If you are building, consider insulating the hull, headliner, and under the cabin soles not only for heat, but for air conditioning. An insulated boat will get by with less than half the BTU capacity than that of a noninsulated vessel.

WATER MAKERS

Up until recently, water makers aboard cruising boats were a joke. They depended on exhaust temperature for evaporation, and the average sailboat auxiliary just didn't have the heat capacity to make a good installation worthwhile. Add to this the complex nature of plumbing and pumps, and the machine's relative unreliability unless used on a frequent basis and one ended up with a pretty poor score. But this was before the advent of compact, reverse-osmosis water makers. The reverse-osmosis water system works by forcing seawater through a membrane, or series of membranes, under very high pressure. The salt and other impurities are removed by this process, leaving pure, potable water (good for batteries, too). Units are available that can be powered directly by the engine or via AC current and that will produce 10 to 12 gallons an hour. If you have the budget and the space, this would more than cover your total water consumption per day.

AUXILIARY GENERATORS

In a boat 45 feet or more, it becomes possible to fit a second small generating plant. This can take the form of either a full Onan or homelight generator/diesel set, or a more modest one-cylinder diesel coupled to an alternator and compressor for use as backup. If you go up one size in the diesel, using the latter approach, you may find that the unit can be used daily in lieu of the main engine. A 5-h.p. water-cooled diesel suitable for marine use can be bought for about $1000. Add to this a few hundred dollars for a compressor, second alternator, and installation (if you install it yourself), and it makes a pretty good backup system to the main engine.

The use of the complete generating sets, unless you are planning on electric cooking, doesn't make sense. The money, weight, and space can be better spent in other areas.

SHAFT-CHARGING SYSTEMS

Part of the joy of cruising is the peace and quiet one (usually) finds at sea. To disturb this on a daily basis by running the engine is more than many people can bear. Yet, we also enjoy the refrigerator/freezer and electricity for lights and pilot, not to mention radio and stereo. There is an answer: shaft-charging systems.

In this set-up the main prop shaft is allowed to spin and an alternator and/or refrigeration compressor is belted on. Rigged properly, there will be huge quantities of power available. If a standard alternator is used, normally a step-up ratio of between 7 and 10 to 1 is necessary before enough alternator R.P.M. is obtained to

Aboard *Intermezzo II* we went for a permanent sea generating propeller installation. This 12″ prop will kick out better than 50 amps if we're moving at over 9 knots. At 6½ knots it generates enough power to supply the autopilot and radar.

make the alternator's output worthwhile (3 or 4 to 1 will do the trick for the compressor). There are several drawbacks to this approach. First, it forces you to use a fixed prop or a variable-pitch unit with the pitch cranked in. If this is done for an hour a day, you can tolerate the loss of speed. But on a constant basis the speed loss is too much. The other problem is noise. The shaft spinning in its bearings and rotating the transmission parts sets up a racket, usually a low-pitched rumble, that is difficult to eliminate.

If you have a modern, flat-bottom boat, consider putting in a small second shaft with a very small prop to do the job. A 12-inch outboard prop, with 7 or 8 inches of pitch, will work well. This allows the main prop to be feathered or folded, and eliminates much of the noise.

The simplest approach, though, is to use a taffrail generator. These units utilize low-R.P.M., permanent-magnet DC motors that are rotated by a prop towed behind the boat. The best unit for the money in our opinion, is made by Ham Ferris of Dover, Massachusetts. His unit, $400 today, will put out 6 to 7 amps at 6 knots of boat speed. It's simple to maintain and gives good service. We carried a unit aboard *Intermezzo* for more than 20,000 miles and several of our friends ordered units after seeing ours. We found that when sailing with the autopilot, which used a fair amount of power, the unit saved us 3½ hours of engine time per day.

75. Electrical Systems

There is an old adage: electricity and salt water don't mix. While this is undeniably true, some of the things that electricity provides when you're cruising are very nice to have—and you *can* have them if you set up your system carefully. One fundamental rule which proves the old adage must be observed, however: anything remotely associated with electricity has to stay dry. There is no way around this axiom. Now for specifics.

WIRING

Only tinned wire (copper wire drawn through a solder bath) should be used on a boat, and the wire must be encased in moisture-resistant insulation. Wire has many grades of flexibility: as the number of strands in a given size increases, so does the flexibility, its longevity, and cost. All connections should be soldered. Even where crimp-on lugs are used, a drop of solder should be applied after they have been attached. If you really want to do it right, smear a little silicone sealant over the end of the insulation to protect it from moisture.

Two potential troublemakers that are seldom fused aboard cruising boats but have great potential for harm are the alternator and starter wiring. A direct short in this wiring could result in a fire. Consider inserting high-amperage fuses at the battery end of these cables. If you go this route, be sure the fuses have mechanical fasteners rather than just large spring clips. The anchor winch should be protected at both the battery end and at the winch end because of its long run.

On deck, electrical gear doesn't work out. After several years you will be lucky if any control switches or meters are still working. After fighting this battle on *Intermezzo,* I finally removed all switches from the deck and placed them below. Usually it is possible to place controls for such things as the autopilot clutch, spreader lights, or engine shutoff just inside the companionway, where they are shielded from the elements.

BATTERIES

Batteries come in many sizes, types, and constructions. The normal automotive battery or starting battery is designed for high-cranking amperage. To accomplish this aim, manufacturers utilize lots of thin lead plates in their construction. This high density of plates leads to a high amp-hour rating. For starting engines they work fine. But on board, we are more concerned with a gradual output for lights, fans, electronic gear, and the like. The best construction for this application involves fewer, thicker, and heavier plates. The instant cranking power is down, but it is possible to take a battery of this construction and run it way down, and then bring it back with a fast charge without damaging the plates. These are called deep-discharge batteries, and generally cost one-third more. What's confusing here is that batteries of the latter type will show fewer amp-hours in their test, but will actually deliver more usable storage capacity and longevity than ordinary starting batteries. From the cruiser's standpoint, we are lucky in that the golf-cart industry has the same application, so the type of batteries we need are manufactured in quantity.

Part of the equation you must look at in your battery bank is how fast they can be charged back up to their full capacity. The larger the bank, the more amperage they will accept from the alternator(s) without overheating. If daily consumption for the vessel is 60 amp-hours and you have the capacity of putting in 60 amp-hours from the alternator, it will take several hours to put all that electricity back in. To begin with, the batteries require about 25 percent more capacity coming in than went out. That is inherent inefficiency. Then, as they come up in their charge, the alternator must taper off so that by the end of the charge cycle you are putting out just a few amps.

One way around this dilema is to increase battery bank capacity. If you go from a 400-amp-hour bank to an 800-amp-hour bank for the same 60 amp-hours of consumption, you can charge at twice the rate as before. In other words, you can double the charge rate by adding a second alternator and cut the time required to put back the 60 amp-hours by half. A bonus is that the double battery bank will last longer.

Another approach to batteries is to use nickel-cadmium construction, or Nicads as they are called. These batteries can be utilized almost to the bottom of their charge capacity and then brought back up very rapidly. Further, they have a very long life. Most Nicads are guaranteed for 10 years.

We have already discussed battery location, but let me emphasize once again that if the batteries can be kept cool, their life will much longer, and they will accept a much faster charge rate.

Other considerations in battery location are serviceability, cleanliness, and gas accumulation. The latter has safety connotations. Hydrogen gas, which is given off during the charging cycle, is lighter than air. If the battery compartment is ventilated, the gas will rise and find its way out of the boat. If not, you can develop a dangerous, explosive situation. Second, it is odorous. If the batteries are under a bunk and your head is over them, you will certainly be able to tell they are there, especially when they're charging.

If the batteries are charged properly, they won't require much maintenance. Check the water levels occasionally, and if you have to add water more than once every six months, something is wrong. A big maintenance factor, however, is cleanliness. Surprisingly, a dirty battery will leak electricity between its terminals. If you think I'm kidding, take a voltmeter, set it on the low scale, and do some checking on the top of a dirty battery. A bad case can utilize as much as 15 percent of a battery's capacity. So keep them clean. Terminals must be kept free of corrosion.

CONTROL PANELS

The range of marine electrical control panels offers many options. It's the one area where even dyed-in-the-wool "simplest is best" folks begin to stray. Everybody likes switches, lights, and dials. Perhaps this is a throwback to watching those old Buck Rogers movies. Still, no matter how complex, a good electrical control panel must be functional.

First you have to decide between switches and fuses or circuit-breaker/switch combinations. The former not only are cheap and easy to utilize, they are prevalent in many parts of the world. But in the U.S. and some areas of Europe, aircraft-type DC circuit breakers have made inroads in the last 10 years. Today, every quality yacht in the U.S. is fitted with circuit breakers. They seem to be reliable and are neat in appearance.

The more the individual circuits are divided, the easier it will be to trace a problem. If there are three bilge pumps, each should have its own remote and manual control. The same with various navigation lights and other accessories.

Consider light-emitting diodes as indicators on key functions such as water pumps and bilge pumps. Manual controls should be handy for all engine-related accessories so they can be shut down in the event maximum power is necessary for the propeller. It's a good idea to have a master breaker for all engine accessories. When the engine is shut down, one switch assures you that all the accessories are turned off.

All engines should be fitted with oil pressure and water temperature alarm systems. These two vital-symptom indicators should make different sounds. If the engine overheats, the world isn't going to end, at least for a short period of time. If you're in the middle of a tricky maneuver, you'll want to keep going. If you lose oil pressure, on the other hand, you will want to know it immediately; then you can weigh the cost of replacing the engine against any damage that might happen to the boat through an immediate shutdown.

If an automatic shutdown system is employed during the times when the engine is used as a generator, it must be disconnected when maneuvering in case it leaves you without power at an inopportune time.

Engine heat and oil pressure gauges should be fitted below as well as on deck. The voltage meter should have an expanded scale. If the amperage output meter is far from the alternator and batteries, use a unit with a separate shunt. This means the current-sensing unit can be located away from the meter itself. By this method you reduce the distance the electricity has to travel from the alternator to the batteries, and with it the resistance that must be overcome.

AC SYSTEMS

Alternating current at high voltages (120/240 volts) aboard a yacht must be treated with extreme care: it is lethal. Properly set up, though, its potential for serious harm can be minimized. Ground-fault-interrupting breakers should be utilized in all the receptacles aboard. The GFI is simply a circuit breaker that trips on very low current, if someone gets a shock. They are so sensitive that it's not practical to have one breaker service the entire vessel. Accumulated leakage over a period of time will set them off. So each receptacle should be equipped with a GFI. Obviously those receptacles that have any chance of getting wet need screw-on positive weather-proofing covers. This is especially true of heads and the galley. The AC circuit board should be plastic and have an insulated box on the back to prevent accidental shocking. For use with shore power, it is essential that an isolation or electrostatically shielded transformer be employed between the shore current and the vessel. This helps solve certain electrolysis problems, but more important, it isolates the ship from the shore ground, reducing the risk of injury through a shock.

Power should come to a master breaker that disconnects all the wires from shore, not just the hot wire. A voltage meter and frequency meter will be needed to keep an eye on what you're getting in the way of power. An amp meter is necessary to watch capacity. These are also helpful to keep an eye on your on-board sources of AC, i.e., inverters, main engine generators, or auxiliaries.

If you'll be spending time in the islands or in other countries and using shore power, you'll need a step-down transformer as well. In other parts of the world, without exception 220/240 volts at 50 cycles is the norm. If you step down to 110 volts via a transformer you'll be okay. The cycles difference means that some appliances will run more slowly, but in general it can be tolerated.

It's also important to have a reverse-polarity-indicating circuit, which tells you if the shore plug is improperly wired. If you have twin shore-power leads and are using both at the same time, have reverse-polarity indicators on both. It is not unknown to find a dock with one plug wired properly and the other reversed!

76. DC-to-AC Inverters

No modern book on cruising would be complete without a word about solid-state DC-to-AC inverters. The advent of the transistor has made it possible to take 12-volt DC out of batteries, turn it into alternating current, and boost it up to 110 volts with transformers. The impact of this technology on cruising comfort is not to be underestimated. For less than $200 you can create plenty of AC to take care of a small vacuum cleaner, galley hand-mixer, blender, ⅜" drill, or orbital sander.

Because they are solid state these electronic inverters are quiet and efficient. When they're working at their most efficient level, the consumption of energy from the batteries will be about 20 to 30 percent more than the appliance itself uses. Compared to the old motor converters, this is fantastically efficient.

Tripp Lite is probably the largest manufacturer of inverters for the recreational market. Units range in size from 100 to 1000 watts. Several of the models are frequency controlled, which means that the inverter will smoothe out the normal battery voltage variations and stay at 60 cycles, to keep tape decks and TVs operating as they should.

Dynamote units are much beefier. They go as high as 3600 watts and will run refrigeration compressors, microwaves, and the like.

One word of caution, though: While the AC amperage is low on these units, they still put a big drain on your 12-volt batteries. If you plan on using an inverter at high loads for any period of time, watch battery voltage carefully or run the engine at the same time so the alternator can help share the load.

8
The Next Boat

Wherever yachtsmen gather there is always talk of the next, the ultimate boat. In many cases this represents an extension of their present yacht. The new vessel will have the same hull characteristics, maybe a little more waterline, and a few more bits of hardware. Once in a while one will run across a really special vessel, different from others and unique in concept and execution.

We have been fortunate in meeting several such yachts and the people who created them in different parts of the world. Three more disparate yachts could not be found than *Masina, Sunflower,* and *Wakaroa.* Yet their owners have in common a love of the sea and the freedom that comes with cruising it. Their cumulative experience includes three circumnavigations and hundreds of thousands of sea miles. Their intimate understanding of the cruising life is reflected, in different ways, in the boats they have created.

Intermezzo II is our own ultimate yacht.

Masina beats slowly offshore with her double-head rig. (Noel Barrett)

77. Masina

I don't fall in love easily. It usually takes a while for me to absorb the qualities of endearment that make such a state possible. There have been a couple of exceptions. Linda was definitely love at first sight. And we have lived happily ever after. The second time there was another man involved and I was "engaged."

I was sitting in our cockpit in Cape Town watching the coal-fired switching engines when out of the corner of my eye I first saw *Masina.* That she was well designed was undeniable. There was something about her graceful sheer, clean foredeck, and short ends

Note the deep reefs in the mainsail and the battens in the Yankee jib leech/foot to prevent chattering.

Noel and Letara Barrett—an iron crew out of a classical mold. (Noel Barrett)

that bespoke power and purpose. She had a conservative cutter rig, well stayed, and as she tacked through the narrow yacht moorings it was apparent she handled with ease.

Had I been a little younger I would have sacrificed anything to own her. At 38 feet overall, with a 34½-foot waterline and an eight-ton displacement, she had to be quick. Her 5½-foot draft made her versatile and her clean ends coupled with a modest 9½-foot beam would keep her running true, even in foul conditions. She was the most beautiful yacht I had ever seen.

But I was engaged by then in a new *Intermezzo,* and Noel and Letara Barrett were already wedded to *Masina.*

Noel grew up with the sea, as most New Zealanders do. He spent 2½ years of part-time effort building *Masina* in New Zealand to a design by Jack Brook (somewhat modified), and his concept of a cruising yacht matched exactly what I would have done in my youth: fast, seaworthy, beautiful, and simple. Noel had been there before: thousands of miles of ocean racing and cruising, including a jaunt down to 60 degrees south latitude just to have a look at the ice pack, and maybe the the Horn.

Masina carried no head in her tiny, functional cabin. She did have an occasionally charged (ashore) battery to run the binnacle light, but no engine, no windvane, no radio gear, and very little maintenance.

Noel built her, strip-planking the hull over sawn and steam-bent frames. Underwater, she had a well-developed fin and a skeg-hung rudder. To ease steering pressure, the bottom section of the rudder projected forward to provide some counterbalance.

The engine that was to have been installed was sold to pay for *Masina*'s spars. As a result Noel fined up her run aft, getting better direction control as a result. Would he do without an engine again? "Yes, I'm a bit inclined that way."

According to the theories presented in this book *Masina* isn't a good candidate for a successful cruiser. She wouldn't keep most women happy, and even her master might tire of her spartan ways.

Has she traveled? Since her launching in October 1972, 80,000 miles have passed under her keel, including the Horn, the North Pacific, Japan to Vancouver, the North Atlantic, and the Southern Ocean, Cape Town to New Zealand. Noel, his iron lady Letara, and his wooden ship seem to thrive on the high latitudes.

That Noel took pride in both his ladies and their accomplishments was evident: Galapagos to the Marquesas (2800 miles) in 18½ days, three days during that run of 210 to 212 miles. They averaged more than 150 miles per day on downwind passages in general, with an overall average of 120 to 130 miles per day including all their doldrums and uphill passages—all on a 34½-foot waterline.

"Why don't you at least have a vane of some sort?" I asked as we shared dinner in our saloon.

"Because they're so damn ugly sticking out there," Noel replied.

"Don't you get tired of hanging onto that tiller day after day?"

"Yes, but I enjoy the challenge."

While *Masina*'s gear was limited, what she had was well thought out. Her double-spreader spar was heavily stayed. The spinnaker poles could be stowed on the mast or on deck.

Her ground tackle was what one would expect on an engineless sea-going yacht—substantial. For everyday anchoring, this lightweight, low-windage yacht carried a 45-lb. CQR and 45 fathoms of 5/16" chain. Next came 60 fathoms of 3/8" chain and a 65-lb. fisherman anchor. Finally she had 35 fathoms of one-inch-diameter rode with a 5-fathom section of chain and a stainless-steel folding North Hill anchor. For running before severe gales they carried, just in case, 60 fathoms of 1¾" nylon warp.

Where *Masina* might be lacking in bangles, she has an exquisite wardrobe in which to dress her spars—two mains; a flat Swedish cut with hollow leeches and no battens; and a conventional main, heavily reinforced. For the forestay she carried an overlapping staysail, to be used with the Yankee, and a high-cut storm staysail for severe weather. She carried three sizes of genoas, the smallest of which worked very well downwind when poled out with its short foot. There was a #4, or storm jib, which they changed down to after the Yankee. For light airs downhill they carried a spinnaker.

Since we sailed out the anchor on *Intermezzo* as often as was practicable, I was interested in Noel's techniques aboard *Masina,* especially in heavy or tight conditions. If conditions got really bad, they hoisted the main, close-reefed so it wouldn't flog. Then the staysail was hoisted in stops. They would then overhaul the anchor, and if necessary, as it was once, slip the chain or rode at the last moment.

The southern summer was advancing, and Noel, Letara, and *Masina* were soon to be off eastbound across the Southern Ocean. They were "curious" about the string of islands in the Southern Ocean between Cape Town and Australia, and intended to do some "interesting gunkholing in the 50s and 60s." We watched as a moderate amount of stores went aboard; the cold-weather clothing was broken out, and finally Noel filled his 75-gallon water tank.

There is always debate about how to handle heavy weather. The definition of extreme conditions varies with one's vessel, experience, and mental outlook. I knew that when Noel and I talked about tactics, his heavy weather would really be extreme.

Anyone who sails the Southern Ocean from the 40s south does so expecting a series of easterly moving depressions with storm-strength winds. On their first leg toward Marion Island there was a series of blows, as expected. The problem these pose for any yacht caught in their path is the abrupt shift in wind direction that occurs with the frontal passage. One then has to contend with breaking seas from two directions.

Noel had *Masina* running before what *he* called a severe storm. Their storm staysail was sheeted amidships, as it had been in previ-

Masina carried her substantial ground tackle well aft. Her twin spinnaker poles were stored on the mast in port or when sailing downwind in moderate conditions. In heavy going they were kept on deck to lower the center of gravity.

Masina's oil-fired running lights eliminate the need for a generator aboard.

ous blows. Now they were trailing all 60 fathoms of their 1¾" warp, with the North Hill anchor attached as well. With the frontal passage and the abrupt shift in wind direction, the sea conditions became chaotic. Towing 420 feet of warp, *Masina* would occasionally slew around on the face of the larger, disturbed seas. One particularly bad one caught her and rolled her down until her masthead was underwater, soaking gear below and emptying their lockers onto Letara in the leeward bunk. The deckhead was dented and splattered from flying gear.

Masina shook herself, straightened out, and continued on to Marion Island where the Barretts dried out and tidied up.

Their curiosity about this first Southern Ocean outpost sated, they headed east toward the French Crozet Islands. An unusual easterly wind forced them south, however, and they decided to have a look at Herd Island, within the Antarctic ice-pack zone. Atlas Cove was the only ice-free anchorage, and after a short stay weather conditions forced them to move on toward Kerguelen just north of the 50th Parallel. More severe weather overcame them and once again *Masina* was severely knocked down and her crew and interior soaked to the core. Cold and wet, they ran off and headed for Hobart, Tasmania, arriving 23 days later.

Noel and Letara are now building a larger yacht. With a brand-new crew member to be fed, diapered, and housed, they need more room. She'll be a conservative ketch, built in wood, maybe with an engine. But Noel is getting rid of the hassle of electricity. His next binnacle will have oil-burning lights alongside.

78. Sunflower

It had been a squally, wet passage to the Shortland Islands in the Solomon group, and we were very pleased to have *Intermezzo* once again in calm, charted waters. Maneuvering toward the anchorage, keeping an eye peeled for coral heads that the cartographers might have missed, out of the corner of my eye I noticed a large yellow beacon. As we worked closer, finally dropping the hook, the beacon turned into a distinctive yellow *Sunflower*. With the anchor set firmly, we put the dinghy over the side to have a better look at our new neighbor.

"Come aboard and set a spell," drawled the skipper. And so began a wonderful friendship.

Even from *Intermezzo,* half a mile away, I could tell that *Sunflower* was no ordinary vessel. Her distinctive shape, high freeboard, and substantial cutter rig had the look of a modern sea-going yacht that was meant to travel.

That Al and Beth Liggett had been there before was obvious not only in the overall design of *Sunflower,* but in the many details that make up this functional cruising yacht.

Listening to Al's easy-flowing voice and feeling his laid-back manner, it wasn't difficult to picture his rowing on the Ohio River in earlier days. Then after a little sailing experience on a 20-foot sloop, he and Beth (who had sailed overnight only once) took off on *Baccus,* an old heavy-displacement, long-keeled woody on what ended up being a four-year circumnavigation.

They settled in Guam on their return, Al going back to his surveying and Beth to teaching, while in their spare time they developed a laundromat business, taught navigation, and made sails.

They were once more, as Al put it, "prisoners of society," and it wasn't long before Al was drawing boat pictures and playing around with designs.

They eventually asked Bob Perry to design them a flush-deck version of the Valiant 40.

When word got around that the Liggetts were doing a new boat, people started asking if they could build one too, and before long there were a number of *Sunflowers* to build. Being in Guam, it was natural for Al and Beth to look at Taiwan for quotes, since they were relatively close by. Wary of the normal Taiwan building practices, they began working with a yard that hadn't built fiberglass yachts before, but were interested in starting. *Sunflower* became the plug for the mold on which the future vessels would be molded.

By visiting the yard monthly during building, they were able to get close to what they considered at the time an ideal cruising yacht.

Sunflower at speed. Her clean deck and conservative cutter rig are the favorite offshore approach of most experienced cruisers. (Al Liggett)

Al and Beth Liggett in the cockpit of *Sunflower*.

Between snorkeling trips to Japanese World War II seaplanes sunk in the lagoon, we had plenty of time to get a good look at Al and Beth's creation.

Sunflower is 42 feet long, 34½ feet on the waterline, and 12½ feet wide. She draws a little over 6 feet loaded and displaces 12 tons, with an additional 2 tons for payload. She is built of fiberglass over a ¾" airex foam core, the laminate averaging half an inch. The keel itself is solid fiberglass with internal lead ballast.

Sunflower was one of the earliest designs that was laid out specifically for the way most people cruise, i.e., for the Liggetts alone, with accommodations for occasional guests. The emphasis was on utilizing the space effectively for Al and Beth on their own.

The cockpit seats are large enough to sleep on, but the well itself is quite small. As you go down below, you are at once struck by the tremendous apparent room of her interior.

That visual (and actual) volume is from two factors. First, the flush-deck design allows the eye to go all the way out to the hull edge, rather than being confined to doghouse or trunk cabin sides. This also adds substantially to the available storage space. Second, Al and Beth prefer a light interior. Most of her vertical surfaces are painted a soft off-white, with lots of teak trim. She has several large hatches for light and ventilation in the tropics, and the interior is further brightened by the blues, reds, and yellows favored by this cheerful and very "up" couple.

You come down the companionway into an L-shaped galley to port with a good-size fridge and freezer running off the main engine. The sinks are amidships where they will drain on either tack. The three-burner propane stove is gimballed to port. Beth has specialized storage areas for dishes, condiments, and other galley necessities. She professes to not having any "special" galley gear other than her large pressure cooker, which she uses occasionally for canning. It was through this galley that we were introduced to Mother Liggett's famous dill pickle recipe (see Chapter 60).

The 35-h.p. Volvo engine is located beneath the galley sink, and

Sunflower anchored at Nissan Island, Papua, New Guinea. The awning keeps her water tanks filled and her crew comfortable.

is easy to get at. Originally it had a direct saltwater-cooled block, but Al later changed to freshwater heat-exchanger cooling. Al is one of the few cruisers we have met who is happy with his Volvo. Their daily charging cycle to top up the two banks of batteries (100 and 320 amp-hours, respectively) and take care of the fridge runs about 45 minutes. Al has manual as well as automatic control on his 35-amp alternator. The engine drives a 16- by 12-inch fixed prop through a 1.9 to 1 reduction gear. With a clean bottom the three-bladed prop will push them at 6 knots at 1800 R.P.M. Their 150 gallons of fuel gives them close to a 900-mile range.

To starboard, opposite the galley is the navigation station. A fairly simple switch panel, and wind speed, boat speed, and depth indicators (all Signet) are there, along with Al's Atlas ham radio rig and a couple of old-fashioned multiband radios. They also have a Loran C receiver, but they now feel that the relatively low cost makes a satellite navigator a more useful and a better investment.

Aft of the navigation station are two features I liked very much. In place of the usual quarterberth, they had fitted a proper chart-stowage cabinet, with pull-out drawers. Next, abaft the removable companionway steps is access to the considerable stowage area under the cockpit. Owing to *Sunflower*'s extreme freeboard this area had good headroom and was efficient, useful stowage.

Going forward, there is a conventional saloon, with L-shaped settee to port and a drop-leaf table for dining. A very attractive open cupboard sits behind the settee—a perfect place to display baskets, shells, and pottery. To starboard is another settee with a pilot berth behind. The Liggetts would not put the pilot berth in again, as it is never used. On both sides are practical and aesthetic book shelves. At the forward end of the saloon is an end table with a Dickinson diesel-fired heater.

The unusual part of the interior develops as you walk forward and see what can be done within a hull like this if you forsake the "pack 'em in" mentality. They have a lovely double bunk to starboard, raised high enough to get width from the topside flare and good storage underneath. Opposite this is a head with separate stall shower, usually filled with spare gear. Forward, where one might normally find two crammed V-berths, are storage areas and a good workbench.

That *Sunflower* is immenently livable is undeniable, and the fact that Al and Beth have been doing that for five years now is proof enough. But does she sail?

Our first experience watching *Sunflower* move was in southern New Guinea where we had spent time together working up the coast of Bougainville Island. We had enjoyed touring an Australian-run cocoa plantation, then sailed out to the Carterette Islands where we watched the colorful pageantry of local outriggers. Sailing overnight, we arrived at Nissan, where we each traded for huge pieces of traditional *kina* (shell money) and were treated to an unexpected chance to watch the men perform a traditional "bird" dance. Here also we shared meals with the good-humored Father Lepping at the Catholic mission and listened to his stories about being a Japanese prisoner of war in Rabaul during World War II. And finally we sailed on to the southern end of New Ireland. It was from this anchorage that we finally left at the same time. The day was bright and windless as we worked our way out of the quiet anchorage we had shared. We were excited about arriving that afternoon in Rabaul, the first big city any of us had seen in several months. Mail and friends awaited us, so we both were cruising along under our "iron genoas."

I went below after a while to take a short nap. When I awoke, a gentle breeze from the southeast had come up and *Sunflower* was flying her yellow-and-black spinnaker, pulling rapidly away from us. Sensing a good photo, we speeded up to a maximum 7½ knots. Having taken our photos (to the accompanying abuse about "stink-potting"), I set *Intermezzo*'s sails and soon had the big spinnaker and mizzen staysail drawing. While we owned *Intermezzo* we never found another yacht of any size that would stay downwind with her in light to moderate going, and I expected to overhaul *Sunflower* in short order. But it wasn't until we had reached the corner of New Britain Island, hardened up, and headed for Rabaul that we finally overhauled Al and Beth and were able to salute them with our double whammy. *Sunflower*'s combination of low-wetted-surface hull and big rig really moved her along.

Having seen *Sunflower* out of the water, I would classify her shape as vintage Robert Perry, with a moderate fin keel, skeg-hung rudder, and full deadrise forward. The Liggetts felt that at speed she had a more lively motion than the heavier *Baccus,* but then they were going a lot faster.

She carried 8-oz. working canvas, main Yankee, and staysail.

When they replaced these sails after 4½ years, they dropped down to 6-oz. material. The staysail is the workhorse of the inventory. There is a 640-square-foot #1 genoa which sees some service, but is really a bundle to handle on the foredeck. The 450-square-foot #2 genoa is used more on passages, and flies better off the spinnaker pole when running. They also carry a storm jib, used occasionally, and a storm trysail that (fortunately) has never seen service. They use their spinnaker on occasion, and recently acquired a cruising spinnaker that gets a lot of service day-sailing.

The old adage that one can tell a cruising boat by its ground tackle is nowhere more true than on *Sunflower*. Two 60-lb. CQRs are carried, one on the stemhead roller, along with a 70-lb. Danforth and a 15-lb. Danforth used as a stern anchor. Their primary chain rode is 300 feet of ⅜" high-tensile chain. There is a second shot of 100 feet of chain for emergencies; 600 feet of ¾" nylon and 600 feet of ⅝" nylon round out their gear. The latter quantities are not so much for anchoring as tying up in the mangrove swamps in the event of a hurricane.

They have slab reefing on the main, using a single line through the clew, and tack to a winch on the boom. All halyard winches are on the mast. Halyards are rope, and when we were together in New Guinea they did stretch a bit.

As one would expect, her high freeboard keeps them dry, and as is typical with modern boats, she doesn't like to get her rail down. They find that she sails better on her feet. In the five years they have been aboard, Al and Beth have averaged about 130 miles per day. She'll do better, perhaps 150 a day. But Al and Beth feel the small amount of time saved isn't worth the discomfort—although Al allows as how he likes the feeling of the faster day, and *Sunflower* has been entered in a number of races.

At sea they use their double-bunk cabin for storage, preferring to sleep in the main saloon. They stand watches of two hours on and two off, and both are awake during doubtful navigational sections. Steering is handled by a Sayes vane (modified by Al with a larger sail) or a Tillermaster when sailing with spinnaker and under power. During the day they don't stand formal watches, and in the evening they rotate the schedule so they don't always have the same hours.

For safety gear they carry a C. J. Hendry raft with a sailing kit and a good deal of survival gear. They have harnesses, but say they don't use them as often as they should. Al made a point of mentioning that they did always wear whistles around their necks at night, and usually carry strobe lights in their pockets. Beth added that she thinks it would be a good idea to add a pocket mirror, since a strobe would not be too effective in a daylight man-overboard situation.

They like to keep things "simple," and thus have no water pressure pumps in the galley. They use hand pumps for salt and fresh water (they carry 150 gallons). For showers they use a solar heater on deck.

We said our last good-bye to Al and Beth in Bali. We were heading for home via the Cape of Good Hope and they were going to fabled Singapore. In the two years since they have been back to Japan (their favorite area for culture), had a near-record crossing of the North Pacific, and cruised Alaska. *Sunflower*'s simplicity must be getting to Al. He doesn't seem to have enough maintenance work to do at present, and he's ruminating about a new ultimate cruiser.

79. Wakaroa

We met Jim and Cheryl Schmidt in the most beautiful island in the world, Fatu Hiva in the Marquesas group. We had been enjoying the peace and solitude of spectacular Hanavave Bay for several days, taking hikes ashore to visit new friends and view the incredible scenery that is a trademark of this magnificent group. I read somewhere that these peaks looked like the Grand Canyon turned inside out—an apt description, but picture them laden with tropical foliage as well.

Our afternoon siesta was interrupted by the unmistakable roar of a GM 6-71 diesel as the Schmidts maneuvered their 70-foot ketch and anchored just behind us. And it wasn't long before we were comparing notes, discussing boats, gear, touring our respective floating homes, and enjoying a new friendship.

Aboard the Sparkman and Stephens–designed *Wind'Son* for din-

The Schmidt family and *Wakaroa* at speed off Suva, Fiji.

ner that night, Jim and I found that we had both been in the construction game at one time and knew a lot of the same people. It turned out that Cheryl and I had been born in the same New York hospital—"years apart," as Cheryl was quick to point out. It was the beginning of a warm and lasting friendship that would span three oceans, a couple of gales, and some awfully good times.

Linda marveled at the provisions Cheryl had to draw on in the galley. She produced real whipped cream, perked coffee, and frozen juices—items we hadn't seen for months. We thought their video machine with library of movies the height of luxury. This was 1977 in the middle of the South Pacific, and such "toys" were unheard of then.

Elyse and Sarah instantly fell in love with their pets Kitty Cat and Shassy, a beautiful doberman who was good with the children. Jim kept them in gales of giggles with his constant teasing, too. Some of

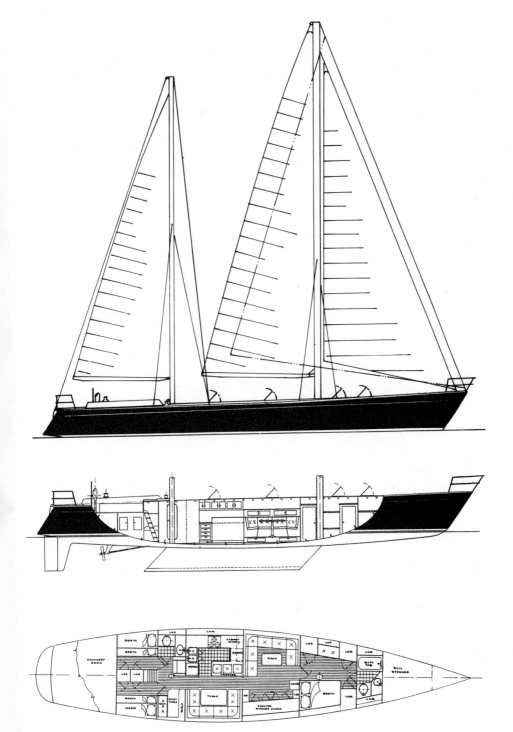

Plans for *Wakaroa*.

Behind-the-mast roller furling on the mainsail is inefficient, but easy to use and relatively reliable.

the pressure was off us as parents providing for all of the children's
needs. Up until now we had been parents, teachers, and playmates.
The Schmidts became an extended family as the children took to
their open warm-heartedness. What child can resist a man who
pretends his shoe is a telephone?

Wind'Son was a classic. A heavily built motorsailor with five
watertight compartments, two generators, and every conceivable
form of electronic gear, she was a very comfortable yacht indeed.

On deck they used Stearns roller furling on the headsails and main,
and did away with the main boom in the process of rerigging her.

Everything about her was massive. And she took some handling.
By the time we reached Papeete, Jim and Cheryl had decided they

Jim and Cheryl Schmidt handle the spinnaker and mizzen staysail with the aid of sail "socks," which can be seen at the head of both sails.

wanted more privacy, and so when the two young men crewing with them returned to Georgia, they decided to go it alone. From French Polynesia on they managed *Wind'Son*'s 65 tons by themselves with an occasional assist from friends or relatives along the way. On their own, even in mid-ocean, they kept formal watches.

It was in Rabaul, Papua, New Guinea, that I had first started to fool around with designs for a new boat. I had looked over the market and didn't really see anything I liked. Constellation Marine was building a 68-foot Peterson-designed light-displacement cruiser in New Zealand, and it appeared that her hull might just work for us. We were after a maximum boat for two people to sail. Long, narrow (by modern IOR standards), and light seemed the obvious way to go. My background and concern with performance had a notable influence on our rigs, layout, and hull-shape designs. Sitting with Jim aboard *Wind'Son,* I would bounce ideas off him and he would come back with a different viewpoint. We always took a lot of kidding from the Schmidts about our little "Tupperware" boat, and they always seemed surprised when we "struggled" (as Jimmy often put it) into port, occasionally after *Wind'Son* on a rough passage.

It was soon time for a sad farewell as the Schmidts headed for Truk Lagoon, on the other side of the equator for the wreck diving that Jim had always dreamed about.

We met up again in Madang, New Guinea. The Liggetts, Moeslys, ourselves, and some of our other friends were having a picnic at Crankett, a local island, when the unmistakable roar of that 6-71 GM diesel split the air. Elyse and Sarah jumped for joy, for soon they would have Kitty Cat and Shassy to play with, not to mention Jim and Cheryl. After expressing his surprise that we were still afloat, Jim asked how the new design was coming.

It gradually came out that he might be interested in a new boat, if I could convince him that it was "safe." And so began one of the more interesting design experiences I have been through.

I was looking for a high-performance cruising yacht, with enough amenities to keep Linda afloat; Jim was after an easily handled cruising yacht with the same conveniences of *Wind'Son* . . . and she had to be "bulletproof."

The most likely occurrence that would damage the yacht was contact with a coral head. In this regard the Peterson hull I was using

The business end of the spinnaker sock.

as a basic model had an unusual advantage over heavier designs. With a long, light boat, the hull depth was actually quite shallow: under 30 inches as it turned out, with the payload Jim wanted to carry. The keel projection would be made of steel. Since a majority of coral is awash two to three feet, that meant that contact would normally be made first by the steel weldment that was the keel. (The Schmidts finally opted for a half-inch-thick stainless-steel construction.)

Next came lying on her side in a grounded situation. Here we were concerned with abrasion more than puncture, specifically between the fore and aft watertight bulkheads. To minimize this risk, we specified an additional tapered laminate of fiberglass, half an inch thick in the turn of the bilge where abrasion was likely to occur, bringing the total to over 2½ inches.

Collision was the next concern, and the risk here was reduced with

The 9'-long galley has the space and conveniences of a modern apartment.

A clever double-door arrangement on the freezer.

Wakaroa has 18′ between her galley and forward saloon bulkheads.

The entertainment center.

a very heavy laminate schedule in the bow coupled with a bronze "shoe" to distribute load. Fore and aft watertight bulkheads, and several intermediate bulkheads, would reduce risk as well.

The next question was draft, a concern that I shared with Jim, having had a close call or two with our 7 feet. At 8 feet, *Wind'Son* had spent some anxious moments in Guam as a typhoon headed their way. She was forced to lie on a dock in the outer harbor unable to seek shelter in the mangroves as the shallower draft yachts had done.

We found that by going to a flush-deck layout and paying careful attention to the center of gravity, we would be able to develop a long ballast shoe with a very low center of gravity and keep draft to 6½ feet, fully loaded. This long keel had the added advantage of containing over 500 gallons of water and 350 gallons of fuel, which added considerably to her stability.

We were in agreement on the rig. A yacht this size, to be handled by two people, would have to be a ketch with some form of roller furling.

Once the basic problems were solved, it was the interior that really held Jim and Cheryl's interest. Sure, the new boat would be fast, but they professed no interest in speed. What they wanted was a comfortable layout that would be warm and cosy at sea or in port. Our concerns in this regard were identical. Not overly worried about a "commercial layout," we were able to take advantage of the very long hull and waterline and work out one of the most interesting interiors I have ever seen on a large yacht. Bear in mind that the boat was being built for a couple with a potential family on the horizon, who might have occasional guests along. The focus of attention would be the living area between the forward and after cabins. With 22 feet of length to work with and the full 14½-foot beam, the space, even by their standards, was huge. Cheryl's galley is as large as that found in many moderate-size apartments. The flush-deck configuration allows her wall cupboards to run right to the deckhead from counter height, providing a tremendous amount of easily accessible storage. There is 25 cubic feet of fridge and freezer, enough space for a year's supply of meat, frozen vegetables, and (for when we visit) ice cream.

Opposite the galley is a conventional C-shaped eating area, making service easy and keeping the mess and spills that occasionally accompany this endeavor confined to an area where they are easy to clean up.

A good-size double bunk with reading material close at hand.

Opposite Jim and Cheryl's bunk are two full-size hanging lockers with a love seat between them.

J.P. has his own "crib" in the port after stateroom.

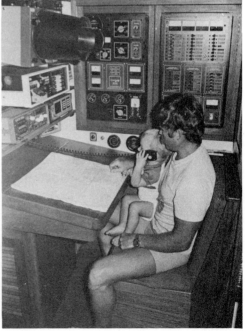

Wakaroa has a very complete navigation station.

Deck beams were drilled in convenient locations for handholds.

Forward of the galley is the main saloon and entertainment center, Jim's *pièce de résistance.* A beautifully crafted settee and coffee table lie alongside the galley counters. To starboard is a built-in cabinet arrangement housing stereo gear, videotape equipment, and their color TV. There is nothing like watching a Mel Brooks comedy to brighten the spirits when you are fighting a heavy blow.

The owner's cabin was placed forward for privacy and to keep it as far away from the engine room noise as possible. With a good-size double bunk, lots of floor space, and a full-width head, it is by any yacht standards very cosy. Aft there is a double cabin on each side of the companionway, with a head (including Cheryls washing machine) to starboard. Opposite the head is the navigation area, compact but efficient. With today's miniaturized components Jim is able to fit in satellite navigation gear, Loran C, weather fax, radar, radar alarm, ham gear, all-band receivers, direction finders, boat speed, and wind gear, as well as VHF and SSB, and a depth sounder. Interestingly, the total price tag was not much more than his satellite navigator aboard the old boat. When everything is going on the electrical control panel, lights glow and flash on and off, and the baby loves to climb up on Jim's lap and watch the "show" (J.P., their new permanent crew member, was born a few months before the boat was launched).

Constellation's subcontractors started work on the boat while *Intermezzo* and *Wind'Son* were in Darwin, Australia, together. We had two things to celebrate: the new boat and Cheryl's announcement that she was expecting.

By the time we had finished racing the Schmidts across the Indian Ocean, and fought a few gales together off South Africa, *Wakaroa*, called a Deerfoot 68 by the builders, was well underway.

Finishing their circumnavigation in February 1980, Jim set about buying special gear and was soon ensconced back in New Zealand with Cheryl and J.P. *Wakaroa* went into the water in January 1981, an exciting moment for all concerned. An incredibly sleek-looking yacht, she has performed up to all our expectations. Jim and Cheryl handle her all-roller-furling rig (except mizzen) and 66,000 lbs. with ease. In the forward triangle they carry two headstays, one slightly ahead of the other, with #1 and #3 genoas in place. There is a roller-furling staysail to be used in heavy air with the mizzen reefed, and a behind-the-mast roller-furling mainsail.

While still protesting that he isn't interested in speed, Jim couldn't resist ordering a cruising spinnaker with a sock to control it, and a gigantic mizzen staysail. During her trials off Auckland, Jim and Cheryl had *Wakaroa* ("long canoe" in Maori) reaching at a steady 13.5 knots in smooth water. On her trip up from the Bay of Islands to Suva, Fiji, they averaged 200 miles per day hard on the wind. Her 15,000-lb, low-aspect-ratio keel hasn't hurt her performance upwind as much as some people expected. Cheryl reported she was able to sleep in their forward cabin even under these conditions.

We were pleased with this last comment, as Cheryl had often been a little green around the gills aboard the stately *Wind'Son*. The one problem Cheryl has had is with Jim's desire to "see what *Wakaroa* will do." He has taken to racing the clock now and then, and anything else that might appear on the ocean.

Jim and Cheryl are not unlike a lot of other friends we have made cruising. Cheryl had never seen a sailboat when she met Jim. Jim's sailing goes back to when he was a kid, but cruising came only in recent years.

Both Jim and Cheryl enjoy the freedom the lifestyle gives them. Exploring, diving on wrecks, investigating new rivers, collecting

Driven off the front end of the 85-h.p. diesel with an angled universal joint, *Wakaroa*'s lay shaft services a refrigeration compressor, water pump, 150-amp DC alternator, 3500-watt AC alternator, water maker, and 80-gallons-per-minute emergency bilge pump.

artifacts, and maintenance keep them very busy. Once or twice a year they take a break, as do many cruisers, and fly "home" to see family and friends. But they're always glad to get back aboard. In their mid-30s, they feel no urge to go back to the "rat race."

Jim's philosophy about complexity is a little different from that of the average sailor today. He feels that if you buy good gear, install it properly, and give it the service it requires, for the most part you can expect trouble-free cruising. *Wakaroa*'s engine room is in the after nine feet of the hull, under the cockpit. There is more headroom than on the old boat, and accessibility to all the gear. She is powered by an 85-h.p., four-cylinder Perkins diesel. Using an angled drive and universal joint, she has a puller prop (as sometimes seen on commer-

Note the pivoting double chain roller in the stemhead fitting.

cial vessels). The prop shaft runs forward rather than aft, and has a variable pitch Hundestadt propeller tucked in just behind the keel. The system works well, and as one would expect, she handles easily under power, cruising at 8 to 8½ knots.

They use the main engine as a generator. Belted to a lay shaft driven by the engine is a 150-amp, 12-volt DC Electrodyne alternator, 3500-watt AC generator, the refrigeration compressor, and an air compressor for filling dive bottles. They also have aboard a reverse-osmosis water maker. Hot water is provided by waste engine heat or electricity, and of course, there is pressure fresh and salt water, and a large Jabsco pump for damage control.

For ground tackle Jim carries as a primary anchor a 110-lb. Bruce on 300 feet of schedule 70, high-tensile 7/16″ chain, worked by a Nillson vertical windlass.

She is steered at sea with hydraulic steering and a Wagner autopi-

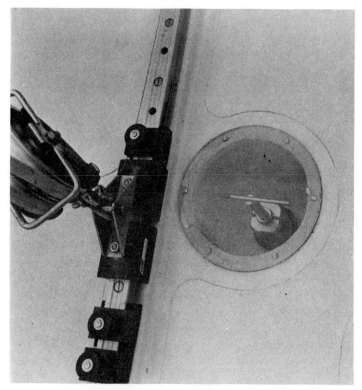

The top of the rudder post is used as a rudder angle indicator.

lot. They can drive their lay shaft by turning the Hundestadt while sailing. They also have a second prop shaft onto which is attached a specially wound alternator for producing electricity at sea. In port, they hoist an eight-foot-diameter windmill in the forward triangle to keep the batteries up. Large inverters can handle the built-in microwave if Cheryl isn't using her propane stove. At dockside, reverse-cycle air conditioning keeps them cool.

The interior is finished off in a combination of light Formica and vinyl for bulkheads with beautifully joined teak cabinetry. They cover all settees and bunks with vinyl to protect the foam, and then in fabric slipcovers that are easily removed for cleaning or washing.

Taking all aspects into account, *Wakaroa* is perhaps the most beautiful, strongly built yacht of her class afloat today. And knowing Jim, I wouldn't be surprised if he may be out to prove that she is also the fastest.

80. *Intermezzo II*

All the way across the Indian Ocean I had been thinking about the
new *Intermezzo*. The experience of working with the Schmidts had
been a good one and I felt the compromise we had worked out from
our opposite positions reflected an excellent choice for us as well. We
were planning on heading from Cape Town to New Zealand on an
airplane to conclude arrangements for our "ultimate" cruiser, then
continue to the States aboard *Intermezzo* and sell her.

In Mauritius I met Yves Betuel, the manager of the Taylor Smith
shipyard there. Yves had been a friend to circumnavigating yachtsmen for many years. A sailor himself, he made everyone's stay in
Gran Baie memorable. Yves couldn't do enough to help people out.
I needed a small piece of stainless welded and Yves took me to the
yard with him. As he escorted me to his welding shop, I looked
around at a large steel-boat building operation in full swing. In spite
of all my arguments about fiberglass with Jim, I had always considered metal to be the safest cruising-hull material. Mauritius had very
inexpensive labor and was certainly a pleasant enough place to spend
some time. What if. . . ? Yves then introduced me to his head
estimator and I began work on the scantlings for a light-displacement
hull in steel. Their quote really opened up my eyes. "But," Yves said,
"You will do it much cheaper in South Africa."

Perhaps it was the lure of working with another material, but I was
convinced to give metal a try.

Once in Durban I began to look around. I talked with a number
of builders, refined my structural details, and finally ran into a group
of builders in Cape Town who were aggressively seeking overseas
business. I sent them a package of drawings and scantlings. A few
days later I had a call: "Yes, we can do it in steel" (And the price
was right), "but why not aluminum?" Aluminum! That was the
dream metal. We could never afford that.

As it turned out, when all factors were considered aluminum
wasn't that much more expensive. A lighter hull meant a smaller
engine and running gear. Rigging, sails, and spars could all be
lighter. The actual painting was cheaper, and while raw material

Intermezzo II under working canvas. Even with the small headsails in Force 4 winds she can reach at better than 220 miles per day. (Phil Harrill)

costs were higher, labor for working and welding aluminum were about the same as for steel. There would be no comparison when it came to resale; aluminum would win, hands down.

A succession of southwesterly gales delayed our departure from Durban for Cape Town. I was fairly bursting to get down and see the people I had talked with. Finally *Intermezzo* was on her way during a brief respite in the weather, and after an arduous, although typical passage toward the roaring 40s that front Cape Town, we were snugged into the inner harbor in the marina of the Royal Cape Yacht Club.

As we would be building in metal, starting from scratch, I wasn't bound by a given hull shape available in a mold. I was introduced to a designer, Angelo Lavranos, who seemed to have designed most of the local boats.

Angelo and I immediately hit it off. He was an alumnus of Sparkman and Stephens, having done his apprenticeship under the tutelage of Angus Primrose in England. On his résumé were listed a number of well-known designs for production boats with builders like Moody and Swan, as well as numerous racing successes. What impressed me most was that Angelo was a numbers man. He had a rare talent in yacht designers—the ability to quantify not only hydrodynamic qualities, but structure as well. In addition he was an inquisitive human being with interests ranging from classical philosophy to mountain climbing.

I gave Angelo our basic parameters: a maximum boat for the two of us, one that we would be able to sail without having to rely on roller-furling aids in the high latitudes. We wanted a maximum draft of six feet fully loaded, and a displacement not over 50,000 lbs. I threw Angelo the rough work I had done and he replied with an enigmatic "We'll see."

Two weeks later I had a set of preliminary drawings in front of me. Angelo felt he could make our light-displacement, shallow-draft cruising concept work.

The numbers that he had come up with indicated that within our 50,000-lb. weight limit we should be able to carry the cruising payload I needed to keep both Linda and myself happy. I expected to give up some performance in light air compared to our present boat, but the exciting prospects of sailing a long, narrow, light hull in a real breeze more than made up for that.

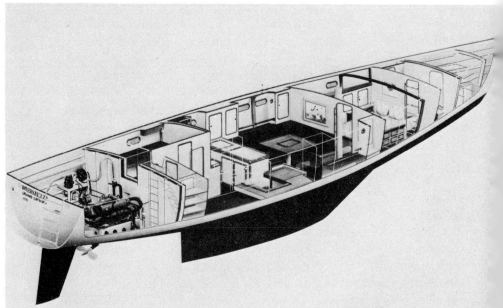

Steve Davis prepared these renderings of *Intermezzo II* for an article in *Sail* magazine. They provide a good overall view of the equipment that makes her so easy to sail and a comfortable home.

During this period we made friends with quite a number of South Africans. The structure of the local marine business seemed efficient, and I sensed that there might be commercial possibilities in boat-building there. The efficiency we had seen in metalwork, joinery, and engineering might make it possible to build a really high-quality cruising yacht at competitive prices.

So we set up a company to build the new boat, and shortly thereafter set sail from Cape Town on a nonstop 6000-mile journey to the West Indies. We were anxious to get back to the States, sell *Intermezzo,* purchase the materials for our new boat, and see about getting an order or two for additional vessels.

Angelo would be sending the lines and construction drawings to us in Miami. Aluminum had been ordered, and by the time I approved the first batch of drawings they were ready to start.

After we cleared Customs, in Fort Lauderdale, our old friend Chuck Adams was next on the list; he had our mail and drawings! Chuck brought them out that night, and I don't think I've ever been more excited than when I undid the careful wrappings on the envelope.

We stretched out the lines and offsets on *Intermezzo*'s saloon table and absorbed what Angelo had created.

She was 62 feet long, 55 feet on the water, and 14½ feet wide. He had caught exactly the flavor of what we wanted, and was able to work in not only the draft requirements but our aft engine room as well. Both factors came together in the hull to form a wide, powerful stern that helped stability, thereby reducing necessary draft, and moved the center of buoyancy aft to accommodate the machinery weight under the cockpit.

As a result, we had a beamy after hull section that would work well with the interior arrangement I had in mind.

One of the advantages of aluminum is its strength/weight ratio. In a 50,000-lb. boat, we could create a hull that could withstand substantial pounding on a reef for less than 12,000 lbs. Angelo had specified a 1-inch-thick keel plate, ½ inch sides, and a hull bottom plating running from ½ inch in the center to $\frac{7}{32}$ inch in the topsides. She was framed longitudinally with 5-inch-deep webs at approximately 5-foot centers over which ran 2- by 2- by ¼-inch angles every 12 inches. All the tankage would be in the keel and just under the floorboards. Within our weight budget we were able to work in 340 gallons of fuel, enough for a 2000-mile range at 7 knots or 1200 miles at 8 knots, and 540 gallons of fresh water.

I had specified fore and aft watertight bulkheads, and Angelo had added a partial collision bulkhead six feet back from the bow. A collision at sea might ruin our day, but it wouldn't sink us.

Our initial experience in meeting *Sunflower* had convinced us about flush-deck interiors which, in our case, by lowering the center of gravity also helped draft. To keep the interior from being too dark we put as many deck hatches in as possible, using the largest commercial hatches we could find. Angelo came up with a sea-going hull window design we liked very much. With an aluminum welded frame, the window itself, of half-inch Lexan, would be set into the hull two inches, minimizing the possibility of damage alongside a dock or another vessel. Further, we would be able to remove a window at sea and regasket it should the need ever arise.

One of the aspects of metal construction which had attracted me was the possibility of having a really watertight yacht. I recalled a conversation in Fiji some years back where we had met an Australian family just finishing their cruise. We were drying out a locker that had gotten wet from an as-yet-untraced deck leak. I commented on how it was one of the things we all must bear in cruising.

"Not us," came the reply. "Metal boats won't leak if you don't drill holes in them."

We took this philosophy to the extreme; there are no holes in the deck between the watertight bulkheads on the new boat. Anywhere that a fitting had to be attached to the deck, a pad was welded and blind tapped. The hatch bases were welded to their combings, and winches were fastened to upstands that in turn were welded to the deck

We had learned the hard way not to keep hatches cracked open when at sea. In order to get comfortable conditions in the tropics and adhere to this philosophy, we allowed for nine Dorade boxes, each one an aluminum weldment, with very substantial upstands on the through-deck pipe. These serve a double purpose on deck because each is equipped with a handrail. They will make working the deck in bouncy weather that much easier.

For lifeline bases we welded sockets to the deck with reinforcing pads underneath. We used 1¼-inch 14-gauge stainless-steel tubing for the stanchion itself, and these were sleeved into a plastic bearing (as

Pipe stubs welded to the aft watertight bulkhead. Various plumbing lines are hose-clamped to both sides of these stubs, keeping the bulkhead itself watertight.

Construction view of welded hatch combing, Dorade vent pipe, and web frame.

Welding the window frames and hull longitudinals.

The support tube for the spade rudder allows for a solid 6″-diameter stock. The shaft is one of the strongest parts of the boat.

was all stainless aboard) to avoid paint electrolysis from dissimilar metals.

The forward 14 feet of the vessel would be used for stowage. Pipe-framed sail bins were welded in on the port side to make handling and stowage of our headsail easier. To starboard we made up two pipe berths which were used as stowage shelves for awnings, fenders, and diving gear.

With one boat being built and a second for sale, we were understandably, if reluctantly, eager to find a buyer for the *Intermezzo* that had served us so faithfully. Tight money was in vogue and people were pulling in their horns, so we sat. The time was approaching when I would have to go down to South Africa to supervise work on the last of the hull and the interior, and we now had one and a half yachts.

It was a slow summer for Florida brokerage, but as the critical time drew near we had three offers for our old friend in a matter of days, and she was soon in able new hands.

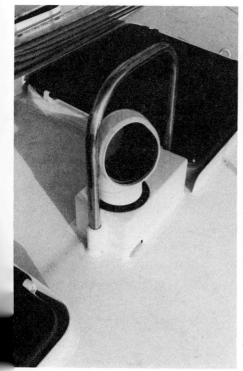

Welded Dorade box with a handrail to make working on deck easier in heavy going. Note the hatch breakwaters protecting gaskets from direct hits by spray.

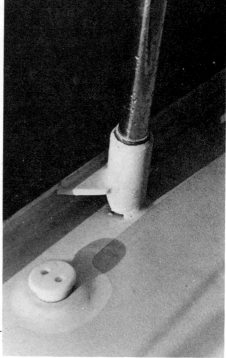

Lifeline stanchions are welded to the deck and combing. A nylon spacer keeps the stainless and aluminum separated to prevent electrolysis.

We concentrated during this period on researching equipment and buying all the hardware bits and pieces that make up a cruising yacht. There were so many new concepts around it was difficult to know which way to turn. Jim Schmidt was a real help during this period, as he had started the same process slightly ahead of us and had researched some good sources.

With our old boat sold and a container of gear on its way to Cape Town, we took a brief visit to California and Idaho, and headed south, this time on the big bird, to see our new *Intermezzo*.

Immediately on arrival we went to the building shed. As the lights went on I was awed by what we had started. Looking at a two-dimensional drawing is one thing; seeing it in three dimensions is another. This was going to be one big, fast boat.

Over the next six months, working at times seven days a week and 14 hours a day, the new *Intermezzo* filled out. We found that the craftsmen we had to work with were productive, good-natured, and quick to grasp what we were trying to create. Irwin Faustman and his crew of carpenters and finishers did a beautiful job for us. Angelo put up with my endless requests for reviews of design data on the rig, weight, and interior, even when we ended up coming back to square one, where he said we should have been in the first place. The rig went back and forth between ketch and cutter. We finally opted for the cutter, as I felt the proportions were modest enough so that I could handle it. It was more efficient than a ketch, cheaper, and would be that much stiffer without the 800 lbs. of mast, rigging, and sail to contend with back aft.

The interior ended up similar to the original concept we worked out with Jim Schmidt in New Guinea, modified for this boat's slightly shorter length. Going for an open, airy approach with light matte-finish Formica and teak trim, we worked hard at overcoming the cave feeling that so many flush-deck racing boats have.

We were concerned throughout the project with safety at sea, and since Linda and I had plans for some cruising in the area of Cape Horn, the interior had to be usable, with minimum risks in severe weather. We solved this problem by putting two aft cabins, each with its own head, on either side of the companionway leading down directly from the cockpit. This provides four good sea berths (two to each cabin) and a secure walkway forward between the cabin bulkheads. In severe weather we can live in the after section of the

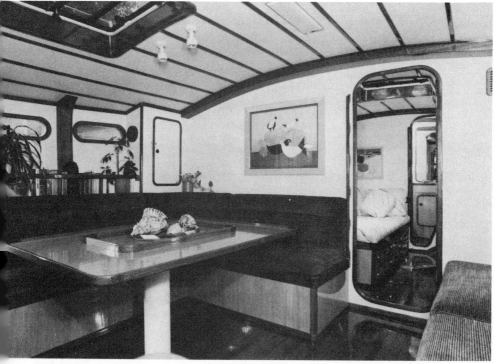

We decided on an L-shaped settee in the saloon for easy access. Note the center fiddle on the table to keep serving dishes in place when at sea. (Phil Harrill)

boat. The open forward sections serve us in port and in reasonable conditions at sea.

Once again we put the owner's cabin forward where it most efficiently uses the space available. There are large lockers on either side and a double bunk somewhat free standing so it is easier to make up. Forward of this cabin is our head with a tub/shower combination to port.

The galley is C-shaped, with the sink placed outboard and the propane stove placed athwartships on the aft bulkhead. We decided to try a nongimballed stove in this location as we felt that the boat would be stable enough to get away without the gimbals. I have always been leery of a stove outboard of, and therefore directly in line with, the cook in heavy going. The athwartship stove has worked out well; we bolted fiddles in place around the burners, which do an

Linda's sea-going galley with a fixed athwartships propane stove. The position was chosen for maximum safety in hard going. The built-in microwave does most of the cooking. Note the high counter fiddles. (Phil Harrill)

excellent job of holding the pots and pans in place at sea. The inconvenience of an off-center sink is not that hard to live with.

The navigation area is simpler than on many large yachts, but also larger. We were primarily interested in a ship's office first and a navigation station second. We wanted enough desk space and storage to spread out our paperwork, typing, or navigation. The saloon doubles for meals when we eat below. We opted for an L-shaped settee to port, with access under the seats for storage, and another settee to starboard. Port and starboard settees are 27 inches wide, so they are comfortable in heavy going if we choose to sleep in the saloon.

We built in a medium-size microwave in the galley and this, along with an assortment of electric frying pans and toaster, has done most of the cooking; Linda has relegated the propane stove to second place, even at sea. The microwave is especially handy for three reasons: (1) it creates no heat; (2) it's easy to clean up; and (3) it's fast cooking.

For refrigeration we went once again to a mechanical compressor-driven holding-plate system. We found a Cape Town firm to custom-make finned evaporators for the holding plates to our specs, so we would have a very efficient fridge/freezer set-up. We ended up with a seven-cubic-foot freezer with six inches of insulation, and a four-cubic-foot refrigerator and an eight-cubic-foot vegetable box, each with four inches of insulation. The reason for the double refrigerator system is so that we can use the smaller box for normal refrigerator storage, thus leaving the larger box free for storing fruits and vegetables when we're on long passages or for stores when we're going to be away from shops for a long time.

One of the aspects that excited me the most about the new boat project was the possibility of getting into the mechanical, electrical, and plumbing systems at the beginning. I had spent so much time dealing with poorly built gear (both on our own and on our friends' boats) that I was anxious for the opportunity of doing things really right. I had learned that a slight increase in the overall cost of materials and a little attention to detail in the building stage could yield tremendous maintenance benefits later on.

It is the electrical system on any sea-going yacht that gives the most problems. To circumvent these, we used tinned wire throughout, and all connections were soldered. By running each wire in one piece from our control panel to its accessory, supplying each with a separate ground wire, and running them all in conduits, we eliminated a lot of future headaches.

Gritting our teeth over the weight (over 900 lbs.), we installed 1100 amp-hours of deep-discharge batteries for ship's lighting. These are charged by a 150-amp brushless Electrodyne alternator. For AC power with the engine running, we belted on a 3500-watt generator that could be used from about 1100 to 1500 engine R.P.M. For AC power when the engine is off there are two inverters: an 1800-watt unit that starts on demand, and a second, smaller 500-watt device for running small appliances or the tape deck. Refrigeration is provided by a mechanical compressor and the 85-h.p. Perkins diesel serves as generator.

The prop shaft, exiting forward of the spade rudder (which I wanted for control) is hooked up via a V-drive. To reduce drag we installed a feathering Max Prop.

With plenty of space in the engine room but a limited weight budget, we looked around for a means of backing up the Perkins diesel. We found a 4-h.p. Yanmar diesel that weighed 120 lbs.; it was water cooled, and can drive a spare alternator and compressor if need be. For damage control we mounted a 200-gallons-per-minute centrifugal pump to the Yanmar and plumbed it to the three watertight sections of the boat.

For electrical power at sea we added a second offset prop shaft. This prop absorbs power from the water as we sail. Belted with a 2 to 1 ratio to a specially wound alternator, it produces, at 6½ knots boat speed, enough juice to power our autopilot, radar, and miscellaneous electrical requirements. At 8 knots it provides enough extra electricity for Linda to cook using the inverters.

We spent the first two months of 1981 in a daze as we worked toward our mid-March launch date. We felt this was the latest we could launch and still have time to run adequate trials before setting

To port is the 5-h.p. Yanmar diesel with a 200-gallons-per-minute damage-control pump mounted on top. On the starboard side are mounted the shaft-driven alternator and compressor. The electric motor on top drives the compressor when hooked up to shore power. A separate set of V-belts is carried to enable the Yanmar to drive the shaft compressor and alternator if the main engine is down. The 85-h.p. Perkins has a 12″-diameter pulley on its power takeoff shaft to drive the main 150-amp alternator, 3500-watt AC generator, and compressor.

A closeup of the shaft-driven alternator and its 8″ drive pulley. The smaller shaft pulley in the foreground is used to drive the refrigeration compressor when underway.

out for the States. We wanted to arrive well before any early hurricanes started brewing. Elyse and Sarah were going to school in Pinelands, where we were living. Their school broke for holidays in late March, and we had our house until April 1, so the timing worked out well.

Finally, on March 22, 1981, a glorious, clear day, ten months to the day from when lofting was started, *Intermezzo II* splashed into Cape Town Harbor. Linda did the honors with champagne on the stemhead the first crack, to the cheers of a large crowd of onlookers and press. A few hours later, our mast partially rigged, we powered around to the Royal Cape Yacht Club where the launching party was already in full swing.

What a joy to be afloat again, to hear the southeaster whistle in the rigging and the lap-lap of the inner harbor wavelets on our transom. Tomorrow would see our first sail and we would know what

The double bunk in *Intermezzo II*'s forward cabin is free standing so it's easy to make up. The forward location of the cabin makes it quieter under power, and we are able to hear the chain if it shifts at anchor. In all but the very worst conditions the motion is acceptable. (Phil Harrill)

we had wrought. Regardless of the outcome, it had been a memorable and enjoyable period of our lives. From the experiences of many acquaintances who had custom-built, we realized how lucky we had been to both enjoy the process and complete on time—and within budget.

Saturday morning dawned bright and clear. Table Mountain was beginning to develop its famous tablecloth, a sure sign of a strong southeaster. Angelo was first aboard as we began to lay out blocks and sails. Most of the running rigging had been cut, spliced, and whipped while we were still in the shed, and it wasn't long before we were ready for sailing trials.

On board was a collection of some of Cape Town's best sailors as we headed out into the South Atlantic. In the protection of the inner harbor we set the main, staysail, and Yankee. We were sailing in light trim, with no personal gear aboard yet, tanks empty, and no supplies. If she was going to be tender, we would soon know. The area to leeward of Table Mountain is marked by a series of wind zones, and

Designer Angelo Lavranos and his happy clients with *Intermezzo II* about to be launched. (Afdeling Fotographie)

as we headed toward the beach after leaving the harbor, we could see the white caps whipping. As the 30-knot southeaster hit us on the quarter, *Intermezzo* leaped forward, leaving a clean, flat wake behind. She was doing a steady 11 knots, about what we had expected, but with much more poise and less excitement than we had projected.

Observing that the mast was reasonably well tuned, and with a full crew of willing hands to do the work, I decided to take advantage of the conditions. Out came the cruising spinnaker, and wham! We were doing 13, then 14 knots and more.

I looked at Angelo and grinned. I couldn't help at least one "I told you so." The microwave, reverse-cycle air conditioning, and plush interior weren't going to hold her back that much after all. At 13 knots we were rapidly eating up ground toward the lee shore, so we jibed and headed back up the coast. As we beat toward the harbor, the wind increased to the high 30s and low 40s, and we shortened down progressively to two reefs in the main and the #2 Yankee. She

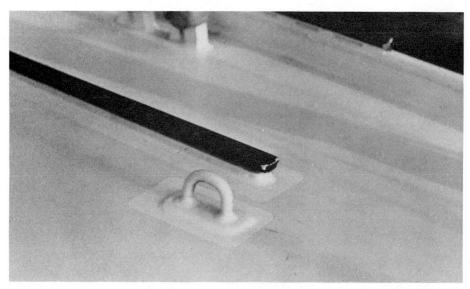

A tie-down bale for the dinghy and blind-fastened staysail track. A flat piece of aluminum is tapped to receive the staysail track, then welded to the deck, eliminating any holes through the deck plating that eventually might leak.

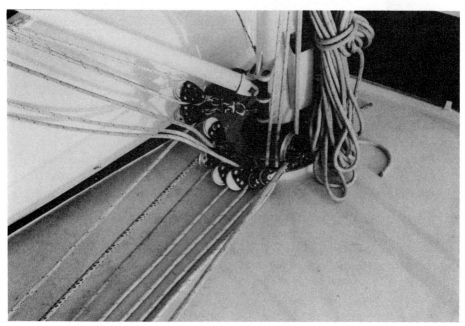

Mast-base turning blocks.

went upwind much better than we had thought she would, and considering her light condition, was very powerful. In the smooth water we were plugging along at better than 9 knots, at about 45 degrees off the wind.

The list of changes and wrinkles to work out was shorter than expected. While Linda busied herself returning our rented home to its owners and stocking *Intermezzo II* for her trip up the Atlantic, I did some organizing for the next boat that would be built in our absence. In the next 2½ weeks we had several sails and a chance to try out our ground tackle. I had opted for a Bruce anchor for our primary hook, and at 110 lbs. it seemed to do an excellent job. We had 280 feet of ⅜" high-tensile chain attached, and a vertical 3000-lb.-pull windlass to do the hoisting. For backup we stowed two large Viking aluminum anchors, each with its own chain, plus 300 feet of ¾" nylon.

Our dodger was fitted and a set of deck awnings made. The twin backstays, fitted to eliminate twist in the masthead from our offset twin headstays, helped tremendously with rigging a large sailing awning. Some minor recutting of sails was needed, and we were ready to go.

We had been ashore for almost a year, and looking at a beautiful 6000 miles of ocean and the possibility of a record passage, not to mention our new *Intermezzo II* waiting for her real christening, it is difficult to describe the excitement we all felt as the moment neared to be off. Last-minute stores came aboard, we said our good-byes, and consulted with the meterological pundits. A deep low was approaching from the southwest, but we should be well on our way before it reached the coast.

Never ones for big send-offs, we slipped quietly away from the yacht club at 2000 Sunday evening. Jeff Stevens rang the bell at the club—as a farewell, good luck, and bon voyage. A light southwesterly greeted us as we headed west to put some distance between ourselves and the lee shore that the coast of Africa formed. We were back in our element.

We set the mainsail first. Its 540 square feet of 9-oz. cloth was much easier to raise than I had anticipated. I found that by going to the mast to heave down the halyard, with Linda or one of the children tailing, I could get it all the way to the masthead without the winch. The #27 self-tailing Barient in the cockpit was used only

The halyard winches for the staysail, two jibs, and the spinnaker pole car drive are all on the starboard side of the mast because our 14′ dinghy is carried to port. The staysail winch doubles on the spinnaker pole topping lift.

for luff tension. Next up went the 600-square-foot Yankee (7¼ oz.) and then our 400-square-foot staysail (9-oz.). We had installed the double-headsail cutter rig to keep our working sails small. While not as efficient as having all the foretriangle devoted to a series of genoas, the double-head rig meant that none of the headsails was so bulky that I couldn't unhank and stow it in the bins forward with relative ease. If bad weather was expected, we could hank on a second, smaller headsail on the other headstay. All sails from the #2 Yankee down through the storm jibs could also be set on the forestay in extreme going.

Angelo had taken freeboard measurements before we left, and with tanks full and all our cruising gear aboard, plus four months of stores, we were somewhat under 50,000 lbs. Even with this full load, *Intermezzo II* accelerated quickly to 8 knots in the 14-knot headwind. As we cleared Table Bay and began to feel the moderate southwesterly swell and wind chop, we had our first experiencewith upwind motion in a seaway.

I had known in advance that our light displacement would make us more lively than heavier yachts of our size. But I felt that this was an acceptable trade-off on the rare occasions when we made passages upwind. We did have a larger yacht than would have been possible by keeping to our 50,000-lb. weight if we had gone to a heavier displacement/length–ratio design. Angelo had projected that the long, close-tucked ballast shoe and the weight of the machinery and ground tackle in the ends would dampen our motion considerably in moderate going (although it would do the opposite in really heavy seas). As the wind and sea built up toward Force 5 and 6, *Intermezzo II*'s motion was very ladylike.

The breeze was influenced by the land, and as we saw the lights of Cape Columbine disappear behind us the wind went with them. Under power shortly thereafter we found that the little diesel would easily move us at 8 knots at 1600 R.P.M. At 7 knots it was very quiet aboard and we used 40 percent less fuel, extending our range to more than 2000 miles.

With the first light of morning I switched up to our 3½-oz. 12.5 percent genoa. The sail had been ordered at the last minute for just such occasions, and while its 1000 square feet seemed daunting, it really was quite easy to handle. The lightweight cloth actually made stowing it easier than the heavier but smaller Yankee jib.

Intermezzo II charging along with her light #1, 125% genoa. In 12 knots of wind she'll reach at better than 9½ knots all day long. Note the circular traveler and radar mast. (Les Abberly)

We found that the combination of stable foredeck, 32-inch-high lifelines, and short overlap on the headsails made them very easy to douse. With the sheets in tight, they would end up on deck, with perhaps a little tug on the leech, when the halyard was released. Compared to our 50-footer's bouncy foredeck, lower lifelines, and longer overlaps, it was easier to change headsails on the larger boat.

With the light genoa up we ghosted along at 7 to 8 knots, close-reaching in 8 to 10 knots of wind. By the end of our second day at sea, with a little help from the current, we had covered 386 miles for an average speed of just over 8 knots.

Linda was performing her usual wonders in the galley. We had settled into our sea-going routine much more quickly than I had thought possible. There were no signs of mal de mer among the crew (which some of us usually suffered from for a day or two when first at sea). The bigger boat and smoother motion must really be helping. We found the forward cabin very comfortable to sleep in, even going uphill. Sarah and Elyse began rehearsals for the big Easter show that was to be held in the port after cabin. Posters began appearing announcing the extravaganza, and they spent hours in seclusion writing the script and rehearsing the characters.

The navigation area worked out well as a below-deck watch station. We had put in some simple wind speed and direction gear with readouts below, as well as a speedometer-odometer combination. With the generating prop kicking out lots of DC power, we ran our 36-mile Furuno radar every evening. We had splurged on a radar alarm and found this amazing little device worth its weight in gold (and peace of mind). In the cool air of the approaching fall we would snug ourselves in at the navigation table, keeping an eye on the elements and any shipping that might be closeby on the radar. We were surprised to find large ships showing up as far as 24 miles away in spite of our low antenna height. Every 15 to 20 minutes we'd go on deck, scan the horizon, and check our sail trim.

On the third day at sea the wind began to freshen from the south-southwest and the Yankee/staysail combination pushed us along, Beam-reaching, in 15 to 20 knots of wind. *Intermezzo II* was really rolling the miles under her keel now. With occasional bursts as high as 13 knots, she was averaging over 9 knots without current. Down below it was quiet, and if we hadn't seen the sea whipping by through the hull windows it would have been impossible to imagine the speeds we were making from the motion or sound. The two-inch foam insulation on the hull and the interior, plus the watertight bulkheads, had made her very quiet down below. Not quite familiar with our Wagner hydraulic autopilot and its several controls, I didn't push as hard as I could have and we ended up with a respectable 228-mile run between sights.

The fourth day gave us an indication of the boat's potential. The wind freshened to 25 to 30 knots and backed toward the south. I was just barely able to carry the Yankee on the spinnaker pole to wind ward. I had thought our 25-foot pole would be a handful, but with a track on the mast allowing for vertical stowage, it was actually quite simple to work with. Once I learned a few tricks, the combina tion of stable platform and mast stowage made the actual work of setting or dousing the pole easier than on the old boat.

A quartering sea running five to eight feet began to lift our stern as we bore off slightly to make the Yankee more efficient. As we accelerated smoothly down the face, I heard a yell from Elyse who was reading at the navigation table: "Sixteen knots," she shrilled. *Intermezzo II* didn't seem to be hard pressed at all, and there was certainly room for higher numbers.

Over the next eight hours we would see speeds in the low teens so often that they no longer caused much comment: 16, 17, 18 knots would be casually announced by whomever happened to glance at the steam gauge as we whooshed down a sea. As the day wore on into early evening the wind continued to back until the main was well out. Still not having the pilot controls sorted out to my satisfaction, I pulled down a reef in the main for the evening.

We had rigged both mainsail clew and tack reefing pendants permanently; both of them led, along with the main halyard, to the cockpit. Without the confusion of all the helpers we had along on our trial sails, it was possible to reef the main in less than three minutes, even though we were broad-reaching at the time.

That night, in honor of our first day of real sailing, Linda really went to work in the galley. We had a huge, crisp green salad, oven-fried chicken with fresh corn and brocolli, and for dessert, lemon meringue pie baked in the microwave. The latter caused us to make a note to get a glass pie plate, as the plastic one we baked it in couldn't be put in the conventional oven for final browning of the crust.

While I was washing up there was a larger whoosh than usual and Linda screamed "22, 23, 24.3 knots!" We were sailing with the main well out and vanged to the rail with the wind on the quarter. As we surfed down the sea *Intermezzo II* seemed to linger on the face, enjoying her own motion. If this kept up, what a day's run we would have!

Alas, the wind began to lighten after midnight and back around farther, and soon we were running almost square; though we still clocked some exciting speeds on the waves, our average speed slipped back toward mediocrity. At noon the next day, after working out my sights, I was disappointed to announce only a 226-mile run. At that rate we would never get anywhere (how quickly one's expectations change).

With the wind now behind us, I decided to drop the staysail and

With her light genoa to windward on the spinnaker pole and the hank-on cruising spinnaker sheeted through the main boom, *Intermezzo II* is moving at better than 190 miles per day in light going.

hoist the light genoa on the leeward headstay. First I had to change the Yankee jib over to weather, and did so without difficulty, leaving the pole guyed in place during the process.

The genoa added enough speed to smooth our ride out considerably, and eased steering as well. It was warm and sunny for the first time since leaving Table Bay, so all hands were on deck enjoying the approaching tropics. With the wind now down to 15 knots, I contemplated setting the cruising spinnaker but decided to wait. We made 201 miles between sights and had now averaged over 195 per day since leaving Cape Town.

It appeared that our daily averages might be even better than the old boat in light downwind going. That would certainly be a bonus. Time would tell, and as we knew from previous experience, there would be plenty of light-air running ahead.

Easter dawned and the children discovered that the Easter bunny had visited during the night, leaving beautiful African baskets stuffed with hand-painted eggs, jelly beans, and a plethora of other Easter delicacies. Elyse and Sarah had colored their own eggs to add to the collection. We had a delicious leg of lamb for dinner and all hands enjoyed the big Easter show performed by Elyse and Sarah, accompanied by Brownie and Bobbie bunny, the monkeys, and all the dolls.

The wind continued to lighten and back until it was just off the stern at an angle of about 160 degrees. We dropped the Yankee and switched the genoa to the weather stay, then hoisted our cruising spinnaker in the lee of the main. The spinnaker hoisted, the mainsail was dropped. With the spinnaker sheet led through the end of the main boom we had 2900 square feet of sail aloft, enough power to keep us moving on the faces of most of the waves. Our apparent wind was down to 4 or 5 knots at about 140 degrees. Boat speed averaged 7 to 8 knots, and we settled down to a routine of 175 to 185 miles per day. The cockpit awning was rigged, a real milestone, and we thought about St. Helena Island.

The previous year we had been in a hurry and had passed right by. It was earlier in the year, and the South Atlantic high was farther south, which meant that stopping at the island would have taken us out of our way. This time we would be going right by it, and considering it might be the last chance for the kids to see it, we decided to stop if an early-morning landfall could be made.

At 0336 on our eighth night at sea we picked up the island at an extreme distance of 42 miles on radar. Still carrying the genoa to weather and the spinnaker to leeward, we were moving along at just under 8 knots average in the 10 to 12 knots of wind.

St. Helena has a fascinating history. Originally settled by the British as a supply base for ships heading toward the Indian Ocean, it is best known as the last prison of Napoleon after his tactical errors at Waterloo. We had talked with friends who had stopped there, and were anxious to sample for ourselves, if only for an afternoon, the charm of its friendly, easy-going people.

By 0830 we were abeam of the island; rounding the northwest corner, we motorsailed toward the main anchorage. The locals were out fishing in seaworthy-looking skiffs, many of them oar or sail powered. The island presented a steep, formidable appearance and the few accesable valleys that opened to the sea were fortified heavily with battlements of stone.

Sarah relaxes in the shade of our large cockpit awning just northwest of St. Helena Island in the South Atlantic.

It wasn't long before the main anchorage hove into view and we saw several familiar-looking rigs, cruising neighbors from the docks of the Royal Cape. With their help we secured bow-and-stern to the local moorings and awaited Customs.

The combination boat watchman/water taxi rowed us ashore after we cleared Customs, so we wouldn't have to launch the dinghy. It was a short walk down the wharf, along the beach to the entrance of George Town through massive wooden gates and across a moat. The town is built in the valley with soaring canyon walls on either side. Many homes and businesses sport antique hand-carved doors; all antiques, in fact, are put to daily use on this island where it is illegal to export the indigenous furniture.

We met a pleasant old gentleman on a street corner who asked if he could help us. When we told him we were looking for a car to tour the island, he volunteered to take us; so arrangements were made to meet him after lunch.

Once we climbed out of the valley into the highlands the characteristics of the island changed from a desert-like facade to lush green foliage. For years the island's economy depended on its hemp industry. But synthetics gradually replaced hemp, and the fields are no longer productive. One highlight of the tour was a stop at the governor's mansion, where we were introduced to the island's oldest living inhabitant—an ancient land tortoise. He has been there since Napoleon's day. A stop at Napoleon's house was the second feature of the day. We were interested to learn that this historical monument was unobtrusively maintained by the guide who also works as gardener. His father was guide and caretaker before him, as was his father's father. The present guide unlocked the door and took us on a tour through history. What an intimate, exciting lesson it was. Napoleon will be much more than a name in history for our children.

The next morning we were underway early, having spent less than 24 hours on beautiful St. Helena. The hurricane season was advancing and there were things to do in the States. We set the spinnaker to leeward and the genoa on the pole again and ran off in the light 10-knot trade winds. The next couple of days saw runs of 180, 199, then 188. In the vicinity of Ascension Island the wind lightened further, dropping at times to 4 or 5 knots. Apparent wind was so light that our wind-speed meter refused to budge. Still, we were able to average 169 miles between sights.

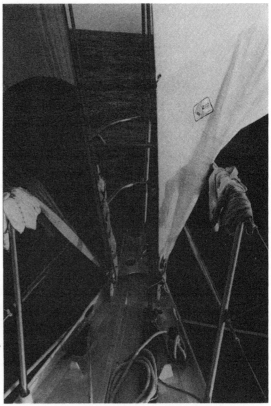

The cruising spinnaker is hanked on the leeward stay and the light genoa is hanked on the weather stay. Note the soft rags used as chafing gear to protect the foot of each sail from the pulpit.

Ascension Island appeared off the starboard bow as a light smudge, and the radar put us 40 miles off. As the island drew abeam I decided to jibe to the port tack and more or less follow what we felt would be the circulation of the high. It would put us on a more westerly course, and if we picked up an anticipated shift to the east farther on we would be able to jibe back and pick up a good wind angle. We decided to try the spinnaker to windward. The pole was shifted to the weather side and the genoa sheeted to the rail. I then put the main back up; the spinnaker would feed the genoa and the main could add some horsepower. The new sail arrangement worked well and our daily runs picked up to better than 190 a day for the next week. The wind was still at 165 degrees true, in the 10- to 12-knot range. Our log of the previous passage in the first *Intermezzo* showed that conditions this trip were lighter if anything, and yet we were averaging 15 to 20 miles a day better than the old *Intermezzo*. Our sail-area/wetted-surface ratios indicated this would not happen. A combination of better stability and taller rig must have made the difference. Whatever it was, we weren't complaining. But we would have liked more wind.

Linda took advantage of the calm weather to do a washing in the compact Maytag washing machine. I strung clotheslines from the mast back to the cockpit and we were able to go to bed with fresh sheets.

We looked forward to each day's session of reading aloud; laughing to the antics of the Marx brothers in Harpo's autobiography *Harpo Speaks,* or thrilling to the romance of *Ivanhoe,* we enhanced family life aboard our 62-foot floating home.

Sarah discovered a new use for the swim platform on the stern. She and Elyse hooked their lifelines to a line in the cockpit, then went down the ladder to the platform where they sat and dragged their feet in the water. It was a good way to keep cool.

We started to get occasional squalls as we neared the equator. They almost always came at night and rarely had any more than a brief increase of wind, which we welcomed. The radar alarm would announce their coming with its loud beeping, then we'd dog the hatches and stand by the autopilot control for any necessary course changes. Occasionally we'd get 20 knots of breeze. On our 15th day at sea, with 2800 miles on the log, it was time for our halfway party.

We were three days ahead of last year's passage. We celebrated with the menu that is a favorite of Linda's mother: roast beef, mashed potatoes and gravy, Jell-o salad, fresh vegetables, and cookies the girls had baked for dessert. Our fresh food was holding out well. Elyse and Sarah opened their halfway presents of books, games, and crafts.

As if the halfway party had put us into a new weather system, our next day dawned overcast, with an ominous-looking cloud buildup behind us. By afternoon we could see the evening's entertainment developing in the form of large, black clouds; that night it was one squall after another. We were up and down constantly trying to keep the boat headed in the right direction without a lot of sail changing. Between squalls the wind dropped away, but in spite of the off-again, on-again weather, *Intermezzo II* had another 190-mile day between sights.

The 17th day at sea was enlivened by two substantial squalls. We

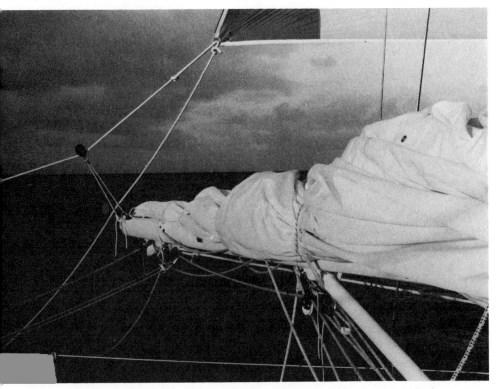

The cruising spinnaker has been hanked on the leeward headstay and sheeted through the end of the main boom.

saw them coming on the radar—12 to 15 miles across. For the first one I decided to be cautious and dropped the spinnaker. When all we had was 30 knots I was disappointed at not being able to let *Intermezzo II* stretch her legs. The next time I was not so cautious.

As the clouds bore down on us I watched the water turn white, and before I could react we were slammed by a 50-knot plus gust. With the spinnaker, genoa, and main set, we were slightly overcanvased. *Intermezzo II* leaped forward, and then in a substantial shift found the wind almost on her beam. Over she went, with the genoa in the water and main boom buried almost to the vang bale. We were knocked down to 65 degrees, with the decks barely awash. We sat like that for several minutes, the spinnaker protesting madly, until a brief lull allowed *Intermezzo II* to right herself and bear off downwind. By this time I had relieved the pilot and was standing in my

Sarah about to take the plunge. Our step works well when swimming or boarding from a dinghy, although the first consideration in its design was the recovery of a person overboard. Note the man-overboard pole in the transom. The louvers on either side of the swim ladder are for engine air, and have a series of four baffles in each to reduce noise transmission.

Steering from one of our twin helm seats is a fingertip affair. A single Barient #35 self-tailing winch does the headsail sheet honors. It can be trimmed without moving from the steering seat.

altogether at the wheel, having the time of my life conning our flyer at speeds to 20 knots. But then the spinnaker tack let go and we settled down to a comfortable 11 to 12 knots under genoa and main.

That last squall helped the average, and a popcorn and pizza party was declared as we had our first day over 200 miles in some time.

During all this slow running I had consoled myself with thoughts of the northeast trades. "Just wait till we get the wind on the beam or forward; then we'll fly," I would tell the crew.

It wasn't far off. We were crossing the equator and seeing the first signs of a doldrum sky. Our average runs dropped toward the 170-mile range. We even had one day of 160 between sights in very fluky weather. I had hoped that a day or two of this weather would put us into the northeast trades.

It wasn't to be. Day after day the wind stayed fluky and mainly in the southeast. Had we been reaching in the light air we would have been moving well, but since we were running not much could be expected. Finally on our 24th day at sea the breeze picked up, still from the southeast. In 12 to 18 knots of wind and carrying everything we could set, we logged another 195-mile day. Not bad, but nothing compared to what we would be doing if the northeast winds came.

Our easy living ended abruptly on the 26th day at sea. The pilot refused to steer to starboard and for the first time in all our cruising we faced the prospect of hand-steering. We had close to 1000 miles to go and I didn't relish the idea of standing watch on watch at the helm, but there was no choice.

We were fortunate in that the wind backed to the east, maintaining its velocity, so we were broad-reaching now in 12 to 15 knots of wind. But the genoa and spinnaker were out of commission, victims of severe squalls and the new boat's power. I had found that by hand-steering, and running off in the puffs, we could leave everything set. The short, squally sail would be exhilerating, and as it passed we would be on our way again. When it really blew into the 40s and 50s, there was an occasional tendency to oscillate when everything was set, and we dipped the main boom now and then. But *Intermezzo II* showed no inclination to head up or broach to. She simply gave no indication she was being overpressed, but the sails were getting more pressure than they could stand. We didn't realize this until it was too late and we had several major repair jobs on our hands.

The wind backed and filled, teasing us with a taste of east-

Sarah contemplates almost 6000 miles of ocean behind us as we near Antigua.

northeast and then back to east-southeast. Not what we had hoped for, but with the true wind on the quarter and the apparent wind forward of the beam, we reeled off runs of 213, 215, 229, and 225 miles carrying working sails only.

Désirade and Guadalupe Islands stood in our wake and Antigua was rising fast on the horizon. Below, Linda and the children cleaned and polished in our usual prearrival flurry of activity. With main, Yankee, and staysail set and the wind finally in the northeast, we were scooting along at just under 10 knots.

We hardened up as the Pillars of Hercules in front of English Harbour hove into view. The trade wind cut off on cue and we ghosted into the outer anchorage. Staysail down, then Yankee; our momentum carried us past half a dozen beautiful yachts. Linda headed us up, Elyse let go the main halyard, and I watched the anchor splash down. As we settled back on our chain, an inflatable powered over to have a look at the new arrival.

"Where from?" they hailed.

"Cape Town."

"How was it?"

"A little light, but pleasant."

"Take long?"

"No, 30 days for 5860 miles."

Intermezzo II had set her first cruising record.

Index

AC systems, 420–21
Adams, Chuck, 457
air conditioning, 413
alarm systems, 419
alternators:
  AC, 411
  DC, 409–11
  diesel driven, 141–42
  Dynamote inverters and, 411, 421
  regulators for, 410
aluminum, 324
Ambrym, 62
American Boat and Yacht Council, 117
anchor chains:
  bow rollers for, 57
  extra links in, 55
  fit of, 55
  galvanization of, 55
  length of, 54–55
  powered windlass for, 56–57
  securing of, 57
  size of, 53–54
  stowage of, 55–56
anchoring, 42, 51–53, 201–6
  with chain rode, 203–4
  compasses and, 202
  crew size and, 298
  defensive, 201–2
  depth sounders and, 202
  dinghies and, 57–58
  with double anchors, 204–5
  floats in, 204
  freeing fouls in, 204
  reference points in, 202
  riding sails in, 57
  with rope rode, 203–4
  sailing in and out, 205–6
  swinging radii in, 202–3
  tides and, 202
anchors:
  Bruce, 49–51
  in coral atolls, 42–45, 210–13

CQR plow, 45–47, 204
Danforth, 46–47, 204
Herreshoff Yachtsman, 49
Northhill sea-plane, 49
number of, 53
rodes for, 53–56; *see also* anchor chains
shock absorbers for, 44–45, 53–54, 56
size of, 45, 51
storm, 188
Viking aluminum, 47–49
Andural, 320
antibiotics, 131
Arion III, 111, 211–13
Armanel, 127, 153
artifacts, 250
Australia:
  animals and, 243
  government correspondence courses from, 280
autopilots, 65–68, 360–61
  control boxes for, 65
  extensions of, 66–67
  installation of, 65
  maintenance of, 65
  power consumption of, 67
Aventura, 69, 309
awnings, 68–76
  attachment of, 75
  battens for, 73
  construction of, 70–72
  design of, 68–70
  materials for, 70
  placement of, 72–73
  roles of, 68
  specialty, 74–75

Baccus, 430, 435
backstays, 343
ballast, 310
Barrett, Noel and Letara, 425–29
bartering, 249–50
battens, 345–46

batteries, 410, 417–18
  location of, 410, 418
  Nicad (nickel-cadmium), 418
Beowulf V, 315
Beowulf VI, 314–16
Betuel, Yves, 451
bilge pumps, mechanical, 412
Blackwell, Tom, 63, 300
boats:
  building of, 295
  purchasing of, 293–96
  size of, 293
  structural condition of, 293
breadfruits, 264–65
breadfruit soup (recipe), 264–65
budgets, *see* cost
bug screens, 124
buoyancy, positive, 326–27

Calvert School, 277–78
Carkhuff, Vickie and Sy, 279
catalogs, 290–91
catamarans, *see* multihulls
Caticus Rex, 48
celestial navigation, 225–27
chafe, 113–16
checklists, 146–49
  for engines, 146–47
  for heavy weather, 147–48
  for moderate climates, 147
  for steering gear, 147
children, 26–27
  bartering and, 250
  dinghies for, 101
  guns and, 138
  library for, 278
  school of, *see* schooling
circuit breakers, 419–20
clearance procedures, 240–42
  Customs in, 241–42
  Immigration in, 242
  port doctor in, 240–41
Clish Ma Claver, 314
clothing:
  on board, 272
  buying of, 276
  clothespins for, 274–75
  footwear, 272
  formal, 271
  maintenance of, 273–74
  sewing machines and, 275
  sheets and blankets, 275
  storage of, 273
  towels, 275
  in tropics, 271
  washing machines for, 273–75

cockpit cushions, 124
cockpits, 389–91
  dodgers for, 391–92
  drainage in, 389
coconuts, 265–66
Cole, Adlard, 321
collisions, 219–20
Cologne, 47
Colvin, Tom, 337
communications systems, 87–95
  antenna couplers for, 92–93
  BFO (beat frequency oscillator) in, 150
  Cat's Whiskers antennas for, 94
  half-wave dipole antennas for, 93–94
  marine single sideband (SSB), 88–90
  receivers for, 94–95
  tape recorders in, 150
  VHF, 87–88
  whip (balanced) antennas for, 93
  wire (unbalanced) antennas for, 92
  see also ham radio
companionways, 80
compasses, 148, 386
  anchoring and, 202
compressors, 85, 411
Constellation, 75, 303
constipation, 133
control panels, 419–20
  alarm systems in, 419
  circuit breakers in, 419
coral:
  anchors and, 42–45
  approaches to, 189–93
  bottom conditions around, 42–45, 199–200
  hull materials and, 322–26
  passes through, 200–201
  piloting in, 193–201
  running aground on, 208–14
  sun angle and, 198
  tides and, 192, 200
  visibility of, 192–93, 195–97
  water clarity around, 197–98
  wave changes from, 192
  weather and, 198–99
cost, 280–88
  of charts, 284
  civilization and, 283–84
  earning money and, 287–88
  of food, 284
  of gear, 286–87
  inflation and, 286
  of insurance, 286
  land expenses and, 286
  of maintenance, 284–86
  vessel age and, 281
  vessel size and, 283

yearly, 281
  see also finances
credit cards, 290
crews, 296–300
  anchoring and, 298
  docking and, 298
  emergencies and, 299–300
  maintenance and, 299
  sail handling and, 298–99
  self-steering and, 299
  standing watches and, 299
Crowther, Peter, 337–38
currencies, 290
currents, speed and, 164
cushions, cockpit, 124
cushions, interior, 382–84
Customs, 241–42
cutter rigs, 335–36

Davis, Steve, 456
Dawn Treader, 101
Decision, 365
deck, working on, 156–57
deck knives, 128–29, 223
Deerfoot, 52, 79, 81, 234, 331–33, 363
depth sounders, 202, 233
design, boat, 295–96, 300–313
  ballast in, 310
  of CCA boats, 307
  displacement in, 305, 307–8
  of double-enders, 309–10
  draft in, 301
  freeboard in, 305–6
  IOR racing rule and, 307
  keel shape in, 308–9
  positive buoyancy in, 326–27
  rudders in, 310–13
  speed and, 304–5
  stability in, 306–7
  trunk cabin vs. flush deck in, 306
  weatherliness in, 301–4
  see also boats; materials; multihulls
diesel engines, *see* engines
dill pickles (recipe), 267
dinghies, 57–58, 95–101
  Avon, 99–100
  inflatable, 99–100, 104–5
  solid, 100
  storage of, 96–97
  in surf, 99–100
  towing of, 100
  as transportation, 97
  waterskiing with, 99
  weight of, 97–98
  Zodiac, 99–100
displacement, 305, 307–8

docking, 298
documents:
  passports, 239–40, 242
  proof of ownership, 238–39
  UN health cards, 240
  visas, 240
dodgers, 391–92
dogs, 135–36, 243, 253
doldrums, 156
Dorade ventilators, 122–23, 458–61
double-enders, 309–10
double-spreader rigs, 349–50
draft, 301
  hurricane holes and, 301
  on multihulls, 320

Eastman, Peter, 129, 213
Eaton, Gerry, 319–20
electrical systems, 416–21
  AC systems, 420–21
  batteries in, 410, 417–18
  control panels in, 419–20
  wiring in, 416–17
Elements of Yacht Design (Skene), 339, 398
Eluthera, 61
emergencies, crew size and, 299–300
employment, 287–88
engine rooms, 386–87
engines, 396–403
  checklists for, 146–47
  diesel, 397–400
  electrical power from, 141–43
  exhaust systems for, 412–13
  Ford, 402
  gasoline, 403
  glow-plug starting, 399–400
  GM, 402
  hand-cranking, 400
  Isuzu, 397
  Perkins, 401–2
  size requirements, 397–99
  speed/length ratio for, 397
  spring starter, 400
Eos, 185–88, 215–16
exhaust systems, 412–13

fans, 119–20
Faustman, Irwin, 462
Ferris, Ham, 416
ferrocement, 325–26
fiberglass, 322–23
Fiji:
  coral around, 189–92, 199
  officials of, 243
finances, 25–26, 289–92
  banks and, 289–90

finances *(continued)*
  catalogs and, 290–91
  credit cards and, 290
  currency and, 290
  power-of-attorney and, 291–92
  taxes and, 291
  travelers checks and, 289
fire, 218–19
  Halon systems and, 219
First Aid Afloat (Eastman), 129
fish poisoning, 134
flashlights, 125–26
Florida, lightning off, 118
flotation, *see* positive buoyancy
foods:
  breadfruits, 264–65
  coconuts, 265–66
  cost of, 284
  dill pickles, 266–67
  herbs and spices, 267
  precooked meals, 270–71
  see also provisioning
foreign bureaucracies, 238–43
  animals and, 243
  appearance and, 242
  clearance procedures of, 240–42
  Customs in, 241–42
  documents needed for, 238–40
  financial regulations of, 240
  guns and, 241–42
  Immigration in, 242
  language and, 242–43
  narcotics and, 241
  port doctors in, 240–41
freeboard, 305–6
French (language), 244

Galaway Blazer, 337–38
galley equipment, 268–70
  for cooking and baking, 269
  dishes in, 269–70
  mugs in, 270
  serving dishes in, 269
  storage containers in, 269
galleys, 367–77
  diesel stoves in, 374–76
  electric cooking in, 376
  kerosene in, 371–74
  propane in, 374
  sinks in, 370
  storage space in, 370, 377
  trash storage in, 376–77
generating systems, wind, 126–28
generators:
  auxiliary, 414
  diesel driven, 141–42

Gibbs family, 91–92
goals, setting of, 25–27
grooming:
  hair and, 276
  in the tropics, 271–76
  see also clothing
ground tackle, 42–58
  see also anchor chains; anchors
guns, 136–39
  Customs and, 241–42
  in foreign ports, 139
  maintenance of, 138–39
  sealable lockers for, 241
  types of, 137–38
  use of, 136–37
Gypsy, 294

halyards, 354–56
ham radio:
  benefits of, 90–92
  licenses for, 92
harnesses, 106–7, 157
Hast, Charlie, 117–18
hatches:
  construction of, 78
  covers for, 78–80
  leakage of, 77–80
  placement of, 77
heads, 380
headstays, 343
health cards, UN, 240
Heart of Edna, 76, 325, 396
heaters, 119
heavy weather:
  advance action for, 188–89
  bottom conditions and, 182
  checklist for, 147–48
  design and, 304
  maintaining speed in, 182–84
  securing interiors for, 109–13
  storm anchors and, 188
  tactics for, 180–89
  towing warps in, 188
  wave systems and, 181–82
Heavy Weather Sailing (Cole), 321
Hicok, Roy, 314
Hotchkiss, Doug and Kristie, 294
hot water, 143–44, 394
hurricane holes, 301
hurricanes, 155
  multihulls and, 321

Immigration, 242
Indian Ocean:
  bottom conditions in, 182, 230, 312
  southwestern, 312

spinnakers in, 170
infections, 133
inoculations, 131–32
insurance, 286
interiors, 362–92
  cockpits and, 389–91
  colors and textures in, 363–64
  cushions in, 382–84
  engine rooms in, 386–87
  galleys in, 367–77
  general layout of, 364–65
  heads in, 380
  lighting in, 384–86
  navigatoriums in, 377–79
  saloons in, 380–82
  sleeping accommodations in, 365–67
  stowage in, 387–89
  visual obstructions in, 364
  watchkeeping and, 386
Intermezzo, 28–42, 294–95
  anchors on, 44, 49, 51, 56
  awnings on, 70–71
  cockpit layout of, 36
  communications gear on, 87–90, 94
  cruising gear for, 33–34
  deck knives on, 128–29
  diesel engine in, 397
  dinghy on, 100–101
  equipment added to, 33–34, 37
  gear stowage on, 148
  in heavy weather, 39, 183
  interior of, 34–39, 109, 364–90
  major changes in, 28–29, 37–42
  propeller on, 405
  purchase of, 29–30
  refrigeration on, 83–84
  sails on, 32–33, 36–37, 40–42, 328
  sale of, 461
  self-steering gear for, 60–61, 65–68
  shaft-charging system on, 416
  shakedown cruise of, 316–19
  speed of, 32, 167, 175–77
  spinnaker on, 167–73
  windows on, 112
  yearly cost of, 281
Intermezzo II, 453–87
  aluminum hull on, 453–58
  anchors on, 50–51, 471
  Atlantic crossing of, 471–87
  cutter rig on, 336, 471–73
  design of, 455–61
  diesel engine in, 400
  electrical system on, 465
  galley on, 368, 359–61
  interior of, 462–65
  lines in cockpit of, 355

  machinery on, 465–66
  "magic box" on, 66
  maiden voyage of, 466–71
  navigation area on, 464, 475
  refrigeration on, 84, 464–65
  sails on, 471–73, 485
  securing of interiors on, 110
  shaft-charging systems on, 411, 466–67
  speed of, 469–78
  ventilation on, 458
International Medical Guide for Ships
  (World Health Organization), 129
inverters, DC-to-AC, 421
Islander, 60, 63, 300

Jenson, Dena, 217
Johnson, Robin Knox, 307
Johnson, Rusty and Lorraine, 309
Johnson, Swede, 30, 31, 36, 65
Joshua, 184
junk rigs, 337–38

ketch rigs, 337
Kewish, Dean, 43–45, 216, 257
knives, deck, 128–29
Kottick, 59

languages, 242–46
  questions and, 246
  technical items and, 246
Lapworth, Bill, 307
LaRue, Frikki, 187
Lavranos, Angelo, 455–58, 468–71
lay shafts, 141
leakage, 77–82
  companionways and, 80
  deck fittings and, 80–81
  galley sink drains and, 81–82
  hatches and, 77–80
  major, 220–21
  windows and, 80
Lee, Dixie, 209–11
Letcher, John, 67
Lewis, David, 193
lifelines, 148
liferafts, 102–6
  gear for, 103–4
  inflatable dinghies and, 104–5
  servicing of, 104
  transmitters for, 105–6
Liggett, Al and Beth, 246, 266, 306, 430–37
lighting, 384–86
lightning, 117–18
  electrical equipment and, 118
lights, running, 121
lines, chafing of, 116

liquor, 241, 247
local conditions:
    acceptance in, 250–52
    bartering in, 249–50
    distance in, 251
    fresh produce and, 267–68
    fruits and vegetables in, 267–68
    hospitality in, 252
    language in, 244–46
    local customs in, 252
    marketplaces in, *see* marketplaces
    "official greeters" in, 252–53
    prices in, 246–49, 264
    privacy in, 253
    supermarkets in, 262
    see also foreign bureaucracies
Long Way, The (Moitessier), 184
Loran C, 237

MacDonald, Bruce and Liz, 278–79
machinery, 396–412
    air conditioning, 413
    alternators, 409–11
    auxiliary generators, 414
    bilge pumps, 412
    engines, 396–403
    exhaust systems, 412–13
    reliability of, 401–2
    shaft-charging systems, 414–16
    transmissions, 400–403
    water makers, 413–14
    see also propellers
mail, 288–89
maintenance, 284–86
    crew size and, 299
    of steel, 323
Makaretu, 91, 189–92, 205, 270
malaria, 132
man overboard, 215–18
    reboarding after, 216–18
    from single-handers, 215–16
man-overboard gear, 107–8, 216
Mar, 188
marketplaces, 246–47, 262–64
    haggling in, 246
    prices in, 246–47
Marquesas Islands:
    food costs in, 284
    "no-no" bugs of, 125
Marriott, Mr. and Mrs., 91, 270
Masina, 423–29
    design of, 426
    ground tackle on, 426–28
    in heavy weather, 427–29
    sails on, 427
materials, 322–26

aluminum, 324, 453–58
    fiberglass as, 322–23
    sandwich construction and, 322–23
    steel, 323–24
    stone (ferrocement), 325–26
    wood, 324–25
medical preparation, 129–34
    antibiotics, 131
    for constipation, 133
    fish poisoning and, 134
    for infections, 133
    inoculations, 131
    salt tablets, 130–31
    for skin fungus, 133–34
    vitamins, 131
messages, 289
Mexico, officials in, 243
Milner, Heinz, 309
Moesly, Carl and Jean, 76, 91, 309
Moesly, Don and Sue, 67, 79, 270, 275, 400
Moitessier, Bernard, 184
Molly, 65
money, *see* cost; finances
Moore, Emory and DeeDee, 102, 130–31, 211–13, 352
Moore, Jim, 124
Moorhardt, Mike, 153
multihulls, 314–21
    advantages of, 319–20
    draft of, 320
    speed of, 320
    suggested ratios for, 321
    weight problems of, 314–15, 321
musical instruments, 251

Naranjo, Ralph and Lenore, 105, 130
narcotics, 241
National Geographic, 251
navigation, 224–37
    celestial, 225–27
    preplanning in, 227–30
    storm seasons and, 229–30
    thoroughness in, 226
navigational aids, 230–37
    accuracy of, 231–32
    alertness as, 231
    charts as, 231–32
    depth sounders as, 233
    electronic, 232–37
    Loran as, 237
    maintenance of, 237
    omega as, 236–37
    pilot books as, 231
    radar as, 233–36
    RDF beacons as, 231, 233
    satellite, 236

navigatoriums, 377–79
Ned Kelly, 320
New Guinea, lightning off, 118
New Zealand:
    animals and, 243
    food costs in, 284
    government correspondence courses from,
        280
Nichols, John, 76, 325, 396
notaries, 292

omega sets, 33, 236–37
Osborne, Bob and Carol, 365
outboards, 101–2
    Evinrude, 102
    fuel tanks for, 101
    Johnson, 102
    Mercury, 102
    Seagull, 102
Overboard (Searle), 156
ownership, proof of, 238–39

Pagan Lee, 209–11
Panama, Gulf of, lightning in, 118
Papeete, Tahiti, 99, 296–97
Parks, Bob, 213
passports, 239–40, 242
Perry, Robert, 306, 308, 426
pilot books, 231
plumbing, 393–96
    drainage in, 393–94
    filters in, 395
    fresh water and, 394–95
    fuel tanks in, 395–96
    in heads, 396
    hoses and clamps in, 393
    pressure pumps in, 394–95
    showers in, 393, 395
    through-hull fittings and, 393–94
poisoning, fish, 134
poisson cru (recipe), 265–66
Porst, Craig, 133
Porter, Larry, 65
positive buoyancy, 326–27
powering range, 405
preparation, 28–144
    creature comforts and, 28–29
    major changes and, 28–29
prices:
    discounting of, 247
    duty free, 247
    haggling over, 246
propellers, 403–8
    drag of, 403
    efficiency of, 403
    feathering, 406

fixed vs. folding, 179
folding, 406
location of, 403–4
reverse power of, 406
R.P.M. and diameter of, 404, 408
Sabb, 404–6
second set of blades for, 406–8
variable pitch, 404–6
provisioning, 253–62
    of bread, 260
    for breakfasts, 257
    canned goods in, 261–62
    cardboard cartons in, 261
    of cheese, 259–60, 268
    of condiments, 257
    for desserts, 258
    eggs in, 261
    flour in, 255
    from foreign markets, 262–68
    of fresh produce, 260–61
    of fruit, 259, 267–68
    of fruit juices, 255–56
    of liquors, 256–57
    meat in, 258–59, 268
    of milk, 255
    nonfood items in, 260
    precruise checklist for, 254–62
    for snacks, 257–58
    soda in, 256
    of staples, 255
    stowing and, 261
    vegetables in, 258–59, 267–68
    washing produce in, 268
    see also foods

radar, 233–36
    advantages of, 234–36
radar reflectors, 162–63
rain catchers, 39, 76–77
    awnings as, 68, 73–74
range, powering, 405
RDF beacons, 231, 233
recipes, 264–67
reefing and furling systems:
    bendy-mast reefing, 334
    boom roller-reefing, 334
    extruded-red headstay, 330
    roller furling, 33, 330–34
    slab-reefing, 334
refrigeration systems, 82–87
    box for, 86
    compressors for, 85, 411
    finned evaporators for, 86
    freezer in, 86–87
    heat exchangers for, 85
    holding plates for, 85–86

refrigeration (continued)
   performance of, 83–84
Rhodora, 259
riding sails, 57
Rigadoon, 76–77, 309, 369, 371
rigging:
   boom gallows and, 352
   boom vangs in, 350–52
   compression struts in, 352
   failure of, 221–22
   halyards in, 354–56
   jammers for, 353–54
   maintenance of, 286
   metals in, 340–41
   reverse cycle loading and, 339
   safety criteria for, 338–39
   sheets in, 356
   size in, 338–39
   spinnaker poles in, 356–60
   stainless-steel wire for, 340
   Sta-lok/Norsemen end fittings in, 340
   stress risers and, 339
   swages and, 340
   topping lifts in, 352
   winches and, 352–53
rigs, 327–60
   aspect ratio and, 335
   cutter, 335–36
   double-spreader, 349–50
   junk, 337–38
   ketch, 337
   mizzens in, 330
   reefing and furling systems in, see reefing
      and furling systems
   relative efficiency of, 329–30
   running backstays and, 348–49
   sailing region and, 328–29
   schooner, 337
   size of, 328–29
   sloop, 336
   sock-sail, 338
   spars in, 341–44
   yawl, 336
Robertson, Dougal, 97, 103
rudders, 310–13
   collisions and, 312
   control and, 312–13
   grounding and, 310–12
   safety and, 313
   threats to, 310–12
   types of, 310–11
running aground:
   anchor winching after, 210–13
   gear for, 213–14
   heeling after, 214
   keel ballast and, 214
   laying down in, 207
   offshore, 208–14
   in protected waters, 206–8
   standard steps for, 208
   tides and, 207
running backstays, 348–49
running lights, 121, 160

Sail, 456
sailing instruments, 121–22
sails:
   aspect ratios for, 335
   battens and, 345–46
   chafing of, 113–15
   crew size and, 298–99
   drifters, 347
   forestaysails, 347
   on Intermezzo, 32–33, 36–37, 40–42
   inventory of, 344–48
   jibs, 346
   light headsails, 346–47
   maintenance of, 285–86
   mizzen staysails, 347
   reefing headsails, 348
   socks for, 441, 443
   spinnakers vs. twin jibs, 169
   stopping quickly and, 222–23
   storm, 347–48
   stretchy luff in, 345
   visibility of, 163
   weight of, 344–45
   windvanes and, 59–60
   see also reefing and furling systems; rig-
      ging; rigs; spinnakers
St. Helena Island, 478–80
saloons, 380–82
   tables in, 381–82
salt tablets, 130–31
Sanderson, Dan, 314
Sandstrom, Mr. and Mrs., 320
sandwich construction, 322–23
satellite navigation, 236
scheduling, 26–27
Schmidt, Jim and Cheryl, 151–53, 185–88, 264,
      433–48, 458
schooling, 276–80
   Calvert School and, 277–78
   high school courses in, 278
   options in, 277
   supplementing of, 278
schooner rigs, 337
screens, bug, 125
Sea, 243
Sea Love, 217
Searle, Hank, 156
security, 134–39